CONTENTS

volume **8** number **2** august **2003**

ANGELAKI
journal of the theoretical humanities

special issue: **the one or the other**
french philosophy today

issue editor: **peter hallward**

ANGELAKI
journal of the theoretical humanities

Subscription Information:
Angelaki: journal of the theoretical humanities is a peer-reviewed journal published three times a year (April, August and December), by Routledge Journals, an imprint of Taylor & Francis Ltd, 4 Park Square, Milton Park, Abingdon, Oxfordshire OX14 4RN, UK.

Annual Institutional Subscription, Volume 8, 2003

Print ISSN 0969-725X   US$269   £164

A subscription to the print edition includes free access for any number of concurrent users across a local area network to the online edition, ISSN 1469-2899.
For more information, visit our website: http://www.tandf.co.uk/journals
For a complete and up-to-date guide to Taylor & Francis Group's journals and books publishing programmes, and details of advertising in our journals, visit our website: http://www.tandf.co.uk/journals

Dollar rates apply to subscribers in all countries except the UK and the Republic of Ireland where the pound sterling price applies. All subscriptions are payable in advance and all rates include postage. Journals are sent by air to the USA, Canada, Mexico, India, Japan and Australasia. Subscriptions are entered on an annual basis, i.e. January to December. Payment may be made by sterling cheque, dollar cheque, international money order, National Giro, or credit card (Amex, Visa, Mastercard).

Ordering information:
USA/Canada: Taylor & Francis Inc., Journals Department, 325 Chestnut Street, 8th Floor, Philadelphia, PA 19106, USA. **UK/Europe/Rest of World**: Taylor & Francis Ltd, Rankine Road, Basingstoke, Hampshire RG24 8PR, UK.

Advertising enquiries to:
USA/Canada: The Advertising Manager, Taylor & Francis Inc., 325 Chestnut Street, 8th Floor, Philadelphia, PA 19106, USA. Tel: +1 (215) 625 8900. Fax: +1 (215) 625 2240.
EU/RoW: The Advertising Manager, Taylor & Francis Ltd, 4 Park Square, Milton Park, Abingdon, Oxfordshire OX14 4RN, UK. Tel: +44 (0)1235 828600. Fax: +44 (0)1235 829000.

The print edition of this journal is typeset by Infotype Ltd, Eynsham, Oxfordshire, UK and printed on ANSI conforming acid free paper by Alden Press, Oxford, UK. The online edition of this journal is hosted by Metapress at http://www.journalsonline.tandf.co.uk

journal of the theoretical humanities
volume 8   number 2   august 2003

I

Among the themes that tend to dominate general discussion of recent French philosophy, four seem to recur with particular frequency. *Complexity*: the field retains a lingering reputation for daunting if not arcane difficulty and sophistication, which restricts access to initiated insiders only. *Subversion*: recent French philosophy is supposed to have broken with the sterile certainties of metaphysics, to have exploded the benign intimacy of the subject, shattered the stability of reflection, undermined every figure of the absolute or immediate. *Eclecticism*: in place of traditional concerns with being and truth, French philosophers are supposed to have drawn their inspiration from the sciences and humanities, from psychoanalysis, from anthropology, from linguistics, from the artistic avant-garde, and more recently from liberalism, analytical philosophy, and so on. *Exhaustion*: over the last twenty years, in particular, our philosophers are supposed to have stepped back from the more radical implications of their most subversive declarations – the end of philosophy, the death of man, the dissolution of the subject – to accept the more humble tasks of remembering historical events, supervising institutional changes, rationalising administrative practices, clarifying logical arguments, resolving methodological disputes, and excavating details about the history of philosophy itself.

Combine the last two themes and you have what is now perhaps the most prevalent picture of contemporary philosophy – a melancholic, chastened discipline more or less resigned to the pragmatic ways of the world.[2] Combine all four

EDITORIAL INTRODUCTION

peter hallward

THE ONE OR THE OTHER
french philosophy today[1]

themes and you've got a discipline in retreat, a despondent branch of learning defeated by its unsustainable ambition and subsequently rearranged by needs external to its own, needs borrowed or imposed by government, pedagogy, science, history.

The grain of truth in this admittedly simplified picture is perhaps just large enough to rule out adoption of its mere inversion as the organising principle for the following survey of the field. Nevertheless, the planning of this issue of *Angelaki*, which set out to provide a broad (though obviously far from comprehensive[3]) overview of the most innovative and most inspiring projects currently underway in the field of French philosophy, was guided by very different presuppositions. Namely:

ISSN 0969-725X print/ISSN 1469-2899 online/03/020001-32 © 2003 Taylor & Francis Ltd and the Editors of *Angelaki*
DOI: 10.1080/0969725032000162549

french philosophy today

1. Just as earlier accounts of French philosophy tended to exaggerate the disruptive novelty of the years of its most dramatic innovations – the decades shaped by Althusser, Deleuze, Foucault, Lacan, Derrida – so too more recent accounts tend to exaggerate the degree of subsequent "decline" or withdrawal. Some things have certainly changed. The *nouveaux philosophes* have left their mark. A reader of Wittgenstein presides over the Collège de France. A critic of *la pensée '68* presides over the nation's education. Established institutions are firmly in reactionary hands. But the work of innovation proceeds apace and reports of exhaustion are greatly overblown. The field remains exceptionally dynamic and inventive, and, when it occurs philosophical thinking usually takes place today as a work of *persistence* and perseverance, terms that figure prominently in the work of many of the authors represented here.

2. Less than an eclectic profusion of interdisciplinary experiments, much of the field remains marked by a stubborn commitment to the specific tasks peculiar to philosophy itself (or its substitute – ethics, theology, non-philosophy, etc.). That these tasks involve philosophy in other disciplines has been obvious since Plato; the fact remains that this involvement is oriented, one way or another, by concepts and priorities internal to the active practice of philosophy as such, however this is prescribed, rather than to its own history or to one or another set of objects or knowledges. Very roughly speaking, "philosophical" here means, negatively, something irreducible to the sociological or cultural, i.e. to the forms and conditions of representation or interpretation whereby certain groups of people make sense of what they know about the world; more positively, it means forms of thought that (i) defy any further analysis and survive, one way or another, any subsequent paralysis of analysis, and that (ii) transform the thinker in ways that could apply, in principle, to all possible thinkers.

3. The majority of contemporary philosophical concepts derive from perfectly traditional metaphysical concerns, i.e. from questions regarding the ultimate nature of being, the forms and foundations of knowledge, the relation between subjects and objects of thought, and so on. In particular, many of the thinkers under discussion here embrace versions of that most quintessentially metaphysical theme: the evocation, as the ultimate point of reference, of an absolute or autonomous principle, one that is effectively self-grounding, self-causing, self-necessitating. They invoke principles that are independent, in short, of any constitutive relation with some *other* principle. That these principles differ from those propounded by Aristotle or Plotinus is again obvious, but no more so than the fact that much recent French philosophy pursues metaphysical aims by non-metaphysical or quasi-metaphysical means. We might say that the most distinctive projects in the field – those most "typical" of the field in general – are precisely those that pursue the most adamantly metaphysical agenda with the most apparently non-metaphysical means. Gilles Deleuze, for example, is perhaps best read as a thinker concerned, through the most varied of contemporary occasions, with the renewal of mainly pre-Kantian metaphysical questions: in terms of his essential priorities he has far more in common with Spinoza or Mulla Sadra than with, say, cultural critics preoccupied with the categories of race, nation or class.

4. What I am calling the most distinctive aspect of the field is best characterised, then, by a sort of *simplicity* in the proper sense of the term – an orientation to a principle marked by its essential singularity, its indifference to the mechanics of mediation and interaction (in particular to the forms of mediation involved in the process of representation, i.e. the process whereby a subject seeks to identify recognisable and classifiable aspects of an object and then organise these aspects in a body of knowledge). The fact that the non-relational principles at issue here are typically principles of radical difference or limitless creativity does not by itself qualify the singularity of the principle itself.

5. There is nothing especially "contemporary" about such a philosophical orientation. On the contrary, the basic parameters of a philosophy that seeks to align itself with a singular principle of absolute creativity are very ancient. Though theology clearly has no monopoly on the articulation of such principles, various forms of

monotheism offer some of the most obvious and most sophisticated examples. Before Deleuze or Henry, before Boehme or Spinoza, the essential distinctions at issue are already well established in the work of a radical theophanist like John Scottus Eriugena (himself working in a neo-Platonic tradition that goes back to Pseudo-Dionysius and Plotinus). Adapting the terms of Eriugena's fourfold "division of nature," we might say that any singular principle of radical creativity will entail the distinction of (a) an uncreated and consequently unknowable or unthinkable *creator*, which in itself can be thought only as no-thing; (b) the immediate and adequate expression of this creator in multiple self-revelations or *creatings* (which are both created and creative); (c) the various *creatures* (created but not creative) that lend material substance to these creatings; and (d) the virtual or uncreated state beyond creaturely perception and distinction to which these creatures are destined eventually to return. Versions of these distinctions recur in any fully singular conception of thought, be it transcendent *or* immanent. For as Eriugena explains, once "every creature visible and invisible can be called a theophany"[4] or manifesting of God, and if God qua creator is nothing, then only nothing separates God from his creation. This is why, he goes on, "we ought not to understand God and the creature as two things distinct from one another but as one and the same: the creature, by subsisting, is in God, and God, by manifesting himself, in a marvellous and ineffable manner creates himself in the creature." Understood in this way, God not only "becomes in all things all things," he "dwells nowhere but in the nature of men and angels, to whom alone it is given to contemplate the Truth."[5] God expresses himself in the infinite multiplicity of his creatings, God *is* only in these creatings, but these creatings remain expressive of a single creative force, "an indivisible One, which is Principle as well as Cause and End."[6]

6. For the same reason, then, the simplicity or singularity at issue here must always be distinguished from mere uniformity or homogeneity. Singularity involves non-relational or immediate forms of *individuation*, precisely, as opposed to both relational or dialectical forms of individua-tion on the one hand and pure dissolution or de-individuation on the other. A singular creative force *is* nothing other than the multiplication of singular creatings, each of which is originally and uniquely individual in its own right, *before* it differs from other creatings. The essential point is that such individuation does not itself depend on mediation through the categories of representation, objectivity or the world. An individual is only truly unique, according to this conception of things, if its individuation is the manifestation of an unlimited individuating power. More crudely: you are only really an individual if God makes you so.

7. Philosophies oriented around a singular principle can only cohere, in the end, as philosophies of the subject in what is again a supremely metaphysical sense of the term – a subject that is itself self-grounding, self-causing, a subject modelled more or less directly on the paradigm of a sovereign actor or creator God. If recent French philosophers have often attacked the philosophical foundations of the Cartesian *cogito* this has most often been in favour of a neo-Spinozist *cogitor*: they have cast doubt on the ontological implications of the "I think" in order to clear the way for the still more absolute implications of a passive "I am thought" or "I am being thought."[7] Thought thinks through me. Illuminated by the absolute, the knowing subject ceases to be a subject in *relation* to an object. The subject of representation, the subject bound up in relations with objects, the subject as ego, tends to yield here in favour of a subject without object, a subject "subjectivised" as the facet of a radically singular or non-relational principle. Such a principle not only acts freely or creatively, it creates the very medium in which it acts. As a result, an absolute subject can never be known through conformity to a model or norm, as the object of knowledge or representation; it can only be accessed through immediate participation in what it does, thinks, or lives. As Corbin explains with particular clarity, absolute creativity, or God, "cannot be an object (an objective given). He can only be known through himself as absolute Subject, that is, as absolved from all unreal objectivity," from all merely "creatural" mediation.[8] Adjusted for different contexts, this

point can be extended to our field as a whole: far from seeking to dissolve the subject, the great effort of French philosophy in the twentieth century, the effort that is broad enough to include Bergson and Sartre, Lacan and Foucault, Levinas and Baudrillard, Badiou and Rancière, is instead to dissolve *everything that objectifies the subject*, i.e. everything that serves to mediate subjective thought through the representation of objects. The most general goal has been to evacuate all that serves to reduce an essentially creative being to the mere creature of objective forces.[9]

8. Subjective participation in the absolute proceeds in an equally absolute indifference to the world, or at least to the principles that shape the prevailing "way of the world." Access to the absolute is not arrived at through some process of approximation or progression, it is not the result of a dialectical revaluation of trends in the world. It is not the culmination of some complex process of mediation. It is instead a point of departure, an original or pre-original affirmation, a sort of axiom, which opens the field of its subsequent effects as a series of essentially internal consequences or implications. Preoccupation with the world or concern with the orderly representation of the things of the world inhibits any such affirmation, which is "extreme" by definition (non-conditional, non-relative, non-derivative). Thinkers as different as Lardreau and Rancière can agree that true thought is compromised precisely when the world succeeds in assigning it a place and making it "fit." The philosopher's concern is instead, says Deleuze, "one of knowing how the individual would be able to transcend his form and his syntactical link with a world" in order to become the transparent vessel for that "non-organic life of things which burns us [... ,] which is the divine part in us, the spiritual relationship in which we are alone with God as light."[10] Or, as Eriugena might remind us: hell is not a place, it is the psychological state to which we commit ourselves in so far as we refuse to abandon the circumstances that sustain our specifically creatural fantasies.[11]

9. Subjective, absolute, such philosophy is indeed best described as "spiritual" in this rather loose sense of the term, i.e. one compatible with

the sort of anti-spiritualist materialism that Lardreau himself espouses,[12] or with the general effort of Bergson and Deleuze's work: the development of ways of thinking and acting "that liberate man from the plane or level that is proper to him, in order to make him a creator, adequate to the whole movement of creation."[13] The absolutely subjective inheres on an exclusively spiritual plane; what remains of the subject in a world purged of spirit is only the corpse, or its equivalent – robot, consumer, citizen ... The persistent effort to deny (or to limit to a recent "ethical" or "theological" turn) the often explicitly spiritual dimension of our field, to insist on its exclusively secular inspiration, is usually just another aspect of the attempt to reconcile it with the way of the world – an attempt vigorously denied by those who, like Corbin and Henry, to say nothing of Levinas or Jambet, are most at ease with the metaphysical orientation of philosophy and its consequent engagement with forms of religion. Such engagement provides, in turn, a basis for the sharpest possible version of the ancient distinction between philosophy and dogma.

10. Spiritual and hostile to the world, the cutting edge of this tendency in French philosophy is for the same reason hostile to any quasi-Heideggerian attempt to re-enchant or "spiritualise" the world itself. There is nothing more irrational or "archaic" in Corbin's work on Avicenna or Ibn Arabi, say, than there is in Deleuze's work on Spinoza or Nietzsche. On balance, most twentieth-century French philosophers have remained faithful to the rationalist principles of their predecessors and presumed the essential autonomy of language, imagination and thought, their independence of mediation through nature or psychology. The formalising priorities affirmed by Lévi-Strauss, Althusser, and *Les Cahiers pour l'analyse* have had a lasting impact. Lardreau and Jambet, no less than Badiou or Laruelle, remain faithful to the anti-hermeneutic orientation of Descartes and Lacan. Even Henry, who of all the thinkers at issue here is the most explicit in its affirmation of an affective vitality, withdraws it from the phenomenological logic whereby this vitality might *show* itself within the world. As for those who, like

Nancy and Lacoue-Labarthe, continue to work through a quasi-Heideggerian inheritance, what is perhaps most distinctive about their work is the lengths to which they go to purge it of its sentimental aura, of its nostalgia for an intimate relation with the sacred, with the authentic or proper, so as to affirm, as the sole medium of thought, a generalised impropriety.

The remainder of this introduction will try to justify this somewhat unorthodox account of the field through the illustration of some salient examples, beginning with the particularly instructive work of Michel Henry and subsequently framed by the more familiar figures of Levinas, Bergson, Deleuze, Sartre, and Derrida, along with a few others. Three qualifications, however, are already overdue.

In the first place, if much of the field is oriented around a singular *one*, then considered in terms of the field as a whole this is a one that, like its Maoist instance, is no sooner one than it immediately "divides into two." Singular thought always polarises between the twin limits of immanence and transcendence (even if, at their own limit, these limits themselves tend back towards a singular indistinction). Deleuze is not "like" Levinas, obviously, nor Rosset like Corbin – the point is that they are all equally committed to non-relational means of orienting or polarising thought.

In the second place, this division of one into two implies the possibility of a third, a sort of situated or localised combining of the two – the scattering of multiple points of transcendence, the deployment of exceptional processes, processes that then open zones of egalitarian immanence or generic im-propriety against a backdrop of inertia, indifference or confusion. As we shall see, such points and processes condition the work of Sartre and Badiou in one sense, and of Derrida (and Lacoue-Labarthe, and Nancy) in another.

Thirdly, and most obviously: the singular orientation of the field is by no means homogeneous or all-inclusive. Far from it. Camus, Merleau-Ponty and Ricoeur have worked mainly against this orientation, for instance, as do, in different ways, Stiegler, David-Ménard, and Bensaïd. Others, like Foucault and Rancière,

operate at its limit or edge. Needless to say, it would be quite impossible to account for so varied and complex a field *within* the scope of a single model. On the other hand, it would be still more unsatisfactory to avoid any attempt at a comprehensive characterisation, to take refuge in an empirical aversion to generalisation. I am not suggesting that all those who embrace singularity do so to the same degree or in the same way: Jambet's orientation is no doubt more adamantly non-relational than is that of Badiou, say, and Rancière is in turn more relational than Badiou. The singular pole of the field is precisely that, a *pole*. It is not the field itself. Nor am I suggesting that *all* significant French philosophy of the past few decades has embraced a singular orientation: my argument is that the most original and most striking figures in the field have tended to embrace such an orientation, and that their innovations have in turn sparked reactions – Merleau-Ponty to Sartre, Rancière to Althusser, and so on – leading to more or less radical reorientations. If anything holds the field together, if anything (beyond the contingency of languages and institutions) allows us to speak here of *a* field and thus to think of these various reactions and innovations together, then it is the continuous persistence of singularity as the strong polarising principle of the field as a whole. It is this principle that "unites" the field, precisely as a field split between its own poles and divided by attempts at its reorientation.

II

The fundamental ideas of what I am calling the strong, singular orientation of the field have seldom been expressed as starkly and insistently as in the work of Michel Henry. Henry's philosophy turns above all on the irreconcilable dualism between "life" and "world," or between immediate subjective reality and illusory objective mediation. The most compressed version of the essential sequence runs as follows. Absolute self-revealing and self-experiencing subjectivity is another name for God, and "God is Life." But since "God's revelation as his self-revelation owes nothing to the phenomenality of the world but rather rejects it as fundamentally foreign to his own phenomenality," so then "living is not possible in the world," "life is never shown in the world," and "as for the natural life that we think we see around us in the world, it does not exist."[14]

The world (as distinct from life) is the place in which objects appear to subjects who see and represent them as external to themselves, as "out there," illuminated by the light of the world. The task of worldly knowledges is to bring the greatest possible number of objects out from ignorant obscurity into the clarity and distinction of well-ordered representation. Likewise, the perspective of a (neo-Kantian or neo-Hegelian) philosophy that is itself mediated by knowledge and the world will be determined in terms of the progressive perfection of these knowledges or the progressive completion of those processes of "objectification" through which spirit, mind or life externalises itself in the world. The world is the place in which what is revealed, in other words, are objects or things other than revealings per se. Things appear and signify in the light of the world, but "things do not rise into the light of this 'outside' except as torn from themselves, emptied of their being, already dead." And since "time and the world are identical," since things appear in the world according to specific determinations of place and time, so then time is *essentially* destructive and the world essentially unreal. "Everything that appears in the world is subject to a process of principled de-realisation [...] – if there existed no other truth than that of the world there would be no reality at all anywhere but only, on all sides, death."[15]

At an infinite distance from this morbid world, however, the real ground of "being is life, the immediate internal experience of the self excluding all transcendence, all representation."[16] What is real is precisely that which appears through "absolute self-revelation," in which the revealing and the revealed, though not merely self-identical, are nonetheless so indivisible that no separation or distance can ever arise between them. Life is defined in terms of its perfectly self-reflexive experience of itself, its sufficiency, its immanence to itself: life is that which immediately undergoes, suffers, or enjoys itself, in the absence of any mediation through object or world. Life only lives, furthermore, through singular lives that are themselves unique and personal by definition. The self-revelation of Life in individual lives is already the absolute differentiation of these lives, again in advance of any relation with the world. Life lives according to modalities (anxieties, concerns, sorrows, joys, etc.) that are expressed in the world but which are not themselves of the world. They are in the world as so many imperceptible exceptions from the world. Nobody has ever seen life because life is exclusively subjective and the essence of subjectivity is affectivity as such.[17] Life must be felt and suffered, it cannot (*pace* Heidegger, or Wittgenstein) be *shown* or perceived.[18] "The absolute revelation of the absolute," life does not appear as a phenomenon according to the light of the world.[19] It has never been and will never be the object of scientific representations, however accurate these might become – biology, for example, exclusively concerned with material and objective processes, knows nothing of life.[20] The attempt to show, represent, objectify or otherwise "externalise" life amounts only to the murderous extinction or abandonment of life.

In other words, life is not something that evolved in the world or that is in any way adapted to the world. Life is the manifestation of a principle entirely independent of the world. Life persists in the absolute sanctuary of its own sufficiency. Wherever there is pure self-revelation there is life, but life never allows itself to become the *object* of a perception. Whatever lives is the manifestation, in short, of an absolute Life, an absolute subject, or God. True reality is based in God's perfectly immediate but endlessly dynamic, endlessly creative (non-)coincidence with himself *as subject* – which is also to say his absolute lack of coincidence with any sort of object, his absolute distance from "the barbarism of mindless objectivity."[21]

Consider briefly the deployment of this singular conception of things according to two of Henry's most thoroughly developed paradigms, which he associates with Marx and Christ, respectively.

As Henry reads him, Marx is the thinker who first developed suitably modern means of liberating an exclusively subjective conception of praxis from the forces that seek to trap and exploit it within the contemporary forms of objective alienation. Most of these forms, of course, are economic – forces of production, patterns of consumption, divisions of labour, relations of exchange, etc. Marx's great achievement, according to Henry, was to realise that praxis or labour is not a commodity or any sort of an economic reality: subjective, invisible, and indivisible, labour is an aspect of *life* alone. Labour is the *doing* of things, and is as irreducible to the world as is, for example, the experience of those running a race from those who merely watch that same race.[22] Far from developing a science that attributes causal primacy to objectively representable modes of production or class struggle, therefore, Henry's Marx moves past Feuerbach and Hegel precisely to the degree that he subtracts life from objective mediation in general and from economic mediation in particular.[23] Processes of objectivation always involve the separating or distancing of a product from a producer, an object from a subject, a world from a spirit – such is the essential basis of all alienation, and the crux of the various ideologies that seek to conceal it. What is truly real, by contrast, is

> whatever excludes from itself this distancing, whatever is subjective in a radically immanent sense, whatever experiences itself immediately without being able to separate itself from itself, to take the slightest distance with regard to itself, in short, whatever cannot be represented or understood in any way at all.[24]

Marx realised, in the face of modern forces of objectification, in the face too of the variously scientistic versions of Marx-ism that would soon come to occlude his philosophy, that such experience is "the single origin, the single creative principle [which] creates the conditions of production, of classes and of ideas."[25] This principle, which is alone productive, is the concrete activity and potential of individuals as they live, work and act.

When in his last books Henry makes the theological orientation of his work fully explicit, the Manichaean division between life and world

becomes still more insistent and allows for the clarification of a number of essential points. First of all, life figures here as a still more emphatically singular process. Christianity declares that "there is only one Life, that of Christ, which is also that of God and men, [...] this single and unique life that is self-revelation." Life is what engenders itself in the movement whereby a Living being (a "Son") manifests or reveals Life as such (the "Father," who in himself, as *pure* Life, transcends any sort of living).[26] Life is that process of revelation that reveals only itself: "life generates itself inasmuch as it propels itself into phenomenality in the form of a self-revelation."[27] Life is not only singular or unique; so are all living beings, which are not particular instances of a more general principle (variations on a generic invariant) but directly individuated selves. Life lives exclusively as self-affection, and every *living* is thus immediately and originally a distinct self.

> What individualises something like the Individual that each of us is, different from every other – each "me" and each transcendental ego forever distinct and irreplaceable – is not found in the world at all [...]. If by man we usually mean the empirical individual, one whose individuality relates to the world's categories – space, time, causality – in short, if a man is a being of the world intelligible in the truth of the world, then we must come to terms with him: this man is not an Ipseity, he bears within him no Self, no me. The empirical individual is not an individual and cannot be. And a man who is not an Individual and who is not a Self is not a man. *The man of the world is merely an optical illusion. "Man" does not exist.*[28]

Instead, "I myself am this singular Self engendered in the self-engendering of absolute Life, and only that. Life self-engenders itself as me."[29] In this sense, "life is the relation that itself generates its own 'terms,'" and "it generates them as internal one to the other, such that they belong together, one and the other, in a co-belonging that is more powerful than any conceivable unity, in the inconceivable unity of Life whose self-engendering is one with the engendering of the Engendered."[30] Our relations with other people are likewise independent of our dealings with variously specified empirical human objects, the bearers of characteristics that are themselves empirical and worldly (matters of culture, gender, ethnicity, etc.). We truly "relate" only with "Sons of life," in whom "all empirical and worldly characteristics are immediately eliminated," beginning with anything that arises from a family genealogy, a sexual identity or a cultural inheritance. Living ethical relations presume the wholesale rejection of all visible characterisation. "What is Identical in each person – the self-giving of absolute phenomenological Life in its original Ipseity – determines in its entirety the Christian theory of the relation to another."[31]

In the second place, while Christ's own living is purely self-activating or self-engendering, human life is engendered *within* this original self-engendering. Like all life, we experience ourselves in a relation of radical intimacy or immanence which knows no separation, which passes through no representation, but we are *given* to experience ourselves in this way by a force in infinite excess of this experience. Life is one, there is only absolute life, which is given to each self or ego just as it is given to itself: this relation, however, is not reversible or reciprocal. The ego receives its life from a principle that remains immeasurably beyond it.

> Such is the paradoxical condition of the ego: that of being wholly itself, having its own phenomenological substance (namely, its own life as it experiences it), yet being nothing by itself, and taking this phenomenological substance (its self-affecting) from a phenomenological substance that is absolutely other than it, from power other than its own, of which it is absolutely deprived, the power of absolute Life to be thrown into life and living.[32]

I affect myself, but I am not myself the source of this self-affecting. I am not the cause of my own condition. Instead "I find myself self-affected." Hence the "passivity of this singular Self that I am, a passivity that determines it from top to bottom," its absolute and unavoidable exposure to the undiluted suffering of its life.[33] Hence, too, the logic of that Passion which justi-

fies the conversion of *absolute* suffering into joy. The ceaseless inversion of suffering into joy proceeds on account of the fact that, when pushed to its limit, the experience of our passivity is simultaneously the experience of divine activity: our total passivity or impotence is what allows us to become an adequate vehicle of the absolutely affirmative Life that lives through us. The more we suffer, the more we are exposed to the "invincible and inalienable power of life [...]. At the summit of its impotence the ego is submerged by the hyper-strength of life."[34] Suffering is both the experience of living and exposure to the absolute principle that expresses itself as *livings*.

> The more life is caught up in the suffering of its being as it is limited and tied to itself, and the more it experiences as a burden the absence and the impossibility of any transcendence, of any overcoming, the more this overcoming is realised, the more one can feel in and through this very suffering the emergence of one's own being, its silent advent and the experience of its ultimate ground. In this way, Kierkegaard was able to conceive of the extreme point of suffering, despair, as leading the self to the most radical test both of itself and of the life within it, to delve through its own transparence into the power that has posited it [...]. In Christ's passion and in his sacrifice the metaphysical law of life is revealed and is expressed, insofar as its essence lies in affectivity [...], insofar as suffering reveals what it is that suffers at the very heart of this suffering, the absolutely living being of life.[35]

The path of redemption leads all the more firmly, then, out of a world that promises only the denial if not the extermination of life. "In granting values to Life, Christianity withdraws them from the world."[36] Christ does not offer an opportunity to revalue or elevate the things of this world so much as provide the basis on which to ignore them altogether. "By defining man as son of God, Christianity rules out any form of thought – science, philosophy, or religion – that holds man to be a Being in the world, whether in a naïve or critical sense."[37] Ignorance and alienation arise precisely because we are led to think of ourselves as worldly beings, as concerned with whatever appears in the light of the world and as dependent upon objects and our representations of objects. Because our experience is essentially passive, because we suffer our life without respite, we are forever tempted to posit ourselves as the source of our own life so as then to posit this life, in turn, as an object that we might study, understand, and enhance. The "transcendental illusion of the ego" begins when the ego, rather than allow life and its powers (to act, think, move, create, etc.) to live through it, instead takes itself as the ground of its Being and in doing so commits itself to the mode of appearing in the world. The more vigorously an ego attributes its power to itself the more it forgets the nature of its life, the more it posits itself as an object – the more it identifies itself, in short, with the worldly cadaver that it will sooner or later become. "The more the ego leans on itself with a view to elevating itself, the more the ground disappears under its feet. But the more the ego forgets itself and confides itself to life, the more it will be open to the unlimited strength of that life."[38]

As in Bergson or Deleuze, as in Corbin or Levinas, as in any configuration of thought that identifies reality with some absolutely creative principle, the immediate consequence of this identity is an irreducible distinction between the *creating* that is alone real and the derivative *creature* that exists only as obscurity or illusion. Creative *natura naturans* is always liable to conceal itself through the creaturely *naturata* that it generates.[39] We can think of our body, for instance, as a real channel of life's auto-affection or as a mere object that I posit as external to myself. "Everything is double, but if what is offered to us in a double aspect is in itself one and the same reality then one of its aspects must be merely an appearance, an image, a copy of reality, but not that reality itself – precisely its double," which is nothing more than a "trap," the basis of "hypocrisy" and "duplicity."[40] As a result, "the extraordinary event by which the ego's life will be changed into God's" can be equally well considered either as the process whereby this ego comes to forget itself through the literal elimination of its worldly self – as the birth of an other-worldly self that "has no image,

no perception, no memory of self, that is not concerned with itself, does not think of itself" and that has thereby purged itself of the very possibility of duplicity – or as the process whereby God alone comes to act through the void left by evacuation of this worldly self.[41] Only God allows us access to himself; only by *living*, i.e. by *being-lived*, can we know life.

Henry's work thus culminates in a rejection of the way of the world as uncompromising as any in recent philosophy. However it happens, once "my being is constituted as an object then it can be taken away from me and handed over to the fate of the world," and the world is essentially the place that leads us astray.[42] The world is the place of our doom. In the world that we know, the world known by science and mathematics, there is no place for life or self. Today's anti-Christ is simply "the world itself," the world governed by the pursuit of profits and the ongoing sophistication of technology. Our world reduces people to robots who programme and consume mere simulations of life. Our world brings universal "desolation and ruin." Reduced to our mere representation in the world, emptied of sentience and sentiment, "counted like animals and counting for much less," we survive only as degraded and despised, in despite of ourselves.[43]

III

Henry's particular *thematics* (Christian, affective, vitalist, etc.) are hardly typical, of course, of all recent French philosophy. In particular, his generally anti-modern stance is in stark contrast to those who seek, one way or another, to radicalise the projects of Enlightened modernity (Sartre, Lacan, Badiou, Laruelle, etc.). The essential logic at issue in Henry's work, however – the singularity of its creative or productive principle, the immediate and non-relational process of individuation that it generates, the radical refusal of mediation or representation that it implies, the redemptive struggle against duplicity that it inspires – is indeed exemplary of what I have called the "strong" pole of the field as a whole. Though there can be no question here of anything but the most cursory survey of additional examples, it may be worth running very rapidly through a number of these in order to lend a little more substance to this preliminary characterisation of the field. Perhaps the simplest way of presenting the material is to retain the traditional distinction of transcendence and immanence as the apparently opposite limits defining the field of non-relational thought. This will take us successively from Levinas, Corbin, Jambet, and Lardreau to Bergson, Deleuze, Rosset, and Laruelle, before leading us to that "third" position variously explored by Sartre, Badiou and Derrida.

Levinas and Corbin propose the most radical (and no doubt the most ancient or archetypal) contemporary versions of transcendent singularity. Both work according to a broadly neo-Platonic outlook. Levinas orients thought entirely towards that which is absolutely other than being or transcendent of being, an infinite "creator," so to speak, that is both the principle of all that exists yet infinitely distant from its creatures and external to the domain of creation as such. "The great force of the idea of creation as it was contributed by monotheism is that this creation is *ex nihilo*," notes Levinas, such that "the separated and created being is thereby not simply issued forth from the father but is absolutely other than him." The creator is entirely separate, entirely other than creation. The essential characteristic of this extreme alterity is simply its axiomatic characterisation as absolutely or infinitely other than all that can be thought or represented *within* the field of being, within the "totality" of creation. However inclusive or anarchic this totality might be, as a field of being Levinas confines it within the ontological category of the *same*. Infinite transcendence or alterity, which is consequently "otherwise than being," thus has nothing to do with an eminent place or form of being: infinite transcendence qualifies only that which reveals itself in being as an exception to being, as the tearing away of being from being and towards the other-than-being. "The idea of Infinity (which is not a representation of infinity) sustains activity itself," including the activity of be-ing.[44] By definition, infinite alterity is infinitely in excess of all knowledge, all mediation, all representa-

tion. "The Other comes to us not only out of context but also without mediation," and in the face of its "immeasurable excess" the world and its objects dissolve.[45]

As otherwise than being, infinite transcendence *is* only in these excessive revealings as such. Alterity is revealed in the ways whereby we are oriented towards infinite alterity. Infinite transcendence "only *happens* [*se passe*] through the subject who confesses or contests it" and "subjectivity" is itself nothing other than subjection to alterity as such. "Responsibility for the other is the place in which is placed the non-place of subjectivity."[46] We are subjects to the degree that we think the infinite alterity that transcends and orients us or, rather, we are subjects in so far as this alterity thinks through us, in so far as we are thought *by* it. We are subjects in so far as that which is otherwise than being manifests itself through us as transcendent of us. No less than in Henry or Corbin, there is thus no relation *between* the subject and the principle that makes-subject. The subject is simply an instance of this principle, i.e. the manifesting of its transcendence of any manifestation. If we are then to be described as "responsible" to this principle, this responsibility will not characterise our relation *with* an other or others so much as express the very principle that makes us what we are. We are responsible to the other as a creature is responsible to its creator. Since the other person is only *other* (i.e. other than a mere creature or being, other than whatever falls within the totality of the same) in so far as he or she is a manifesting or "trace" of the absolutely other, so then my relation with the other can only be a "relation without relation."[47] In my relation "with" the other, therefore, "the other remains absolute and absolves itself from the relation which it enters into."[48] I only relate to the other as its "hostage," through forms of "unconditional obedience" or "persecution." More graphically: "I expose myself to the summons of this responsibility as though placed under a blazing sun that eradicates [...] every loosening of the thread that would allow evasion." The subject of responsibility is an instance of radical "denudation": "he does not posit himself, know or possess himself, he is consumed, he is delivered over, he de-situates himself, loses his place, exiles himself […], empties himself into a non-place."[49] He is evacuated of all creatural substance.

Since I remain *I* precisely in so far as I suffer this evacuation, however, the latter must not be confused with the mere dissolution of the subject. It is above all the determination to avoid this confusion that inspires Henry Corbin's epic engagement with Islamic conceptions of "Creation as theophany," i.e. creation as the immediate revelation of God.[50] In terms that resonate closely with those of Michel Henry, Corbin conceives of a theophanic or "angelic" conception of divinity as the only adequate bulwark against contemporary nihilism, where nihilism is defined as the belief that representation of subjects and objects in the world exhausts what we can know of reality. Nihilism has its root precisely in our attempt (dramatised in the Ismaili account of the origins of humanity) to know the absolute *in*-itself rather than *for*-itself, i.e. to know God as *Ens supremum*, as supreme creature rather than as singular creator (as a supreme being rather than as the "act of being" that makes all beings be).[51] By attempting to know God as an object while admitting the necessarily inaccessible transcendence of this object, orthodox monotheism prepared the way for its own demise. Since nothing can be positively known of such transcendence, since all that can be predicated of the divine as such is simply the projection of human or "creatural" qualities, there is nothing to block the eventual conclusion that the absolute is itself nothing and that the creatural is all that exists (or alternatively, though the result is the same: that we are ourselves "divine" or transcendent).

Corbin's defence of apophatic theology prevents this disaster by (a) preserving the inaccessible dimension of God as such, who remains utterly impervious to any mediation through creation, history, or the world (i.e. impervious to any quasi-Hegelian conception of spirit) and (b) insisting, consequently, on the *necessity* of another dimension of God: the revealing of God in the infinite variety of creation. Since any "*Ens*, any being, refers by its essence to that which is beyond itself, to the *act* of being that

transcends it and that constitutes it as *a* being," so each living soul is the direct and immediate expression of this transcendent act, i.e. a sufficient facet of God's self-revelation, a moment in "eternal birth of God."[52] Each of these souls is absolutely unique but they all express and multiply the same creative force. Infinitely multiplied ($1 \times 1 \times 1 \times 1 \ldots$), the One remains one. Apophatic theology prepares the way for the unlimited differentiation of theophanies or self-revealings of God.

Those who see only the creatural are condemned to nihilism, those who look only for the creator are condemned to blindness. The true task is instead "simultaneously to see divinity in the creature, the One in the multiple, and the creature in the divine, the multiplicity of theophanies in the Unity that 'theophanises' itself."[53] In a crucial passage of *Nietzsche and Philosophy*, Deleuze distinguishes Nietzsche's emphasis on creative individuation from the Schopenhauer who concludes that humans are "at best beings who suppress themselves."[54] In much the same way, Corbin distinguishes between two mystical conceptions of creation: one that follows the path of individuation or "personality" (epitomised by Jacob Boehme) and another that pursues pure impersonality or detachment (epitomised by Meister Eckhart). For Eckhart, the effort to rejoin the Creator requires the dissolution of *all* particularity and all sense of personality or self.[55] Boehme's deepest conviction, by contrast, is that though undifferentiated and inaccessible in himself, God *expresses* himself as "a personal Being, a living person, conscious of himself" through all the individual consciousnesses that he creates.[56] God is precisely the creative movement that proceeds from undifferentiated abyss (*Ungrund*) to fully determined creatings or self-revelations; to try to reverse this movement is thus to work directly against God. Understood along these lines, redemption has nothing to do with annihilation of the self through mystical fusion with the divine; it is rather through "the realisation of that which is most personal and most profound in man that man fulfils his essential function, which is theophanic: to express God, to be a *theophore*, a vehicle of God."[57]

11

In short: God as creator is forever unknowable but his creatings are immediately knowable in so far as the creatures to which they give rise are capable of knowing themselves as these very creatings. This process requires evacuation of the creaturely as such, the conversion of material creatures into transparent prisms for the purely spiritual light that alone sustains them.

The point I want to emphasise is that such individuation remains fully singular in that non-relational sense I am concerned with here. An individual does not become an individual as the result of psychological development or through relations with other individuals, let alone through worldly interaction with various socio-historical forces: what individuates a particular creature is exclusively that divine creating which its existence reflects. In the Persian theological traditions that most interest Corbin and Jambet, these creatings figure as "angelic," i.e. as purely spiritual forms that are directly expressive of the divinity they contemplate. As an absolutely creative force, God expresses himself in every possible way, including ways that, like matter, are only passively expressive of him, i.e. ways that are most obviously expressive of their creatural distance from God. Human creatures appear, then, as ambiguous entities, part spiritual, part material, and only the spiritual component (the "creating") is *actively* expressive of God. "A human person is only a person thanks to this celestial, archetypical, angelic dimension; this dimension is the celestial pole without which the terrestrial pole of his human dimension is completely *depolarised*, disoriented and lost."[58] Corbin's major effort involves the "preservation of the spiritual from all the perils of socialisation," from its "subjection to time" and "historicism" – in short, the redemption of spirit from Hegelianism and its consequences.[59] Today's despiritualised and depolarised world is a place in which people are manipulated as de-individuated objects, a place of devastation and death.[60] For Corbin, as for Bergson, the worldly or material dimension remains forever undifferentiated and resistant to all individuation: the door to the realm of the spirit opens only when the material door is closed, through "suspension of the external senses and of all preoccupation with the external world."[61] And since human beings begin their lives plunged in the exile of material obscurity they will remain so unless they find ways to "de-materialise" themselves, to empty themselves of all creaturely opacity and thereby rejoin, in a purely spiritual, purely theophanic or "imaginal" sphere, the angel who personifies that aspect of God which their existence reveals.

Working along paths opened in the wake of Corbin's work, it is Christian Jambet and Guy Lardreau who, marked by their experience of Lacan's teaching and Lin Piao's Cultural Revolution, have since developed the most striking variations of a transcendent conception of singularity. Lardreau's primary inspiration comes from those early Syriac ascetics who were motivated by an absolute renunciation of the world, of the body and of sexuality – "this surreal crowd that swarms in the deserts of the Orient, these monks with wasted bellies, their bodies lacerated with chains, these ruined figures whipped by wind and rain, these worm-eaten but radiant stylites, these voluntary madmen." They illustrate a logic (and a destiny) that would be repeated with equal enthusiasm in what Lardreau takes to be the climactic moments of Maoism, likewise motivated by a determination to purge revolt of any objective mediation (any past, tradition, familiarity, continuum, institution, order, etc.) so as to confront undiluted the irreducible "real of dualism" that divides those who work with and through the world from those who reject it altogether and who make of this rejection, this antagonism, the exclusive "foundation" of thought.[62] Lardreau's subsequent work has persisted in a starkly "negative" conception of philosophy, in ardent indifference to the world.

Following more directly in Corbin's footsteps, Jambet's work offers, all by itself, a sort of compressed microcosm of our field as a whole. It experiments with both poles of singular theophany, from the immanent pantheism affirmed by Mulla Sadra to that transcendent "creative imperative" embraced by Ismaili thinkers like Abu Yaqub Sijistani and Nasir ad-Din Tusi.[63] What holds Jambet's work together is again the essential unity of that "real act" that makes all being be and which we, as beings endowed with creative speech, can articulate as the immediate revelation of God. As the super-infinite basis of being, there is nothing "thinglike" about God. Though all that *is* is the expression of God, only direct illumination or inspiration allows participation in the *expressing* as such.[64] We grasp the pure appearing or manifestation of things to the degree that we can see past (or dissolve) the merely manifested or apparent.

Like Corbin and Henry, Jambet everywhere assumes the radical "autonomy of spiritual meanings," the non-relational isolation which enables "visionary assumption of the internal singularity of the spirit."[65] Nowhere is the affirmation of this autonomy more striking than in the episode analysed in Jambet's most remarkable book to date, *La Grande Résurrection d'Alamût*. Inspired above all by "the desire to experience divinisation here and now, by the determination to interrupt the way of the world" once and for all,[66] this exemplary eschatological sequence (which began in northern Iran in 1164 CE) is organised entirely in terms of the consequences of a "liberated" or "unveiled contemplation of the divine unity." Alamut is the privileged historical moment during which, to the exclusion of any law-based representation of God, "human freedom experienced itself as the expression of the unconditioned liberty and spontaneous constituent power of God."[67] Since an absolute creativity must by definition be unlimited by the mediation of being (or the world, or history, or society, or the self, etc.), it is only because we can embrace imperatives that cohere with a force beyond being and beyond the world that we can, exceptionally, act as absolutely and "unsayably" free. This is the point, Jambet implies, that Sartre and Deleuze fail to grasp even when they realise that absolute freedom is indistinguishable from absolute necessity: the ultimate imperative "let be!," which is the "real of being," the "making-be" which sustains all being, is not itself articulated from within being or indeed from within any conception of "within."[68] The foundation of being is itself without foundation. Radical liberation includes liberation from being itself.

Although Bergson and Deleuze seek to purge philosophy of every trace of transcendence, they pursue an equally singular or non-relational programme of creatural evacuation. Bergson's guiding idea is precisely that living time (or dynamic creativity) is not itself directly mediated by the world of matter or space. As a general rule, "everything is obscure if we confine ourselves to mere manifestations," for instance manifestations of society or intelligence; "all becomes clear, on the contrary, if we start by a quest beyond these manifestations for Life itself," i.e. that which actively manifests itself as creativity.[69] Living time is singular, self-generating and self-sustaining, driven "in all places as at all times" by a "single impulsion [...], in itself indivisible," that "makes of the whole series of the living one single immense wave flowing over matter."[70] Life itself figures as a purely spiritual force once "we understand by spirituality a progress to ever new creations."[71]

That life lives *through* matter does not mean, then, that it is mediated *by* matter in the sense that relations between living objects, living organisms or species, might be directly constitutive of life. On the contrary, matter simply resists life. Most of the time, life "cannot create absolutely because it is confronted with matter, that is to say with the movement that is the inverse of its own."[72] Matter forces life to follow divergent paths of actualisation (vegetal and animal, instinctual and intellectual, intellectual and intuitive). "Life is essentially a current sent through matter, drawing from it what it can." This current is not itself weakened or altered, however, by what it traverses. Matter is the element in which life is individuated in particular organisms or souls; without dividing it, matter forces "the great river of life" into myriad and divergent channels. But "the movement of the stream is distinct from the river bed," just as "consciousness is distinct from the organism it animates," and there is at least one channel through which life has indeed escaped material mediation, the channel in which consciousness finally appears as "essentially free, as freedom itself." If the story of evolution is the story of compromises life has been forced to make with and in matter, the climax or "end" of this story is precisely the moment when, with humanity, life or consciousness invents a form that is finally capable of bypassing all material, organic, social or intellectual obstruction, of advancing on a purely spiritual (or purely dematerialised) plane. "Everywhere but in man, consciousness has had to come to a standstill; in man alone it has kept on its way. Man, then, continues the vital movement indefinitely."[73] We accomplish this every time we transcend mere matter-oriented intellect in favour of life-oriented intuition.

As Bergson defines it, intuition is an immediate participation in creativity as such, which eludes any mediation of a space, object or thing. Static objects, or "creatures," are mere illusions of a mind that through pursuit of its creatural interests has become more comfortable with the representation of material things than with the intuition of spirit.

> Everything is obscure in the idea of creation if we think of *things* which are created and a *thing* which creates, as we habitually do. [... For] there *are* no things, there are only actions [...]. God thus defined has nothing of the already made; He is unceasing life, action, freedom. Creation, so conceived, is not a mystery; we experience it in ourselves when we act freely.[74]

In other words, living time does not pass *through* objects in space, it creates and distributes them over the course of its own unfolding (just as spiritual mind, or memory, is not mediated but only filtered and limited by the organic functions of the brain). Our intuitive experience of time is immediate, indivisible, sufficient, absolute. It leaves no place for the concepts presumed by any operation of re-presentation–distance, nothingness, absence, negation, void, etc. Mysticism thus figures as the logical culmination of Bergson's system because

> the ultimate end of mysticism is the establishment of a contact, consequently of a partial coincidence, with the creative effort which life itself manifests. This effort is of God, if it is not God himself. The great mystic is to be conceived as an individual being, capable of transcending the limitations imposed on the species by its material nature, thus continuing and extending the divine action.[75]

The great mystics are people who become perfectly transparent vehicles for the singular creative force that surges through all living things. By leaping across all social and material boundaries, they achieve "identification of the human will with the divine will." They "simply open their souls to the oncoming wave" and become pure "instruments of God," such that "it is God who is acting through the soul in the soul."[76]

With Deleuze this creation-centred conception of things becomes more absolute, not less.[77] His philosophy everywhere relies on the point of departure he adapts from Bergson in opposition to Hegel: whereas according to Hegel "the thing differs with itself because it differs first with all that it is not," with all the objects to which it relates, Deleuze's Bergson affirms that a "thing differs with itself first, immediately," on account of the "internal explosive force" it carries within itself.[78] Fully creative "difference *must relate different to different without any mediation whatsoever* by the identical, the similar, the analogous or the opposed."[79] But unlike Bergson, Deleuze seeks precisely to elaborate a singular conception of creation that might include matter itself – a creation unlimited by *any* medium external to itself. Deleuze equates being as such with absolute creativity. To put things in unabashedly simplified terms, this equation again implies: (i) that all existent things exist in one and the same way, univocally, as so many active creatings; (ii) that these (virtual) creatings are themselves aspects of a limitless and consequently singular creative power; (iii) that every creating gives rise to a derivative (actual) creature whose own power or creativity is limited by its material organisation, its situation, its capacities, its relations with other creatures, and so on; (iv) that the main task facing any such creature is to dissolve these limitations, in order to become, broadly in line with Corbin's "angelic" conception of things, the immaterial vehicle for that virtual creating which alone individuates it. In the case of human creatures, this involves first and foremost the dissolution of all those mental habits which sustain the illusion we have of ourselves as independent subjects preoccupied with the representation of other subjects or objects; it also involves the dissolution of all the psychological, social, historical, territorial and ultimately organic structures which enable these habits to continue. Rather than supervise the rational coordination of representations, Deleuze orients his philosophy in line with that immediate, overwhelming participation in reality which in *Anti-Oedipus* he and Guattari attribute to the figure of the schizophrenic – a participation which "brings the schizo as close as possible to the beating heart of reality [...], to an intense point identical with the production of the real."[80]

Absolute creativity can only proceed through the eventual evacuation of all actual or creaturely mediation. Purely creative thought can only take place in a wholly virtual dimension and must operate at literally infinite speed. Any particular creature can reorient itself in line with the virtual creating that it expresses through a series of transformations or "becomings" directed towards what Deleuze presents as their exclusive telos: their "becoming-imperceptible."[81] Every organic creature, for instance, coordinates sensations and reactions through some sort of sensory-motor mechanism and thereby subordinates the perception of movement to the creaturely interests of that organism. However, "as soon as it stops being related to an interval as sensory-motor centre," as soon as it escapes the mediation of representation, then creative "movement finds its absolute quality again" and returns to the primordial "regime of universal variation, which goes beyond the human limits of the sensory-motor schema towards a non-human world where movement equals matter, or else in the direction of that super-human world which speaks for a new spirit."[82] The question: how, as creatures, "can we rid ourselves of ourselves?"[83] thus finds an answer in the promise of

> imperceptibility, indiscernibility, and impersonality – the three virtues. To reduce oneself to an abstract line, a trait, in order to find one's zone of indiscernibility with other traits, and in this way enter the haecceity and impersonality of the creator. One is then like grass: one has made the whole world into a becoming because one has suppressed in oneself everything that prevents us from slipping between things ...[84]

In his determination to affirm the implacable "stony" presence of things,[85] their cruel indiffer-

ence to all the various meanings or expectations that we project upon them, Clément Rosset takes the critique of transcendence one step closer towards an integral materialism on the Lucretian model. Of all the thinkers under consideration here, Rosset is the one who most emphatically repeats the essential principle that polarises our field as a whole: the real, each real, is singular, unique, self-sufficient, and "the destiny of every experience of reality is to be immediate and only immediate."[86] Since many if not most such experiences are unpleasant if not "hideous," we spend most of our time concocting ways of keeping them at a safe distance. We protect ourselves from the real behind suitably contrived illusions or masks. Rosset conceives of his project as a generalised unmasking or dis-illusionment (which clears the way, in turn, for an unconditional affirmation of the real behind the mask). He denounces whatever pretends to mediate, distance or otherwise anaesthetise our access to the real. The real is experienced immediately or not at all. The real exists in the absence of any principle other than itself, in the absence of any representation or image, any "double" of itself; our knowledge of the real is consumed in the (inexhaustible) tautology whereby the real simply is what it ineluctably is, to the exclusion of any alternative mode or way of being. Every reality is thus marked above all by its "idiotic" or "stupefying singularity," and in so far as it is always "singular, the real is that which authorises no guarantee of its existence other than itself."[87]

Relentless critic of that "metaphysical illusion" whereby (on the model of Plato's allegory of the cave) the real can only be recognised as real if it expresses some higher or ideal reality which alone is authorised to explain it,[88] Rosset might seem at first glance to have nothing in common with those who, like Corbin or Henry, preach renunciation of the world in favour of an other-worldly truth. Obvious differences of priority aside, however, this is not at all the case. Rosset's primary principle is no less absolute, no less self-sufficient than those of Corbin or Henry. All three thinkers share an equally vigorous revulsion for representation, i.e. the attempt to conceive of the real as an object which might then be doubled with an image and a meaning and thus with a recognisable place in a series of recognisable similarities and differences. Rosset's real, no less than Henry's life, is precisely *not* an object in the ordinary (i.e. representable or "creatural") sense of the word. "The real is that which, lacking any double, remains resistant to any identification […], foreign to all characterisation" or "description," and the "more an object is real, the more it is unidentifiable." The more "intense is the impression of the real [*le sentiment du réel*], the more it is indescribable and obscure."[89] Rosset is as disturbed as is Corbin or Henry by "that eminently terroristic idea according to which all persons are like one another."[90] No less than Henry's Living, his real is so radically unique as to be essentially "silent" and "invisible."[91] Rather than some well-defined objective thing, rather than "something that preserves itself, the real is instead that which is present at every instant, an offering [*offrande*] of being against the ultimate backdrop of non-being, which is of value only in the instant in which it is." Rather than a present or presentable thing, the real consists, according to a formula that will reappear in the work of Jean-Luc Nancy, in "the perpetually renewed *gift* of presence."[92]

Less than *a* being, in other words, Rosset's real concerns what Corbin and Jambet call, after Mulla Sadra, the creative *act* of being or making-be. It is clearly the intuition of this act (rather than its result) that underlies Rosset's secularised conception of beatitude or grace, which he names "joy [*allégresse*]."[93] Joy is the experience of the real as utterly sufficient in itself. If joy is a "loving knowledge of the real" the difference between joy and love is precisely the fact that love remains limited by its need to be complemented by a direct object (its need for a *complément d'objet*) whereas joy consists in an approval "situated above and beyond all the performances and possibilities of love." Joy is above and beyond every specifiable object. Love is nothing more than "a little joy directed by chance to some particular object," whereas joy embraces that "absolutely undetermined object" which is life in general. The object of joy is nothing other than "the fact that the real exists, that there is something rather than nothing," i.e.

the act of being as such.[94] In its non-relational integrity, in its absolute indifference to any specific object, "joy is an all-or-nothing proposition" – this is what accounts for what Rosset himself is prepared to call its "totalitarian nature."[95]

Once again, then, what's real is the dynamic creating rather than its derivative creature. The real conforms to both a "principle of sufficient reason," such that its attestation requires no reference to anything other than itself, *and* a "principle of uncertainty," so that every real can appear as either substantial or "evanescent," on the model of love, which never loses the "double power to appear and to disappear, to be and not to be." Such is "the ambiguity inherent in every species of reality."[96] (Such too is the ambiguous persistence of duality in philosophies directed to the abolition of every figure of doubling or representation.) As a result, "the identity of the real cannot be known directly," i.e. as an object, but only in so far as it fails to coincide with any duplication or representation of the real.[97] The real is that non-coincident, non-identical thing to which we can never become accustomed, which we will never be able to anticipate or recognise. "The real is nothing stable, nothing constituted, nothing that has been brought to a stop." So we experience the real when, negatively, all that solidifies or consolidates our (invariably futile) attempts to represent or escape it suddenly collapse,[98] just as we flee the real when we seek refuge in a version of what Sartre calls bad faith, when we adopt a role or image which we hope will provide (always ineffectual) security from real instability. As Oedipus comes to understand too late, the real emerges only amidst the ruins of creatural illusions.[99] The necessary price for any genuine "enjoyment of life" is a radical "indifference to yourself": if you are to know and love yourself as yourself, you must first "abandon your image in favour of your self as such, i.e. yourself as invisible, as inestimable or imperceptible [*inappréciable*]." It is only as *inappréciable* that you can ever be worthy of love.[100] "Romantic" is the label that Rosset assigns to those who fail to understand this point. Like Girard before him, what Rosset identifies as the Romantic delusion par excellence is the determination to cultivate your identity or image as such. But the truth is that as the bearer of an identity you can never amount to anything more durable than those identity papers which alone reliably identify you as this or that creature. The creature qua creature is no more substantial than paper itself.[101]

By the same token, however, we experience the positivity of the real when we ourselves manage to act as channels for a non-representative or un-mediated creativity. If music figures here as the "exemplary reality" this is not because it offers an especially appropriate or eminent *image* of the real but because it illustrates "its principal and characteristic performance, which is to exist on the basis of its own authority, independently of any origin or *raison d'être*." The most obviously non-representative of the arts, music is for that very reason free to express the real as such. Music is entirely absorbed in *this* particular real that it is. "Music is creation of the real in its raw state, without commentary or image [*réplique*]; it is the only form of art that presents a real as such," precisely because it alone among all "human creations" avoids duplication or imitation of something other than itself.[102]

It is because he affirms the immediately singular quality of the real, finally, that Rosset must also share Corbin's ultimately apophatic orientation. Since the real, "as singular, can never be seen or described," so then, as Rosset is quite happy to admit, "the ontology of the real can only be a 'negative ontology'" on the mystical model, in accordance with Meister Eckhart's principle that where God (or the real) is concerned "we can see only when we cannot see and understand only when we do not understand ..."[103] Singular in both occasion and motivation, "the intervention of joy is forever mysterious."[104]

Perhaps the only feasible way to refer here to the exceptionally abstract non-philosophy of François Laruelle is as a still more immediate, still more anti-relational variation on the pattern that has emerged thus far. His concern is again with a principle that must be thought as self-sufficient, indivisible, as immanent and immediate to itself, but thought now in such a way as to

singularise its singularity as such. If the singular always involves absolution from relation, Laruelle aims to absolve from relation this very absolution from relation. He presumes that rigorous singularity can only be thought if it is posited in such a way as to withdraw it from *every* possible relation with another principle (being, life, difference, etc.), along with any form of "self-relation."[105] The One must even be thought in such a way that it remains unaffected by this thinking itself. "The founding axiom of non-philosophy is that the One or the Real is foreclosed to thought."[106]

Pushing past Levinas, Derrida and Deleuze, Laruelle wants to escape entirely from what he calls the lingering "realist presupposition" of contemporary philosophy, its pretension to account for or describe what still figure, precisely, as *accountable* characteristics of the real. He achieves this, quite simply, by positing the real in such a way as to guarantee that it will remain forever stripped of every conceivable characteristic. What this means is that the real, or one, must be thought in an *exclusively axiomatic* way, rather than as the object of any sort of intuition or experience (let alone any sort of representation or knowledge). Just as mathematics grounds the reality of its elementary terms – an empty set, a geometric point – in their exclusively axiomatic assertion as operationally reliable but strictly undefinable or indescribable terms (thereby opening the door to wholly unrepresentable, wholly unintuitable configurations of thought, on the model of non-Euclidean geometries and post-Cantorian set theories), so too Laruelle insists that the indivisible individual or one presented by a non-philosophical "science of man will be real because *posited* as irreducible reality." What currently go by the (philosophically authorised) name of "human sciences," by contrast, are not interested in indivisible humanity as such but only in the description of those various "attributes that allow for our division – man as speaking or sexual being, as social or economic, etc."[107]

Whereas philosophy, including the philosophies of difference advanced by Deleuze and Derrida, always involves the combination of at least two terms (the one and the multiple, or being and appearing, or presence and absence, etc.), Laruelle's "non-philosophy" posits the individual or one as an identity without either separation or combination. His one is without *mélange*, it can only be thought in so far as it "knows itself immediately and without any distance from itself."[108] As one of the clearest available introductions to his work explains:

> this is an identity even more radical than the immanent life uncovered by Michel Henry. The latter, precisely because of its *in*-visibility, is the result of a refusal of philosophy or philosophy's object, the world, and hence ultimately remains caught up within the philosophical web of combination or Difference. Instead of constituting an immanence or a transcendence that exceeds philosophy, thereby maintaining an ultimate relation to it, the One is a radically autonomous term: *it implies no relation whatsoever, not even one of rupture or refusal, with philosophy or the world.* Laruelle breaks with philosophising, but if this break is not to remain illusory, it has to be a consequence – and only a consequence – that follows from an *identity-without-difference*: the identity of the One which, since it does not refuse (or accept) anything in and of itself, determines man as what is radically Immanent, without-time and without-space, simply because it is without-philosophy. And since it is radically autonomous and cannot be gauged either in terms of thought or language, the One is *no more thinkable than unthinkable, no more sayable than unsayable.*[109]

In other words, rather than think *of* the individual in relation to some universal (being, nature, reason, etc.) that it individuates or transcends, Laruelle seeks to "think the individual directly, from itself."[110] Of all the thinkers under consideration here, Laruelle goes to the greatest lengths to refuse thinking the individual as in any way mediated by anything other than itself, by anything that relates to society or history or the world. Mediated by the world, the individual only ever appears as a certain *kind* of individual, never as individual per se – it appears only as an organic individual, a social individual, an historical or psychological individual, etc., i.e. as a particular kind of being qualified by particular

sorts of attributes. Laruelle asserts, by contrast, the empty and inconsequential individuality of the individual (and the consequently dispersive discontinuity of multiple individuals, or "minorities") as its singular and exclusive characteristic.

Particularly in his most recent work, Laruelle is careful to present non-philosophy as a theory destined *for* philosophy (which means, in his terms, for the world).[111] He adheres, nonetheless, to the essential principle polarising our field as a whole, whereby you are only truly an individual if you are so absolutely. "Man is only given as man to man insofar as he is given in his *sufficient humanity*, rather than as a being of language, sexuality, power, and so on." The sufficiency of this giving is simply a measure of its singularity as such, i.e. the immediacy of its own self-assertion as "already given," as "*donation immédiate ou absolue.*"[112] That "the irreducible structure of the individual resides in its absolute and immediate coincidence with itself" implies its equally absolute "indifference" to the world and thus its invulnerable resistance to any form of philosophical manipulation.[113] In other words, what individuates the individual is again absolved from any process that might mediate it through the categories of knowledge, representation or the world. It is as if Laruelle has decreed that prospect of radical de-individuation so dreaded by Henry and Corbin impossible in advance. "Not everything is philosophisable," Laruelle tells us: "such is the good news I bring."[114]

If Levinas and Deleuze have pushed a singular conception of thought to its opposing limits, Sartre situates punctual and contingent (and mutually exclusive) instances of the absolute in each individual consciousness.[115] Consciousness is primary and self-causing, it "determines its existence at each moment [...;] each moment of our conscious life reveals to us a creation ex nihilo."[116] Pure creating without a creature, consciousness is not an object, it has no inside. Grounded in the power of imagination to negate the world we observe, consciousness has no structure or depth that might allow it to "digest" the objects it perceives. So although consciousness is always intentional, always conscious *of* something, consciousness is doubly independent of any mediation through objects in the world. Lacking any inside, it is immediately exposed to the (attractive, repulsive, fearsome, etc.) qualities of the object, such that "if we love a woman it is because she is lovable."[117] For the same reason, consciousness remains forever free to decide on *how* it is to be conscious of its objects (as passionate, or jealous, or indifferent, etc.). It is always a subject who invests obstacles or misfortunes, for instance, with their adversity. Strictly speaking, "a meaning can only come from subjectivity itself."[118]

A situation of consciousness, in other words, is precisely not constituted as relation of "*knowledge* or even an affective understanding of a state of the world by a subject," but is immediately constituted as an immediate "*relation of being* between a [conscious] for-itself and the [objective] in-itself that it negates."[119] So although consciousness is always conscious of something, these somethings remain merely the occasions of consciousness: they do not mediate or otherwise affect the way consciousness is conscious of them. Since the "self" of self-consciousness is nothing more than another object of consciousness, consciousness as such is grounded only in the "nothingness" of an objectless or non-thetic being *for*-itself. If I take myself as the object of my consciousness, for example, I may know that (as an object) I am happy or sad; my knowing this, however, is not itself happy or sad. This knowing, this non-thetic or pre-reflexive consciousness, can never itself be taken as object. It eludes all identity and all description. It is only as nothing for itself that it can be truly *for* itself, i.e. pure evasion or flight from itself.

The elusive logic of Sartre's for-itself thus conforms in most respects to the more general difference between an (objective) creature and a (subjective) creating: if a creature is defined by its nature, by what it is in-itself, a creating is precisely never identical to itself. The negation of any identity or "self," the for-itself never coincides with itself, it is nothing other than freedom or creativity as such.[120] Just as from a theophanic perspective there is no relation *between* the subject and the thinking that thinks through the subject, so too Sartre's *pour-soi* is thought through by a self-positing consciousness to which

the categories of relation do not apply: in either case there is no "outside" the subject, or rather, the subject is nothing other than a vehicle for the process that constantly displaces it outside itself. Creator of the meanings that I attribute to things, responsible for the very fact "that there is a world," accountable for its every subjective quality (including those I am obliged to suffer, receive, or inherit), it can make no more sense for me to complain about what happens to me than it would for God to regret what happens on earth.[121] By the same token, my world remains exclusively mine. Though I can only justify what I do in terms that apply in principle to what everyone should do, this is precisely because I am not constrained by relations with others that might limit my responsibility for what I do (or what everyone does). Absolute, singular and immediate, consciousness persists by definition in a "primary absence of relation."[122] Another subject can only be an object for me, or vice versa: it is impossible to think of two absolute subjects *together*. It is impossible, in other words, to relate to a nothingness.

Absolute freedom and universal responsibility are points of departure for Sartre, grounded in the self-causing operation of consciousness as pure subject (or pure non-object). Very roughly speaking, we might think of Alain Badiou's project as an evolving effort to reconceive these points in terms of *processes* that occasionally come to pass. What Badiou calls "truths" are singular procedures that take place from time to time in situations governed by a given regime of representation; subtracted from the grip of this regime, truths generate un-representable statements which eventually come to acquire a universal subjective validity. No philosopher could be further from Henry's vitalist theology than Badiou. It is all the more striking, then, that, no less than Henry (or Laruelle), Badiou grounds his project on the integrity of a "subject without object."[123] No less than Sartre (or Jambet), this primacy is itself grounded on the literally foundational role played by that which figures as void in the situation, i.e. that which cannot be counted or represented as an object of any kind. By grounding, in turn, the truths of ontology upon the object-less or void-based operations of elementary mathematics, Badiou further evacuates being itself of that opacity and inertia which continue to characterise Sartre's in-itself – in this sense we might say that Badiou is to Sartre somewhat as Deleuze is to Bergson. On the other hand, by thinking of the subject as abruptly "induced" by a truth that is itself sparked by an exceptional and ephemeral event (a revolution, a mobilisation, an invention, an encounter, etc.), Badiou insists on the rarity of the subject in terms that break decisively not just with Sartre's early conception of absolute freedom but equally with Sartre's later, more dialectical conception of relative emancipation (i.e. Sartre's insistence on the fact that, though circumstances beyond our control largely make us what we are, "we can always make something of what we are made to be"[124]).

Sparked by an event that occurs at the "edge of the void" of a situation, a truth proceeds as the universalisable collection of elements of the situation according to initially unrecognisable criteria that are consistent with the anarchic being of these elements themselves, i.e. with "being in its fearsome and creative inconsistency, or in its void, which is the without-place of every place."[125] Despite his emphatic distance from the theophanic perspectives embraced by Jambet or Corbin, say, Badiou would at least agree that "creative inconsistency" can only be thought by a subject whose principle of subjectivation is subtracted from mediation through the world as we know it. Inconsistent or creative being can only be thought through the affirmation of a truth as it "bores a hole" in the forms of knowledge and representation that sustain a world.[126] In every case, "the truth is not said of the object, but says itself only of itself."[127]

Of all the thinkers at issue here, Jacques Derrida is the most notoriously resistant to rapid characterisation, but since no survey of this kind would be complete without some reference to his work we might at least suggest that he is best read in terms of a more occasion-dependent conception of transcendence than the version affirmed by Levinas. No less than Levinas (indeed no less than Sartre[128]), Derrida orients thought to the purely elusive or non-identical work of a "creator" utterly beyond creation and

thus purged of any presence or proximity, any tacit complicity with its creatures – purged, in short, of that whole thematics of intimacy, home, dwelling, and so on, that Derrida discerns in Heidegger's work.[129] But he accepts the fact that we can only so orient thought from the occasions offered by readings of particular texts or instances of thought. A logocentric text is precisely a creating that seeks to establish itself as an independent creature, one that, on the model of Plato's conception of authoritative speech, attempts to grasp *itself* as present and autonomous, in denial of the evasive dynamism of writing or signification which in fact sustains it. Derrida "define[s] writing as the impossibility that a signifying chain might come to a stop with a certain signified"[130] before immediately starting off again in an unending sequence of supplements and substitutions. Writing, or différance, is nothing other than the infinitely non-identical proliferation of creatings that only ever appear to come to a stop in the textual creatures to which they give rise. "It is the determination of being as presence or as beingness that is interrogated by the thought of différance," since différance thinks only creatings as such. It is because the movement of creating per se can never present itself as a creature (however eminent) that we already *know* that différance must always remain

> unnameable, because there is no name for it at all, not even the name of essence or of Being, not even that of "différance," which is not a name, which is not a pure nominal unity, and which unceasingly dislocates itself in a chain of differing and deferring substitutions.[131]

Stretching things a little, we might say that Derrida writes a version of Bergsonism adjusted to the (considerable) consequences of the linguistic turn.

The point is, again, that the singular productive principle at work here is not itself essentially mediated by the unstable, if not illusory, objects it creates. "Since being has never had a 'meaning,' has never been thought or said as such except by dissimulating itself in beings, then différance, in a certain and very strange way, (is) 'older' than the ontological difference, or than the truth of being,"[132] and it remains so all through the infinite play of differences to which it gives rise and whose deconstruction it anticipates. There is nothing particularly strange about this priority in a theophanic context, however: if "nothing precedes différance," this is again because no more than Bergson's creator is différance a thing standing outside of other things. "Différance is the structured and differing origin of differences [...], the difference that produces differences," which is also to say that it figures as non-origin, or as pre-original.[133] The play of différance is "unlimited" precisely because it precedes the question of the world as such and transcends, in its anarchic creativity, any limitation by an *Ens supremum* or transcendental signified:

> One could call play the absence of the transcendental signified as illimitation of play, that is the crumbling of onto-theology and the metaphysics of presence [...]. This play, thought as absence of the transcendental signified, is not a *play in the world*, as it has always been defined, for the purpose of containing it, by the philosophical tradition [...]. To think play radically the ontological and transcendental problematics must first be seriously exhausted.[134]

Différance leaves *traces* in being (in creation), in other words, because it meets the condition that Levinas sets for any such tracing: "only a being that transcends the world, an ab-solute being, can leave a trace."[135]

Similarly, the general effort of Derrida's more recent reflections on friendship, ethics, forgiveness, the gift, and so on, is perhaps best summed up as an attempt to preserve the creative "undecidability" that is at work in any genuinely ethical decision, and thus to keep every such decision open, elusive, non-identical. Everything turns on "the decision of the absolute other in me, the other as the absolute that decides on me in me," but "since each of us, each other is infinitely other in its absolute singularity, inaccessible, solitary, transcendent, nonmanifest," so then my relation to the other develops in keeping with that paradigmatic "non-relation" of creature to Creator dramatised in Abraham's relation to God – a relation to the other as absolutely other (*tout autre*).[136] Every true decision must proceed,

in other words, as a vessel for that unconditional and ultimately "secret" undecidability that works through it.

> The crucial experience of the *perhaps* imposed by the undecidable – that is to say, the condition of decision – is not a moment to be exceeded, forgotten, or suppressed. It continues to constitute the decision as such; it can never again be separated from it; it produces it *qua* decision *in and through* the undecidable.

Hence the undecidable inconsistency characteristic of any creating suitably oriented to that absolute (i.e. absolutely non-identical) creativity which alone sustains it, i.e. that elusive inconsistency which appears as the complement to any creaturely consistency and which "always consists in not consisting, in eluding consistency and constancy, presence, permanence or substance, essence or existence, as well as any concept of truth which might be associated with them."[137] Sartre and Badiou could only agree: for all the obvious differences between their work, the articulation of inconsistency and decision is essential to all three thinkers.

IV

Such is the inconsistent consistency of the ways in which recent French philosophy has tended to orient itself towards a singular conception of individuation. Needless to say, this review is far from complete: a more inclusive introduction might include reference to Bataille, Blanchot, Girard, Althusser, Baudrillard, Serres, Lyotard, along with certain aspects of the work of Lacan, Barthes, Kristeva and Foucault; it might also venture comparisons with Negri, Agamben and Žižek. This clearly is not the place to hazard a substantial explanation of why versions of this configuration of thought should have inspired so many French thinkers during the twentieth century. By way of a conclusion, however, it may be worth returning briefly to Michel Henry's own suggestive account. Corbin again anticipates the essential point: by definition, "history is not the place in which supreme divine consciousness develops." On the contrary, "history as such dissolves or vanishes" in the face of theophany.[138] In equally adamant opposition to the Hegelian conception of things, Henry likewise insists that the absolute "does not produce itself in history" and remains independent of historical development. "The idea that the absolute might reveal itself progressively, bit by bit, is absurd."[139] Absolute immediacy excludes historical or worldly mediation as a matter of course. Variations on this principle have been endorsed by all of the thinkers we have reviewed thus far, including the most emphatically atheist among them – Badiou, Deleuze and the early Sartre.

Unsurprisingly, then, Henry identifies the crucial philosophical error with mediation itself. The error, he says, is to believe that the absolute can only express itself through relative means, that being must reveal itself through appearing, that absolute subjectivity can only know itself in so far as it externalises and distances itself over time in a world of objects. Apart from a few exceptional thinkers (Meister Eckhart, Jacob Boehme, Maine de Biran, etc.) who recognise that living self-revelation owes nothing to time or to its manifestation in a world and who insist instead that we are ourselves the immediate incarnation of timeless creativity, the entire Western philosophical tradition, Heidegger included, is marked by its persistence in this false conception of manifestation as visible exteriorisation-temporalisation. For obvious reasons it is the modern phase of this tradition, the phase that begins with Kant and that revels in its growing mastery of objects and its unchecked domination of the world, that is most grievously guilty of the charge. Kant's critical idea is that thought avoids delirium only in so far as it is mediated through that which is other than thought, i.e. through the categories that allow for our knowledge of objects. Thought will advance as it develops more reliable means of representing that which appears as "external reality." As far as Henry is concerned, Hegel simply confirms Kant's essential principle when he conceives of the absolute as the historical process of its own self-externalisation or self-objectification, such that spirit only becomes one with itself by passing through the mediation of the world. That spirit is itself the principle of this world leaves

the basic error intact, namely the understanding of creation as mediated by the objective qualities of its creatures rather than as immediately expressed in the subjective sufficiency of its creatings. By obliging spirit to work through the world Hegel completes the secularisation (or annihilation) of spirit. This is the long error that Henry's Marx finally corrects when, in his *Theses on Feuerbach*, he

> moves from an intuitive subjectivity that establishes and receives the object, an "objective" subjectivity, to a subjectivity that is no longer "objective," to a radical subjectivity from which all objectivity is excluded [...]. Reality, that which up to the present has been understood as the object of intuition, that is, as object, as sensuous world [...], is originally nothing of the sort.[140]

We might say then, very approximately, that French philosophy from Descartes to Brunschvicg tended to adhere to versions of the modern objectivist paradigm, whereby rational progress coincides with the development of ever more adequate forms of representing the world and ever more universally acknowledged forms of resolving conflicts and dilemmas in the world. During the nineteenth century, in particular, the world remained a tolerable partner for thought, or at least offered no significant "objection" to thought. The world seemed to make itself available to rational observation and administration (to say nothing of exploitation, commodification, colonisation, etc.). But from Bergson to Badiou, the most forceful French philosophers of the twentieth century would decide, in effect, that the world had become essentially intolerable. The gap that Levinas opens at the beginning of his *Totality and Infinity* locates the philosophical space he shares with the majority of his contemporaries: "'True life is absent.' But we are in the world." Our contemporary world, Badiou will conclude, is organised as an "obstacle to the desire for philosophy."[141] This world invites passive complacency at best, barbarism or despair at worst. Recent French philosophers came to embrace a singular conception of thought to the degree that they judged the world incapable of redemption.

This judgement is not itself an undifferentiated one, of course. It ranges from *contempt* if not hatred for the world (Corbin and Lardreau) through a somewhat gentler *compassion* for the world (Bergson, Levinas) to a rigorously dispassionate *indifference* to the world (Badiou and Laruelle).[142] It may well be that this judgement was, for a time, the condition of philosophy's survival. Perhaps it remains so to this day. Today's world is one in which judgement is ever more coercively aligned, one way or another, with the prevailing way of the world as such, in keeping with the global movement of "investment" and privatisation, the global coordination of communication, the global dynamic of systemic exploitation, i.e. in keeping with the movement that tends to inhibit genuine forms of intervention in the world – it is for this reason that Badiou declares that today "there is no world" at all.[143]

In such circumstances it is certainly essential that philosophy do something other than merely react (or resign itself) to the world, even a non-existent one. During the 1980s and 1990s, years in which many thinkers, French included, made a positive virtue of such resignation, our anti-worldly philosophers allowed philosophy itself to continue. It is hard to think, today, of a philosophical project worthy of the name that does not continue in this continuation.

We will never change tomorrow's world, however, on the basis of a non-relation.

Many of the contributions to this issue of *Angelaki* will demonstrate, I hope, the enduring depth and provocative power of a non-relational conception of thought. About half of the contributions will also indicate divergences, resistances, complications, more or less explicit reactions against it. By reading them together we can begin to consider, above and beyond the persistence of certain familiar themes common to virtually every thinker in the field (the affirmation of the open-ended destiny of thought, of that which is to-come (*à-venir*), of the generic or anti-communitarian address of philosophy, its unclassifiable im-propriety, its complex universality, and so on), how far these divergences might be thought as variations on a non-relational logic, as reactions against this logic, or as neither one nor the other. Indeed, so long as such questions are posed in terms of one *or* the other – pure singularity or pure alterity – then the non-relational orientation common to both will persist unchanged. Something different may begin when we start to rethink what is involved in the *and* of "one and the other."[144] Tomorrow arrives through its relation with today, and the task of changing the world will only proceed through forms of militant mediation that involve both terms: change *and* world.

Today's French philosophers have developed a conception of singular or non-relational thought as varied and ingenious as any in the history of philosophy. The task of tomorrow's generation of thinkers may be to develop an equally resilient relational alternative.

acknowledgements

I am very grateful to Françoise Anvar, Amandine Sossa and Julie Poincelet for transcribing some of the interviews, to Antoine Hatzenberger, Sinéad Rushe and Sarah Hirschmuller for helping with several of the translations, and above all to Alberto Toscano, Ray Brassier and Bruno Bosteels for engaging, with their usual brilliance and enthusiasm, with many of the most challenging aspects of this project.

notes

1 I would like to thank Ray Brassier, Bruno Bosteels and Christian Kerslake for their helpful and incisive readings of an earlier version of this essay.

Where a reference contains two page numbers separated by a forward slash, the first number refers to the original edition and the second to the translation listed in the bibliography; "tm" stands for "translation modified." When no note accompanies a quotation, the reference is included in the next note.

2 For example, Gary Gutting concludes his useful and substantial history of twentieth-century French philosophy with an emphasis on pragmatic pluralism and fatigue. Now that the distinctive effort of this philosophy – its elaboration of

competing accounts of radical freedom – seems to be "essentially exhausted," it is apparently easier to realise that "experience can be read in many different ways, each with its own plausibility, self-consistency, and limitations [...]. Philosophies are like novels, not alternative absolutes among which we must choose the 'right one' but different perspectival visions [...], all of which have their relative values and uses" (Gutting, *French Philosophy in the Twentieth Century* 385–86, 390). Exceptions to this trend include Michel Haar's Heidegger-inspired critique of the metaphysical tendencies in the work of Sartre, Levinas, Henry and Derrida (Haar, *La Philosophie française entre phénoménologie et métaphysique*) and Judith Butler's suggestion that for Lacan and Deleuze, along with other thinkers marked by a "residual Hegelianism," "a version of absolute presence, albeit internally differentiated, is the final aim or *telos* of desire" (Butler, *Subjects of Desire* 216). I presented an initial characterisation of the singular orientation of the field in my "The Singular and the Specific: Recent French Philosophy" (2000).

3 Although the editorial priorities behind the present issue are perfectly transparent, the reader will appreciate, I hope, that not every major figure in the field was willing or able to participate in a project of this kind. The original list of invitations also included Juliette Simont, Jacques Derrida, Pierre Macherey, Julia Kristeva, Jean-Claude Milner, Michèle Le Doeff, and Barbara Cassin.

4 Eriugena, *Periphyseon* III 681A.

5 Eriugena, *Periphyseon* III, 678C, V, 982C.

6 Eriugena, *Periphyseon* II, 528B.

7 See, in particular, Jambet, *La Logique des Orientaux* 118, 224–25.

8 Corbin, *Histoire de la philosophie islamique* 357; Corbin, *Philosophie iranienne* 118; cf. Jambet, *La Logique des Orientaux* 38. Or, as Michel Henry would put it: rather than initiation through a text, an image or a representation, it is "Truth and Truth alone that can offer us access to itself [...]. More radically, divine essence consists in Revelation as self-revelation, as revelation of itself on the basis of itself. Only one to whom that revelation is made can enter into it, into its absolute truth." And then there is "no separation between the seeing and what is seen, between the light and what it illuminates" (Henry, *C'est moi la vérité*

17/9–10, 36/24; cf. Henry, *L'Essence de la manifestation* 69).

9 Descombes recognises a version of this point in his critique of the Nietzsche-inspired movements of the 1960s and 1970s – "French Nietzscheanism claims to overcome the subject when in fact it suppresses the object," i.e. the referent of the text, the fact behind an interpretation, the event behind an historical account, the world behind a perspective (Descombes, *Modern French Philosophy* 189). Though more daring and inventive a field than Anglo-American analytic philosophy, French philosophy is thus also in a sense more concentrated in its approach: its subtractive orientation tends at least *towards* the evacuation of any object external to philosophical thinking itself, whereas Anglo-American philosophy is more directly caught up in problems of scientific method, in the real practice of experimentation, in questions concerned with cognitive and psychological development, with neurology and biology, with empirical language analysis, with applied mathematics, and so on.

10 Deleuze, *Logique du sens* 208/178; Deleuze, *Cinéma I* 80/54.

11 Eriugena, *Periphyseon* V, 977A–978B.

12 Cf. Lardreau [originally published as anonymous], *Vive le matérialisme!*

13 Deleuze, *Le Bergsonisme* 117/111.

14 Henry, *C'est moi la vérité* 40–70/27–52.

15 Ibid. 27–30/17–20. "For any living being, to come for good into the world, and to no longer be anything other than what is exhibited in the world as such, amounts to being offered as a cadaver. A cadaver is just that: a body reduced to its pure externality" (79/59).

16 Henry, *Marx* 162.

17 Henry, *C'est moi la vérité* 36/25, 104/81; Henry, *L'Essence de la manifestation* 595.

18 As far as Henry is concerned, Heidegger remains very much a thinker of the world rather than of life, a thinker for whom being is what appears in the light or clearing of the world. Henry reads Heidegger's conception of the sacred as that which illuminates being as nothing more than a denial of the sacred, and he reads his attempt to conceive of life in the form of a being-in-the-world as little short of its attempted murder (Henry, *C'est moi la vérité* 198/157, 62/46).

19 Henry, *L'Essence de la manifestation* 860.

20 Henry, *C'est moi la vérité* 52–53/38–39.

21 Henry, *Marx* 32.

22 Henry, *C'est moi la vérité* 303–04/243.

23 "Considered in itself, reality is nothing economic," and the economy acts precisely as "the mask of reality" (Henry, *Marx* 224, 228; cf. *C'est moi la vérité* 304–09/244–47).

24 Henry, *Marx* 160.

25 Henry, *Marx* 171. Communism figures here, then, as the moment when, "with the abolition of all mediation, subjectivity will be restored to itself" (199).

26 Henry, *C'est moi la vérité* 49/36; cf. 128/101.

27 Ibid. 75/56.

28 Ibid. 156–57/123–24.

29 Ibid. 133/104. Against Schopenhauer, against the Romantic affirmation of an anonymous power of impersonal life, Henry insists that "the individual can be identified with universal life only on the condition that an essential Ipseity does not disappear but is maintained – in the individual as well as in life itself" (153/121).

30 Ibid. Hence the

> relation between Individual and Life is precisely not a relation in the ordinary sense, that is, some sort of link between two separate terms each of which can exist without the other. Nor is it a "dialectic" relation, as defined by modern thought: a relation between two terms in which the one could not exist without the other [...]. The relation between Individual and Life in Christianity is a relation that takes place in Life and proceeds from it, being nothing other than Life's own movement. (150–51/119)

31 Ibid. 309–17/248–54.

32 Ibid. 263/210.

33 Ibid. 136/107.

34 Ibid. 263/209.

35 And Henry goes on, in terms that spell out the immediate link between Marx and Christ:

> as has been rightly said: the proletariat is Christ. The proletariat is the one [...] who must go to the very limit of suffering and of evil, to the sacrifice of his being, giving his sweat and blood and ultimately his very life, in order to reach – through this complete self-annihilation, through this self-negation which is a negation of life – the true life which leaves all finiteness and all particularity behind, which is a complete life and salvation itself. (Henry, *Marx* 73–74)

36 Henry, *C'est moi la vérité* 247/197.

37 Ibid. 123/97.

38 Ibid. 177/140, 264/211.

39 As Deleuze admits, creative "difference is explicated in systems in which it tends to be cancelled" (Deleuze, *Différence et répétition* 293/228). *Unlimited* creation cannot proceed without generating creaturely limitation, if only because it cannot itself be limited by anything at all. Though perfectly dynamic in itself, "life as movement alienates itself in the material form that it creates; by actualising itself, by differentiation itself, it loses 'contact with the rest of itself'" (Deleuze, *Le Bergsonisme* 108/104). Or as Levinas puts it: "it is certainly a great glory for the creator to have set up a being capable of atheism" (*Totalité et infini* 52/58).

40 Henry, *C'est moi la vérité* 245/195.

41 Ibid. 214/169, 210/166.

42 Henry, *Marx* 60–61.

43 Henry, *C'est moi la vérité*, 337–41/269–71.

44 Levinas, *Totalité et infini* 58/63,13/27. "The idea of Infinity is revealed [se révèle] in the strong sense of the term," and "the absolute experience is not disclosure but revelation: a coinciding of the expressed with him who expresses, which is the privileged manifestation of the Other" (*Totalité et infini* 56/62, 61/66).

45 Levinas, "Meaning and Sense" in *Basic Philosophical Writings* 53. Most famously, as Levinas describes it "the relation with the face [of the other] is not an object-cognition. The transcendence of the face is at the same time its absence from this world into which it enters" (*Totalité et infini* 72–73/75).

46 Levinas, *Autrement qu'être* 244, 24.

47 Levinas, *Totalité et infini* 79/80.

48 Levinas, "Transcendence and Height" in *Basic Philosophical Writings* 16.

49 Levinas, "Truth of Disclosure and Truth of Testimony" in *Basic Philosophical Writings* 104; "Transcendence and Height" in *Basic Philosophical Writings* 19–20; *Autrement qu'être* 216.

50 Corbin, *Le Paradoxe du monothéisme* 17.

51 Ibid. 11, 84–85. Cf. Jambet, *L'Acte d'être*.

52 Corbin, *Le Paradoxe du monothéisme* 12, 193.

53 Ibid. 17.

54 Deleuze, *Nietzsche et la philosophie* 93–94/83–84; cf. Deleuze, *Différence et répétition*, 332/258.

55 Meister Eckhart, *Vom Abgeschiedenheit (On Detachment)* in Eckhart, *Sermons and Treatises* III, 117–29.

56 Koyré, *La Philosophie de Jacob Boehme* 315, quoted in Corbin, *Le Paradoxe du monothéisme* 197. More frequently in Corbin's work a similar contrast is made between the generic or non-individuated conception of creation he associates with Averroes (in rationalist form) and al-Hallaj (in mystical form), on the one hand, and the singularising or immediately individuating theophanic conception he associates with Avicenna and Suhrawardi, on the other (Corbin, *Histoire de la philosophie islamique* 343; Corbin, *Avicenne et le récit visionnaire* 84; cf. Jambet, *La Logique des Orientaux* 130–32).

57 Corbin, *Le Paradoxe du monothéisme* 200.

58 Ibid. 203. The Angel is "the form under which the *Absconditum* is revealed to you according to your own essential being" (89). According to Suhrawardi's conception of things, the angel is that fully (divinely) individuated spiritual or celestial person from which the material creatural person "proceeds in a theurgic manner. All the natural relations and proportions that we might ascertain of the bodily entity are the shadow, image or icon of the spiritual relations and modalities of light that constitute the angelic hypostasis and its noetic activity" (50–51).

59 Corbin, *Histoire* 58; Corbin, *Philosophie iranienne* 16, 130–31.

60 Corbin, *Le Paradoxe du monothéisme* 126.

61 Ibid. 147. Hence Ibn al-Arabi's conclusion that it is in fact "our world that is hidden and which never appears, whereas it is Divine Being that is made manifest and which can never be hidden" (quoted in Corbin, *Le Paradoxe du monothéisme* 18).

62 Lardreau, "Lin Piao comme volonté et représentation" in *L'Ange* 109, 153. For these "souls purified of this world and wholly directed to the other" there is no greater vice than that "duplicity" or "hesitation" (89) which consists in trying to make of *any* activity in this world, including the most "liberated" forms of desire and jouissance, the means of an eventual redemption – a vice incarnated, in *L'Ange*, by Sade and Lyotard.

63 Jambet, *La Grande Résurrection d'Alamût* 179.

64 Jambet, *L'Acte d'être* 10–11; Jambet, *La Logique des Orientaux* 38; Jambet, *La Grande Résurrection d'Alamût* 81, 197. Cf. Corbin, *Histoire de la philosophie islamique* 78–79.

65 Jambet, *La Logique des Orientaux* 265, 82; cf. Jambet, *La Grande Résurrection d'Alamût* 104.

66 Jambet, *La Grande Résurrection d'Alamût* 11.

67 Ibid. 139, 143.

68 See, in particular, Jambet, *La Grande Résurrection d'Alamût* 143–44, 175–85. As Jambet himself observes, the most pertinent contemporary point of comparison for this conception of a creative *event* that is itself founded on the void of being and prompted by something other-than-being is the (radically secular) work of Alain Badiou (192, n. 228).

69 Bergson, *Les Deux Sources de la morale et de la religion* 103/101.

70 Bergson, *L'Evolution créatrice* 271/271, 251/250.

71 Ibid. 213/212. On the spiritualist orientation of Bergson's work see, in particular, Jankélévitch, *Henri Bergson* 86, 95, 247–52.

72 Bergson, *L'Evolution créatrice* 252/251.

73 Ibid. 266–70/265–70.

74 Ibid. 249/248–49.

75 Bergson, *Deux Sources* 233/220–21. The mystic is that person to whom "creation will appear as God undertaking to create creators, that He may have, besides Himself, beings worth of His love" (270/255).

76 Ibid. 242/229, 101/99, 332/311, 245/232.

77 I have developed this reading of Deleuze in my "Deleuze and Redemption from Interest" (1997); "Deleuze and the World without Others" (1997); "The Limits of Individuation" (2000); and "'Everything is Real'" (2003).

78 Deleuze, "La Conception de la différence chez Bergson" 96/53, 93/51. Henry again offers another useful point of comparison, in so far as "the revelation of absolute being is not separate from it, is nothing external to it, nothing unreal, is not an image of being but resides in it, in its reality as identical to it, as being itself" (Henry, *L'Essence de la manifestation* 859).

79 Deleuze, *Différence et répétition* 154/117.

80 Deleuze and Guattari, *L'Anti-Oedipe* 26/19 tm, 104/87.

81 "The imperceptible is the immanent end of becoming, its cosmic formula" (Deleuze and Guattari, *Mille plateaux* 342/279; cf. Deleuze, *Dialogues* 56/45). The crucial thing is always "finally to acquire the power to disappear" (Deleuze, *Cinéma 2* 248/190).

82 Deleuze, *Cinéma 2* 57–58/40.

83 Deleuze, *Cinéma 1* 97/66.

84 Deleuze and Guattari, *Mille plateaux* 342–43/279–80.

85 Rosset, *Le Réel* 43–44.

86 Rosset, *Le Principe de cruauté* 31. Every refusal of the real is precisely a refusal of its "immediacy," its "presence," its self-signifying sufficiency, its tautological redundancy – hence a major difference with Lacan's conception of the real as that which is "missing from its place," or that which signifies only through a register other than itself (through the symbolic or, rather, through gaps in the symbolic) (Rosset, *Le Réel et son double* 61, 75–76).

87 Rosset, *Le Réel* 41; Rosset, *L'Objet singulier* 34. When Rosset comes to respond directly to those who accuse him of always saying essentially the same thing he makes no effort to evade the charge: it is instead those false or pseudo-tautological discourses (*lapalissade*, pleonasm, truism, redundancy, and so on), discourses which seem to say that A is A but that in fact provide a *double* of A which they then employ to indicate some additional, albeit redundant, information about A, that are limited to an impoverished verification of the identity of A (the mere *equation* of A with A). As for tautology proper, which restricts itself to the affirmation that A *is* A (to the exclusion of *any* relation of A *with* A), Rosset maintains that it alone is adequate to the inexhaustible depth of A as such (Rosset, *Le Démon de la tautologie* 12, 33, 48).

88 Rosset, *Le Réel et son double* 60.

89 Rosset, *L'Objet singulier* 33.

90 Rosset, *Joyful Cruelty* 10–11.

91 Rosset, *Le Réel* 42.

92 Ibid. 79–80; my emphasis. For Rosset, as for Deleuze or Corbin, then, experience of the real involves a kind of dematerialisation, the "dissipation of ordinary forms of representation" and the evacuation of all "weight," all "intellectual or psychological heaviness" (*L'Objet singulier* 34, 97).

93 Rosset identifies his *allégresse* with Pascal's grace (Rosset, *Le Principe de cruauté* 23).

94 Rosset, *L'Objet singulier* 95, 101–02; Rosset, *Le Réel* 76.

95 Rosset, *Joyful Cruelty* 3.

96 Rosset, *Le Principe de cruauté* 55.

97 Rosset, *L'Objet singulier* 20–21. The ontological profile of Rosset's real, in other words, is much closer to what Sartre describes as the for-itself than to what remains simply (identically or objectively) in-itself.

98 Rosset, *Le Réel* 21, 45.

99 As a general rule, you trap yourself in the creatural by trying to avoid the creating that you are given to express. "It is by refusing to be that which you are […] that you become precisely that which you are"; it is precisely by trying to avoid seeming undesirable, for example, that you come to seem undesirable (Rosset, *Le Réel et son double* 99, 101). You will be what you must be, whatever happens, such is the inescapable cruelty of the real. But by trying to escape yourself (by trying to maintain a certain "image" of yourself in the eyes of others) you simply return yourself to yourself in the mode of creatural passivity, i.e. deprived of any possibility of joy. Such is the lesson incarnated by Oedipus in many of Rosset's books: it is by trying to avoid that which he is cruelly destined to become that he becomes it in the cruellest possible way, i.e. in such a way as to allow for no other way out than self-inflicted blindness (see, for instance, Rosset, *Le Réel et son double* 28–41). It is by trying to be other than what you are that you confirm yourself as *merely this* particular creature or object, and thereby lose any chance of affirming the creative singularity to which your existence attests.

100 Rosset, *Le Réel et son double* 112–14.

101 Ibid. 116–18; cf. Girard, *Mensonge romantique et vérité romanesque* (1961).

102 Rosset, *L'Objet singulier* 59–63. Likewise, a genuine metaphor deserves recognition as an *effet de réel* in so far as it indicates "the thing itself" but *as* something hitherto unrecognisable, something seen afresh, as part of a world that has itself been "made anew" (Rosset, *Le Démon de la tautologie* 43).

103 Rosset, *L'Objet singulier* 28–29. "Deprived of all ground," "indifferent to every objection," unable to account for itself, joy remains an "inexpressible hypothesis." By insisting on the "incompatibility between joy and its rational justification," Rosset implies that it is precisely the fact that joy cannot explain or justify itself that makes it truly joyful rather than simply pleasant or agreeable. "There is no true joy unless it is simultaneously thwarted, in contradiction with itself [...]. There is no joy which is not completely mad [*folle*]" (*Joyful Cruelty* 4–5, 16–17). There is indeed little that might distance Rosset from Corbin's acknowledgement of the ultimate transcendence of the *Absconditum* once he concludes that "the most direct relation of consciousness to the real is one of ignorance pure and simple" (*L'Objet singulier* 23).

104 Rosset, *Joyful Cruelty* 19.

105 Cf. Laruelle, *Le Principe de minorité* 125.

106 Laruelle, *Principes de la non-philosophie* vi. What Laruelle calls the process of non-philosophical "unilateralisation" involves the abrupt and unconditional isolation of an identity from any relation in which it might be (philosophically) implied, i.e. the invention of ways of "thinking that allow us exclusively to think the terms of a relation without reference to their relation itself" (Laruelle, *En tant qu'un* 217).

107 Laruelle, *En tant qu'un* 213–14. It is thanks to its strictly axiomatic basis, the fact that "the one is not a self-affecting logos," is not caught up in any sort of self-reflection or relation with itself (or with whatever might be other than itself), that Laruelle declares the "real and absolutely indivisible immanence of the One to be undeconstructible" (231). It is this same axiomatic determination that aligns non-philosophy with what Laruelle describes as the essentially "passive" relation of science to the real, i.e. the

sort of "naivety, the unnoticed and opaque immediation through which science relates in the last instance its procedures, equipment and theories to a real that figures as its required point of reference yet which is nevertheless never present as such" (237).

108 Ibid. 244.

109 Hugues Choplin, "François Laruelle"; I am grateful to Ray Brassier for providing me with this reference. Given the uniquely daunting scope and density of Laruelle's work I limit my few references here to the most accessible of his presentational texts; for a more substantial and more reliable introduction see Brassier's recent article "Axiomatic Heresy" (2003).

110 Laruelle, *En tant qu'un* 208.

111 Cf. Brassier, "Axiomatic Heresy" 33. According to Brassier, "Henry's work still effectively mediates between non-relational life and worldly relationality: it relates relation and non-relation. Laruelle's non-philosophy exemplifies a quite different logic: that of the non-relation of relation and non-relation" (Brassier, correspondence with the author, 9 September 2003; cf. Brassier, "Axiomatic Heresy" 27).

112 Laruelle, *En tant qu'un* 229.

113 Ibid. 211, 237. The individual as such is "really distinct from the world" (Laruelle, *Une biographie de l'homme ordinaire* 7). What Laruelle calls "ordinary man" as opposed to "generic man" refers "to the essence of the individual insofar as this does not belong to the world." Non-philosophy thus leads directly to "a sort of 'dualist' thesis: on the one hand there is [individual] man and on the other hand there is the World with all its attributes, its great characteristics, Language, Sexuality, etc." Purged of every organic or social attribute, sustained in his "absolute sufficiency," "by his very existence the individual holds the world at a distance in an irreversible or 'unilateral' way" (*En tant qu'un* 221, 210, 219). Laruelle makes no secret, meanwhile, of his interest in the more extreme forms of heretical mysticism and gnosticism; his current cycle of publications, beginning with *Le Christ futur*, is organised around the forthcoming treatise *Théorèmes mystiques*.

114 Laruelle, *En tant qu'un* 246.

115 "Consciousness is its own foundation, but it remains contingent that there be a consciousness,

rather than purely and simply the in-itself, ad infinitum" (Sartre, *L'Etre et le néant* 120).

116 Sartre, *Transcendance de l'ego* 79/98–99.

117 Sartre, "Une Idée fondamentale de la phénoménologie de Husserl: l'intentionnalité" in *Situations philosophiques* 12.

118 Sartre, *L'Etre et le néant* 538, 597.

119 Ibid. 607.

120 Ibid. 114–17.

121 Ibid. 612–13. "There are never any accidents in life" (613). As Michel Haar observes, Sartre is at every point determined to preserve an absolute or "sovereign" conception of the subject: "man as cause of himself occupies entirely the place of God." Sartre is determined to avoid both Heidegger's cooperative and enabling conception of being-with others (along with his conception of an authenticity that emerges *from* its initial anonymity among the "they" of ordinary social existence) and Husserl's tendency to "make sense of the relation consciousness-world primarily in terms of the relation of knowledge" (Haar, *La Philosophie française entre phénoménologie et métaphysique* 63, 39).

122 Sartre, *L'Etre et le néant* 275.

123 Cf. Badiou, "On a Finally Objectless Subject" (1989). Bruno Bosteels draws attention to important differences between the quasi-dialectical conception of event and intervention that Badiou develops (particularly in the work up to and including *Théorie du sujet*) and the more absolute, more all-or-nothing "speculative leftism" Badiou associates with Jambet and Lardreau (cf. Bosteels, *Badiou and the Political*, forthcoming). I would argue, however, that these differences are internal to the broadly singular or non-relational conception of thought common to all three thinkers; I discuss the non-relational aspects of Badiou's philosophy in my *Badiou: A Subject to Truth* (24–28, 271–91) and "Consequences of Abstraction" (forthcoming).

124 Cf. Sartre, *Critique de la raison dialectique* 76; Sartre, *Situations IX* 101–03. As Sartre becomes progressively more concerned with the practicalities of "changing the world," so too does his later work attenuate his initially absolute (and initially "imaginary") point of departure with various forms of mediation in the world. It is perhaps no

accident that Badiou himself, as he has shifted his philosophical conception of change from the circumstances of generalised war to the circumstances of an uncertain "peace," has directed much of his recent work to a new conception of "worlds" (cf. Badiou, *Logiques des mondes*, forthcoming; Hallward, *Badiou*, chapter 14).

125 Badiou, *Court traité d'ontologie transitoire* 200.

126 Badiou, *Manifeste pour la philosophie* 60; cf. Badiou, *L'Etre et l'événement* 365–77.

127 Badiou, "Saisissement, dessaisie, fidélité" 21.

128 Christina Howells has long drawn attention to the similarity of both Sartre and Derrida's refusal of self-coincidence or self-presence (see, in particular, Howells, "Sartre and the Deconstruction of the Subject" in *Cambridge Companion to Sartre*).

129 See, in particular, Derrida, "Les Fins de l'homme" in *Marges de la philosophie* 148–61/124–34. "L'être est depuis toujours sa propre fin, c'est-à-dire la fin de son propre" (161/134).

130 Derrida, *Positions* 109–10.

131 Derrida, *Marges de la philosophie* 22/21, 24/23. Despite Derrida's (qualified) denial of the negative-theological resonances of his argument here, much of what he associates with différance fits smoothly with the apophatic-theophanic tradition, starting with the fact that "différance is not. It is not a present being, however excellent" (22/21).

132 Ibid. 23/22.

133 Derrida, *Positions* 40; *Marges de la philosophie* 12/11 tm.

134 Derrida, *De la grammatologie* 73/50 tm.

135 Levinas, "Meaning and Sense" in *Basic Philosophical Writings* 63. Like any creating, the trace is forever non-coincident with itself, never present to itself: "always differing and deferring, the trace is never as it is in the presentation of itself. It erases itself in presenting itself" (Derrida, *Marges de la philosophie* 24/23).

136 Derrida, *Politiques de l'amitié* 87/68; Derrida, "Donner la mort" 76–77/78.

137 Derrida, *Politiques de l'amitié* 247/219, 47/29.

138 Corbin, *Histoire* 58; Corbin, *Le Paradoxe du monothéisme* 55. Cf. Corbin, *Corps spirituel* 8–9;

Corbin, *Philosophie iranienne* 16. According to Jambet's terse summary, "Corbin thinks of the tearing away from history as the true meaning of human existence" (Jambet, *La Logique des Orientaux* 17). And Levinas: "when man truly approaches the Other he is uprooted from history" (*Totalité et infini* 45/52).

139 Henry, *L'Essence de la manifestation* 203–04, 859.

140 Henry, *Marx* 144–45.

141 Levinas, *Totalité et infini* 21/33 tm; Badiou, *Infinite Thought* 40–42.

142 This is a point made forcefully by Brassier, who insists on the difference between "two very different kinds of anti-relationality: the religious, archaic *refusal* of relation or the world, à la Bergson, Henry, Corbin, and Levinas; and the radical enlightenment, anti-phenomenological, ultra-modernist *indifference* to relation or the world peculiar to Badiou and Laruelle" (Ray Brassier, correspondence with the author, 9 September 2003). I accept that the thematic expression of this difference is readily apparent; the question is whether the slender resources of anti-relationality themselves allow, in the end, for much more than an apparent distinction between ("progressive") indifference to the world and ("reactionary") denial of the world.

143 Badiou, "The Caesura of Nihilism" (2002).

144 This *and* is qualitatively different from that differential multiplication of the one affirmed by Corbin or Henry ($1 \times 1 \times 1 \times 1 \ldots$) or that univocal repetition of difference affirmed by Deleuze (AND AND AND …).

bibliography

Badiou, Alain. "The Caesura of Nihilism" [unpublished lecture given at the University of Cardiff, 25 May 2002].

Badiou, Alain. *Court traité d'ontologie transitoire.* Paris: Seuil, 1998.

Badiou, Alain. *L'Etre et l'événement.* Paris: Seuil, 1988. *Being and Event.* Trans. Oliver Feltham. London: Continuum, 2004.

Badiou, Alain. *Infinite Thought: Truth and the Return to Philosophy.* Ed. Justin Clemens and Oliver Feltham. London: Continuum, 2003.

Badiou, Alain. *Logiques des mondes.* Paris: Seuil, forthcoming 2005.

Badiou, Alain. *Manifeste pour la philosophie.* Paris: Seuil, 1989. *Manifesto for Philosophy.* Trans. Norman Madarasz. Albany: State U of New York P, 1999.

Badiou, Alain. "Saisissement, dessaisie, fidélité." *Les Temps modernes* 531–533 (1990, 2 vols.). Vol. 1: 14–22.

Badiou, Alain. "D'un sujet enfin sans objet." *Cahiers Confrontations* 20 (1989): 13–22. "On a Finally Objectless Subject." Trans. Bruce Fink. *Who Comes after the Subject?* Ed. Eduardo Cadava et al. London: Routledge, 1991. 24–32.

Badiou, Alain. *Théorie du sujet.* Paris: Seuil, 1982.

Bergson, Henri. *Les Deux Sources de la morale et de la religion.* 1932. Paris: Presses Universitaires de France, 1997. *The Two Sources of Morality and Religion.* Trans. R. Ashley Audra and Cloudesley Brereton. Notre Dame: U of Notre Dame P, 1977.

Bergson, Henri. *L'Evolution créatrice.* 1907. Paris: Presses Universitaires de France, 1941. *Creative Evolution.* Trans. Arthur Mitchell. Mineola, NY: Dover, 1998.

Bosteels, Bruno. *Badiou and the Political.* Durham, NC: Duke UP, forthcoming.

Brassier, Ray. "Axiomatic Heresy: The Non-Philosophy of François Laruelle." *Radical Philosophy* 121 (Sept. 2003): 24–35.

Butler, Judith. *Subjects of Desire: Hegelian Reflections in Twentieth-Century France.* New York: Columbia UP, 1999.

Choplin, Hugues. "François Laruelle." *Encyclopédie Universalis.* Paris, 2002.

Choplin, Hugues. *La Non-Philosophie de François Laruelle.* Paris: Kimé, 2000.

Corbin, Henry. *Avicenne et le récit visionnaire.* 1954. Paris: Berg, 1979.

Corbin, Henry. *Corps spirituel et terre céleste: De l'Iran mazdéen à l'Iran shî-ite.* 1961. Paris: Buchet-Chastel, 1979.

Corbin, Henry. *Histoire de la philosophie islamique.* 1964, 1974. Paris: Gallimard, "Folio," 1986.

Corbin, Henry. *Le Paradoxe du monothéisme.* Paris: Livre de Poche, 1981.

Corbin, Henry. *Philosophie iranienne et philosophie comparée.* 1977. Paris: Buchet-Chastel, 1985.

Deleuze, Gilles. *Le Bergsonisme.* Paris: Presses Universitaires de France, 1966. *Bergsonism.* Trans. Hugh Tomlinson and Barbara Habberjam. New York: Zone, 1988.

Deleuze, Gilles. *Cinéma 1: L'Image-mouvement.* Paris: Minuit, 1983. *Cinema 1: The Mouvement-Image.* Trans. Hugh Tomlinson and Barbara Habberjam. Minneapolis: U of Minnesota P, 1986.

Deleuze, Gilles. *Cinéma 2: L'Image-temps.* Paris: Minuit, 1985. *Cinema 2: The Time-Image.* Trans. Hugh Tomlinson and Robert Galeta. Minneapolis: U of Minnesota P, 1989.

Deleuze, Gilles. "La Conception de la différence chez Bergson." *Les Etudes Bergsoniennes* 4 (1956): 77–112. "Bergson's Conception of Difference." Trans. Melissa McMahon. *The New Bergson.* Ed. John Mullarkey. Manchester: U of Manchester P, 1999. 42–65.

Deleuze, Gilles. *Différence et répétition.* Paris: Presses Universitaires de France, 1968. *Difference and Repetition.* Trans. Paul Patton. New York: Columbia UP, 1994.

Deleuze, Gilles. *Logique du sens.* Paris: Minuit, 1969. *The Logic of Sense.* Trans. Mark Lester with Charles Stivale. New York: Columbia UP, 1990.

Deleuze, Gilles. *Nietzsche et la philosophie.* Paris: Presses Universitaires de France, 1962. *Nietzsche and Philosophy.* Trans. Hugh Tomlinson. Minneapolis: U of Minnesota P, 1983.

Deleuze, Gilles and Félix Guattari. *L'Anti-Oedipe.* Paris: Minuit, 1972. *Anti-Oedipus.* Trans. Robert Hurley, Mark Seem and Helen R. Lane. Minneapolis: U of Minnesota P, 1977.

Deleuze, Gilles and Félix Guattari. *Mille plateaux.* Paris: Minuit, 1980. *A Thousand Plateaus.* Trans. Brian Massumi. Minneapolis: U of Minnesota P, 1986.

Deleuze, Gilles with Claire Parnet. *Dialogues.* 1977. Paris: Flammarion, 1996. *Dialogues.* Trans. Hugh Tomlinson and Barbara Habberjam. New York: Columbia UP, 1987.

Derrida, Jacques. "Donner la mort." *L'Ethique du don: Jacques Derrida et la pensée du don.* Ed. Jean-Michel Rabaté et al. Paris: Métailié-Transition, 1992. *The Gift of Death.* Trans. David Wills. Chicago: U of Chicago P, 1995.

Derrida, Jacques. *De la grammatologie.* Paris: Minuit, 1967. *Of Grammatology.* Trans. Gayatri Chakravorty Spivak. Baltimore: Johns Hopkins UP, 1976.

Derrida, Jacques. *Marges de la philosophie.* Paris: Minuit, 1972. *Margins of Philosophy.* Trans. Alan Bass. Chicago: U of Chicago P, 1982.

Derrida, Jacques. *Politiques de l'amitié.* Paris: Galilée, 1994. *Politics of Friendship.* Trans. George Collins. London: Verso, 1997.

Derrida, Jacques. *Positions.* Paris: Minuit, 1972.

Descombes, Vincent. *Modern French Philosophy.* Trans. L. Scott-Fox and J. M. Harding. Cambridge: Cambridge UP, 1980.

Eckhart. *Meister Eckhart: Sermons and Treatises.* Vol. III. Ed. Maurice Walshe. Rockport, MA: Element, 1992.

Eriugena, John Scottus. *Periphyseon (The Division of Nature).* Ed. and trans. Inglis Patrick Sheldon-Williams and John O'Meara. Montréal and Paris: Bellarmin, 1987.

Girard, René. *Mensonge romantique et vérité romanesque.* Paris: Grasset, 1961.

Gutting, Gary. *French Philosophy in the Twentieth Century.* Cambridge: Cambridge UP, 2001.

Haar, Michel. *La Philosophie française entre phénoménologie et métaphysique.* Paris: Presses Universitaires de France, 1999.

Hallward, Peter. *Badiou: A Subject to Truth.* Minneapolis: U of Minnesota P, 2003.

Hallward, Peter. "Consequences of Abstraction." *Think Again: Alain Badiou and the Future of Philosophy.* Ed. Peter Hallward. London: Continuum, forthcoming 2004.

Hallward, Peter. "Deleuze and Redemption from Interest." *Radical Philosophy* 81 (Jan. 1997): 6–21.

Hallward, Peter. "Deleuze and the World without Others." *Philosophy Today* 41.4 (1997): 530–44.

Hallward, Peter. "'Everything is Real': Gilles Deleuze and Creative Univocity." *New Formations* 49 (spring 2003): 61–74.

Hallward, Peter. "The Limits of Individuation, or How to Distinguish Deleuze from Foucault." *Angelaki* 5:2 (2000): 93–112.

Hallward, Peter. "The Singular and the Specific: Recent French Philosophy." *Radical Philosophy* 99 (Jan. 2000): 6–18.

Henry, Michel. *C'est moi la vérité: pour une philosophie du christianisme.* Paris: Seuil, 1996. *I Am the Truth: Toward a Philosophy of Christianity.* Trans. Susan Emanuel. Stanford: Stanford UP, 2003.

Henry, Michel. *L'Essence de la manifestation.* 1963. Paris: Presses Universitaires de France, 1990.

Henry, Michel. *Marx: A Philosophy of Human Reality.* Trans. Kathleen McLaughlin, reworked and abbreviated by Michel Henry. Bloomington: Indiana UP, 1983.

Howells, Christina. "Sartre and the Deconstruction of the Subject." *Cambridge Companion to Sartre.* Ed. Christina Howells. Cambridge: Cambridge UP, 1992.

Jambet, Christian. *L'Acte d'être: la philosophie de la révélation chez Mollâ Sadrâ.* Paris: Fayard, 2002.

Jambet, Christian. *La Grande Résurrection d'Alamût: les formes de la liberté dans le shî'isme ismaélien.* Lagrasse: Verdier, 1990.

Jambet, Christian. *La Logique des Orientaux: Henry Corbin et la science des formes.* Paris: Seuil, 1983.

Jankélévitch, Vladimir. *Henri Bergson.* 1959. Paris: Presses Universitaires de France, 1999.

Koyré, Alexandre. *La Philosophie de Jacob Boehme.* Paris: Vrin, 1929.

Lardreau, Guy. *Vive le matérialisme!* Lagrasse: Verdier, 2001.

Lardreau, Guy and Christian Jambet. *L'Ange: pour une cynégétique du semblant.* Paris: Grasset, 1976.

Laruelle, François. *Une biographie de l'homme ordinaire: des autorités et des minorités.* Paris: Aubier, 1985.

Laruelle, François. *Le Christ futur: une leçon d'hérésie.* Paris: Exils, 2002.

Laruelle, François. *Le Principe de minorité.* Paris: Aubier-Montaigne, 1981.

Laruelle, François. *Principes de la non-philosophie.* Paris: Presses Universitaires de France, 1996.

Laruelle, François. *En tant qu'un: la "non-philosophie" expliquée aux philosophes.* Paris: Aubier, 1991.

Levinas, Emmanuel. *Autrement qu'être, ou, au-delà de l'essence.* Paris: Livre de Poche, 1974.

Levinas, Emmanuel. *Emmanuel Levinas: Basic Philosophical Writings.* Ed. Adriaan Peperzak et al. Bloomington: Indiana UP, 1996.

Levinas, Emmanuel. *Totalité et infini.* 1961. Paris: Livre de Poche, 1961. *Totality and Infinity.* Trans. Alphonso Lingis. Pittsburgh: Duquesne UP, 1969.

Rosset, Clément. *Le Démon de la tautologie: suivi de Cinq petites pièces morales.* Paris: Minuit, 1997.

Rosset, Clément. *Joyful Cruelty: Toward a Philosophy of the Real.* Ed. and trans. David F. Bell. Oxford: Oxford UP, 1993.

Rosset, Clément. *L'Objet singulier.* Paris: Minuit, 1979.

Rosset, Clément. *Le Principe de cruauté.* Paris: Minuit, 1988.

Rosset, Clément. *Le Réel et son double: essai sur l'illusion.* 1976. Paris: Gallimard, 1985.

Rosset, Clément. *Le Réel: traité de l'idiotie.* Paris: Minuit, 1977.

Sartre, Jean-Paul. *Critique de la raison dialectique.* 1960. Paris: Gallimard, 1985.

Sartre, Jean-Paul. *L'Etre et le néant.* 1943. Paris: Gallimard, 1976.

Sartre, Jean-Paul. *Situations IX.* Paris: Gallimard, 1972.

Sartre, Jean-Paul. *Situations philosophiques.* Paris: Gallimard, 1990.

Sartre, Jean-Paul. *Transcendance de l'ego.* 1937. Paris: Vrin, 1988. *The Transcendence of the Ego.* Trans. Forrest Williams and Robert Kirkpatrick. New York: Noonday, 1957.

Peter Hallward
French Department
King's College London
The Strand
London WC2R 2LS
UK
E-mail: peter.hallward@kcl.ac.uk

journal of the theoretical humanities
volume 8   number 2   august 2003

introduction

peter hallward

Born in Algiers in 1949, Christian Jambet specialises in Islamic philosophy. He emerged in the late 1970s as the most brilliant of Henry Corbin's students, and has now taught philosophy for many years at the lycée Jules Ferry, at the Institut d'Études Iraniennes (University of Paris III) and the École Pratique des Hautes Études. Influenced by Mao and Lacan, the translator of Rumi and Oscar Wilde, an attentive reader of Foucault, Deleuze, and Badiou, Jambet's range of interests makes mainstream work in comparative philosophy look positively parochial. Whatever its immediate occasion, a genuine "philosophical act takes place when its subjects overturn their conception of the world," when, breaking with prejudice or habit, they devise ways of thinking along lines indifferent to all received representations of the world. Philosophy is not a matter of knowledge or opinion, it is not a matter of internalising "correct" ideas: it is a reflexive work of transformation applied upon oneself, an entering into "discord with oneself" so as to accord with a way of thinking that holds, in principle, for anyone at all.[1]

As a student, inspired by the events surrounding the Chinese Cultural Revolution and May 1968, Jambet was a member of the Maoist groups Union des Jeunesses Communistes (Marxistes-Léninistes) and Gauche Prolétarienne. When he visited China in 1969 he was witness to "the configuration of a world in which it seemed that the masses themselves were the active subject of politics."[2] Disappointment with the direction subsequently taken by Maoism in both China and France led to Jambet's eventual break with organised revolutionary politics and provided the

christian jambet

translated by andrew asibong

SOME COMMENTS ON THE QUESTION OF THE ONE

immediate occasion for his early collaborative writings with Guy Lardreau. The uncompromising or "angelic" theory of subjectivity developed in their books *L'Ange* (1976) and *Le Monde* (1978) is designed to preserve a purely revolutionary commitment, one that is both irreducible to dialectical forms of antagonism and independent of any doctrinal, institutional or historical contamination.[3] Revolution, in short, becomes an essentially spiritual affair, and its most immediate enemies are those (Pol Pot, Khomeini, etc.) who seek to harness its force to merely social or historical ends. Jambet's preferred interlocutors, by contrast, remain those who both in their lives and their philosophies sought to maximise the gap between spirit and historical world, to attribute to spirit an absolute freedom and

ISSN 0969-725X print/ISSN 1469-2899 online/03/020033-09 © 2003 Taylor & Francis Ltd and the Editors of *Angelaki*
DOI: 10.1080/0969725032000162558

creativity. Jambet's decisive encounter with Corbin during these same years is what determined him to look for such points of reference primarily in esoteric Shi'ite philosophy, in which the struggle between world and spirit (between a literal or law-bound conception of the *Qu'ran* and one that urges the invention of new forms of interpretation) is particularly acute. The question posed today by the likes of Khomeini and bin Laden is the question that has divided Islam from the beginning: is God's will essentially mediated by rules and institutions and thus caught up in the enforcement of law, or "is God creative freedom, pure spontaneity, such that true believers express this divine freedom in their own spiritual practice," as so many instances of "boundless spontaneity"?[4]

Any conception of spirit as absolute creativity must have at least three fundamental attributes, which return again and again as the dominant themes of Jambet's work. In the first place (for reasons similar to those embraced by Spinoza), an unlimited creative force can only be singular, unique. The most basic tenet of Islamic faith concerns "the identity of God and the 'One,'" and much of Jambet's work concerns the ontological implications of the effort to think being in terms of a One that is both beyond being and the "real" of being.[5] In the second place (for reasons similar to those embraced by Hegel), pure creativity can only be thought as subject rather than as object, and the only subject adequate to the One is God himself. God cannot be conceived or represented as any sort of objective thing, he can be conceived only as he conceives himself, as absolute subject. In the third place, then (for reasons similar to those embraced by Bergson), we ourselves can know God only in so far as God thinks through us, in so far as we are directly inspired by God. The only true principle immune to radical doubt here is not "*I* think" but "I am thought (by God)" – *cogitor* rather than *cogito*.[6] Understood in this sense, truth is indifferently a matter of invention or of revelation, and the whole effort of spiritual Islam is to transcend the apparent difference between the two, so as to realise the "prophetic essence of man." We speak truly in so far as we are spoken *by* God and thereby experience, in

the endless analysis of this speech, both the infinite gap between absolute Speech and its human voice, and the essential univocity that expresses itself in the thinking of this very gap – this gap which is nothing other, for the Jambet who reads Mulla Sadra in the light of Lacan, than the real of thought.[7]

Roughly speaking, Jambet's three major works to date correspond to three of the most consequential inflections of this otherwise broadly consistent set of principles. In *La Logique des Orientaux* (1983), a book dominated by the figure of the Iranian mystic Suhrawardi (1154–91), absolute creativity is expressed in terms of light and imagination, and is limited by whatever offers an opaque resistance to light (corporal solidity, stasis, prejudice, etc.). The One as such, the source of light, is hidden and inaccessible. What emanate from the One, according to a broadly neo-Platonic logic, are so many reflections or "images" of light which cohere on an "imaginal" plane of pure inspiration.[8] Human beings begin their lives in relative shadow, in an "occidental exile" from the light that is their source: redemption involves pulling away from the shadows so as to become a translucent prism for the radiance of the creator. Our access to the light is always refracted through particular souls, particular acts of imagination or spirit. Jambet distinguishes, in this way, such *Ishraqi* illumination from the simple extinction of the individual in mystical union with the One: the imaginal plane corresponds precisely with an intermediary or "angelic" revelation, where the angel appears *between* the divine and the human intelligence. "The Angel is what is accorded to us from the absolutely hidden Other" or One.[9] Suhrawardi's angel is a figure with two wings, one in shadow and one in light, and his imaginal world is populated by individuals conceived as immaterial but distinct "imaginings" of God.

In *L'Acte d'être* (2002), Jambet turns his attention to Iran's most celebrated philosopher, Mulla Sadra (1571–1641). Inspired by Suhrawardi, among others, Mulla Sadra's great effort is to think *all* being in terms of the self-sufficient, self-necessitating or divinely creative *act* that sustains it, i.e. to think (again in terms that resonate with Spinoza, to say nothing of

Deleuze) the whole of being as unceasing and infinitely mobile creation, framed by the fundamental "equation of the real, of being, and of the One."[10]

If Mulla Sadra seeks to bend Suhrawardi's angelic orientation towards a fully immanent conception of being, Nasir ad-Din Tusi (1201–74) and the other Ismaili thinkers studied in Jambet's *La Grande Résurrection d'Alamût* (1990), by contrast, reinforce the dualism implicit in the transcendence of a one beyond being. What Jambet analyses here as the "paradoxical One" is a "superinfinite" creativity unmediated, so to speak, by any creaturely persistence (any *quidditas*) at all.[11] Reality erupts into being from a real that itself remains unintelligible, unsayable. This apophatic conception of God opens, as the space of true spiritual experience, a searing gap between reality and the real, between historical time and messianic revelation, between the world of experience and a pure "imperative" that commands with a force indifferent to the distinction of freedom and necessity.[12]

notes

1 Jambet, "Interview avec Christian Jambet" (1997).

2 Jambet, "Un souverainiste nommé Mao" (2000). Today, remembering his Maoist affiliation, Jambet accepts its lack of immediate historical consequence in France: less than a sequence endowed with an "historical posterity," he thinks of it in terms of its "trans-historical" persistence, along the lines illustrated in a different context by Joan of Arc (whose impact endures despite or perhaps because of her lack of direct historical influence) (ibid.).

3 The "transcendental question" at issue in these books, and sustained in a different form in the remainder of Jambet's work, concerns the "possible autonomy of revolt" (Jambet, "Allez!" in *L'Ange* 233). For more on *L'Ange*, see the introduction to Guy Lardreau's essay in the present issue.

4 Jambet, "Entre Islam spirituel et Islam légalitaire, le conflit est déclaré," *Le Monde* 25 June 2001; cf. Jambet, *L'Acte d'être* 21–24. Corbin's influence is especially important here: see, for example,

Henry Corbin, *Le Paradoxe du monothéisme* (Paris: L'Herne, 1981) and Corbin, *Philosophie iranienne et philosophie comparée* (Paris: Buchet-Chastel, 1985).

5 Jambet, *L'Acte d'être* 9. As the fundamental *Qu'ranic* verse (112: 1) declares: "Say: He, Allah, is One."

6 Jambet, *La Logique des Orientaux* 118, 224–25.

7 Jambet, *L'Acte d'être* 10–11; cf. 63–64.

8 Jambet, *La Logique des Orientaux* 37–51. As one commentator explains it, "the imaginal world [... is] that world whose dimensions and extension fall only within the purview of imaginative perception. It is the world of autonomous imaginal Forms, that is to say, Forms un-mixed with a corruptible substrate, but suspended, like images suspended in a mirror" (Qotboddin Shirazi, quoted in Henry Corbin, *Corps spirituel et terre céleste* (Paris: Buchet-Chastel, 1979) 154). Bachelard concludes, in a somewhat similar sense, that "the imagination is not, as its etymology suggests, the faculty of forming images of reality, it is the faculty of forming images that exceed reality, that sing reality. It is a superhuman faculty" (Gaston Bachelard, *L'Eau et les rêves* (Paris: Corti, 1942) 23).

9 Jambet, "Présentation" in *Henri Corbin, Cahiers de l'Herne* (1981) 14.

10 Jambet, *L'Acte d'être* 14.

11 Jambet, *La Grande Résurrection d'Alamût* 139–76. The historical occasion for the elaboration of this doctrine is the messianic declaration, sustained by the Ismaili Shi'ites of northern Iran from 1164 to 1210, of an end to the reign of law and the beginning of a life entirely oriented towards the immortal and divine.

12 Jambet, *La Grande Résurrection d'Alamût* 175–85.

some comments on the question of the one

christian jambet

If there is one conviction shared by the majority of contemporary philosophers, this is it: the one is not [*l'un n'est pas*]. It seems that in order go along with the demands of the modern scientific age we must renounce any philosophy founded on some ultimate principle of existence, such as it was conceived in the theology of the various religions of the Book, i.e. through the equation of being, the one, and the real. Once affirmed, this conviction converts smoothly into various systems of thought, until either every attestation of the real is renounced, or at least until the real is thoroughly separated from its theological identity with the one. Lacan, Deleuze and Derrida are clearly recognisable here, in all their conflicting orientations.

Whatever the merits of this decision may be, its unavoidable consequence is to conceal what is at stake, metaphysically, when the mind acknowledges that the highest power resides in the one. This is borne out, I think, by the way in which most contemporary thinkers have worked against Hegel, in the margins of Hegel, or with the express aim of breaking with Hegelian logic. This anti-dialectical thematic has been pursued in various ways. Foucault, for instance, deploys it in order to expose the way war – the constant, silent war that animates the field of social forces – has been hidden or overshadowed by the great concepts and figures of sovereignty. By reaching the end of the royal road that led thought to the state, to the totalising one, Hegel is supposed to have concocted the most dangerously attractive of philosophical responses to this war. This response consisted in positing that negation is the truth of the one, in such a way that negation itself – the absolute transfigured into the negative – might be overcome in an ultimate affirmation of its own resolution. Whether the one is posited in the element of identity or swallowed up in the "Bacchic delirium" of its negative development, whether it be conceived as substance or subject, whether it be the cause of causes or the becoming of itself – all this would appear to change nothing, in the final analysis, since the one remains the major figure of mastery, which tames every danger and squashes any new irruption of discourse.

The Deleuzean critique of dialectics, as is well known, follows a quite different path. It affirms the rights not of war but of difference, the kind that need never succumb to the simplifying abstractions of duality or contradiction. The Deleuzian critique of contradiction is homologous to the Bergsonian critique of language. Like the latter, it maintains that real singularity remains outside the grasp of the kinds of categories and judgments that, from Aristotle to Hegel, map out a syllogistic logic.

It is Lacan who must be credited with the most radical dismissal of any theology of the one. Lacan distinguishes the imaginary thesis "the one is [*l'un est*]" (which he identifies with the thesis "everything is everything," everything is whole, or all) from the thesis appropriate to the real of the subject: "there is one [*il y a de l'un*]" (itself a consequence of the thesis "nothing is everything," nothing is whole or all).[1] Perhaps we need to take a closer look, and ask ourselves why Lacan tried to introduce such a break into the domain of ontology.

The source for a first reason is easily found, in the earlier break brought about by Galileo. I agree here with Jean-Claude Milner, who describes this point in terms of "Koyré's theorem." The break on which modern science is founded consists, according to Alexandre Koyré, in the mathematisation of an infinite universe. It seems to follow that the very concept of the universe, understood in the sense of the *universum* of the existent, falls apart: the infinity of the universe implies the dissolution of that pair of concepts on which ancient cosmology was founded: the universe, and that which lies outside the universe. In a sort of post-Galilean Epicureanism, Lacanian logic disqualifies both the one situated outside the universe and the one understood in the sense of the universe itself. It is clear that such a deduction presumes a preliminary identification of the one with the most perfect being (according to the theological

36

argument) and of the one with the all or whole (according to the definitions of rational cosmology).

For my part I have tried to show that this Lacanian gesture broke with all the metaphysical consequences of what I call philosophy's "Avicennian moment." Without going into a detailed analysis of the great Iranian philosopher's metaphysics, physics and eschatology, let me simply draw attention to the fact that the main Avicennian decision, which consists in distinguishing "the meaning of the thing" from the "meaning of existence," is connected to another, equally important decision. This is the claim that necessity is the very reality of the act of existing: it is the real as such. The existent, located in the universe, is necessitated by the other [nécessité par autrui], and consequently requires an ultimate cause in something that necessarily exists through itself: the real one [l'un réel]. This strikes Avicenna as incontestable not only because he is faithful to the Aristotelian cosmological schema but also because, in its logical and ontological basis, the very meaning of the act of existing is necessity.

It is perfectly obvious that Lacanian logic targets precisely this assumption of necessity, in so far as it undoes the structure of the three modalities: the necessary, the possible and the impossible. It replaces them with a structure in which the circle of the real is no longer identified with the modality of necessity, in which necessity slides, so to speak, over to the place where the symbolic is tied to the imaginary. The knot that ties the symbolic to the real, on the other hand, is marked by what ancient metaphysics understood in terms of the idea of contingency. As for the impossible, it no longer refers to the nonexistent, but to the domain where, in so far as we are able, we must strive to conceive the object of desire, the cause of the subject – where, in short, we conceive the very link between the modalities of being. What any such logic or arrangement will lack, henceforth, is a place of total enjoyment, a place that Avicenna situated in God, i.e. in the one, defined as the subject which is "itself for itself," which enjoys itself eternally, infinitely.

We should perhaps note in passing that this Lacanian reformation of ontology implicates, in the general ruin of metaphysics, not just Avicenna but Spinoza as well. And also that the discovery of the unconscious implies nothing less than the repudiation of any conception of the real that might situate it in the identification (whether immediate or eventual) of the one and of being. The proposition "there is one [il y a de l'un]" wants "one [de l'un]" to count only in the non-total constitution of the subject, i.e. in the primary affirmation of the subject, an affirmation without foundation in being, since its being, the being of a pure subject, can only be expressed negatively. More than Spinoza it is Fichte, the thinker of infinite freedom, who would be relevant here, if, in its turn, his "Ich" was not caught up in an historical sequence of its own, one that Freudianism understands in quite a different way than did Fichte and then Hegel.

Such are the conditions, it seems to me, under which I have had to pursue my own project. I have mentioned them very allusively here, and have skipped over a number of points of reference and mediation. I accord much importance, for example, to the early Wittgenstein, and also to Strawson. Since it would be presumptuous to try to say something about them in so short a space, I would rather move on to a task that is no less delicate but rather easier to justify: the identification of some of the questions that I have been trying to address in the work I have been carrying out over the past few years.

The first of these questions is not very far removed from what drove Foucault in his research on "war." It can be formulated as follows: how are we to recognise the demands of the two, of non-dialectisable duality [dualitude]? I have long shared the fairly common conviction that the general movement of German idealism since Kant, modern philosophy in other words, led to the erasure, the foreclosure, of such a duality. My early training, under the powerful theoretical influence of Althusser, encouraged me in this conviction, as did, a little later, the imperious torsion that revolutionary political thought (incarnated, for me, by Mao Tse-Tung) operated upon dialectics itself. "One divides into two," we used to say at the time. It is remarkable that when Foucault, in his thoroughgoing critique of dialectical thought, seeks to derive dialectics from conceptions of state sovereignty, he criticises not only (and without naming him) Carl Schmitt as a reader of Hobbes, but also Hegel, Marx and Mao (without naming him either). Foucault entertained few illusions about the possibility – one that I used to find fruitful – of keeping alive a philosophy of decision and sovereignty while at the same time transforming, in a revolutionary way, the classical conception of dialectics (dialectics as it began with Aristotle and ended with Hegel). To maintain that "one divides into two" means that the "two" is primary and that the one is in no sense a principle – but according to Foucault, to maintain this is a task that is destined to fail. The conclusion I draw from this differs from that of Foucault. I take seriously that conjunction of the one, the real and the absolute which has been assumed by the various theologies, in order to ask myself how, on the basis of the one, identity and war, unity and radical duality, might be arranged in a constantly reversible pattern – one that allows us to think, alternately, both the nature of order and the process of tearing away from the world as it is.

I am led in this direction by the empirical work that I embarked upon, following my teacher Henry Corbin, in the field of Islamic systems of thought. Why this interest in Islam? Why am I so interested in Islam, why has it become for me the object of a constant philosophical preoccupation, given that I am fully aware that the theological era has come to end in the West, given that I have myself been marked, from the beginning of my philosophical education, by those critical proposals that I have already mentioned (and which have done everything possible to lead us away from an exhausted metaphysics)? It is in no sense, I hasten to say, a "return to religion." Less still is it a "sociological" interest in a culture that might seem out of synch with the times, a culture that might seem worthy of a little general discussion before it moves on to join the various other forms of spirituality that lie in the pantheon of dead ideas.

First and foremost, I set out from this observation: that "war," the endlessly renewed confrontation between the forces of submission and those of liberation, found its chosen terrain in the sphere of the religions of the Book, no doubt because, in them, the one foments submission as much as it does liberation. Contrary to what is presumed by the positivist schema adopted more or less unthinkingly by all modern thinkers, the God whose being is "one" cannot be considered as purely imaginary. Not only is God the existence which (because it exists necessarily) was necessary to the foundation of ancient philosophy, God presents himself, in transhistorical fashion, as that point of the real without which the histories of the monotheistic West and East remain unintelligible. Not an "illusion" of consciousness, but the real itself, a real about which, no doubt, our various forms of knowledge have nothing to say, but whose obvious impact and reality govern a considerable portion of the knowledge essential to our present history. In this sense Hegel was not behind us but ahead of us when he perceived God as being the position of the subject. God is in the position of the subject not because he is the totalising "one," the ultimate pure cause of cosmology, but that he is the transhistorical name of absolute subjectivity. God is thus not the opposite of freedom but the name under which the unfounded act of freedom can be thought, at least when this latter is not thought as the simple empirical independence of an isolated entity or existent.

Since Erasmus, even since Saint Augustine, we can follow the way in which, in the West, the notion of free will has developed as a concept essential to our modern institutions. It is clear that the dissolution of the space of theology and the disqualification of the one have enabled the more recent elaboration of several alternative conceptions of singularity, of the one detached from any apprehension of some kind of whole. Even more than that of Locke or of the other thinkers of natural law, it is the work of Hume, in all its profundity, that is indicative of this irresistible victory. But is it not obvious this "victory" has only been won because we have allowed ourselves to forget the prodigious achievements of two older systems of thought: neo-Platonism and the dualist theologies? They may seem "outmoded" to us but the present moment reminds us of their importance, and Islamic thinkers have developed their implications brilliantly. In their improbable but real combination, the Platonic idea of *the one which is not* and the Manichaean notion of the *foundational two*, which enter into both conflict and harmony in the metaphysics of Shi'ite Islam, have allowed me (within the framework of those messianic movements that punctuate, in cyclical fashion, the time of oriental Islam) to bring to light "forms of freedom" that are also forms of servitude. This is borne out by the history of Ismaili Shi'ite Islam in particular, and also by the remarkable synthesis of Islamic metaphysics, in terms that remain broadly faithful to Plotinus, carried out by Mulla Sadra Shirazi and other thinkers of the School of Ispahan in the seventeenth century (CE).

If freedom has "forms," if it is indeed what Hegel said it was, i.e. the infinite real under multiple forms, this in no way means that the freedom of the "Orientals" is superior to our own, or that it has a prestige that might justify anything and everything. But it does mean that philosophy must take up once more (and no doubt in ways that differ from those pursued by German idealism) the idea defended by Hegel or Schelling – that the question of the one, and not the question of being, is the question of questions. Or, to put it more precisely: how does the real that is one (without prejudging its truth with respect to our modern sciences) produce not only "truths," a schema of truth, but schemas and forms of existence? How is the one immanent to the constitution of transhistorical subjects?

It seems to me that it is possible, in this way, to reactivate a set of questions that have otherwise remained foreign to the recent era of philosophy. Foucault alone tried to speak of "spiritual politics," when it seemed important to him to understand what was happening in Iran. Everyone knows the uncomprehending furore this provoked.[2] I had quite a few conversations with him at the time. I had already embarked upon my work in the field of oriental studies, work that has continued ever since. It seemed pointless to me (and pointless to Foucault as well, I believe) to pretend that ontologies of the

one could be treated as superficial forms of ideology, as foreign and lifeless. To mention just one major theoretical issue: it is obvious that the concept of "Islamic revolution" would not be what it is, with all its considerable and now familiar consequences, if it did not translate (and distort, but in ways that remain analysable) the concept of "substantial movement," of "revolution in the act of existing," as it was rigorously thought out by the great Iranian metaphysician Mulla Sadra (who died in 1644). Must we not pay attention, then, to the emergence of this conception of a substance at once indivisible and plastic, a substance-subject that owes nothing to its formal definition but everything to the infinite and variable emanation, from world to world, of the unique act of existing – in short, the emergence of the one adequate to being [*l'un adéquat à l'être*]?

How can we understand the question of authority, of power, of the mastery of true speech in Islam, without studying henologies (systems of the one) in which it appears that the one is not? We need to realise that our definitions of the one as totality, as total and necessary existent entity, are inadequate. We need to go back and think anew the hypotheses of the *Parmenides* – not in order to lend metaphysics a sterile sophistication but so as to inform living, concrete ways of thinking the institution of order, the subject, and sovereignty, that are also ways of thinking revolt and insubordination.

What I am now trying to study are the ways in which politics, negative theology, and morality, but also infinite freedom and order, are intertwined, within a philosophical universe closely connected to our own – a universe which in my view is essential to our understanding of ourselves.

notes

1 The French formulation of the two theses – *tout est tout* and *rien n'est tout* – allows in the second case for a sort of double or unequivocal negation that is difficult to convey in English. [Translator's note.]

2 Jambet is referring to articles that Foucault wrote about the Iranian Revolution in 1979, which have often been criticised as idealistic or naive. See, in particular, Foucault, "Useless to Revolt?" and "Open Letter to Mehdi Bazargan" in *Power: Essential Works of Foucault III*, ed. James Faubion (New York: New Press, 2000), and "Iran: The Spirit of a World without Spirit" in *Politics, Philosophy, Culture: Interviews and Other Writings*, ed. Lawrence Kritzman (London: Routledge, 1990). [Translator's note.]

works by christian jambet

With Guy Lardreau. *L'Ange: pour une cynégétique du semblant*. Paris: Grasset, 1976.

Apologie de Platon: essais de métaphysique. Paris: Grasset, 1976.

With Guy Lardreau. *Le Monde: réponse à la question, qu'est-ce que les droits de l'homme?* Paris: Grasset, 1978.

(Ed.). *Henry Corbin: cahiers de l'Herne*. Paris: Herne, 1981.

"La Grande Résurrection d'Alamût d'après quelques textes ismaéliens." *Apocalypse et sens de l'histoire*. Ed. Jean-Louis Vieillard-Baron et al. Paris: Berg, 1983. 113–31.

La Logique des Orientaux: Henry Corbin et la science des formes. Paris: Seuil, 1983.

(Ed.). *Le Crépuscule des idoles*. By Friedrich Nietzsche. Paris: Garnier-Flammarion, 1985.

"Introduction." *Le Livre de la Sagesse Orientale*. By Shihab Al-Din Yahya Suhrawardi. Ed. and trans. Henri Corbin. 1986. Paris: Gallimard, 2003.

"Preface." *Heidegger et le Nazisme*. By Victor Farías. Paris: Verdier, 1987.

"Alain Badiou, *L'Être et l'événement*" [Review essay]. *Annuaire philosophique* 1. Paris: Seuil, 1989. 141–83.

"Constitution du sujet et pratique spirituelle." *Michel Foucault philosophe. Rencontre internationale. Paris 9, 10, 11 janvier 1988*. Ed. Georges Canguilhem. Paris: Seuil, 1989. 271–87.

"L'Expérience de la terreur." *Présences de Schopenhauer*. Ed. Roger-Pol Droit. Paris: Grasset, 1989. 124–34.

"Sohrawardî." *Encyclopaedia Universalis*. 3rd ed. Paris, 1989.

"Y a-t-il une philosophie française?" *Annales de Philosophie de l'Université Saint-Joseph* (Beirut) (1989): 85–97.

La Grande Résurrection d'Alamût: les formes de la liberté dans le shî'isme ismaélien. Lagrasse: Verdier, 1990.

"L'Autre est-il pensable?" *Revue des Deux Mondes* (June 1991): 146–52.

"Le Concept et la langue." *Revue des Deux Mondes* (Nov. 1991): 79–86.

"Lire le Coran au présent?" *Revue des Deux Mondes* (May 1991): 171–78.

"Pour Louis Althusser." *Revue des Deux Mondes* (Jan. 1991): 103–10.

"Les Conditions religieuses et philosophiques de la révolution islamique." *Rue Descartes* (May 1992): 121–39.

"La Pensée fondatrice de l'Islam." *Histoire de la philosophie, tome I: Les Pensées fondatrices*. Ed. Jacqueline Russ. Paris: Armand Colin, 1993. 163–85.

(Ed. and trans.). *La Ballade de la Geôle de Reading, suivie de Pour un portrait de Sébastien Melmoth*. By Oscar Wilde. Lagrasse: Verdier, 1994.

(Ed. and trans.). *La Convocation d'Alamût: somme de philosophie ismaélienne. Rawdat al-taslim (Le Jardin de la vraie foi)*. By Nasir ad-Din Tusi. Lagrasse: Verdier, 1996.

"Interview avec Christian Jambet." Conducted by Stéphane Gatti and Michel Séonnet. *Le Banquet du livre à Lagrasse* 30 (12 Aug. 1997). Available online at <http://www.editions-verdier.fr/banquet/97/n30/jambet1.htm>.

(Ed. and trans.). *Soleil du Réel. Poèmes d'amour mystique*. By Jalal ad-Din Rumi. Paris: Imprimerie Nationale, 1999.

"Postface." *Les Sept Portraits*. By Nezami. Trans. Isabelle de Gastines. Paris: Fayard, 2000.

(Ed. and trans.). *Se rendre immortel: suivi du Traité de la résurrection*. By Mulla Sadra Shirazi. Saint-Clément-de-Rivière: Fata Morgana, 2000.

"Un souverainiste nommé Mao: entretien avec Christian Jambet." *Immédiatement* 14 (June 2000). Available online at <http://www.immediatement.com/numeros/immed14/souverainistemao.htm>.

"L'Islam et ses philosophies (entretien)." *Esprit* 8–9 (Aug.–Sept. 2001): 186–201.

"Preface." *Kant entre désespoir et espérance.* By Élodie Mailliet. Paris: Harmattan, 2001.

L'Acte d'être: la philosophie de la révélation chez Mollâ Sadrâ. Paris: Fayard, 2002.

"L'Islam se réduit-il à l'islamisme?" *Revue des Deux Mondes* 4 (2003): 97–103.

Christian Jambet
Lycée Jules Ferry
77 Boulevard de Clichy
75009 Paris
France

Andrew Asibong
French Department
King's College London
The Strand
London WC2R 2LS
UK
E-mail: andrew.asibong@kcl.ac.uk

Routledge
Taylor & Francis Group

ANGELAKI
journal of the theoretical humanities
volume 8   number 2   august 2003

introduction

emma campbell

Jean-Luc Nancy taught philosophy for many years at the Marc Bloch University in Strasbourg, before retiring in 2002. Like his close friend and collaborator Philippe Lacoue-Labarthe, Nancy has been strongly influenced by his careful readings of Heidegger and Derrida, and much of his work deals with issues long associated with deconstruction: identity, indeterminacy, alterity, freedom, community, ethics. Contrary to what some might expect from a deconstructive thinker, however, Nancy's primary concerns are with presence and meaning – a "birth to presence" understood not in terms of being or identity (what presence might *be*) but in terms of an opening or coming *to* presence (a coming into that lack of form or identity that characterises a pure opening as such); an articulation of meaning or sense (*sens*) understood not in terms of recognisable signification but as a space that opens up after the collapse and abandonment of all given meanings, as the meaning of this very collapse. For all its playful variety, then, Nancy's work is characterised by a certain ascetic or subtractive quality, a sort of elusive "nudity."

Nancy's early collaborations with Lacoue-Labarthe criticised, among other things, the totalising theory of literature developed by German romanticism (*The Literary Absolute*, 1978) and the degree to which Lacan's innovative conception of language and signification is limited by its reliance on metaphysical or pre-Heideggerian understandings of being, coherence and truth (*The Title of the Letter*, 1973). Nancy's many other books are made up of reflections on the body, art, poetry, freedom, religion, and globalisation, as well as detailed responses to

jean-luc nancy

translated by emma campbell

"OUR WORLD"
an interview

philosophers ranging from Plato (*Le Partage des voix*, 1982) and Descartes (*Ego sum*, 1979) to Hegel (*The Speculative Remark*, 1973; *The Restlessness of the Negative*, 1997) and Kant (*Le Discours de la syncope*, 1976; *The Experience of Freedom*, 1988). But Nancy's eclecticism does not prevent the recurrence of dominant motifs: again and again he ponders concepts of finitude and community fundamental to an understanding of existence as both singular and shared. These concerns find some of their most striking formulations in *The Inoperative Community* (1986) and *Being Singular Plural* (1996).

In *Being Singular Plural*, for example, Nancy argues that the question of the particular or proper must be posed in terms of the common or

ISSN 0969-725X print/ISSN 1469-2899 online/03/020043-12 © 2003 Taylor & Francis Ltd and the Editors of *Angelaki*
DOI: 10.1080/0969725032000162567

43

indifferent. This involves a reconsideration of the proper as a form of being that is at once proper and improper to the subject, a form of being that might therefore provide the foundation for an alternative conceptualisation of both community and subjectivity. Rather than as an essence that might transcend and ground the subject, he considers existence in terms of a constitutive exposure to the finitude of one's own being. According to Nancy, such an exposure can occur only in the context of a communal co-presentation (*comparution*) of singularities, where finitude appears through its presentation to others who are similarly finite. Being is always already "in common" in so far as neither singularity nor finitude has an ontological status independent of its presentation or exposure to others. Being-with others, then, is neither an essence proper to the individual nor an essence possessed by the community; it is a form of being that refuses to establish essence *tout court*. In keeping with a logic typical of Nancy's general project, co-presentation "denudes" both singularity and community through a gesture that suspends rather than creates being, that carries both terms to their limit.

Confronted with the familiar Heideggerian themes of finitude and the "end" of philosophy (themes which return in his readings of Kant, Hegel, Nietzsche, Freud and Marx), Nancy's response is thus to embrace them as the condition of possibility for a philosophy that exposes itself to its own end in a way that gives it new meaning and direction (*sens*). "The end" does not simply mark the termination of a certain idea or concept; it indicates the erasure of any clearly assignable meaning associated with that concept or idea. Likewise, the recognition of finitude does not ground a concept that replaces it; it "establishes" new concepts as evacuations of meaning, as meanings that – in being continually exposed to their own limit – are never established or complete.

More than anything else, Nancy's recent work is a sustained meditation on the aesthetic, political and philosophical implications of the crisis of meaning associated with "Western modernity," very broadly understood. By paying attention to the socio-political dimensions of this crisis, Nancy has developed an enriched practice of deconstruction that enables reconsideration of metaphysical questions about the nature of being and existence within the framework of an historically informed investigation of the processes that make and unmake meanings, identities and communities. If we now find ourselves in a world that is inessential, dispossessed and fundamentally non-appropriable, Nancy suggests that it is the task of art and philosophy to expose us to this world and to the impropriety of our being within it. This is fundamentally a *shared* project in so far as it concerns a mode of being that is at once common and proper to all – the true place of the philosopher, we might say, is both with and at the limit of the community.

"our world": an interview[1]

jean-luc nancy

Peter Hallward: Which questions have remained fundamental for you over the course of your work? Do you think that your work has evolved in a fairly continuous way, or has it been marked by specific breaks or changes of direction?

Jean-Luc Nancy: It's rather difficult for me to answer that question. I'm not somebody who is very self-aware, I don't really have much of a conception of my own historical trajectory, if indeed there is one. I see myself rather as someone carried on the tides of a history that isn't mine, a history that is a time and a place: the end of the twentieth century in Europe, the beginning of another world (which will be precisely something other than Europe). I would simply point out, in retrospect, certain constants: the so-called question of "religion" (an interest that extends from my Master's thesis to the course I've just taught, this year), which as posed is poorly stated (is it religion or faith? Or "god," or "name of god," or the "sacred"?) Also, the question of meaning [sens], of another meaning of "meaning." This latter issue is fundamental. Philosophy for me has always been a matter of meaning. Then I discovered writing (through Derrida) and literature (through Lacoue-Labarthe), that is, the interminable act of "absent meaning" (Blanchot). Then "community," that is, the impossibility of a "meaning for one alone" (Bataille). All of this falls under the aegis of the "meaning of being" (Heidegger) and of the notion that the "Absolute wants to be near to us" (Hegel). Such are my "moments" and their interconnections.

Along with all this there is what was, for me, the most unexpected thing: art (painting, cinema, dance, music). And this came to me, as was the case for many of my contemporaries, as a result of the immense unrest of art over the last fifty years – art's "crisis," as they say, but that simply means an emphasis of the need to re-make forms for meaning. Meaning makes new demands on form, on perceptible meanings [des sens sensibles] ...

As for "evolution": I wouldn't use that word. It's more like a combination of marking time (one never ceases to jump up and down at the same place of thought) and of making leaps or strides (one jumps from one place to another while simultaneously staying in the same place). And also, all the while, of breaks, defections, jumps out of philosophy: the lassitude of discourse, a need for images, for manual work, for ordinary life, for in the end it's there that it happens, this "meaning" ... I'm not an "intellectual," I'm a bit of a peasant, a bit rustic, a bit of a manual worker. I work "in strength [en force]" as they say, and I forget all the time what I've already done. I advance like an animal.

P.H.: Let's stick with the first two points for the moment. Traditionally, hermeneutics has linked the interrogation of meaning to a more or less explicitly theological orientation. Your work doesn't bear much resemblance to that of, say, Paul Ricoeur, and still less to that of Gadamer. But should we nevertheless think of your conception of meaning – the meaning of the contemporary absence of meaning, the deferred meaning which subsists after or rather through the end of "solid" meaning, i.e. of recognisable if not "mythical" meaning – as part of the hermeneutic enterprise? Or as an anti-hermeneutics?

J.-L.N.: It depends on what one understands by "hermeneutic." That word has been used to refer to a vast philosophical domain, without me ever quite understanding this extension of the notion (which is often opposed, in this context, to "structuralism," a term which is more consistent although sometimes improperly used – on the whole, people used to oppose meaning to structure and this opposition itself seems to me to be a pointless one; we'll come back to it perhaps).

If hermeneutics designates in its habitual usage (the usage that is coloured chiefly by the names of Gadamer and Ricoeur) the interpretation, firstly, of texts, and then of all the data of experience which seem to yield some meaning, under the guiding light of an inexhaustible meaning which is always renewed and always carried further by the act of the reader-interpreter, then I would say that this is what we must do, with respect to our very provenance (and it's because of this, to make the point in a symbolic and formulaic way, that we never stop reading Plato ... and all the others after him). Why? *Because our provenance has its source in nothing other than a withdrawal of meaning, a non-donation of meaning. Philosophy and monotheism (in – at least – its later Jewish and then Christian and Muslim elaboration) are both essentially positions modelled upon such a non-donation. Meaning is not given, is not available, even if there are texts, even if there is a "revelation" and/or a "logos."* Or, rather: "revelation" and "logos" constitute the double word for the same non-donation. Revelation reveals that there is something to be revealed, infinitely. The logos offers itself as the process, which is infinite in principle, of auto-foundation (of a "justifying of itself"). The two belong to a world (the Western world) where language signifies rather than names (I mean naming in the sense of calling, invoking, summoning things in their being). Hermeneutics in this first sense is of a kind with a language that defines itself above all by the fact that it is both always inadequate and confines you to the silence of a supreme and impossible showing or proof [*monstration*].

But on the other hand there is this other meaning of hermeneutics, which Heidegger sought to expose (please allow me to refer you to my essay "Le Partage des voix" – I feel obliged to make this reference, since what I wrote in this text is – for me – essential to what I am saying now[2]). That is to say: the reader-interpreter is the one who "interprets" in the sense that he or she "plays," "executes," "performs" or "stages" a word. This word is "divine" (as it is at the end of Plato's *Ion*). Its meaning is drawn back into the divine order, and it is not to be extracted by signifying in various ways but to be communicated through the kinds of "performance" I have just indicated. In other words there is no meaning, but there is a diversity of singular voices executing (singing, miming, accentuating, articulating, modalising, tonalising ...) language

[*parole*] without voice, or inaudible language. Put yet another way, the originary "meaning" here would be nothing, silence or an unnameable name, but we will each of us be engaged in "executing" a voice, a register, a timbre of this aphasia. Each voice would be a musical phrasing [*un phrasé*] of aphasia.

You see, therefore, that it is neither exactly a "variant" of hermeneutics nor exactly "anti-hermeneutic." It is something else, because it begins with a different interpretation of the word *hermeneia*. That is, a different interpretation of interpretation. The theatrical sense or the musical senses of the word *interprétation* are suggestive here – as in playing or interpreting a role, or a sonata. That is to say, it is a written text that is at issue in each case, but it is written with something other than its meaning in mind; it's written out of a concern for an excess of meaning, an excess that makes up its most proper meaning. A meaning outside meaning, and the delivery (*hermeneia*) of this outside of meaning.

P.H.: To get to grips with this other interpretation a little more precisely, could you elaborate a little on the two criteria of distinction implied in your response – the Western world as opposed to the non-Western world, and the work of interpretation as opposed to the work of analysis? (Perhaps these refer back to one and the same point.)

In the first case, you manipulate the distinction between Western and non-Western or oriental in a way that complicates, of course, any opposition that might work along the lines of "modernity vs. tradition" or "scientific disenchantment vs. sacred primitivism."[3] The work of orientation, of finding a meaning or direction [un sens] in a world that is not itself organised in terms of an Orient, is precisely a work common to all, a condition of being in the world. But in that case, what distinguishes the Occident, the West? Why continue using the word at all? (Buddhist texts, for instance: are they to be read in terms of "naming" or of "signifying"?)

In the second case, and bearing in mind the immense import of this question for a broadly Heideggerian conception of philosophy, how then are we to think the relation between a reflection on how we make sense of our being in the world (our preoccupation with the withdrawal of meaning, its non-donation, as you put it) and the work of formal or scientific analysis which, since Descartes, since Darwin, since Cantor, since Freud, is essentially indifferent to the question of meaning (be it recognisable or withdrawn, given or non-given)? Clearly this is another way of asking, once again, the question of how meaning and structure might be related.

J.-L.N.: I'm quite happy to grant you that the difference between East and West is a difference impossible to pin down in terms which are – shall we say – geocultural, geophilosophical or geotheological. One could say that these terms refer to certain valencies or tendencies which move across and accentuate each formation of thought in various ways, depending on the circumstance. The case of Buddhism, particularly the form it takes in Zen, is especially remarkable in that it situates itself at the point of overlap between the two, being itself a phenomenon contemporary with and comparable to that of the philosophical, monotheistic West.

It is therefore necessary to say two things at once. On the one hand, there are these variable emphases, which are perhaps present everywhere, in every culture, like gradients that can vary from a minimum to a maximum. But, on the other hand, there is a certain history, there is a Western displacement [*il y a un déplacement occidental*] (and, once again, Buddhism and no doubt Taoism and Confucianism also share with this displacement a time and a motif: the motif of a world without gods, or a world in which the gods, along with their particular powers, withdraw more or less behind other schemas of thought and action, other combinations of power and weakness).

In keeping with this displacement which took place in history and which displaced the world, which began roughly speaking in the eighth century BCE, one must think that there is not or that there has not been in all times and in all places an "effort to orient oneself," as you put it. When meaning is given [*donné*], its donation is repeated through culture, stories, rites. When it is not given, the question of "orientation" pres-

ents itself. However, there is nothing to stop us from asking if there isn't a common element to these two great positions: the element whereby we relate to meaning, precisely, whether meaning be given or not given. This element is never of the order of knowledge. It is always of another order: that which the West calls "faith," and which distinguishes itself from what is called "belief." "Belief" is a weak, hypothetical or imaginary kind of knowledge: it is against belief that Kant directs his revolution, and it is against belief that Buddhism is essentially organised. Diametrically opposed to belief are both science and faith. Science, as you say, is indifferent to meaning. Freud says that from the moment you ask yourself about the meaning of life you are a neurotic. Lévi-Strauss reasserts that the whole network of myths and symbolic systems ultimately falls back on the physico-chemical structure of life. But what is remarkable is that both of them, along with every other great scientist, and even if one overlooks all other considerations (does their work harbour a more or less secret question of meaning? I'm thinking, for instance, of the way that the question of "G.od" appears sometimes in the work of certain physicists, in Einstein's work in particular), both of them *give or find meaning through the enjoyment* [jouissance] *of making and manipulating those combinatory and energetic structures or systems which become the main focus of their work.* This enjoyment is not a simple aesthetic pleasure: it is the substantial meaning of their entire theoretical practice and technique. It is the very thing that mobilises this practice. I would say that it is their faith. Faith means a confidence powerfully invested in something that is not of the order of representation, of concepts or of comprehension, but which is precisely of the order of power or strength [*force*]. The power of mythic constructions: that is what motivated Lévi-Strauss. In this sense, he has faith in myths in a way that is completely different from having a "belief" in them.

Now, if one thinks – as Lévi-Strauss did in *La Pensée sauvage* – that thought previously said to be "primitive" (thought that treats meaning as given) is indeed thought, then one understands that it doesn't rely on "false [childish, naive,

47

'primitive'] representations," but that it relies on something totally different: on relationships of power and force — or of the communication of forces — with the world and with existence in so far as existence is in the world, both before the world and separate from it. On this basis we begin to understand how all that is called "magic" doesn't just emerge from cognitive illusions (how many billions of men would have been and still would be imbeciles, if this were the case!) but rather from an experience of this communication of forces. And in a similar way we can understand that there is nothing in any culture that might forgo this communication without paying the price of sinking into the most profound melancholy: and when that happens there is "crisis."

Thus Plato's *hermeneia* is precisely, in the first instance, this relationship of the power of a first utterance to its interpretation through rhapsody, a relationship rendered metaphorically in the *Ion* through magnetism (a chain of magnetic rings). No doubt this seemed suspect to Plato, but like all that he found suspect (poetry, art, enthusiasm ...), it also designates a point of fascination for him: he wants the power of the *mythos* for the *logos* or, rather, he wants this power itself. He wants a magic of the logos, and wants to acquire it through a (critical) logos of magic. Who is Plato's Socrates if not, above all, a magician, a miracle-worker: the good miracle-worker as opposed to the bad miracle-worker represented by the sophist (*thaumatopoesis* in the *Sophist*)? Socrates is the figure of strength that is the basis or at the heart of the philosophical act ("the torpedo fish," the strength to "hold one's wine," the strength of military courage, etc.). It seems to me that this is an important line of thought when it comes to thinking our relationship to our provenance in a different way. I would call faith the element of "magic" invested in the order of calculating and concluding rationality. And this is also how I would understand the way this faith has become a fruitful motif for a monotheism that defines itself through the rejection of "beliefs" (the rejection of "idols": the idol is a representation without strength, a concept without intuition ...).

P.H.: Which relations of force with the world and with existence sustain your own version of such faith? How, as relations, are they individuated? Or rather: in the end, are they themselves sustained by a sort of opening out onto relationality (or being) in general, an opening which in a sense tends towards the dissolution of the individual qua individual?

J.-L.N.: It's true that I might have seemed to edge towards such a "dissolution" of the "individual." However, this is not at all the case. The individual is at once a fortunate and an unfortunate term. Unfortunate, because it immediately evokes individualism, the atomism of the "solitary crowd," the scattering of little egos floating in an empty space or else savagely exercising the rights of the strong over the weak who have no rights at all. The celebration of the individual is a cross that theoretical, political and moral thought in the modern world has to bear. But, seen from another angle, the individual as an atom ("undividable" is the meaning of both the Latin and Greek terms) must in some sense refer to indivisibility — to the unity that is atomic and possibly empty (like the Kantian "I," and, if one looks at it carefully, like the Cartesian "ego") but to which "an" existence is joined or from which the incessant movement of such an existence springs forth. All the divisions, demolitions or fractures of the "subject" are always separations that happen to such a "unity" or, rather, such a "uniqueness," which thereby shows, in its very uniqueness, that it is not a unity or that it is only one in so far as it is a unity of movement, a repetition of "self" that occurs throughout the invention and/or the indeterminate flight of the same "self." Furthermore, this same atom indicates the space around him, the Democritian space of his fall and of his *clinamen* (or I should say, his *clinamina*). Such is his exposition [*exposition*].

There would not be any exposure without individuals, nor any individuals without exposure. What is exposed is, essentially, a uniqueness — if it were otherwise it would merge into that to which it is exposed, and thereby suppress the exposition. Thus, perhaps Leibniz's monad might be treated in two ways: as exposed, but also as closing any exposure in upon itself. The atomicity of the "I" is also therefore – or also conceals therefore – the quality of strength or force [*force*] that at once exposes the "I," and thus exposes itself, and in exposing it to the outside exposes its "inside" as something that has not come to pass [*en tant que non advenu*], as a repetition of its not having come to pass, clearing the way for its "history" (or its "destiny"). The "faith" that I am trying to speak of is the force that exposes in this sense: the sense in which a new-born child "trusts in" or "is entrusted to" the other and to itself, to the double assignation of the other and the same, of outside/inside. This confidence [*confiance*] trusts in [*se fie à*] the *cum*: in the *with*. If the child doesn't con-fide in this sense, it is autistic. If it de-fies too much then it risks one or another form of psychosis. (What "too much" here might actually mean is another question … One could argue that the child cannot con-fide too much, but rather that it risks moving beyond trust in general, neither *confiding* nor *defying* – playing on words in a way that only works in French, one might call it an *infiant*–, in which case it wouldn't even be in autistic withdrawal: it would remain beneath all "trust" and "trust in.")

So there is the force of a "trust" which is a "trusting in" or a "confiding in": one entrusts oneself to the other, gives back to the other the care of "oneself" [*le soin du "se"*] and, at the same time, one addresses oneself to him, addresses to him the "oneself," which, considered from this angle, doesn't need looking after … The two movements are simultaneous. On the other hand, this con-fidence presupposes a "we" in which the "I" arises. The "we" must also individuate itself as circle, clan group, family, people … (here I would refer you to certain analyses of Bernard Stiegler, in his latest book[4]). It's very important to take into account the various ways in which a "we" comes to be individuated, if we are to save the individual from the individualism in which he gets lost, and if we are to open up the "communities" that barricade themselves in their communitarian enclaves.

All individuation, be it of an "I" or of a "we" (and the one implies the other, without there

ever being a *general* "I" or a *general* "we," i.e. in non-individuated form: a general individual would be a *contradictio in adjecto*), implies the relation of forces that separates one singular entity from another and thereby creates a tension between them (repulsion/attraction). Language delivers this relationship to the power of representation: I show you that "I" am "I," an "I" like you and also therefore a "you" like you. (Clearly the various resemblances and differences between vegetable, animal and linguistic individuations would need to be assessed more carefully, though I will skip over them here.) "Confidence" is the power that enables one to represent – which is to say to "present (to) oneself" [*se présenter*] – the sameness of the other and the alterity of the same. It is therefore also that which initiates and engages [*engage*] meaning: meaning ensures that between the one and the other there is not simply a break. Truth is that which makes a break: that which maintains a single "one" on either side of itself, a "one" that is unattributable and empty (dead) for as long as it remains thus.

P.H.: Neither individualism nor communitarianism, ok. But can we really conceive of relation (or sustain a relational conception of individuation) within the subtractive constraints of what you call, in Being Singular Plural, *"the ontological nakedness [*dénudement*] of being-with," that is to say a "with deprived of substance and relation [*liaison*], stripped of interiority, of subjectivity and personality."[5] How exactly are we to think the relation between such quasi non-relational being-with and being-this or being-that, i.e. a* with *that is specific to a particular struggle, history or place?*

And about truth: isn't it possible to share a truth? Isn't there a with *to truth?*

J.-L.N.: Yes, certainly there is a "with" to truth. There is even only that: truth is nowhere if not in the with. Solitude is absolute un-truth: it is death, or madness, or hateful introversion. The truth of the "I" is always in the Cartesian *ego*, which is only true in the moment of its articulation, and in the Kantian "I," which is an empty point through which my representations are indeed "mine." This "I" is ready to stifle us as soon as we pay attention to it: this is why it is necessary to turn away – not through altruism but through *egotism*, an egotism that forgets the "ego" (which is of no interest since it prevents the "I" from moving forward).

Having said that, the *with* is of course full of reality, of space-time. I say that it is "denuded" in so far as it does not, as such, provide a frame of reference: it is nothing but this trajectory in the world from an empty point. As such, it should be forgotten, it shouldn't even be spoken about. On the other hand, of course, this trajectory passes through places, through precise histories. All that counts in my life (work, love, friends, pleasure and pain) carries very precise markings – names, faces, distinctive features – and "I" "am" nothing but the insignificant result of all these encounters. When I say "insignificant result" I am not being nihilist: I mean that what "I" am, or who "I" am (or, rather, the various characters that "I" am), is, as such, only worth something for those others for whom he played or plays a role in an encounter. But for "me," that has absolutely no interest, no weight and it leads to nothing. One must neither return to oneself, nor come to oneself. You must not "become what you are": you must become ... the becoming, or that which you become.

The "me" always encumbers and restrains. That's why shared truth marks the fading away of the "me" (in the plural). If we talk together in order to talk of something, and not in order each of us to think of ourselves or the "me" of the other person, we share truth. It might be a truth of agreement or disagreement, of commitment or indifference, but it is a truth – which is to say precisely something which disdains "egos." Death, birth, love, hate, work, madness: these sweep aside egos, these create so many *he, she* or *it*, in the plural [*des "il"*]. When a new-born baby dies it is only possible to speak in terms of he or she, and the same applies, fundamentally, to the person that loves, hates, creates a work or becomes mad.

The "he" or the "one" (the Heideggerian *das Man*, the "they" [*le "on"*]) is hugely misunderstood. For the he is neither anonymous, nor general, nor held at a distance: he is an I that is not concerned with the I, or even with you or we. He is not eager to identify himself or to identify others. Perhaps he concerns itself with nothing, but he does things, he advances. Like a sleepwalker? Perhaps, but a sleepwalker who knows that he is sleeping and that it is dark, who doesn't seek to escape. He doesn't deaden himself, he isn't on drugs: he has other things to do, he rolls himself a cigarette, or a concept, he watches television or he reads Duns Scotus, he loves a girl or a guy, he gets pissed off, he gets carried away, he shuts up. What's important is not his "me" but what "he" does, even in doing nothing. And that is his own mark and his own trace, it is his sign and his thought, it is his place, which is as singular and irreplaceable as the space that awaits him at the cemetery. It is both ludicrous and sublime, this idea of the "he-every-one" [*il-chacun*]!

P.H.: So what is at stake for you here is a sort of liberation of the "he" in this sense? Sticking with this Heideggerian frame of reference: how do you understand, today, the distinction between inauthentic and authentic? If it's still possible to move from the one to the other, must we think this movement as within *the neutral and indifferent world of the* they?

J.-L.N.: Yes, there you touch upon an essential point for me. The distinction between the authentic and the inauthentic absorbed me, as you probably know, for a whole essay ("La Décision d'existence"[6]), which is not nearly enough. The whole of *Being and Time* should be reconsidered from this perspective (I'm forever saying, by the way, that that book should be written again differently, taking *Mitsein* or *das Man* as the point of departure ... it's a good indication of what motivates me ... taking into account the fact that there is of course no sense in rewriting a book ...).

Let's go back a bit: there are two problems. The first is one of translation: *eigentlich* is not the same as "authentic" (which is *echt*, a word that appears here and there in the book), it means own or proper, "a matter of the *eigen*." Now, the proper is entirely the concern of Dasein: his "proper" is putting his own being in play in the putting into play of being in him or by him. So everything plays upon an inappropriation, depropriation, *reappropriation*, or, as Derrida says, an "exappropriation." It's an essential lever in the Heideggerian project: to carry the "proper" (which had already become indefinite and/or infinite in Kant, as that which is proper to man as a being "of ends," and in Marx as the produced, alienable and reappropriable property of the social/individual being) to the power of that which lies out of reach at the heart of existence itself, and which thus constitutes the *proper of the ex-* or the *ex- as proper*. For don't forget that this *eigen* is precisely that which returns in and as *Ereignis* (*Enteignis*, *Zueignis*) through the so-called *Kehre*. The *Ereignis* is already at issue in the *Eigentlichkeit* of *Being and Time*.

Secondly, a remarkable ambiguity runs through this book. The *eigentlich* is opposed to the *uneigentlich* (the "they," the "he/one") but it is also said that it need only be a "modified grasping of the *uneigentlich*." This is the whole question of the everyday. What's at stake is not just a concern for the banal trivia of ordinary life (but even so … this life is precisely other than heroic, is indifferent to destiny, and in this very sense it appears as inappropriable!). The everyday constitutes above all the order of "each time" and the "each time" is the *jemein*, the "each time mine," the instant of appropriation. If you don't want the proper to be left "floating around" (I'm quoting Heidegger), if you don't want it to be the projection of an exceptional ideal, how is it to inscribe itself or take place in the everyday? How does the *Jemeinigkeit* communicate with the *Alltäglichkeit*? This question concerns me a great deal. How to open oneself here and now to the "proper" as precisely that which doesn't allow itself to be presented and appropriated *hic et nunc*, that which doesn't allow itself to be posed here in front of me, such that instead, on the contrary, it's "myself" that is ex-posed? This is how we should formulate the problem.

Heidegger betrays this formulation (which he precisely fails to articulate) by discrediting the they [*das Man*] a priori. He posits it only as a mediocrity, and to this extent he remains firmly attached to the idea of the solitary, haughty, heroic individual. It's this which makes him conservative, yet it's also this which later leads him to oppose Nazism (in particular, when he comes to say that the "people" is not everyone but rather the few exceptional voices of the *Gründer*).

I don't mean to say that singular, aristocratic voices might not be decisive (for me, this is the meaning – or at least part of the meaning – of the writer in Blanchot's thought), I mean that these voices don't make meaning; they are only voices to the extent that something of everyone's ordinariness passes through them. They are not heard by all, but the fact that they resound gives form (accent, tone, texture) to the indistinct murmur of the everyday of each- and every-one.

The *Ereignis* is also in this appropriation that appropriates nothing but the ordinary condition that consists not of being ordinary for being but, on the contrary, of not being "for" anything. The everyday is for nothing, it goes on for nothing and *one* lives for nothing, one lives for the sake of living … This meagre truth hides an excess of meaning, an excess that is strictly inappropriable. But one appropriates it: one does nothing but that … one, we …

P.H.: Branching out a little now: it seems to me that one of the most widely shared projects in contemporary French philosophy is precisely this effort to think the "proper" together with the refusal of all propriety and property. Do you think of your own work as part of a more general project in this sense, one that tries to link the conception of radical singularity with the categories of the anonymous, the indeterminate, the indifferent, the open, the generic, the whatever [quelconque], etc.? At a fairly abstract level, there's something here that links the otherwise divergent projects of Foucault, Lyotard, Deleuze, Badiou, Rancière, Rosset, Laruelle, Derrida, Agamben too – to mention but a few. Obvious differences aside, do you recognise yourself as part of this extraordinary generation of thinkers, or is such an inclusive characterisation too loose to be of any use?

J.-L.N.: I'm not sure that I can situate myself in the sense of locating points of reference left, right and centre … but I am certainly "in there" or rather I am "with" those you have named, as well as a few others. It's a "with" that is heavily marked like the ... dare I say "community"? ... in any case, with the *summoning* [*la comparution*], yes, of around two generations (1960–90) which corresponds at the same time to a period of economic, social and cultural mutation, of a new global order, of the expansion of the middle classes and the "service" sector, of information technology, of the awareness that I call ecotechnology [*l'écotechnie*], of the retreat of republican democracy and the rights of man, of the "end of history" and the (re)birth of the event, of art grabbing ferociously at its own "artisticness" ... Through all this, there is of course a total metamorphosis of the "proper" [*propre*] as you have defined it, i.e. as that which owes nothing to the other. For each of the traits that I have chosen as symptoms of the present time carries a precise modality of reference to the other, of dependence or of contagion, of a sign of alterity or of alteration. Our time has witnessed a general confusion of properties ("globalisation" is also the cancerous infection of so-called "private" property, which creates in reality new public–private spaces) and of new anxieties surrounding the "proper" (identity, minority, singularity).

So how are we now to re-pose the question of the "proper"? As far as I'm concerned, I'm especially interested in two ways of tackling this question: on the one hand, the "common" and, on the other hand ... the "common" again! I mean: on the one hand, the ordinary-common, the anonymous, the everyday, the indeterminate, the substitutable, and, on the other hand, the common-with, being next to and sometimes face to face with, being among, in the middle of, or mixed up with ... Both aspects are linked: everyday and with go together.

The first kind of common means that there is nothing of one's "proper" that is not also ordinary, that we don't also all share (birth, death, love, reason, un-reason). This ordinary sharing, this sharing ordinariness, ensures that, for example, "my own death" is only my own in so far as in it I disappear into the most ordinary part of all that is ordinary, and it's thus – in this disappearance – that I can identify myself as a singular point of disappearance. The second kind of

common means what I "properly" am can only exist in so far as it is addressed to others or is called by them, in so far as it is exposed and exposing. What is proper to me is not my property closed upon itself, it is my self in so far as it opens up. This image of openness is very Christian, sentimental and militant, but how are we to replace it? In any case, what I'm trying to say is that it's not a matter of "opening" as if one were a private mansion opening its doors for a charity gala! But almost the reverse: *be an opening* and be nothing else. Have the contours and the emptiness of an opening. When I speak, my mouth forms a contour, it's my own mouth, my own lips, doing their own work, which is to open a cavity from which flows a call or a response to the possibility of meaning that circulates everywhere, i.e. to that which has appropriation at its disposal through singular outbursts, along a network without end and without any ultimate form of property.

In this we are always already together, in the ordinary and the exceptional, in what is ordinary in the exceptional and in what is exceptional in the ordinary, and particularly all of us – the names that you have mentioned – to which others should also be added, some less known or unknown, some very young, some writers, artists and poets too ... But also, to conclude (and to carry on indefinitely), all those with whom we share the inappropriable transformation of the property [*la propriété*] of the world without even knowing it. This world, whose world is it? It's no longer God's, it's no longer Man's, it's no longer Science's. So? It's *ours*. What does that mean? *Ours* ... if you'll allow me to make a joke using free-association (as if you were an analyst!): *Le Nôtre* was the name of Louis XIV's gardener, who designed the park at Versailles ... Could our [*notre*] world be a royal park? Must it only be a wasteland? Or will we be able to create a *wastepark*?[7]

notes

1 This interview was conducted via e-mail during April and May 2002.

2 Jean-Luc Nancy, "Sharing Voices" trans. Gayle L. Ormiston, in *Transforming the Hermeneutic Context: From Nietzsche to Nancy*, eds. Gayle L. Ormiston and Alan D. Schrift (Albany: State U of New York P, 1990) 211–59.

3 See, for instance, Nancy, *The Sense of the World* 77–78.

4 Bernard Stiegler, *La Technique et le temps III: le temps du cinéma et la question du mal-être* (Paris: Galilée, 2001).

5 Nancy, *Être singulier pluriel* 56–57.

6 Nancy, "La Décision d'existence," *Une Pensée finie* (1990), translated in *The Birth to Presence* (1993) and *A Finite Thinking* (2003).

7 The translation-resistant original reads: *"Le Nôtre, permettez-moi une plaisanterie par association libre (comme si vous étiez un analyste!): Le Nôtre était le nom du jardinier de Louis XIV, qui organisa le parc de Versailles … Notre monde pourrait-il être un parc royal? ou bien ne peut-il être qu'un terrain vague? ou bien serons-nous capables d'inventer un parc vague?"* [Translator's note.]

works by nancy

La Remarque spéculative: un bon mot de Hegel. Paris: Galilée, 1973. *The Speculative Remark: One of Hegel's Bons Mots*. Trans. Céline Surprenant. Stanford: Stanford UP, 2001.

With Philippe Lacoue-Labarthe. *Le Titre de la lettre; une lecture de Lacan*. Paris: Galilée, 1973. *The Title of the Letter: A Reading of Lacan*. Trans. François Raffoul and David Pettigrew. Albany: State U of New York P, 1992.

Le Discours de la syncope. Paris: Aubier-Flammarion, 1976.

With Philippe Lacoue-Labarthe. *L'Absolu littéraire: théorie de la littérature du romantisme allemand*. Paris: Seuil, 1978. *The Literary Absolute: The Theory of Literature in German Romanticism*. Trans. with an introduction and additional notes by Philip Barnard and Cheryl Lester. Albany: State U of New York P, 1988.

Ego sum. Paris: Flammarion, 1979.

With Philippe Lacoue-Labarthe (eds.). *Les Fins de l'homme: à partir du travail de Jacques Derrida:*

colloque de Cerisy, 23 juillet–2 août 1980. Paris: Galilée, 1981.

Le Partage des voix. Paris: Galilée, 1982.

L'Impératif catégorique. Paris: Flammarion, 1983.

La Communauté désœuvrée. Paris: Christian Bourgois, 1986. *The Inoperative Community*. Trans. Peter Connor et al. Minneapolis: U of Minnesota P, 1990.

L'Oubli de la philosophie. Paris: Galilée, 1986. *The Gravity of Thought*. Trans. François Raffoul and Gregory Recco. Atlantic Highlands, NJ: Humanities, 1997.

L'Expérience de la liberté. Paris: Galilée, 1988. *The Experience of Freedom*. Trans. Bridget McDonald with a foreword by Peter Fenves. Stanford: Stanford UP, 1993.

Une Pensée finie. Paris: Galilée, 1990. *A Finite Thinking*. Ed. Simon Sparks. Stanford: Stanford UP, 2003.

"Introduction." *Who Comes After the Subject?* Ed. Eduardo Cadava et al. London: Routledge, 1991. 1–8.

Le Mythe Nazi, with Philippe Lacoue-Labarthe. La Tour d'Aigues: L'Aube, 1991. "The Nazi Myth." Trans. Brian Holmes. *Critical Inquiry* 16.2 (1990): 291–312.

Le Poids d'une pensée. Sainte-Foy, Québec: Le Griffon d'Argile. 1991. *The Gravity of Thought*. Trans. François Raffoul and Gregory Recco. Atlantic Highlands, NJ: Humanities, 1997.

"La Comparution/The Compearance: From the Existence of 'Communism' to the Community of 'Existence.'" Trans. Tracy B. Strong. *Political Theory* 20.3 (1992): 371–98.

Corpus. Paris: Métailié, 1992.

The Birth to Presence. Trans. Brian Holmes et al. Stanford: Stanford UP, 1993.

Le Sens du monde. 1993. Paris: Galilée, 2001. *The Sense of the World*. Trans. Jeffrey S. Librett. Minneapolis: U of Minnesota P, 1997.

Les Muses. Paris: Galilée, 1994. *The Muses*. Trans. Peggy Kamuf. Stanford: Stanford UP, 1996.

Être singulier pluriel. Paris: Galilée, 1996. *Being Singular Plural*. Trans. Robert D. Richardson and Anne E. O'Byrne. Stanford: Stanford UP, 2000.

"our world"

Hegel: l'inquiétude du négatif. Coup double. Paris: Hachette, 1997. *Hegel: The Restlessness of the Negative*. Trans. Jason Smith and Steven Miller. Minneapolis: U of Minnesota P, 2002.

With Philippe Lacoue-Labarthe. *Retreating the Political*. Ed. Simon Sparks. London: Routledge, 1997.

"The Calculation of the Poet." Trans. Simon Sparks. *The Solid Letter: Readings of Friedrich Hölderlin*. Ed. Aris Fioretos. Stanford: Stanford UP, 1999. 44–73.

"Foreword." *Enigmas: Essays on Sarah Kofman*. Ed. Penelope Deutscher. Ithaca, NY: Cornell UP, 1999.

"On Evidence: *Life and Nothing More*, by Abbas Kiarostami." Trans. Verena Andermatt Conley. *Discourse* 21.1 (1999): 77–87.

"Entre deux." *Magazine Littéraire* 392 (2000): 54–57. "Between Story and Truth." Trans. Franson Manjali. *The Little Magazine* 2.4 (2001). Available <http://www.littlemag.com/jul-aug01/nancy.html>.

Le Regard du portrait. Paris: Galilée, 2000.

La Communauté affrontée. Paris: Galilée, 2001.

"*Dies Illa*: From One End to the Infinite, or of Creation." Trans. Ullrich Haase. *Journal of the British Society for Phenomenology* 32.3 (2001): 257–76.

L'Il y a du rapport sexuel. Paris: Galilée, 2001.

La Pensée dérobée. Paris: Galilée, 2001.

"The Two Secrets of the Fetish." Trans. Thomas C. Platt. *Diacritics* 31.2 (2001): 3–8.

Visitation (de la peinture chrétienne). Paris: Galilée, 2001.

La Création du monde, ou, la mondialisation. Paris: Galilée, 2002.

A l'écoute. Paris: Galilée, 2002.

"L'Intrus." Trans. Susan Hanson. *New Centennial Review* 2.3 (2002): 1–14.

"Is Everything Political? (A Brief Remark)." Trans. Philip M. Adamek. *New Centennial Review* 2.3 (2002): 15–22.

"Literally." *Angelaki* 7.2 (2002): 91–92.

"The Confronted Community." *Postcolonial Studies* 6.1 (2003): 23–36.

"Consecration and Massacre." *Postcolonial Studies* 6.1 (2003): 47–50.

"Deconstruction of Monotheism." *Postcolonial Studies* 6.1 (2003): 37–46.

Noli me tangere: essai sur la levée du corps. Paris: Bayard, 2003.

"The War of Monotheism." *Postcolonial Studies:* 6.1 (2003): 51–53.

Jean-Luc Nancy
c/o Éditions Galilée
9, rue Linné
75005 Paris
France

Peter Hallward
French Department
King's College London
The Strand
London WC2R 2LS
UK
E-mail: peter.hallward@kcl.ac.uk

Emma Campbell
French Department
King's College London
The Strand
London WC2R 2LS
UK
E-mail: emma.e.campbell@kcl.ac.uk

ANGELAKI
journal of the theoretical humanities
volume 8   number 2   august 2003

introduction

jane hiddleston

Marked above all by the influence of Jacques Derrida and the ambivalent experience of his long engagement with Heidegger, Philippe Lacoue-Labarthe has taught for many years at the University of Strasbourg, alongside his close collaborator Jean-Luc Nancy. He has made a major contribution to the emergence of deconstruction as a distinctive philosophical project. His expert interest in the history of music and his active involvement in theatre have also played important roles in the development of his thought.

The historical range of Lacoue-Labarthe's frame of reference is unusually broad, and stretches from Plato and Aristotle to Lacan and Lyotard, via Rousseau, Diderot, Hölderlin, Hegel, Nietzsche and Freud, among others. What recurs as a common thread linking these otherwise varied analyses is the problem of mimesis. Lacoue-Labarthe is interested not so much in making broad philosophical claims as in tackling the specific conundrum of representation itself, in tracking the way its myths and paradoxes weave themselves elusively in and out of philosophical discourse. Mimesis, for Lacoue-Labarthe, repeatedly "falls away" or "desists" (to use Derrida's term), escaping the grasp of the philosopher and resisting attempts to generalise or celebrate its delusory power. It is propped up by myth, and closer investigation of its mechanisms demonstrates the absence of that which it set out to represent. The philosopher interested in mimesis needs to learn from literature, from the notion of writing as fiction or fable, that masks the gap between form and its elusive and inaccessible "subject."

philippe lacoue-labarthe

translated by jane hiddleston

STAGINGS OF MIMESIS
an interview

Lacoue-Labarthe's most important essays are collected in the books *Typography* (1989) and *The Subject of Philosophy* (1993). In the former, through a reading of Heidegger, Lacoue-Labarthe conceives mimesis as the decline of *aletheia*, its disinstallation or obfuscation. Mimesis is not a process of imitation, in that it cannot imitate some prior subject or essence, but consists in the production or fabrication of the subject. Lacoue-Labarthe charts the failure of a thinker such as Girard to find the hidden essence or specific properties of mimesis, which turns out to have no origin or "proper" substance of its own. Similarly, in *The Subject of Philosophy*, Lacoue-Labarthe explodes, through a reading of Nietzsche, the myth of the opposition between appearance and reality, the straightforward

ISSN 0969-725X print/ISSN 1469-2899 online/03/020055-18 © 2003 Taylor & Francis Ltd and the Editors of *Angelaki*
DOI: 10.1080/0969725032000162576

coupling of representation with the external subject it represents. Language is a figure or a trope that conveys no pre-existing knowledge; representation precedes presence. Language destroys any possibility of locating an originary myth of identity or being; it is shown to speak no truth outside itself. The "subject" of the collection's title for this reason never coincides with its speaking voice. Lacoue-Labarthe reinforces such analyses through sustained reflection on theatre and artifice. He maintains that we are all actors, possessing no properties of our own but playing instead a series of hollow, fictional roles. Actors create models with which they cover the emptiness of human nature.

This denunciation of the myth of mimesis has political repercussions, and Lacoue-Labarthe is especially careful to separate his use of Heidegger's philosophy of being from his unwavering condemnation of Heidegger's conception of politics. Lacoue-Labarthe effectively uses quasi-Heideggerian means to distance himself from Heidegger's own political ends, and it is in this sense that he rejects notions of "Heideggerianism," or the possibility of belonging to a "Heideggerian circle" of thinkers. In *Heidegger, Art, and Politics* (1987) he argues that Heidegger's problem was that he insisted on conceiving "historial" Dasein as the Dasein of a distinct community or people. The thought of history becomes inextricable from this notion of a people, one equipped with a language, an art and a myth. Such art gives rise to "national aestheticism," the all-encompassing spiritual myth that for Heidegger defines and presides over political hegemony itself. Nazism is the most extreme assertion of such a myth, which involves elimination of the Jews in so far as they embody the refusal to enter into this process of self-fictioning. Working with the philosophical insights that emerge from notions of unveiling, art and imitation, Lacoue-Labarthe unequivocally condemns the political uses to which Heidegger puts these concepts.

A reading of Celan, in *Poetry as Experience* (1986), provides a counterexample to such myths. Here, art is divorced from any notion of "the proper" and poetry is upheld as the event and affirmation of singularity. In *Musica ficta*

(1991) Lacoue-Labarthe again examines Heideggerian aesthetics, alongside Wagner's myth-making compositions and in conjunction both with Baudelaire's search for unity through anamnesis and with Mallarmé's exploration of pure representation. A recurring theme of both books, and of much of Lacoue-Labarthe's recent work, is the politicisation of aesthetics (or the aestheticisation of the political); this theme was at the heart of the re-evaluation of community and politics undertaken by Lacoue-Labarthe and Nancy at their Centre de recherches philosophiques sur la politique. They proposed a "retreat" from politics (*la politique*) in order to encourage reflection on the central patterns, figures and modes of thought that inform political awareness (*le politique*) in our time: the collapse of communism, the critique of sovereignty and the withdrawal from transcendence into the realm of the specific (see, in particular, Lacoue-Labarthe and Nancy, *Retreating the Political*, 1997). As Lacoue-Labarthe and Nancy conceive it, the only viable notion of community is one emptied of any substance or essence, one that figures instead as the "compearance," the coexistence or mutual exposure, of singular beings.

stagings of mimesis: an interview[1]

philippe lacoue-labarthe

Peter Hallward: Your philosophy begins – even if the word "begins" is not entirely appropriate – with a recognition of the properly primordial status of mimesis. What do you mean by this, broadly speaking, and what made you consider this question in particular?

Philippe Lacoue-Labarthe: Behind my interest in philosophy there is a sort of passion, in the strongest sense of the word, for literature; I would even say it is a vocation. At the very end of my school studies, I read Girard's *Deceit, Desire and the Novel*, which is entirely based on the distinction that mimesis (in a relatively simple, classical sense inherited from Greek and Latin poetics) allowed him to make, a distinction that I nevertheless found extremely rich.[2] The novel is understood as a denunciation of the practically unconscious submission to mimetic processes (heroes, plots are *exempla*), demonstrated through stunning readings of Stendhal, Cervantes and Dostoyevsky. I was immediately interested in this because I was already fascinated by literature: for two years I had followed the teaching of Gerard Genette, who had also inspired in me a very strong desire to try my hand at literary criticism. It was Genette who advised me to read this book, as well as the work of Roland Barthes, among others. But it was above all Girard's book that made an impact on me, and from there I became interested in the question of imitation. Moreover, it was also at that time that I read Gilbert Durand's *Le Décor mythique de La Chartreuse de Parme*, the title of which is itself eloquent. And for a while I was unsure about this vocation that I just mentioned: I was fascinated by cinema, I wanted to make films myself and was interested in actors' performances – and this was before I became interested in theatre. At that time, and especially where I was, in Bordeaux, when I was twenty years old or a little more, there simply was no

theatre. I had even begun to make a film with some friends at that time, which we had to abandon due to lack of money. It was a filmic essay on Hölderlin's stay in Bordeaux.

Then I set about studying this question more and more, which I found had been reopened by Nietzsche (with *The Birth of Tragedy* and all the texts on theatre, opera, Wagner, and so on), and which for me took shape via an increasingly assiduous reading of Heidegger. First I looked at Heidegger's texts on art. I was fascinated by his hostility towards everything that could derive from the metaphysical concepts of Western aesthetics, in particular, apart from the paired concepts of *morphe* and *idea*, the categories that stem from the opposition between the sensible and the intelligible, and thus from the ultimately Hegelian definition of the work of art as the sensible presentation of an ideal or "spiritual" content. But from the beginning Heidegger had always violently criticised the notion of mimesis – and very early on this astonished me – in terms that, though admittedly rather under-developed, seemed to resonate strangely with Plato's condemnation of mimesis, to which he would not ordinarily have subscribed. For example, there is a moment in one of the three papers on the origin of the work of art where he says that Greek tragedy is not theatre – it is perhaps, to use Hegel's expression, the site of the struggle of the new gods against the old gods, but it has nothing to do with theatrical performance and production, with the *mise-en-scène*, with the presentation on stage. The result is that Heidegger appears to be anti-Platonic (his admiration for tragedy is immense and he claims to be, fundamentally, a tragic thinker) but his fearsome condemnation of theatre is Platonic in style, not least because he insists that, all things considered, theatre is not an art form.

From there I moved, a little shakily I must admit, between two different fields, on the one hand writing texts that could be called literary, and on the other trying to write critical texts. And in the end I came to philosophy by way of a precise question, that of the relation, in reality, between literature and philosophy. For example, why did Plato write dialogues, i.e. why did he adopt a form of literary expression that he is the first to condemn? Why is Nietzsche so keen to rehabilitate literature?

P.H.: Was there also in your work at this time something akin to what Girard calls, as distinct from the delusions of Romanticism, novelistic truth [la vérité romanesque]? I mean the idea of a definitive, quasi-mystical escape from any experience of imitation, of mediation by a third party, etc.? It seems that very quickly you became critical of this idea, but did it tempt you for a while?

P.L.-L.: At the beginning it did, on my first reading I was very impressed, and it is indeed from there that my attention was drawn to the problem of imitation. Even if I did not at the time perceive in it what you term the "quasi-mystical," which only became evident later on. Moreover I had read very early on texts such as those of Le Bon (*The Crowd*) and Tarde (*The Laws of Imitation*), as well as some of Freud's first texts on hysteria, along with his major texts on culture and politics. And it suddenly seemed to me that Girard's stance against imitation, against the rivalry of mimesis, in short all that he had learned from Kojève's teaching on Hegel (as Kojève read the dialectic between the master and the slave precisely in terms of a triangular desire), that it all stemmed for him from a fundamental *belief*. That also coincided with the time when I read Derrida's first texts (1962–63), in which he was beginning to articulate his critique of the metaphysics of presence, of presence to oneself, of authenticity, of the proper, etc. This put me on the alert. I wondered, as a result, whether the thematics at the heart of Girard's book – the only one I knew at the time – was not fundamentally Christian. It is clear that the only imitation that Girard tolerates, the only imitation that does not arise from triangular desire and from mimetic imitation, from possession by mediation, is precisely the imitation of Jesus Christ. And in the end Girard turned out, indeed, to be a profoundly Christian thinker. From then on I found the orientation of his thought problematic.

P.H.: The point of departure then, to summarise things rather quickly, is the absence of the "proper," *the opening out onto the non-proper as a condition of the being of Dasein. A large part of your work then consists in deconstructing a certain number of mechanisms by means of which, confronted by this absence or this impropriety, thinkers have tried to unify it, to identify it, to fill it in, to purify it, in short to ap-propri-ate it. This attempt at appropriation, in the way that you describe it, is usually constituted by means of a model, a form, a setting-into-form, a fiction, a figure [Gestalt], a type, etc., and ultimately by means of a myth, conceived precisely as a sort of auto-conception of the self. The myth is here the height of identitarian thinking, "the dream with which I identify myself," and identify myself unreservedly.[3] Are we speaking, then, of a sort of continuum, where what differentiates the myth from the type, for example, is essentially a difference of degree?*

P.L.-L.: All these attempts to reduce the improper, these attempts at cleaning, at "purification," are part of a great machinery of identification which is entirely founded *upon* imitation itself. I would not establish any fundamental difference, or in any case a difference of level, either qualitative or quantitative, between *Gestalt* and myth. In the modern form of mythology it is *Gestalt* that is primary – this is something that Heidegger first pointed out very well in the work of his friend Jünger, and that is what enabled him to liberate himself from the Nietzschean influence that had shaped much of his political conduct.

The use of such terms is for me in every case critical; I deplore the idea that political mythologies can be born from it. I believe, in fact, that the greatest endeavours of political mythology are founded on the erection of a figure. In the three ideologies that dominated the last century, in Marxist ideology (that is to say, in reality, Leninist ideology), in Nietzschean ideology (that is to say Nietzscheo-Wagnerian), and in Freudian ideology (that is to say the psychologisation at work in liberal societies), in each case there is a figure: the Proletariat; the Worker or Soldier (as Heidegger was still saying in 1935–36), if not the Superman; and Freud's Oedipus. This functions along the lines of the arrangement that Plato denounces when he attacks ancient aristocratic pedagogy, based on examples and mythical models.

I know that by criticising this figuration, this mythologisation, this practice of imitation, there is a risk of repeating Platonic gestures – unless we try to show that in the process of mimesis itself, precisely, identification is not possible, that there is undoubtedly a desire for identification but it is precisely this desire for identification that is perpetually foiled.

P.H.: Would you be willing to pick out, very briefly, the decisive moments that punctuate the history of philosophy seen from this perspective, that is to say as a sequence of attempts at "anti-mimetic" figuration? I assume we'd need to start with The Republic, *books II and III – texts to which you have frequently returned.*[4]

P.L.-L.: It isn't easy. We should first of all note that Plato excludes above all and almost exclusively the tragic poet and the theatre – and it follows that art in general is also excluded. On the other hand, Plato doesn't always ban poetry. In *The Republic* he maintains the dithyramb, and then he pays homage several times and with much respect to someone like Pindar. It is to theatre that he is the most hostile. It is a question of "the rivalry of mimesis," which is manifest everywhere, right through to *The Laws*.

This condemnation of the theatre was subsequently adopted, more or less unchanged, by Christianity and the Fathers of the Church. (By the way, a long time ago, at the request of the director of the Theatre National de Strasbourg, Jean-Pierre Vincent, Jean-Luc Nancy and I arranged a little theatrical show in Avignon in which actors performed some of the texts in which theatre is condemned: we found texts that were well known by historians and scholars, from a whole series of priests, all of whom, unanimously and in terms borrowed from Plato, condemn theatre absolutely.) Theatre was condemned for a very long time; as little as two centuries ago those who worked in the theatre, actors in particular, were totally despised and excluded (in particular from Christian rituals). Had it not been for the Italian Princes,

Shakespeare in England, courtly theatre ("classicism") in France, and the European intelligentsia of the end of the eighteenth century, this situation could have lasted for a long time!

It is thus essentially theatre that is targeted, not just the spectacle but above all the *miming* of human action and the provocation from it of a certain number of emotions that are thought to be dangerous, in particular emotions that are said to be tragic.

P.H.: Is this because these emotions are merely appearances, cut off from the actual circumstances of their occasion? Because they are no longer present to themselves?

P.L.-L.: Yes: these emotions, these affects are not only worthy of condemnation in themselves (in general they are "weaknesses," indications of passivity); in addition, they are merely "mimed" by the actors that "perform" them. It is an illusion. Those who speak on the stage have nothing to do with the characters that they incarnate, nor with the situations in which they pretend to find themselves. Quite simply, they do not speak in their own name nor on their own initiative. They are spokespeople. The author himself does not say directly what he has to say, and it is this whole system of indirect presentation that is condemned. What Plato wants, on the contrary, is people who, in the name of the knowledge they have, come and say in person, directly in front of other people, what they think and what it is necessary to do. Theatre mounts a show [*montre*], it exhibits, but it does not demonstrate [*démontre*]. Worst of all, no "personal" responsibility is taken there. Anything can be offered with impunity. In contrast, Plato's ideal is that of a properly assumed discourse.

P.H.: Which in the light of recent political trends might not be such a bad thing! But let's move on to Aristotle, because it is from him that you take your definition of mimesis in general. With him things become more complicated, more ambiguous.

P.L.-L.: The most theoretical part of Aristotle, what has been preserved at least, has remained perfectly obscure on the two main points.

First of all there is the question of what I would call the "mathematical" significance of mimesis (mimesis allows one to learn, according to Aristotle), and as a result Aristotle acknowledges that mimetic presentation, whether it is theatrical or not, *is* philosophical. It entails knowledge (on humans, on action in general, even the world), it makes one think. This is what Plato had impugned. Of course this was noted at the time of the Renaissance, by the Italians, but not before – this recognition comes very late.

Next there is the matter of catharsis, the famous chapter on catharsis, of which no one understood anything, I would say, right up until today: I still do not know who has explained in a truly convincing manner that renowned sentence which states that it is the mimesis of action that provokes catharsis, through pity and fear, of pity and fear themselves. This was rediscovered, with difficulty as it happens, first of all when the translation into Latin appeared, then when the translation came out in the common tongue, as they said in Italy in the fifteenth and sixteenth centuries: immediately Aristotle was taken for a defender of theatre (which is incontestable), for a philosopher who, on this point at least, was rigorously opposed to Plato. And this opposition to Plato and Platonism signified at the time, in one way or another, an opposition to Christianity, to ecclesiastical condemnation.

Catharsis was understood in two distinct ways, following Aristotle's conception of catharsis as the catharsis of *pathemata*, thus of affects, in particular of painful affects.

On the one hand it was linked in a very curious way to one of the only things that was known regarding the Greeks' theory of the passions, the essence of which comes from Plato. I am alluding here, on the one hand, to the general devalorisation of what is (passively) endured – let's say, to be brief, *pathos* itself; on the other hand I have in mind a certain hierarchisation (and thus a certain exclusion) of the different modes of *pathos*, according precisely to the criterion of activity (which is virile) or passivity (which is feminine); lastly, there is the "physical" or even "physiological" definition of the passions, always linked to organs or functions of the body, which

implies that they obstruct the free activity of the mind, of thought or of the soul. This was further linked to the pathetic nature of the different musical modes (Lydian, Phrygian, etc.) in so far as they "represented" mimetically affects such as grief, joy, courageous exaltation, etc. and even, by means of a sort of very mysterious contamination, in so far as they could provoke these affects, such as in a trance or in instances of "possession." And since it was known on the other hand that Greek tragedy was accompanied by music, every effort was directed towards the reconstruction of ancient tragedy with music and thus with the effects of pathos that this music, associated with the text, could provoke. The Italian Academies (like the Bardi Academy in Florence), the princely courts where the arts were cultivated (as in Padua), the works of the scholars and sages (Galileo's father, for example): everywhere people looked into this question and this resulted, if you like, in the art of Monteverdi (the "representative" style) and in the birth of opera. And from there one is led directly to Wagner, and even beyond.

On the other hand, catharsis was understood as the moral effect that theatre could produce; here the word was inflected with the sense it retained, though less frequently, in antiquity, that is the medical sense (*catharsis* in Greek means "purge," "purgation," and refers mainly to the homoeopathic techniques that can be found in Hippocrates' texts). As a result it was possible to say things like: "the Church condemned theatre as immoral, but it is not true; in reality we can see that theatre can have a moral effect, it can serve as a remedy." For example, with regard to comedy, the famous Latin expression was seized upon (doubtless taken from Horace): *rigendo castigat mores*: laughter refines (or corrects) one's manners. This in any case is the version that I would roughly call that of French classicism. Nevertheless, people continue to speak in terms of the purging of passions, and no one understands quite what that means; Rousseau was at least honest enough to confess that he did not understand it. It would be necessary here to go over the whole question of "drugs," in both senses of the term (the Greek *pharmakon*[5]).

60

When I began working on Hölderlin I came across people who worked in theatre who were Brechtian in origin, the young generation educated by Roland Barthes. So I read Brecht, if only to be able to communicate with them, and I realised that there is a strange contradiction in Brecht's work: while he wanted to oppose Aristotle, I believe that of all the major authors of our time he was the most faithful to Aristotle. One can think what one likes of his submission to one ideology or another, to one piece of propaganda or another, of the cunning he had to use in order to accommodate himself with the Soviet bloc, etc., but he did not write his didactic plays by chance. He thought that theatre was bound up with *intelligence*. And that is perfectly Aristotelian. But he thought this while imagining at the same time that Aristotle represented on the contrary an apology for the "pathetic" identification of the spectator with the character and that as a result he condoned what were in his eyes the worst aspects of the theatre: psychological, naturalist, sentimental theatre, etc. You know to what extent the theory of identification was powerful at that time and up until Freud.

P.H.: By the way: are you familiar with the work of a contemporary English playwright called Howard Barker, who has begun to revive the tradition of defamiliarisation in theatre, by means of what he calls "a theatre of catastrophe"?

P.L.-L.: No, not yet! Unfortunately.

P.H.: I'd like to continue this attempt to reconstruct the history of mimetic thought and the development of strategies designed to contain or pacify mimesis. You quickly identified the important role played by Diderot in this history, his recognition of the profoundly artificial nature of theatrical representation, and you have just written a book on Rousseau who likewise recognised the inaugural absence of a defined human nature.[6] Man is the creature who, lacking any specific properties, can simulate any property. From this point of view, man is the creature who can play any possible role, having no prescribed role (even if for

Rousseau it's important to play these roles "sincerely").

What made this reconceptualisation of the "original theatricality" of man possible? What was the contribution of Descartes, and of the scientific revolution, for example? How does one take on board the status of a science that is more and more explicitly founded on an axiomatic basis and that as a result proceeds more and more independently from any question of imitation or representation – in short, in a way that is increasingly distant from any Aristotelian conception of science?

P.L.-L.: I cannot answer you on this point, I don't know enough about it, particularly about the history of science. Phenomena such as the rediscovery of perspective in painting are certainly linked to the work of the geometers, mathematicians and physicists of the time (for instance that of Galileo the younger). We would have to take into account the science of optics, and the progress accomplished with the help of "machines" (mirrors, lenses, etc.) in pictorial representation. We should also think again about the new theories of the passions (Descartes' *Treatise*, Spinoza's *Ethics*, among others) and the general progress made in the field of what we now call "psychophysiology." But in any case I am not so sure if science can be detached so quickly or so abruptly, by axiomatics, from the Aristotelian conception of it. The work of people like Descartes is riddled with powerful theatrical metaphors at decisive moments (at least the famous *larvatus prodeo*, "I advance masked," *prodeo* being the term that was used to designate an actor who came to the front of the stage). But it would be difficult for me to establish a precise relationship between a certain pattern in the history of the interpretation of mimesis, and thus of theatre, and the epistemological patterns of modern science; my vague guess is that there is a relationship but I do not know how to construct it.

P.H.: On the other hand Diderot's The Paradox of Acting *provided you with one of your clearest examples. He isn't a writer who can easily be situated within a roughly Heideggerian conception of things. What led you to analyse this text?*

61

P.L.-L.: Diderot in no way belongs to the philosophical tradition in the way that Heidegger conceives it. I don't suppose that he ever read him. Furthermore, he does not take into account the reference to *Jack the Fatalist*, a reference that subtends Hegel's analysis of mastery and servitude (which does not only concern slavery, as it is always translated). Diderot was read a lot in Germany at the turn of the nineteenth century. It was Goethe who did the first edition of *Rameau's Nephew*. Heidegger is evidently not interested in this sort of thing. Having said that, this is not a reason for considering this text as an "example." Diderot did nothing less than rethink, comprehensively, and against a whole tradition that I have already evoked, that which makes theatrical performance possible. He carried out an (already) transcendental investigation, one stimulated by a mode of thinking that was (already) that of Rousseau. And this investigation is above all, but not only, "paradoxical" in this sense. It begins "against all expectations" (and consequently against established opinion) with a hitherto unfamiliar logic, which was, to explain things very quickly, a logic of contradiction without resolution: the less the actor is "himself," the better he is able to act. The logic was not unknown but had generally been condemned. Diderot, by contrast, sees in it a totally new possibility for thinking about art, about sociality, about the humanity of man ...

Diderot's *Paradox* is something that I began to read and study when I started working on theatre. I remember it very well: I began working on theatre when I was invited to do so by some people from here [Strasbourg], during the rather glorious time when Jean-Pierre Vincent was the director of the Théâtre National de Strasbourg (TNS). My friend Michel Deutsch, a writer and dramatist, asked me among other things to retranslate Sophocles' *Antigone* from German into French, which we staged twice, in two different versions. Next, my wife and I translated Euripides' *The Phoenician Women* from the Greek, again after being asked by the TNS. More recently, but in less agreeable conditions, I worked on Sophocles' and Hölderlin's *Oedipus*.[7] And I had a few other experiences of theatre along the way. It was when I was confronted all of a sudden with the *work* of an actor, of which I had only ever seen the result, that I thought to myself: "so it is first and foremost here that it all happens." There is a tendency to confuse the production [*la mise en scène*] with the scenography but this is not correct. Production is above all the work with the actors. And at that point, while I was working on *Antigone* – a horribly difficult text (already Sophocles is not easy, but Hölderlin makes it even more opaque, even if he violently brings to light certain aspects) – I had a sort of realisation: I suddenly understood that actors are or should be *very* intelligent. They must above all know and understand what they are saying. It is easy to distinguish between a good and a bad actor. It is purely a difference in intelligence. And since in 1979 I had been asked to teach a seminar on mimesis and theatre for a semester in the USA, I did a seminar on Diderot and Rousseau, but mostly focused on a reading of *The Paradox of Acting*; then I gave a lecture on it in Berkeley, and that was the text that was published.

P.H.: So does your reading of Rousseau date from the same time?

P.L.-L.: I started at that time my reading of Rousseau's texts on theatre. This was indispensable, since as far as the theatre is concerned there is of course an open polemic between Rousseau and Diderot. Whilst everyone says that Rousseau just repeated the discourse of the Church (by way of the reformed Genevan church), that it all came from Plato, etc., from the beginning it was clear to me that in many respects Rousseau and Diderot share several presuppositions in their approach to theatre. They believe that the actor is by necessity a "man without qualities" (or without "properties," to use Musil's term); that there is no such thing as human nature, other than in a purely hypothetical sense; that the primordial moment of the constitution of the humanity of man passes through a process of imitation and identification with the other (in the case of Rousseau, through pity and fear). Of course, Rousseau seems to say the opposite of Diderot. In any case it seems that their valorisations of these concepts are at odds.

But this is not so clear when one reads their texts closely. Something to do with mimesis begins to be *rethought*.

P.H.: Carrying on now with this historical perspective: next there comes the essential separation, established by Kant, between the domain of appearance (thus the domain of imitation and identification) and the domain of essence, of the real, inaccessible to science and to sensible intuition. Is the Kantian crisis insurmountable for the whole of modernity?

P.L.-L.: In my opinion, yes.

P.H.: Nevertheless the appearance of this separation, essential to any conception of mimesis, is immediately threatened by an immense speculative endeavour: Schelling and Hegel's efforts to eliminate the gap between appearance and reality, precisely, via their progressive reconciliation in the Absolute. After Plato and before the Nazi mythologists, it is this speculative project that seems to have attracted your most severe criticism. Is this the great temptation of modern thought?

P.L.-L.: Speculative thought is indeed the great temptation, but at the same time I think it is a mode of thought that has remained under the hold of the Kantian revolution; it is after all merely a way of interpreting that revolution. In spite of its dangers, its apparent drive towards conciliation or appropriation, a certain tradition of speculative thought – such as when it insists on the primacy of negativity – has the merit nevertheless of following the Kantian move towards the transcendental. Kant's achievement was in my view to have tried to conceive of the effects of negativity (see his 1763 essay on negative magnitudes). The very formulation of the transcendental principle as a *condition* of possibility (and thus an operative negativity) resides at the very foundation of what is called speculative thought, in spite of the "rerouting" ["*détournement*"] performed upon the Kantian interpretation of dialectics.

P.H.: And Hölderlin figures as one of the heroes of modern thought, then, because he more

or less manages to escape from the temptations of speculative thought even though his work begins very much from within that tradition?

P.L.-L.: Hölderlin understood very well the stakes of speculative thought, and for good reason, since he was one of its inventors, and he did all he could to rid himself of it and to destroy its very principle. I think that it was essentially his work on tragedy that allowed him, if you like, to reduce [*réduire*] speculative thought: to measure its dangers as well as its greatness, and to throw a curious light on this mode of thought that had not failed until now. Why? Because in his own way (I do not know how) he finds this logic at work in both Rousseau and Diderot, taking into account the contrast between them, and then in Kant, who becomes his only reference – though he read Rousseau a great deal, there's no doubt about that. The thinking of negativity allows him to articulate a way of thinking the essence of tragedy in a way that no one had done before. To paraphrase an expression of Pascal's, written in the Christian context, we can say that for Hölderlin the tragic character is one who falls (infinitely) further the more he wants to rise (infinitely). In contrast with the sort of "optimistic tragedy" implied by dialectical-speculative thought, Hölderlin's ultimate thought is radically tragic. "One can fall into greatness as easily as one can into the depths," he wrote in a note somewhere, in which he seems to remember the double meaning of the Latin term *altus*. Such is the very nature of tragic thought. "Metaphysical" elevation is punished.

P.H.: Do you think that modern thought is essentially tragic thought? What are the implications of such an identification?

P.L.-L.: I don't think that all modern thought or philosophy is tragic. Quite the reverse. For every great example of tragic thought, such as Benjamin (in spite of, or perhaps as a result of, his messianism) or Heidegger (in the context of the 1930s in particular, i.e. in a terrifying political context), there are so many more other, more "optimistic" thinkers … It is not enough simply to proclaim "the tragic," as Nietzsche, when all is said and done, was tempted to do. It still needs to be thought through, without *pathos*. Cases of this are very rare. Perhaps Bataille, in France, would be one.

P.H.: Going back again to our historical sequence: before (in the chronological sense) Heidegger, the question of mimesis is taken up in different ways by Wagner, Nietzsche and Freud. Nietzsche, for example, in addition to his interest in theatre and representation, is as you explain someone who attributes a certain "figurative" power to fiction, who attacks the mystification of "truth." At the same time he insists on the importance of being absolutely oneself, of refusing the interiorisation of any models of behaviour and morality (except that non-example offered by the Greeks, who alone deserve imitation precisely because they are beyond any possible imitation).[8] Freud's famous "double bind" operates somewhat according to the same logic: in the Oedipal model, the father tells his son "imitate me, if you want truly to become yourself."

P.L.-L.: To answer very quickly, I think that in that context some of Girard's analyses, his later ones (and in particular those he made after reading the Palo Alto school on psychosis and on the *double bind*), describe very well these sorts of circular mimetic structures: the more I imitate the more I want to be myself. Freud had perceived this very clearly, and this same logic worked for Nietzsche as well. Nietzsche clings to this expression in his final months: "become what you are." And then there are those notes he sends, towards the "end," to Cosima Wagner and to his last friends (such as "I am all the names of history." "I will govern Europe after shooting the emperor," "Ariadne, I love you" – signed "Dionysus," etc. – I'm quoting approximately).

The two things are always linked, I think. The powerful underlying idea remains that one imitates in order to become oneself. This is what is perfectly evident in the French verb *s'identifier*: one identifies with someone else in order to identify oneself reflexively, to become identical with oneself. And this is to put oneself in an impossible situation. For a long time, and above

all since psychoanalysis, this was described as the psychotic situation par excellence. I've often been struck by the phenomena of collective psychosis brought about by identity crises or by types of brutal desire, affects and forms of identification. The case of Germany is in this sense exemplary, so to speak.

I also think that what is universally confused under the name of Islam is in our time something of the same nature. It is a phenomenon that exists for precise reasons, in different places, but when it occurs more generally it becomes a sort of mass psychotic phenomenon. This interests me a great deal from a political point of view. On the one hand, it was often suggested that totalitarianism was pathological, but in fact what was really being referred to was the pathology of the leaders and their almost hypnotic power over the masses and the crowds (even Freud had a tendency to see it in this way). On the other hand, the pathology in question was never studied close up. I believe, though this is just a hypothesis, that if we were to determine the role of mimesis in politics, we might more easily manage to explain phenomena of collective psychosis.

P.H.: How then should we understand the American position, in the current state of things? I'm thinking of the extraordinary conviction they retain, perhaps sincerely, about both the exceptional nature of "the American way of life" and about the validity of this principle for the whole world.

P.L.-L.: I may be wrong, but it seems that up until now there have not been any *serious* problems regarding American identity – except of course the always underlying, unresolved problem of race, the relation between blacks and whites, to put it brutally. Not to mention the broadly "successful" foreclosure of the original genocide, the killing of the Native Americans. Or rather, if there is a problem of identity in the USA, the social organisation or infra-organisation is such that it gives rise to neurosis rather than psychosis. There have been some very impressive movements in the USA, movements that might be seen as mimetic because they are carried out by extremely conformist people: from the moment when they define themselves according to such and such a category they are all the same and indistinguishable. I observed this phenomenon when I was there, notably among gays in San Francisco: it was the great moment of that movement. It was truly impressive: there was the "wild western" group, the group of "opera lovers," the group of "Greek Adonises," etc. There were forms of collective behaviour that were very crafted, very uniform, which mixed with one another, without violence, but in the same way that the black and white communities did: without overlapping. But I have the impression that the sort of fusion that happened at the time of Nazism or of fascism more generally in Europe has never occurred in the USA. It is too legalistic a culture, too anxious regarding individual freedom to accept any adhesions of this sort. But I may be wrong. What looks today like a sort of American "political theology" seems very worrying.

P.H.: But doesn't precisely this absence of "society" allow for the direct, paranoid identification of a dispersed collection of individuals with a sort of national myth or fantasy ("the American dream")? A myth that is all the more dangerous, all the more likely to incite instinctive or aggressive reactions because it is so ignorant of itself, so poorly thought through, so thinly mediated by the collective body of the civil society?

P.L.-L.: Undoubtedly, but that has not yet given rise to any collective psychosis. Of course, since September 11 (which the USA seems to consider to be a global fracture, an event of "historial" importance, which I very much doubt) we are witnessing a revival of American nationalism. It is quite strong, and at the moment it supports the imperialistic and fairly aggressive policies of George Bush, but I don't have the impression that it has given rise to any mass phenomena comparable to the European ones. "Massification" in America does not seem to me to be directly political, contrary to what has been said about "democracy in America." It is "sociality" that is in question above all. And law. On

every level, even the most microscopic. To say more one would need to develop forms of analysis that I don't think I'm capable of.

P.H.: I'd like now to move on to the climax, so to speak, of our historical sequence: to Heidegger, who in a sense has dominated it from the beginning. You seem to have remained faithful to the deepest movements of Heideggerian thought, to the logic of de-propriation at work in Dasein, in spite of the trenchant critique you offer of that "national aestheticism" in which, as you are the first to acknowledge, Heidegger was so profoundly implicated.[9] What does being Heideggerian mean for you today?

P.L.-L.: To tell the truth, I have never thought of myself as "Heideggerian." Of course, I got into philosophy through reading Heidegger (and through the teaching of Gérard Granel, at the beginning of the 1960s). But this reading was indissociable from that of the German "idealist" tradition (Kant and Hegel), from that of Nietzsche, and from that of Marx as well. I believe that Heidegger's thought dominates every determination of philosophy or of "metaphysics" today, that his teaching is extremely powerful (as Hegel's was in his time), and that he still opens up real possibilities in philosophy. But my reservations have always been very substantial – with regard to his politics, obviously, but also with regard to his "ethos," which to put it briefly is very Neolithic, very archaic, and with regard also to his occasionally scandalous discussion of Hölderlin's poetry, etc. It would take a long time to explain this in detail. It's for this reason that from the beginning I was always very much influenced by Derrida's "critique," and that my relationship with Heidegger has always been "agonal," if it is not too pretentious to say it in this way: I've been in a long "argument" ["*explication*"] with him. Furthermore, I have never been part of the French "Heideggerian circle," I have never shared that sort of "religious" attitude towards Heidegger. And other contemporary thinkers, such as Benjamin (above all Benjamin), have also made a great impact on me.

P.H.: Far from making any sort of apology for Heidegger's Nazi involvement, you have marked out a reading whereby it would be possible to detach a version of Heidegger's way of thinking from this involvement and all its implications. And you formulate this reading mainly through means inspired by Heidegger himself. I know that you have often been asked this question, but in your opinion, why was Heidegger himself so unenthusiastic to follow this route?

P.L.-L.: It is very strange. He had every means at his disposal to do so. Except that he was very profoundly reactionary. I recently spoke about him in terms of "archi-fascism." He believed that he held the truth of a configuration of the world that had lost its way politically, and he witnessed the abortion of the national-socialist revolution. But he did not say anything decisive about it. He believed that one should not broach the subject of Germany, nor question it at all. His great weakness resides in this, let's say, "archi-nationalist" blindness, which is a term that he would have challenged …

P.H.: Why did you decide to remain faithful to him, up to a point? I know you read him very early on, and very carefully. Did you go through some genuine crisis of faith at any moment, or were you from the beginning determined to hold to this rather curious course, a kind of leaving Heidegger by way of Heidegger?

P.L.-L.: I don't think one can speak in terms of "faithfulness." I lived at a time when one had to make choices: in my teens the memory of fascism was still very much alive, Franco's Spain was still a reality, as were the communists, and it was obvious that all the great thinkers had chosen one side or another. You say I defended Heidegger. I do indeed believe that the question of being is, philosophically, the most influential question to have been raised since Kant's conception of the transcendental. Fine. But that does not prevent me from condemning absolutely his approach to politics. And perhaps above all his *post*-war approach: the fact that he never recognised certain things, nor wanted to speak of them, other than in an extremely

furtive, distorted way (for example, but what an example … of the Extermination). All this is unacceptable. And what strikes me more and more is his idea that he and several others could form an elite group of thinkers in the future. His last texts began to resemble a sort of religious preaching that annoys me more and more. Everything that he was able to build up by tampering with and manipulating Hölderlin's texts, in terms of the proximity of the sacred, the "last god," the god who is to come, that god could only reveal himself to *one* people (the German people, obviously), etc., all this comes to be unbearable.

P.H.: All the same, the reading of Heidegger that you have proposed, alongside Derrida, Nancy and several others, has surely inspired one of the most remarkable sequences in contemporary philosophy. Is there a new generation of thinkers who are beginning to explore some of the paths that you and your colleagues have opened up? It is obviously impossible to say, but do you think that the Heideggerian tradition might be remembered as a thought of the end, *a reflection on forgetting, and therefore in some sense a thought of the past? Or do you think of it more as an opening onto an uncertain future, inspired by a watchful uncertainty? Or rather neither one nor the other?*

P.L.-L.: This reading of Heidegger doubtless marked certain patterns prevalent at the time; and it is undeniable that it had significant repercussions to some extent all over the world. I do not know if this is a lasting phenomenon. In the USA, where everything is historically indexed, or "periodised," there is already talk of "postdeconstructionism"! But certain effects can still be felt. And above all, even if Heideggerian thought is a thought of the *end*, it invites at the same time the opening up of another mode of thinking. This can be seen in Derrida's work, and in that of Nancy (who is a true philosopher, even in his style, while I am just an essayist – that is the great difference between us). In the European philosophical tradition, in any case, a reference to Heidegger is indispensable, even if this involves challenging him. No great thought is a thought of the past [*pensée du passé*], even less a thought that is itself "*passée.*" This can only be said of its "doctrinal" aspect.

P.H.: I'll move on now to my last questions, which are rather eclectic, in keeping with your own interests. First of all, music. Anti-mimetic reduction can already be found in periodic rhythm, in repetition, and it develops with the introduction of melody and harmony – so many ways, I suppose, of imposing a type upon sound. A music worth its name, then, will it be something like the music that Adorno dreams of – a music that refuses any form of reconciliation, that avoids calculable or predictable associations? An art that could in some way access the uninhabitable, the unstable, the non-identitarian, if not the inimitable?

P.L.-L.: To push things to the limit, I would be tempted to say that living in the uninhabitable is the very definition of existence. Or, on the other hand, the whole effort that we could provisionally and rather vaguely call "life" consists in constantly trying to make the uninhabitable habitable. This is the reason behind much of my distance from Heidegger's later work: there comes a moment when, having started out from quite a harsh conception of existence, he begins instead to elaborate a whole soothing thematics of dwelling, proximity, the presence of things, the remoteness of the gods (which is also their presence), the earth, the sky, immortals – all that sort of religiosity associated with proximity, the nearby, the neighbouring, habitation and dwelling.

P.H.: Hence your affinity for Derrida's thought.

P.L.-L.: Yes, certainly. When I first read Derrida I thought: at last here is someone who knows about Heidegger, who has read him, has understood him and is able to take his distance from him. And who, since in passing you picked up on Habermas' term, thinks with or against (or rather, if you like, "between") him, who does not merely interpret or repeat him but who uses him as a base from which to think. Derrida's debate with Heidegger, the *Auseinandersetzung* as he

called it, was very fertile. Something similar was to take place a little later with Nancy, and several others.

P.H.: And do you also share Derrida's proximity with Levinas' explicitly theological orientation? When I read Derrida on Heidegger and proximity I think at once of the sin that consists, in a certain tradition of divine transcendence, in conceiving of God as within the field of his own creation, as if God himself was a creature among other creatures, more or less close to them, in relation to them. Whereas the conception of the other as wholly Other, in Levinas' and Derrida's work, seems to rest on the affirmation of an infinite, inaccessible, or secret transcendence that is beyond any proximity and even beyond any relation (what Levinas calls "relation without relation": this relation of unconditional responsibility to the other as Other). By contrast it seems that for you the thought of alterity is something altogether other than the thought of transcendence.

P.L.-L.: I must say that I do not hide my reticence vis-à-vis any "theological" inflection of philosophy. Hence I have certain reservations with regard to Levinas, and towards certain Christian Heideggerians. Having said that, I don't for an instant challenge the notion of transcendence. Nor that of Alterity. But for me, the thought of alterity is more the thought of the intimate, a paradoxical way of thinking the intimate. This is why, without being a Lacanian, I recognise precisely the meaning of the word "extimacy," which Lacan audaciously derived from the word "intimacy." Behind this word "intimacy," this Latin word, there is the German word used by Hölderlin: *Innigkeit*; and also St Augustine's Latin formula for defining God: *deus interior intimo meo*, a God "more internal than my own intimacy." And I know that we need to look for this intimacy in what we call God, while I also hold very strongly, perhaps because of my reading of Benjamin, that God is nothing other than the *event* of language, the *there is* of language [*le qu'il y a du langage*]. And the abyss of that origin within us, i.e. of our origin. This is what the

Jews understood perfectly, and it is what we find in the Gospel of St John: the origin is language. But I don't challenge the notion of transcendence as alterity, even if my reading of Levinas comes more from Blanchot, in whose work I first saw the expression a "relation without relation," which can be set alongside so many similar expressions concerning essentially this other (this same) abyss: our being already dead, originally dead: the impossibility of dying, which is one of the major aspects of the contestation of Heidegger.

P.H.: It is also Agamben's starting point, in a sense.

P.L.-L.: Yes, I believe so; we've talked about that. But our thinking moves in very different directions.

P.H.: You also seem to share with him (and also doubtless with Lyotard, with Derrida again, even with Rancière, or Serres, each in their different ways) a serious reservation regarding everything to do with the will, with decision, rupture, militant engagement, etc. – perhaps even going so far as a certain idea of truth, of clarity and distinction. I think I can see how these concepts have been contaminated, according to a whole generation of philosophers, by decisionism and fascism. Nevertheless it seems to me that contemporary circumstances, in politics as in philosophy, make the need to renew forms of thinking conviction and affirmation more urgent than ever. Don't we need a mode of thought capable of militant decisions – thus a thought capable of suspending this interminable process of questioning?

P.L.-L.: This is the whole problem of ethics. If I say I agree with you, it's as I said earlier, that we have to occupy the uninhabitable. We can have no certainty that there exists some kind of good, as they say, no certainty even about the appropriateness, the truth, the authenticity of what we have chosen to do or not to do, if we do not try by any means (avoiding of course voluntarism and decisionism, which are always founded precisely on prior certainties) to be faithful to

this truth: that we are also without truth, separated from it, as if deported from it. And that at some moment or other, then, "we must" ["*il faut*"] do this or that. The French *il faut*, like the Latin, has the two meanings of obligation and failure. This is what makes me like everyone else: if there is a political decision to be made then I make it. If I need to be faithful to what I believe is essential (or against what I believe is unacceptable) then I will be. If I can see, from a distance, that this is more just than that, I recognise this and adopt its cause. I do not refuse any form of political engagement, quite the reverse. I have never been "militant" (what a word!) but I have often participated in political projects – to be brief, I would situate myself on the revolutionary (and anti-Leninist) far left, in some form or other. But I try to stay on the threshold of this lack of truth that constitutes and dissolves us at the same time, so it is a risk. I would prefer to talk of these things in terms of risk, without ever refusing the risk in question.

P.H.: You say somewhere that "the subject of mimesis, if the concept of the 'subject' has any relevance here, is nothing in itself, strictly 'without qualities,' and able for this reason to 'play any role': it has no being of its own."[10] *I have found a number of variations on this relationship between nothing and everything in the work of your contemporaries – including, for example, in that of someone who works on topics as distant from your own interests as Michel Serres. What for you is the status of such a declaration? What authorises it? Evidently, people who ground their work in cognitive science, or developmental psychology, would have difficulty in accepting it straight off. Can we really play any role?*

P.L.-L.: Evidently not, because we are not all actors. At least, not always ... or without knowing it. Nevertheless, the very *fact* of language makes all of us "actors."

P.H.: Even actors, can they really play any role?

P.L.-L.: Yes of course. A genuine actor can play any role.

P.H.: But actors learn to act, don't they?

P.L.-L.: Of course. Look at what Diderot said: speaking of little "Clairon," an actress, who becomes the great Agrippine, he says that one has to create a model. She needs a very precise model of what she is going to do. It is a construction. An act of intelligence, as I said earlier. This entails learning and understanding: what Aristotle calls *mathesis*.

P.H.: They learn to act, so their being-nothing, their lack of a being of their own, comes to be as the result *of a process. Is this the case for the subject or non-subject of mimesis "in general"? What is the difference between this "acquired" lack, so to speak, this evacuation of a preliminary presence, and the apparently primordial lack of the proper presupposed by any process of imitation? What is the difference between the actor who masters his or her role and the subject of primordial mimesis who seems to be deprived of any sort of mastery? For example the child who masters strictly nothing, but who is nonetheless not un-formed or without form?*

P.L.-L.: Is there really "presence"? I spoke of the abyss. On this point I can see in Heidegger an initial and very powerful intuition: Dasein is that remarkable being that can engage being [*l'être*] in its very being (but it is also itself a being [*un étant*], with a body, which is predetermined in certain ways, which has its own chemistry, etc.). As a result, Dasein ek-sists in its relation – or perhaps without relation – with "nothing of what is": nothingness.

P.H.: Up to a point this was also the opinion of the early Sartre, who tried to reconcile corporality with what he also called the being-nothing of the subject (of consciousness). Being nothing, nothing prevents the conscious being from playing all sorts of roles. And, as you know, Sartre likewise condemned subjects who identify with their role and who in so doing abandon their freedom (their ability, so to speak, to imitate everything or to make any choice) in bad faith. Is there not a mimetic

lacoue-labarthe

logic at work in his philosophy, at least in his early writings on imagination, on consciousness, etc.?

P.L.-L.: If I don't mention Sartre in my works it is accidental, it is simply a question of my generation. I did not read him, or not much, as a student, if only because I was politically mistrustful. I could have paid more attention to that thematic in his work.

P.H.: Was he too much in the limelight, for a certain time?

P.L.-L.: Yes, and in my view he made too many political mistakes. I myself have always been a revolutionary thinker, but anti-Stalinist and anti-Leninist. If I have any political models they are rather in the vein of anarcho-syndicalism, of "*conseillisme*" in general. Whereas Sartre joined up with French Maoism (to my mind, a sort of hyper-Stalinism), I was very much affected by *Socialisme ou Barbarie*, and by the Situationists. For me Sartre was the person who said that we had to vote communist so that the workers of Billancourt did not despair, that we had to remain silent about Budapest, that we had to be on the side of the Party. I found this absurd. And harmful. In addition, remember that in the 1960s all our good leftist teachers, or most of them, were Sartreans, and this became tedious. On the other hand, I read Merleau-Ponty's political texts carefully.

P.H.: To finish, I'd like to come back to something that is perhaps linked to the tragic aspect of your thought. For example, you say that the mimetic subject (and hence the subject in general) is always "already hollowed out, corroded, undermined by an unassignable gap, a kind of hiatus or gaping hole that nothing can ever close or fill up, since it is anterior to any opening, any virtuality."[11] *This vocabulary of corrosion is not neutral. But if the hollow of the non-proper is properly originary, even pre-originary, what justifies the use of such pathos? By saying that* absence *or the non-proper is originary don't you effectively maintain some kind of still more primordial presence or propriety,*

69

one that has precisely been taken away, annihilated? Why do you have recourse to these tragic affects, in this context? "Corroded" is a strong word.

P.L.-L.: Yes, it is a strong word. On the one hand it is perhaps an expression that is over-determined autobiographically, so let's leave that to one side. On the other hand it is at heart quite close to something that I recognised relatively late in Blanchot. I alluded to it earlier: the idea that what authorises our birth is death. Not at all in Heidegger's sense when he says that a three-day-old child is old enough to die, but in the sense that the very fact of being born is already inscribed in death. Corrosion is already there at birth, but our notion of what *is* is that of being-present. The ordeal or experience of that corrosion of the present is tragic. We can imagine this as the problem of time ..."Pathos"? Yes, in the proper sense: we suffer, we endure [*nous subissons*].

P.H.: Are you also thinking of the link between sexuality and death?

P.L.-L.: Certainly that too. It is also there that we find the idea of corrosion or erosion, even if the word is a little strong. The lesson comes from Bataille, essentially. And partly from Lacan.

P.H.: What you retain by using that expression is nevertheless the idea that thought is essentially linked with our mortal "substance" – precisely, a corroded, emptied, fragile substance, etc. Is this the best way of conceiving thought? How should we understand its power of abstraction, its capacity to formulate itself in terms that seem to be indifferent to any substance, including mortality? Do you think this is an illusion of Cartesian thought, or something like it?

P.L.-L.: This would rather bring us back to ancient doctrines of the immortality of the soul and therefore to Greek *sophia*: the Greeks had a conception of immortality in so far as they got rid of any notion of a substance at the centre of

thought. I would say that, while remaining very careful, what we are speaking of stems ultimately from phenomena of an ecstatic nature. I am still thinking of the expression that Heidegger uses to determine time: it is the originary "outside-the-self." And this seems to me to hold also for our existence. In a certain sense, Heidegger "withdrew" (as he says of Kant) in the face of this gaping outside. Not to re-establish some sort of "certainty," in the Cartesian sense, but to celebrate presence. This is the enigma, if you like, that has "oriented" me in the effort to think. As best I can.

notes

1 This interview was conducted in Strasbourg on 4 November 2002.

2 René Girard, *Deceit, Desire, and the Novel; Self and Other in Literary Structure* [1961], trans. Yvonne Freccero (Baltimore: Johns Hopkins UP, 1965).

3 Philippe Lacoue-Labarthe and Jean-Luc Nancy, "The Nazi Myth" 305.

4 See, in particular, Lacoue-Labarthe, "Typography" [1975] in *Typography* 74–80.

5 Lacoue-Labarthe is referring here to Derrida's text "La Pharmacie de Platon" [1968] in *La Dissémination* (Seuil: Paris, 1972) 69–180. [Translator's note.]

6 Lacoue-Labarthe, *La Poétique de l'histoire* (2001).

7 Lacoue-Labarthe is referring to his translations of Hölderlin, *L'Antigone de Sophocle* (Paris: Christian Bourgois, 1998) and Hölderlin, *Œdipe le Tyran de Sophocle* (Paris: Christian Bourgois, 1998). [Translator's note.]

8 Lacoue-Labarthe, "Histoire et mimésis" in *L'Imitation des modernes* 100–03.

9 Lacoue-Labarthe, *La Fiction du politique* (1987).

10 Lacoue-Labarthe, "A Jean-François Lyotard: Où en étions-nous?" in *L'Imitation des modernes* 276.

11 Lacoue-Labarthe, "Typography" in *Typography* 137.

works by lacoue-labarthe

With Jean-Luc Nancy. *Le Titre de la lettre: une lecture de Lacan*. Paris: Galilée, 1973. *The Title of the Letter: A Reading of Lacan*. Trans. François Raffoul and David Pettigrew. Albany: State U of New York P, 1992.

"Typographie." *Mimesis: des articulations*. By Sylviane Agacinski et al. Paris: Flammarion, 1975. 166–275. "Typography." Trans. Eduardo Cadava. *Typography: Mimesis, Philosophy, Politics*. By Philippe Lacoue-Labarthe. Ed. Christopher Fynsk. Cambridge, MA: Harvard UP, 1989. 43–138.

"Theatrum Analyticum." Trans. Robert Vollrath and Samuel Weber. *Glyph* 2 (1977): 122–43. Reprinted in *Mimesis, Masochism, and Mime: The Politics of Theatricality in Contemporary French Thought*. Ed. Timothy Murray. Ann Arbor: U of Michigan P, 1997. 175–96.

With Jean-Luc Nancy. *L'Absolu littéraire: théorie de la littérature du romantisme allemand*. Paris: Seuil, 1978. *The Literary Absolute: The Theory of Literature in German Romanticism*. Trans. with an introduction and additional notes by Philip Barnard and Cheryl Lester. Albany: State U of New York P, 1988.

Portrait de l'artiste, en général. Paris: Christian Bourgois, 1979.

Le Sujet de la philosophie: typographies I. Paris: Flammarion, 1979. Partially translated as *The Subject of Philosophy*. Ed. and trans. Thomas Trezise. Minneapolis: U of Minnesota P, 1993.

With Jean-Luc Nancy (eds.). *Les Fins de l'homme: à partir du travail de Jacques Derrida: colloque de Cerisy, 23 juillet–2 août 1980*. Paris: Galilée, 1981.

L'Imitation des modernes: typographies II. Paris: Galilée, 1986. Partially translated as *Typography: Mimesis, Philosophy, Politics*. Ed. Christopher Fynsk with an introduction by Jacques Derrida. Trans. Barbara Harlow et al. Cambridge, MA: Harvard UP, 1989. [The chapter "Talks" (on Jean-François Lyotard) appears in a separate translation by Christopher Fynsk in *Diacritics* 14.3 (1984): 23–37. The chapter "Oedipus as Figure" appears in a separate translation by David Macey in *Radical Philosophy* 118 (Mar. 2003): 7–17. Several other chapters remain untranslated.]

La Poésie comme expérience. Paris: Christian Bourgois, 1986. *Poetry as Experience*. Trans. Andrea Tarnowski. Stanford: Stanford UP, 1999.

La Fiction du politique: Heidegger, l'art et la politique. Paris: Christian Bourgois, 1987. *Heidegger, Art, and Politics: The Fiction of the Political*. Trans. Chris Turner. Oxford: Blackwell, 1990.

"Required Reading." [Review of Victor Farias, *Heidegger et le nazisme*, 1987.] *Diacritics* 19.3–4 (1989): 38–48.

Musica Ficta: figures de Wagner. Paris: Christian Bourgois, 1991. *Musica Ficta: Figures of Wagner*. Trans. Felicia McCarren. Stanford: Stanford UP, 1994.

With Jean-Luc Nancy. *Le Mythe Nazi*. La Tour d'Aigues: L'Aube, 1991. "The Nazi Myth." Trans. Brian Holmes. *Critical Inquiry* 16.2 (1990): 291–312.

"The Response of Ulysses." *Who Comes after the Subject?* Ed. Eduardo Cadava et al. London: Routledge, 1991. 198–205.

"Sublime Truth." *Cultural Critique* 18 (spring 1991): 5–32.

"Il Faut." Trans. Jeff Fort. *Modern Language Notes* 107.3 (1992): 421–40. Reprinted in *Qui Parle* 10.2 (1997): 33–60.

"Introduction to Walter Benjamin's *The Concept of Art Criticism in the German Romantics*." Trans. David Ferris. *Studies in Romanticism* 31.4 (1992): 421–32.

Pasolini, une improvisation: d'une sainteté. Bordeaux: William Blake, 1995.

With Jean-Luc Nancy. *Retreating the Political*. Ed. Simon Sparks. London: Routledge [Warwick Studies in European Philosophy], 1997.

Métaphrasis; suivi de, Le Théâtre de Hölderlin. Paris: Presses Universitaires de France, 1998.

"L'Agonie de la religion." *Revue des Sciences Humaines* 253 (1999): 227–41.

"Poetry's Courage." *The Solid Letter: Readings of Friedrich Hölderlin*. Ed. Aris Fioretos. Stanford: Stanford UP, 1999. 74–93.

"Fidelities." Trans. Michael Syrotinski. *Oxford Literary Review* 22 (2000): 132–51.

Phrase. Paris: Christian Bourgois, 2000.

Heidegger: la politique du poème. Paris: Galilée, 2002.

Poétique de l'histoire. Paris: Galilée, 2002.

Philippe Lacoue-Labarthe
Département de Philosophie
Université de Strasbourg II
22, rue Descartes
67084 Strasbourg Cedex
France

Peter Hallward
French Department
King's College London
The Strand
London WC2R 2LS
UK
E-mail: peter.hallward@kcl.ac.uk

Jane Hiddleston
French Department
University of Warwick
Coventry CV4 7AL
UK
E-mail: J.Hiddleston@warwick.ac.uk

Routledge
Taylor & Francis Group

ANGELAKI
journal of the theoretical humanities
volume 8   number 2   august 2003

introduction

andrew goffey

Born in 1939, educated at the École Normale Supérieure in Paris and lecturer in philosophy at the University of Nice for 31 years, Clément Rosset published his first book of philosophy, *La Philosophie tragique*, at the age of 21. One of the few philosophers in France to have taken Schopenhauer's work seriously, Rosset consciously sets himself against the dominant trends of post-war philosophy and more generally against what he calls "naturalism." In the foreword to *L'Anti-nature* (the published version of his doctoral thesis) he remarks that "the idea of nature – by whatever name it goes – [...] appears as one of the major screens isolating man in relation to the real, by substituting the ordered complication of a world for the chaotic simplicity of existence."[1] In all his writings, Rosset analyses – with a remarkable blend of acuity, concision and humour – what he diagnoses as the incurably tragic nature of existence. He seeks to reconcile an unconditional love or affirmation of existence with the set of plausible or reasonable arguments which contribute to its demolition. Such a project immediately raises a practical question of sincerity, the question of "knowing whether it's possible to love life *in good conscience*, that is to say, without being obliged to lie to oneself a little everyday."[2]

It is in the nature of the existence of every existing thing to be absolutely singular – unique, unrepeatable (the universe, according to Ernst Mach, is absolutely unilateral, without mirror image). And the singular nature of existence makes it at once infinitely precious and yet consigned to the oblivion of significance. To love or to affirm *this* is clearly difficult since to love

clément rosset

translated by sepideh anvar

DESPITE EVERYTHING, HAPPINESS IS STILL HAPPINESS
an interview

existence unconditionally means to be cheerful without having reason and thus implies an acceptance of its tragic quality. The dishonesty arises when we start to find reasons – intellectual argument, neurotic obsession, paranoia and religious faith are some examples among many – for our happiness. Rosset offers several interpretations of the Christian *credo quia absurdum* so as to sum up the problem: in the mode of nihilism we love life *although* this love is absurd, in the mode of affirmation *because* it is absurd.[3]

It is not easy to situate the writings of such an idiosyncratic thinker. Like many of his contemporaries he studied at the École Normale Supérieure, but unlike most of them Rosset has little interest in the epistemological tradition of thinking developed via Althusser, nor has he

ISSN 0969-725X print/ISSN 1469-2899 online/03/020073-11 © 2003 Taylor & Francis Ltd and the Editors of *Angelaki*
DOI: 10.1080/0969725032000162585

ever shown much of an inclination for Kant and the post-Kantians (Schopenhauer, of course, does not really fit into the post-Kantian trajectory). And his emphasis on the insignificance of the real will not ally him to any variety of text-based critique of the variety practised by Derrida and *Tel Quel*. So perhaps the best way to illustrate the ambit of Rosset's practice of philosophy is to take a look at the reading of Parmenides which he develops in his *Principes de sagesse et de folie*. Parmenides remains a foundational figure for several major traditions of thought – not only the metaphysical tradition but also various strands of the recent general effort, both after and sometimes against Heidegger, to overcome metaphysics.[4]

Parmenides states that "what exists exists and what doesn't exist doesn't exist" and that "you will never force to exist what doesn't exist."[5] These tautologies and the diacritical gesture that inspires them have led many philosophers to try to distinguish the unity of what really is from the transitory and illusory appearance of what is merely in a multiple state of becoming. Parmenidean thought has been read in ways that either reinforce or (with Nietzsche) undermine this distinction; either way, it is held to operate within the framework of an opposition between the ideal and the sensory expressed as a relationship between the one and the many. According to Rosset, by contrast, the tautologies themselves – which are, and with good reason, of an astonishing banality – contain nothing that might help confirm *any* of the interpretations that philosophers from Plato to Heidegger have made of Parmenides' text. Instead, the ostensible father of Western philosophy turns out to be an exemplary thinker of the tragic nature of existence. How so? If Parmenides speaks of the unchanging nature of what exists, this is simply in the sense that as soon as the real presents itself it is by definition unchanging: in this sense (and this sense alone) the real is incontrovertible. Nothing here implies the existence of some superior entity which could assign a cause or reason to the brute facticity of the real. On the other hand, what doesn't exist simply doesn't exist. If we talk about the way sensory reality changes or is altered – becoming in the Hegelian sense – we

are not talking about anything real because, as Rosset puts it, "a reality submitted to alteration, to the past, to becoming, is an *unreal* reality."[6]

Faced with this banality of the real, so clearly stated by Parmenides, philosophy has been tempted to find a superior truth in the fragments of his verse – in the Heideggerian tradition, for instance, the distinction between the paths of being and non-being (what exists and what doesn't exist, in Rosset's version) testifies to a poetic experience of the revealing of Being as such and its "ontological difference" from beings (existing things). But in such semantic inflation one falls into the trap which the real sets for anyone who seeks to escape it – or, as Parmenides has it: "little matter from where I start because I will always return here."[7]

The real – namely everything that exists as a function of the principle of identity, which simply states that A is A – is the unilateral focus of Rosset's work. Typically, this principle has been held to be rather uninformative – Wittgenstein once argued that tautologies (and contradictions) were unable to tell us anything about reality, so one might think that a philosophy organised around a tautology could only be utterly banal. However, there is more than one way of understanding the proposition A is A. In the first instance the very syntax of the proposition implies a certain distinction: one might suspect the fact of identification to conceal an implied difference. At the very least, the identification of A with itself might be taken to sanction the possibility of articulating reality in language, the possibility of a rational discourse. Etienne Balibar has recently argued that the tautological proposition bears the traces of a conflict over truth.[8] In any case, the equivocation of the *is* has been the source of great philosophical difficulty. The sophist Gorgias used it to great effect in his critique of Parmenides – if one says "non-being *is* non-being" are we using the verb in the logical sense of a judgement or in a more "existential" sense?[9] It is particularly tempting, given the separation of A from A implied by the use of the copula, to give some substance to this separation, such that A very quickly ceases to be A and becomes instead something else.

Such, in general, is the problem of duplication. The Lacanian notion of the phallus is a good example. According to Rosset, Lacan's logic is symptomatic of the iterations and negations to which the principle of identity can give rise: "the penis is the phallus only insofar as it is not [the phallus], and vice versa; being is not being, or rather only is [being] insofar as it isn't [being]; white is black only insofar as it isn't [black] or is [black] only to the extent that black is, precisely, white."[10] (It is perhaps not surprising, then, that Hegel could find in the writings of Presocratics such as Parmenides the starting point for his *Science of Logic*.) However, for Rosset the tautological nature of the real must not be a pretext for any such form of evasion. Against Wittgenstein, Rosset argues that a discourse inspired by tautology can be rich in teachings. The crucial point is that for a philosophy of tautological inspiration, to say A is A is to say that A is *nothing other than* A, which implies full acceptance of the fact that A is manifest by itself and as itself, without recourse to anything other than itself. In particular, the manifestation of A *as* A requires no totality of determinations or horizon within which it might acquire a sense: not only is the real insignificant and idiotic, but "nothing is as 'rapid,' if I may say so, as the real, which occurs so quickly that for it to be perceived requires, like a complicated musical score, a virtuoso deciphering. And nothing is as close either: it is proximity itself."[11] The directness of the real is its most troubling quality, which is why Rosset claims that far from offering the serene certainty of an anchoring point for reality, Parmenides' poem is in fact terrifying. It states the absolute constraint of the immanence of the here-now. The real is that from which one cannot escape.

In one of his earlier books, *Logique du pire*, Rosset analysed a certain strain of philosophical thought, the terrorist strain of "tragic philosophy" – a tradition that might seem at first glance to be far removed from the serenity usually associated with Parmenides. Tragic philosophy (Rosset's examples include Lucretius, Montaigne, Balthasar Gracian, Spinoza and Nietzsche) is philosophy that seeks to "think the worst" – the complete absence of any underlying order, any necessity or logic to what is. Any such logic or order would amount to a denial that what exists exists by (and as) itself, without reason, and would thus constitute a depreciation, however subtle, of existence. Tragic philosophy seeks to enunciate this silent intuition of that which is sufficient to itself, that which lacks nothing. It does this in order to enable immediate and unconditional affirmation: "affirmative thought is terroristic because in its eyes terror is the *philosophical* condition of all thought of affirmation."[12] In truth, affirmative thought cannot even *think* existence although it can discuss its affirmation – the singularity of existence entails a plurality which is refractory to concepts – but that is precisely why the jubilation of existence is invulnerable. At the same time that is also why tragic philosophy has to think the worst: precisely in order to experience the invulnerability of tragic joy. Rosset's philosophy mixes a kind of aleatory materialism with an apophatic vision of the multiple.

Despite the terror Rosset associates with tragic philosophy, despite the vigour with which he attacks those (such as Lacan) who in one way or other denigrate existence, who seek to attenuate the cruel indifference of its sufficiency, Rosset's philosophy is not a form of critique. His attacks on the "intellectual submission" of Lacan's Parisian followers, on the "imaginary Marxism" proposed by Althusser and his disciples, on the excesses of a certain critique of power,[13] morality, ethics and so on, do not derive from a sense of superior reason. For Rosset, thinking must *begin* from the beatitude of unconditional affirmation. Affirmation is not something arrived at via some kind of process whereby existence might be divested of everything negative. The mental restrictions we thereby place on the real will always prevent us from seeing that, despite everything, happiness is happiness.

notes

1 Clément Rosset, *L'Anti-nature* 5.

2 Rosset, *Le Choix des mots* 16.

3 See Rosset, "La Joie et son paradoxe" in *Le Choix des mots*. Rosset argues that "although" intro-

duces a measure of doubt and reservation, suggesting that what is senseless might not be quite so absurd after all.

4 For example: the hermeneutic tradition (gathered around Heidegger), which gives his poem an ontological interpretation, and the analytic tradition (exemplified by Jonathan Barnes), which gives it an epistemological interpretation. See Barbara Cassin, "Parménide faitiche" and "Analytique/herméneutique" in her edition of Parmenides, *Sur la nature ou sur l'étant* (Paris: Seuil, 1998).

5 Parmenides, *On Nature*, fragments 6 and 7. (It should be noted that Rosset takes considerable liberties with his translation.)

6 Rosset, *Principes de sagesse et de folie* 17.

7 Parmenides, *On Nature,* fragment 5.

8 See Etienne Balibar, *Lieux et noms de la vérité* (Paris: Aubé, 1994).

9 On this point see Barbara Cassin, *L'Effet sophistique* (Paris: Gallimard, 1995).

10 Rosset, *Le Réel et son double* 7.

11 Rosset, *Le Démon de la tautologie* 51.

12 Rosset, *Logique du pire* 52.

13 In *Le Philosophe et les sortilèges* Rosset attacks what he sees as a certain trend in contemporary philosophy to confuse "reflection" and "accusation" and to conflate issues of freedom with issues of power. The reasoning which says "I am what I am not prevented from being" fails to grasp that not being prevented from being or doing something does not imply that one is able to be or do that thing.

despite everything, happiness is still happiness: an interview[1]

clément rosset

Nicolas Truong: Your latest book on philosophy, Loin de moi *[1999], deals with the question of identity. What is yours?*

Clément Rosset: I became Niçois, a resident of Nice, only by chance. Back in 1967, when I was looking for a teaching position, my applications were rejected by every university except the University of Nice. And I stayed there until 1998 when I took early retirement. This random turn of events made me Mediterranean twice over, in fact, because in the time just before I was born, my parents had spent fifteen years in Bilbao and Madrid where my father was an engineer. I remember that during the Second World War they brought back lots of things from Spain – records by people like Manuel de Falla, crockery, books by Federico García Lorca and others. When I was young that whole Spanish world had a big influence on me. I came to love Seville ham, I enjoyed the music of de Falla and Granados. My father even bought a little house in the Majorcan mountains which he later left to me. With the result that whenever I left Nice it was to go to my little patch of Majorca. So I effectively became Mediterranean even though my father was originally from Paris and the Dauphiné and my mother always remained very much a native of Cotentin, in Normandy. All the same, during the many years I've spent working in this pleasant university, I've often missed the rain, the storms, the seaweed washed up on the beaches ...

N.T.: Why did you choose to study philosophy?

C.R.: On the face of it I was headed more towards a career in music. I was quite a good pianist, although I couldn't read music very well. However, my love of Montaigne, Pascal, Nietzsche won the day; reading them had a pro-found impact on me. And then when I was nineteen I was suddenly gripped by an idea, the idea of tragedy, which I developed into a book, *La Philosophie tragique*, in 1960. So I became a writer and philosopher very early on, almost in spite of myself, simply because I had stumbled upon an idea that I couldn't let go of. Basically, I have only ever had two ideas in my life: the notion of tragedy and the notion of the double (which I began to formulate around 1975). Those are the two ideas that I have constantly come back to in all my books, apart from *Route de nuit* [1999], my only non-philosophical book.

N.T.: How did you arrive at this notion of tragedy?

C.R.: It started well before I was nineteen, actually, even though I didn't manage to formulate it until that age. To answer your question properly I'd have to go back much further, back to Maurice Ravel who has always played a very important role in my life (even though I prefer Mozart's music, which is truly in a class of its own).

As an infant – *infans*, before I'd learned how to talk – I was already so passionate about music that when I'd come home from holidays all I wanted to do was to listen to records on the gramophone. Although I couldn't reach the table in the dining room, I'd manage to climb up to it on telephone books stacked on the floor, and then I'd crank the handle and listen to all four Polydor sides of a recording of *Bolero* directed by Ravel himself.

At a time when I knew nothing about life or death, I had the feeling that the secret of all things had been revealed to me. This music had given me a universal knowledge. Years later (I was nineteen), when I listened to *Bolero* again – this time in Carteret, the village where I was born – the music allowed me to realise that pure tragedy and pure joy, far from being antithetical, were in fact identical. And since at that age that I was strongly opposed to the discourse of morality, I understood that this identity was precisely what that discourse sought to conceal or evade. I recognised the similarity between joy and knowledge of the tragic aspect of life –

77

obviously I took my cue here from Nietzsche's *The Birth of Tragedy*, inflected with a few twists of my own.

N.T.: Can you explain why Ravel's Bolero *struck you in this way, as a kind of summary of the very essence of life?*

C.R.: At the time, of course, I was incapable of explaining it. Today, I believe that it's linked to what Schopenhauer describes very well in his two chapters on music in *The World as Will and Representation*, namely the feeling provoked by the continual repetition of something that remains essentially the same. At the same time, in *Bolero* what repeats is a very rich melodic theme. Ravel himself was a little offhand about it – "I know it's rubbish," he said, "but I had to come up with something." Repetition isn't everything, but something still has to be repeated. "Don't you think the theme has a certain insistence?," Ravel would ask. It is insistent, it has a sort of authority, and it recounts, to quote Debussy on the subject of the wind, "the history of the world."

Having said that, I feel the same way about all music in general; music makes me feel as I've been given a kind of adequate knowledge of the aims, origins and *raison d'être* of all things. That is my metaphysical, ontological, materialist principle. Music is not a metaphor for life, it is life in its purest form, the quintessence of life.

N.T.: For you the real lacks any double;[2] there is no other world, no other moral or religious realm. Yet people are forever trying to push the real aside, to take refuge in delusions so as to avoid acknowledging what you call the "cruelty" of the real. How did you arrive at this notion?

C.R.: It's even more anecdotal and even more difficult to explain than the notion of the tragic, but it's also linked to music. I began to formulate the idea sometime in 1974–75. I was listening to a performance of George Enesco's opera *Oedipus* on the radio. When Oedipus learns that an oracle has decreed that he is to kill his father and marry his mother, he flees in the hope of avoiding his destiny. I'd been thinking of versions of the work that emphasise the parallels between tragedy and the kinds of enigma explored in detective fiction (you're looking for something, but in fact you're always just looking for yourself). I was also thinking of Freudian analysis (every boy wants to kill his father and marry his mother, etc.). But then I realised that the crux of *Oedipus Rex* concerned something else: the way an oracle is fulfilled in the process of avoiding it. In that same flash of inspiration I understood that Oedipus was in fact fulfilling his destiny in the most direct and most predictable way possible. From there I began to think about the real more generally, the way we continually replace it with doubles, in order to forestall a direct intuitive experience of things – a line of thought that brought me close to the theories of intuition developed by Plotinus and Bergson, who both see the real as something essentially simple, something impervious to analysis.

The invention of doubles and the recourse to moral categories are both ways of denying reality, of turning your back on tragedy. They are two aspects of the same problem. Every double is an illusion. Whenever reality seems unpleasant, people find extraordinarily imaginative ways of creating a substitute for reality, which acts like a curtain hiding whatever might be raw, unpalatable, or otherwise intolerable about the real. Moral discourse has always involved talking about what should and should not be, without paying any attention to what actually is.

N.T.: Have you never yourself experienced that protest against the real, against existence, that feeling which Cioran traces to the "the inconvenience of being born," and which you called, in Force majeure *[1983], his "dissatisfaction"?*

C.R.: Not in the way that Cioran experienced it, no. Cioran, incidentally, was a model of urbanity and kindness; I was very close to him and spent many wonderfully amusing and memorable evenings with him. But I did not experience the real as he did because for me the experience of the real is itself what motivates the *joie de vivre*. I do indeed believe that it's possible to marry lucidity – awareness of the fact that life is absurd, ridiculous – and happiness [*allégresse*]. Despite everything, happiness is still happiness.

N.T.: What do you remember about your teachers? And what role did they play in the development of your philosophy?

C.R.: During my last year of secondary school, I thought that most of what my teachers were saying was very dull, which is why I wrote a large part of *La Philosophie tragique* during my philosophy classes. My teacher in Lyons, Jean Lacroix, was so kind to me that I listened to him rather more. But at the time I was most impressed by my history teacher, Joseph Hours, a cynical materialist who, as I relate in *En ce temps-là* [1992], was like a machine that spat out every illusion that people had ever managed to swallow.

Jean Hyppolite was the head of the École Normale Supérieure at the time; he was a great Hegelian, devoted to the timeless truths of philosophy, the first translator of *Phenomenology of Spirit*, and a man of thoroughly liberal views. To such an extent that Madame Dury, a woman of an entirely different persuasion who was head of the girls' school in Sèvres at the time, apparently had an unforgettable exchange with him just before everything boiled over in May 68. Legend has it that, tired of the nightly escapades of her charges, she went to see Hyppolite and gave him a lecture that ended with the words: "The time has come to put an end to this brothel run by a monk." To which Hyppolite is said to have rejoined, with his ready wit: "Better that, perhaps, than a convent run by a whore." And it has since been shown that her refusal to allow her students to meet boys in general, and boys from the École Normale in particular, was one of the causes of the events of May.

My first tutor at the École Normale – we called them *caïman*s – was Louis Althusser. My relationship with him was limited to three essays, one poor, one reasonably good, and one very good, on the basis of which he decided I was ready for the *agrégation* exam. He did not convert me to Marxist-Leninism nor win me over to the Communist Party, but he left me with a most beautiful definition of materialism, which

for him began when you "stopped lying to yourself." Later came Jacques Derrida; at first I thought was a "*Sioux*," which was what we then called the janitors and cleaning ladies at the École Normale. I never got along especially well with him, and even less with what he wrote. On the other hand, I was very good friends with Vladimir Jankélévitch. We were very close, particularly because of our shared taste for music and appreciation of Ravel, about whom he wrote an admirable book.

N.T.: You taught for thirty-one years at the University of Nice, from 1967 to 1998. What were the ideas behind what and how you taught?

C.R.: I had a lot of trouble securing a position, to begin with. I'm not surprised, actually, as what I was publishing was not considered "academic." I must admit that my doctoral thesis, which was published in a prestigious collection ("Quadrige," at the Presses Universitaires de France), caused me no end of trouble.

As far as course content was concerned, I always wanted it to be varied. I assigned many different authors, until in the end I wound up covering the whole history of philosophy and all of its themes, so that although I was pretty ignorant when I started out, by the end of my career I had a pretty solid grasp of the subject. Which entitles me to vindicate something Althusser once said, that "in order really to read philosophy, you have to sit the agrégation exam." Though it should perhaps be said that he did not quite apply this principle to himself, as he admitted in his later and posthumous books that he had only ever read two authors – not Freud and Marx, whom he seemed to hold in such high esteem, but Malebranche and Descartes.

N.T.: You don't seem particularly receptive to recent ideas about pedagogy that have been floated in intellectual and government circles. You've even complained about an excess of pedagogical interference. Why?

C.R.: I've always tried to provoke my students, make them more curious, more critical, and a result I've always been violently opposed to the post-war craze for the teaching of communications, psychology and pedagogy. On the one hand, these disciplines teach you nothing since it's a matter of "learning to learn"; on the other hand, they promote a sort of sheep-like mediocrity. Pedagogism became very influential once it was taken up by a particular teacher's union, the SGEN (Syndicat Général de l'Éducation Nationale) and by successive socialist governments. The first person seriously to propose that universities should become places to meet and understand other people, to communicate and learn citizenship and all sorts of similar nonsense was Alain Savary. Yes, pedagogism took over as early as 1981 and, in a way, you could say that Claude Allègre has been education minister for almost twenty years![3]

Universities, and secondary schools along with them, have become part of an increasingly oppressive machine that weighs ever more heavily upon those who teach in them, only to produce ever more limited results. The drop in standards has been dizzying, and you're now expected to teach forms of ignorance, if not stupidity. Students should instead be learning about culture and cultivating, in the case of philosophy, a sense of critical discernment – and some still manage, certainly, to learn something along these lines. But much has changed with the influx of students sporting dubious versions of the baccalaureate, earned as a result of the fact that everyone agrees, in line with current pseudo-democratic principles, that the baccalaureate should now be awarded to almost everyone. The truth is that we're taking advantage of these students, they've been paid in false coin. But let me qualify my point: it's true that the number of good or excellent students is not falling, they're just lost in the mediocrity of the mass, in the movement of "massification" that should never be confused with democratisation.

N.T.: In 1976, under a pseudonym, you published a play called Les Matinées structuralistes, *along with a* Précis de philosophie moderne, *in which you poked fun at the intellectual trends and philosophical luminaries of the time – Foucault, Deleuze, Lacan, Derrida ...*

Were you inspired by a taste for polemic, or by your unshakeable commitment to the expression of philosophy in clear and accessible language?

C.R.: *Les Matinées structuralistes* was commissioned by Jean-François Revel. I wanted to write about those years at the École Normale when we were caught between the Communist Party, Althusser, Lacan, and the newly crowned glory of Derrida, whom I imitated in a speech on writing – writhing [*l'écrithure*], with an "h" between the "t" and the "i" – in which I distinguished between the notion of writing without an "h" and the notion of writing with an "h," in the exact words used by Derrida in that famous article on difference with an "e" and différance with an "a." Hence the master's great rage!

In fact, what I was rejecting was this all-too-typical way of being both unreadable and boring. As I say in *Le Choix des mots*, I continue to believe that writing is not a "dangerous supplement," as Derrida said after Rousseau, but that it is simply thought itself. And as such a philosophy's strength lies in its clarity, its language.

I suppose I should add that I also have a slightly Voltairian habit of always making daft and mildly hurtful comments whenever the opportunity arises. I'm afraid that I pay no attention to La Bruyère's observation, in a passage of *The Characters*, that a man who fails to resist the pleasure of causing laughter at the expense of another is not a man of honour. For me, laughter is the most important thing, above everything else. If it's funny, I can't help myself. Not out of cruelty, but if there's a way of exposing something comical about a situation then I can't resist it. Of course I apply the same principle to myself – in *Les Matinées structuralistes*, I too figure as a grotesque character. And I'd hardly have published *Route de nuit* [1999], a personal and peculiar book in which I describe certain rather dramatic mood swings, had I not found them to be very funny.

N.T.: Your work consistently refers not just to various philosophers but also to Tintin, Tati or Marivaux. Aside from the delight you clearly take in such apparently incongruous conjunctions, what is their purpose, what is their effect?

C.R.: This omni-referential system in which film, literature and comic strips all operate at the same level is first of all just my way of responding to a sort of writer's instinct. I delight in finding parallels between fields that might otherwise seem as distant and as incongruous as can be. As soon as you look carefully at any first-rate work in any particular field, you find proof of cultural traffic moving between all these different fields. And there's another reason for this tendency in my books, which is that my training was more literary than philosophical. I've read more Shakespeare, Balzac or Dostoyevsky than I have philosophy, which I read mostly for professional reasons. So I indulge in the writer's pleasure of wandering off the beaten track and drawing an arc through completely heterogeneous points of reference, in order then to demonstrate their fundamental homogeneity. It's a bit like the mathematical curve that Leibniz describes – only God knows the function that makes it follow its strange course.

N.T.: Is literature simply a means for you of illustrating various philosophical points, or does it convey a particular way of apprehending the world?

C.R.: It makes me very uncomfortable to read books that refer exclusively to philosophical works. I feel like I'm suffocating, I feel as if life cannot reach these abstract places; on the other hand, principles proposed by Hegel or Nietzsche can come vigorously alive if you can find a way of showing how they relate to what the fishmonger says, or to the way you make bouillabaisse. Philosophical arguments become weak and anaemic once they refer only to themselves. In his *Oneself as Another*, for example, Paul Ricoeur (for whom I happen to have a great deal of respect) somehow manages to refer only to philosophical texts over the course of three or four hundred pages, which makes his work very forbidding. If I refer as much as I do

to Saint-Simon, Dostoyevsky, Balzac, Gogol, Aristophanes, Sophocles or Joseph Conrad it's partly because of my early training but mainly because they are all truly remarkable experts on human nature.

N.T.: Le Démon de la tautologie [1997], a work in which you respond directly to those who accuse you of always repeating the same points, was also a study of identity. Why come back to the question of identity now in Loin de moi?

C.R.: During a series of chronic nightmares that I suffered over the course of several years, I often experienced a sort of loss of identity. After these nightmares I'd have the feeling that the one who had just dreamt what I'd dreamt was not me, that whoever delivers dreams had got the address wrong and made me dream the dreams of someone else. I'd find myself face to face with a signifier that had no significance for me, which is an extremely anguishing experience. I try to I describe what it's like, in my usual way, with the example of an anecdote drawn from the comic strip *Bécassine*. It's the story of a man from the 1910s–1920s, living in a building whose concierge has just quit. All of the residents of the building are worried about how they'll now receive their mail, so they ask this man to help them out. The next day, the man sets himself up in the concierge's lodge and receives such a stack of mail that he asks Bécassine to come and help him open it. Absorbed in the confusion of all this mail, understanding absolutely nothing of what the letters say, he tears his hair out trying to make sense of what it's all about and then suddenly realises that he has become the building's temporary concierge. Well! That's a bit how it was in these nightmares.

In order to come to terms with this experience I wanted to write a book on the feeling of identity – a theme masterfully explored by David Hume. I wanted to say that the feeling of personal identity is a matter of pure fantasy, and that what you lose when you say that you've lost your identity is just your social identity, not your intimate identity. *Loin de moi*, the title of the book, also evokes a way of distancing your-self: the self is something that I keep at a dis-tance from myself, I am "far from me."

N.T.: Route de nuit *(published at the same time as* Loin de moi*) is a startling book which might also have been called* Hors de moi,[4] *since in it you describe a strange and painful disease that you've endured for more than ten years now, which makes you live as if outside or to one side of yourself, so to speak. Why did you write this book?*

C.R.: *Route de nuit* breaks with everything else I've written, even with my most peculiar books, like *Le Choix des mots* [1995]. *Route de nuit* is a purely descriptive and experimental book, and has more in common with fantasy fiction than with a philosophical essay. It describes the trau-matising experiences that have cast a distressing shadow over my daily life for the past ten years. It's made up of notes, points of reference for the observation of my disease. Ten years on, I showed these notes to a psychiatrist who advised me to publish them, as he thought they described a new condition, a condition that I call *"hasofin"* for short, partly on the model of Maupassant's *"Horla."* *Hasofin* is an abbrevia-tion that sums up the major symptoms that I've suffered from, and continue to suffer from: *hyper-activisme semi-onirique de fin de nuit* (semi-dreamlike end of night hyper-activism). I then went over my notes again and added some analyses and illustrations from literature. It involved a new way of writing for me, and I decided to publish it on account of its fantasti-cal and comical quality.

N.T.: Did it help you to understand your dis-ease?

C.R.: Not at all, because the whole book con-firms my belief that there is nothing to under-stand. Diseases without a cause are also diseases without a cure. No doubt there are what Aristotle would called efficient causes at work here, factors that have had some impact on my psyche. But now the disease lives on in a com-pletely autonomous way.

N.T.: Couldn't you say that this is a meta-physical disease, and that the double whose forms you tracked down so relentlessly has since come back to haunt you?

C.R.: Of course I thought that I was being pun-ished for my ideas and that the gods, irritated by my unwavering philosophy, had decided to give me a good thrashing. Actually, Philippe Sollers, the editor of this book at Gallimard, told me that it was all about a "little metaphysical crisis"!

notes

1 This interview was conducted by Nicolas Truong and first appeared in *Le Monde de l'Éduca-tion* in November 1999 under the title "Etre heureux, c'est toujours être heureux malgré tout." It was reprinted in *Le Monde de l'Éducation* 294 (July 2001): 29–32.

2 *Le Réel est sans double.* In keeping with standard usage, I've translated *le réel* as the real and *la réal-ité* as reality, throughout. Unlike Lacan, however, Rosset tends to use the two terms interchange-ably. Although Rosset's understanding of the real as "cruel" bears some resemblance to Lacan's early conception of the real as traumatic, as indif-ferent to representation, etc., it bears little resemblance to his later and more developed versions of the concept – Rosset's *réel* is pre-cisely independent, for instance, of any constitu-tive knot that might tie it to the imaginary and the symbolic. [Translator's note.]

3 Alain Savary was Minister of Education from 1981 to 1984; Claude Allègre was Jospin's Minister of Education from 1997 to 2000. [Translator's note.]

4 *Hors de moi* could be translated either as "out-side myself" or, drawing on a more colloquial usage, as "off my head." [Translator's note.]

works by rosset

La Philosophie tragique. Paris: Presses Universitaires de France, 1960.

Le Monde et ses remèdes. Paris: Presses Universitaires de France, 1964.

"Le Sentiment de l'Absurde dans la philosophie de Schopenhauer." *Revue de Metaphysique et de Morale* 69 (1964): 41–78.

Lettre sur les chimpanzés: plaidoyer pour une humanité totale. Paris: Gallimard, 1965.

Schopenhauer, philosophe de l'absurde. Paris: Presses Universitaires de France, 1967.

L'Esthétique de Schopenhauer. Paris: Presses Universitaires de France, 1969.

Logique du pire: éléments pour une philosophie tragique. Paris: Presses Universitaires de France, 1971.

L'Anti-nature. Paris: Presses Universitaires de France, 1973.

Le Réel et son double: essai sur l'illusion. 1976. Paris: Gallimard, 1985.

Le Réel: traité de l'idiotie. Paris: Minuit, 1977.

"Interieurs romantiques." *Nouvelle Revue Française* 321 (1979): 108–13.

L'Objet singulier. Paris: Minuit, 1979.

"L'Écriture violente." *Nouvelle Revue Française* 328 (1980): 60–65.

"Images de l'absence." *Nouvelle Revue Française* 330–331 (1980): 168–73.

La Force majeure. Paris: Minuit, 1983.

"Une Littérature pour rire." *Raymond Roussel en gloire.* Ed. Anne-Marie Amiot. Lausanne: L'Age d'Homme, 1984. 39–40.

Le Philosophe et les sortilèges. Paris: Minuit, 1985.

Le Principe de cruauté. Paris: Minuit, 1988.

"Reality and the Untheorizable." *The Limits of Theory.* Ed. Thomas M. Kavanagh. Stanford: Stanford UP, 1989. 76–118.

Principes de sagesse et de folie. Paris: Minuit, 1991.

En ce temps-là: notes sur Louis Althusser. Paris: Minuit, 1992.

Matière d'art: hommages. Nantes: Le Passeur-Cecofop, 1992.

Joyful Cruelty: Toward a Philosophy of the Real. Ed. and trans. David F. Bell. Oxford: Oxford UP, 1993.

"Du Terrorisme en philosophie." *Chance, Culture and the Literary Text.* Ed. Thomas M. Kavanagh. Ann Arbor: U of Michigan P, 1994. 65–85.

Le Choix des mots: suivi de La Joie et son paradoxe. Paris: Minuit, 1995.

Le Démon de la tautologie: suivi de Cinq petites pièces morales. Paris: Minuit, 1997.

"Là où j'admire." *Magazine Littéraire* 352 (Mar. 1997): 37–39.

Loin de moi: étude sur l'identité. Paris: Minuit, 1999.

Route de nuit: épisodes cliniques. Paris: Gallimard, 1999.

Propos sur le cinéma. Paris: Presses Universitaires de France, 2001.

Le Régime des passions et autres textes. Paris: Minuit, 2001.

With Michel Polac. *Franchise postale: courrier, mai 2002–décembre 2002.* Paris: Presses Universitaires de France, 2003.

Clément Rosset
Université de Nice
Faculté des lettres et sciences humaines
98, boulevard Edouard Herriot, BP 209
06204 Nice Cedex 3
France

Nicolas Truong
c/o *Le Monde*
21 bis, rue Claude-Bernard
75242 Paris Cedex 05
France

Andrew Goffey
Media, Culture and Communications
University of Middlesex
White Hart Lane
London N17 8HR
UK
E-mail: a.goffey@mdx.ac.uk

Sepideh Anvar
5 rue Planchat
75020 Paris
France

journal of the theoretical humanities
volume 8   number 2   august 2003

introduction

peter hallward

Born in 1947 in Paris, Guy Lardreau teaches philosophy at the Lycée Carnot in Dijon. Although his work ranges across a wide spectrum of radical political and spiritual themes, his specialist training is in Syriac and Coptic studies. His books include a reflection on the forms and implications of cultural revolution (*L'Ange*, co-authored with Christian Jambet, 1976), a monograph on the early Syrian bishop Philoxenus of Mabbug (*Discours philosophique et discours spirituel*, 1985), a trilogy of meditations on crime, science and fantastic fiction (*Fictions philosophiques et science-fiction*, 1988; *Présentation criminelle de quelques concepts majeurs de la philosophie*, 1997; *Intuition philosophique et présence fantastique*, forthcoming), a brief critique of Deleuze occasioned by the latter's readings in the history of philosophy (*L'Exercice différé de la philosophie*, 1999), the more substantial treatise *La Véracité* (1993), and the manifesto *Vive le matérialisme!* (originally published as anonymous, 2001). Like Badiou and Jambet, Lardreau emphasises the systematic and uncompromising orientation of philosophy, one marked above all by Mao and Lacan; unlike Badiou or Jambet, however, Lardreau accords Kant a central place in his effort to reconcile a post-Maoist conception of politics with a rational but fully "negative" – or "non-dishonest" – conception of philosophy.

The question that guides much of Lardreau's work is most starkly posed in the sections of *L'Ange* that refer to the exemplary experience of those early Christian ascetics (Saint Jerome, Chrysostomos, etc.), who both lived and declared a particularly intransigent form of "absolute

guy lardreau

translated by peter hallward

THE PROBLEM OF GREAT POLITICS IN THE LIGHT OF OBVIOUSLY DEFICIENT MODES OF SUBJECTIVATION

revolt" against the prevailing way of the world.[1] The early monastic thinkers, inspired by a resolutely Manichaean conception of reality, propose their own version of "cultural revolution" *avant la lettre*: they invert every accepted form of value, renounce all inheritance, refuse any loyalty to family and familiarity, deny the body, reject sexual difference and desire, pursue a heroic anonymity, adopt a permanent posture of self-criticism, embrace the most severe forms of frugality, discipline and elation. They accept, in short, that "the path of saintliness is a path of struggle *alone*."[2] How could it happen, asks Lardreau, that this uncompromising posture of revolt was then so easily and so quickly accommodated within a new configuration of mastery? How could a discourse of pure revolt, directed

ISSN 0969-725X print/ISSN 1469-2899 online/03/020085-12 © 2003 Taylor & Francis Ltd and the Editors of *Angelaki*
DOI: 10.1080/0969725032000162594

85

against the figure of mastery as such, directed against the very survival of society, in turn become the witless "instrument of the Master," i.e. allow itself to be used, as a sort of safely marginalised lunatic fringe, in ways that help consolidate the social and institutional mainstream? Or, in short, how was the discourse of saints bent to the needs of a *church*? The answer: through the conversion of cultural revolution into a merely "ideological" revolution. Whereas cultural revolution rejects every form of mastery in the un-mediated dualism of oppression/revolt, ideological revolution mediates subjective responses to socio-historical "causes" or conditions and integrates rebellion within a rational historical order or development – and in the process it transforms the critique of mastery into the mere substitution of one master for another.[3]

The writing of *L'Ange* coincided with the realisation that the Maoist rebellion that Lardreau had so enthusiastically embraced was vulnerable to a similar outcome.[4] Both historical sequences seemed to culminate in newly extreme forms of obedience (to the Church, to the party). Was it then the necessary fate of radical revolt to end in radical submission? Lardreau's own answer to this question, here and subsequently, is to rebel against the very form of the question itself: revolt persists as an "unreasonable" and unreasoned "wager" against history, against desire, against every form of reconciliation or deduction. "Once again we will make the senseless wager: the Angel has always been defeated – but he will triumph, in the end, in an unprecedented revolution"[5] Unlike more orthodox versions of Maoism, Lardreau makes of this un-reasonable and discontinuous quality of revolt its highest virtue, an index of its unassimilable resistance to integration in the rational progress of history.

It is in the form of a pure wager, then, that Lardreau and Jambet seek "to preserve, against all forms of power and domination, the hope that a different world, despite everything, is possible," by "pushing the logic of rebellion to its limit, to the point of paroxysm."[6] This involves, among other things: (a) the refusal of conventional forms of "coherence" (hence the book's disjointed composition and syntactical complexity); (b) an acceptance, in the wake of

Lacan, that there is no possible liberation within the field of desire, that *all* desire is subject to mastery and law (hence the critique of Sade, Deleuze, and Lyotard: the free circulation of desire is a contradiction in terms); (c) a consequent insistence upon the "total disjunction of sexuality and rebellion" (hence the affirmation of "Angelism" as indifferent to sexuality, and in particular as indifferent to what Lacan describes as the sexual non-relation[7]); (d) a refusal of historical time, i.e. of the dialectical or "ideological" coordination of structural conditions and subjective responses (hence the presumption that "the past doesn't exist – and this is precisely our most profound metaphysical thesis, our 'esoteric' thesis ..."). The Manichaean dualism of revolt prevails solely in the purity of the present. In contrast to more orthodox conceptions of Maoism, such Angelic subjectivity cannot simply be derived from collective struggle or dialectical progression; it can only arise abruptly, immediately, in a sort of sublime indifference to any dialectical impasse.[8]

Lardreau thus persists in a project that most of his Maoist fellow travellers were soon to abandon as indefensibly utopian. At the same time, however, he has always insisted that the real "enemy is semblance" and dissemblance.[9] Beware of affirmation, he warns Deleuze, since it provides cover for many falsehoods. Against all imaginary delusions, against all reassuring conceptions of wholeness, against every figure of reconciliation, Lardreau perseveres in his starkly negative path. "Negative philosophy is ineluctably worth more than any affirmation for, affirming nothing, it has no interest in betrayal, and it never lies."[10] It is this peculiar combination of uncompromising principle and remorseless negativity, this *systematic scepticism*, that best characterises Lardreau's conception of philosophy. "To philosophise any given statement," he writes at the end of this same rejoinder to Deleuze, "is to confront it with its nullity" – but only on this condition: that the statements thus nullified come from anywhere, from any source (religious, fictional, rational, "opinionated," etc.), without concern for their dignity or worth. This ardent indifference is itself the sole basis for "the dignity of philosophy." It's on this basis that a genuinely negative philosophy can proceed as "super-affirmation, as pure affirmation."[11] Philosophy is the only discourse that is active solely when it welcomes statements that are "absolutely heterogeneous" with if not implacably "hostile" to it.[12] Lardreau takes up the spiritual discourse of Philoxenus, for instance, in order to show (among other things) how, confronted by philosophy's insistence on systematic reasoning, it sustains an irreducible resistance to this reasoning – how it remains "incommensurable" with the world.[13]

As a general rule, therefore, philosophy reflects upon statements or situations drawn from other discourses in so far as these present themselves as inaccessible to all reflection, in keeping with a logic that resembles a generalised negative theology. "Every form of intelligibility stumbles upon a remainder, a left-over, which interrupts its closure. This remainder is the real itself," which persists as "that which can neither be said nor understood."[14] Forever lost behind the "wall of words," this ungraspable real "tolerates only oblique statements" which evoke its absence. Philosophy itself can only pursue such evocation through non-philosophical – non-systematic, non-rational, non-totalisable … – discourses. In this context the proper function of fiction, for instance, is not to create imaginary realities that we might "possess" but rather to indicate the cruel limit of all imagination, to dramatise the irreducible disjunction between discourse and world, to allow for the experience of "an object of which no image might form."[15]

Lardreau provides the most substantial and coherent statement of his position in *La Véracité: essai d'une philosophie négative* (1993). His opening question is not complicated: at the most abstract level, is there or isn't there something like a nature or norm that guides the spontaneous activity of a subject? Is the constituent activity of a subject rule-bound or anarchic? Is the subject constituted or constituent? In short: "is the principle subject, or the subject principle?" That Lardreau opts for the second answer will come as no surprise. The *pure* affirmation of a constituent subjectivity only holds up, however, in so far as it is in turn able to negate or transcend itself, in so far as subjective constitution recognises itself

as not-all (the subject is never simply a part of the empirical world, any more than it is able to constitute every aspect of that world). The "real subject is non-constituent and non-constituted", it is independent of the operations whereby, along conventional Kantian lines, the constituent subject orders its world: it endures in an excess in which the subject counts for nothing, in which collapse all distinctions between matter and form, between the one and the multiple, between God and his creation.[16] Here, as everywhere in his work, the guiding idea is not so much Wittgenstein's notion that we must keep quiet about that which cannot be said (and which is alone of any genuine value) but, on the contrary, that "we cannot *not* say that which we cannot say."[17]

Roughly speaking, the basic argument of the book involves a sort of combination of Kantian and neo-Platonic ideas (filtered through various "knottings" of the Lacanian categories of real, symbolic and imaginary), in such a way as to distinguish alternative versions of three fundamental concepts: a totalising from a non-totalising conception of subjective *constitution*, a conventional or "abject" from a super-affirmative or "heroic" conception of *negation*, and a harmonious or "eclectic" from a discontinuous yet "hierarchical" (Leibniz-inspired) conception of *symphony*, or composition.[18] From Kant, Lardreau assumes the noumenal or inaccessible status of the real, along with the constituted–constitutive (or passive–active) ambiguity of subjective experience. The variably active aspects of the subject ground both the constituent dimension of language (Lacan's symbolic) and the constituted dimension of sensibility (Lacan's imaginary), while the subject's passive aspect bears witness to the utterly unconstitutable (unsayable, insensible, incommensurable, etc.) dimension of the real. However passive it might be, this bearing-witness is nonetheless enough to demonstrate that the real never simply escapes articulation altogether; from the neo-Platonic tradition, then, Lardreau retains the negative yet imperative qualities attributed to a One beyond being. Neo-Platonic, Kantian and Lacanian inspirations combine here to secure the rights of an unsayable real precisely *within* discourse, to compel the respectful articulation of that which is as much beneath contempt as it is indifferent to scorn.

Again broadly in line with Kantian categories, Lardreau then applies such non-contempt to the fields of politics, morality, and aesthetics. This implies, more concretely: in politics, the celebration of pure, sublime revolt, revolt independent of all but the most evanescent of objects, revolt for its own sake ("for two cents …"), always at the risk of a "barbarous" indifference to the other; in morality, a compensatory compassion in the face of suffering, pity for the other as victim, always at the risk of a quasi-quiescent passivity; in aesthetics, a sensitivity to the sensual presence or "jubilant" particularity of things, always at the risk of nostalgia for the figural, the sacred, or the ineffable.[19] Taken together, the result resembles nothing so much as a deliberately perverse version of the categorical imperative: a commandment to rebel for rebellion's sake, which avoids barbarism only to the extent that it turns this commandment against itself in a sort of permanent crucifixion of reason – the unending and eternally dutiful negation of duty as such.

notes

1 Lardreau and Jambet, *L'Ange* 99.

2 Ibid. 148.

3 Ibid. 151–52. In the case of the early Orthodox Christians, such an ideological revolution turned on the reduction of asceticism to a *merely* monastic ideal, the matter of an exceptional and therefore harmless "vocation," which precisely as an exception can be brought to sit comfortably alongside the normal order of work and procreation in the world (ibid. 112ff.).

4 Ibid. 152.

> I finally came to understand, as our own cultural revolution began to wane, how we too had no doubt been merely a moment in an ideological revolution that made use of us, and that in a sense we had never understood […]. We had set out to make war against the philosophy of will, understood as the thought of *conatus*, of survival, but in the end we found only a philosophy that led us to

renounce our *own* will – in other words, a philosophy of the Master's will. (Ibid. 135)

Because it seemed critical of the violent consequences of Mao's Cultural Revolution (a theme which emerges more explicitly in its sequel, *Le Monde* [1978]), *L'Ange* has often been associated with the emergence, in the late 1970s, of the mainly liberal *Nouveaux philosophes*. Apart from a shared horror of state-managed violence, however, it is difficult to imagine two more antithetical approaches to philosophy. Lardreau and Jambet themselves quickly sought to distance themselves from this association (see, for instance, their article "Une dernière fois: contre la 'Nouvelle Philosophie,'" *La Nef,* Jan. 1978), and have denied it ever since. "I don't pretend to write anything other than a Maoist philosophy," Lardreau insists in this book which continues "to provide intellectuals reasons to take up the cause of the people" (*L'Ange* 91, 42 – and as for "the masses, they don't need the Angel, as they are themselves angelic" (79)).

5 *L'Ange* 152.

6 Lardreau and Jambet, *L'Ange* 10, 13; cf. 22, 67.

7 Ibid. 34, 102.

8 Ibid. 21, 57.

9 Ibid. 22, 37.

10 Lardreau, *L'Exercice différé de la philosophie* 88. Point by point, Lardreau opposes his negative and materialist philosophy, oriented towards transcendence and death, to Deleuze's "affirmative" and "spiritualist" philosophy, oriented towards immanence and life (84–85).

11 Lardreau, *La Véracité* 94–96. "Such is the little Copernican revolution on offer here: that we should start out from the certainty that there is no need for a revolution, or if you prefer, that it has always already happened. When you're hungry everything tastes good, and philosophers, like butchers, know that you can use all of the pig but the squeak [*dans la philosophie, comme dans le cochon, tout est bon*]" (17).

12 Lardreau. *L'Exercice différé* 89, 21; *Présentation criminelle* 115.

13 Lardreau, *Discours philosophique* 13–15.

14 Lardreau, *Fictions philosophiques et science-fiction* 271–72; cf. *L'Ange* 36.

15 Lardreau, *Fictions philosophiques et science-fiction* 145, 45–46. Science fiction thus proceeds, notes Lardreau, with a sort of exuberant rational autonomy comparable to that embraced most dramatically by Leibniz. Lardreau likewise finds parallels between the structure of certain kinds of philosophical "inquiry" and the empiricist presuppositions of detective fiction, and finds echoes of classical conceptions of chance and fortune in the moments when a master criminal accidentally loses his grip on a situation, and so on (cf. *Présentation criminelle* 22ff.).

16 Lardreau, *La Véracité* 32, 51, 46.

17 Lardreau, *La Véracité* 15; *Fictions philosophiques et science-fiction* 272–76.

18 Lardreau, *La Véracité* 16–18.

19 Ibid. 249, 183–84, 314.

the problem of great politics in the light of obviously deficient modes of subjectivation[1]

guy lardreau

For a long time now I have been haunted by a problem as massive as it is crude: how can something undertaken in order to make things better eventually take a turn for the worse – and this not because the will behind this undertaking became lazy or forgetful,[2] but on account of this will itself?

Couched in such general terms, versions of this problem have existed ever since people first began trying to connect an intention to discernible changes (henceforth envisioned as its "effects"), and to judge the validity of the former by the consequences of the latter.[3] The problem is no less ancient in its political guise – as ancient, no doubt, as that mode of reflection which compared, as Herodotus did, various types of constitution so as to identify the best among them. It was then enough, in order for our problem explicitly to be recognised as such, to introduce movement and change into the field of comparison, to begin thinking of politics in the context of innovation and possibility, of desirable transformation – in short, in the context of history. This was the step taken by Plato, when he came up against the drama of *metabole*, or change.

However, there is no denying the fact that it is only in the modern age that this problem has come to acquire its extreme urgency. This is because, first of all, the modern age is properly the age of Great Politics (a phrase I borrow from Nietzsche, along with its programme: the effort to "break the history of the world in two" – or as the Cultural Revolution was to say, "to change the very essence of man"). The modern age decided that it is in politics that the supersensible vocation of culture can and must become sensible. In the second place, this is because the modern age is the age that was empirically determined by two sets of events which, as a matter of fact if not as a matter of principle, seemed to provide their contemporaries with proof for their belief that all Great Politics was destined to end in disastrous and criminal failure. These events were the French Revolution (in so far as the Terror is held to be its truth) and the Communist Revolutions (in so far as these are supposed to find their ultimate expression in the camps). In the wake of these events, many other efforts to bend figures of political power to the highest ends of reason will likewise be shown to result in the necessary reversal of best into worst.

The point is then: how are we to avoid responding to this crude problem with an equally crude solution? This is all the more important since theoretical crudeness (which makes do, in the main, with "human nature"[4]) is here, at one and the same time, practical servility (which eternalises failure and exults in garrulous moaning and mourning).

It is important to remember, in this context, that when I say that this problem haunts me, I certainly do not mean that I *myself* pose the problem (which is of no interest either way), any more than I mean that it poses *itself* (i.e. that it is imposed by the real – a question that will be left unanswered here). I simply observe that *it is posed*: as far as general opinion is concerned, the problem exists.

In other words, the problem raised by the fact that revolutionary intentions may be inverted is a problem that can itself only accede to the transcendental regime (understood as the interrogative work whereby something can be analysed in terms of its a priori conditions of possibility) if it is displaced, i.e. if it no longer concerns this inversion as such, but rather the fact that this inversion *appears* as problematic in the eyes of opinion (in short: if the problem itself becomes its own object).

For if we simply suppose that, thus far, every popular uprising for the sake of the good has always turned bad – and even if this continues into the future (as often as you like) – still this supposition will never concern anything more than an empirical question. In each case it will concern a determinate inversion of good into bad, one that determines its particular and contingent conditions of possibility in a particular way. In order that we might ask how such inversion is possible a priori, we must be in a position to affirm it as necessary (whereas, conversely, when others ask why it always seems to happen this way, they provide, in the very form of the question, just that eternalising response they were looking for). But it is precisely this that is altogether impossible, for the very same reasons that Kant (when he comes to consider the idea of progress) rejects the "terrorist" position along with those he characterises as "eudemonist" and "abderitist."[5]

It might perhaps be objected that, taken in itself, the problem's own existence is no less particular and contingent – is not precisely this contingency emphasised in the referral of its urgency to those sets of events I have already mentioned? In response to this I say that while both the genesis and the individual existence of the problem are indeed empirical matters (and as such can be treated as objects of investigation), this in no way alters the fact that our problem poses itself as necessary and universal, and it is from this sole pretension that it exists, not *tout court*, but precisely *as* a problem. The logic here is similar to the logic that allows us to conclude, when all is said and done, that it does not much matter if aesthetic judgement is always empirically determined (here again it is Kant who guides us): what alone distinguishes it is the way it claims for itself the *form* of a universal and necessary validity.

We're now in a position to realise that what has both lent our problem its crudeness and servility and made it so obscure that it continues to haunt me to this day, is the fact that it confuses an empirical question (which deals with the object to which the problem refers) and a transcendental question (which deals with the problem itself). By resolutely choosing to consider only the latter question we are free to dismiss both what we might call the question "of principle," i.e. the false transcendental question (which asks, why *must* rebellion always turn into barbarism?) and what we might call the question "of fact," i.e. the false empirical question (which asks, why is it that *all* rebellions end in crime?).[6]

What we are left with is indeed, at least to begin with, a matter of assertion [*constat*], but what is asserted is not a fact but an *appearance*: the appearance of a problem. And we need not even concern ourselves with whether this problem is well or poorly founded, but only with what its pure existence as appearance implies.

By thus asking questions about an appearance, however, we obviously stop thinking in terms of nature or substance, so as to think instead in the terms of a subject. So the question must be: which subject, or rather (since the subject summoned by politics, albeit a constituent subject, is itself initially constituted), which mode of subjectivation does the existence of this other subject imply – this other subject (who may well be grammatically indistinguishable from the first) who remains "haunted" by the problem? The question, however, must be put in the plural, since the appearance itself is plural, and since it is in all the diversity of its various forms that the reversal of good into bad is "attested." And finally, since what is experienced in each of these forms is the experience of a deficient world, and since this deficiency can only stem from the subject that constitutes this world, so then our question finds its very last refinement in these terms: which deficient modes of subjectivation are revealed by that appearance which the problem of Great Politics produces (and on whose basis this problem then grounds itself)?

It seems to me that the Lacanian doctrine of the "knot," at least in the rather liberal if not heretical use that I tend to make of it, provides us with a reliable guide for the investigation and identification of these modes.[7]

I will assume here a certain familiarity with the letters R, S, I, along with the concepts (real, symbolic, imaginary) to which they refer; I will also take for granted the idea that the real is the very knot that entwines the other rings, rather than one of the rings themselves.[8] It follows that it is crucial to distinguish not only the real from reality (which is the imaginarisation of the real) but also the real of the knot from the real *in* the knot (R). We should also observe, furthermore, that there is one way of failing the knot [*manquer au noeud*] that is widely recognised by those who make use of these three letters, and to which they often refer in order to explain various social phenomena, namely imaginarisation, to which I referred a moment ago as if it was a "familiar" concept. What does imaginarisation involve? The contamination, in short, of R and S by I, i.e. the extension to the entire knot of that which applies to only one of its rings.

The hypothesis to which we must now turn, it seems to me, is that it is possible to raise up each one of the letters in this way, into the position of the real of the knot, i.e. to expand each one of them to the point that it alone occupies the sole place of the knot. Imaginarisation, drawing its energy from the obviously imaginary character of its own version of the knot, demonstrates that the imagination is a creative agency [*instance*];[9] in much the same way, symbolicisation triumphs in so far as it is able to say that everything is a matter of language, and *real*isation [*réellisation*] proceeds in so far as it is able to exploit the homonym that blurs the difference between the real of the knot and the real in the knot. To be sure, this homonymy fails to dispel the graphic artifice adopted here, because this artifice is not accidental but essential. Indeed, if the name of one of the rings of the knot finds itself chosen to designate the very truth of the knot itself, this is because what it designates is precisely the refusal of all ties, all relations, all properties, all predictability – in brief, the refusal of all "essence" (as understood in Hegelian logic) – such that the knotting can itself only be grasped by whose who have first of all accepted that the truth is not whole, or lacks everything [*la vérité manque de tout*].

In this way, the image, the name [*le nom*], and the no [*le non*] can each, in turn, come to figure betrayal of the knot.

To my mind, it is clear that the three deficient modes of subjectivation that can be inferred from these three mutilated configurations of the knot should be recognised as sources of aberrant effects for every possible regime of experience, and as capable of subjecting all representations to their perverse deformity.

For the time being I will content myself with a consideration of their effects in the field of politics: my argument is that these three modes

suffice to account for the full range of those monstrous dreams in which Great Politics comes to founder.

And since I have already suggested, elsewhere (with Christian Jambet, some time ago now), that the subject of Great Politics should be given the name *Angel*, so now I need three angelic names in order to designate the three aspects of the Fall towards which tumble our three deficient modes of subjectivation.

I will only mention, here, the Angel responsible for *real*isation [*réellisation*]. This is not an arbitrary choice: I have already shown how the homonymy that affects the word "real" proceeds *pros hen*, to use Aristotle's phrase (i.e. with respect to one underlying principle),[10] such that it indicates a certain privilege of R over the two other rings – as if, to put it crudely, R is "more true" [*plus vrai*] than S and I, in so far as it exists alongside them in a non-reciprocal manner (since R is precisely what remains when S and I are taken away). I think it is reasonable, then, to suppose that this privilege extends to the deficient mode of subjectivation that follows from the expansion of its agency [*instance*], and that this deficient mode relates to those that follow from expansion of the other two agencies in the same way that R itself relates to these latter. But what are we now to say of this Angel, this Angel who thus appears in a certain sense as "more veracious [*plus vérace*]" than the two other sinful Angels?

If, at the heart of the knot, R is the letter that demonstrates, with respect to whatever thing we refer to it, the fact that nothing can combine with nothing [*rien n'a avec rien puissance de mélange*],[11] so then *real*isation (the attribution of exclusive power to R) will amount to the inflated affirmation that I is only a delusion, that S is only a lie, that neither a "well-founded" world nor a well-made language exists. The Angel of *real*isation will be *the will* to bring every world back to the chaos that is its truth, to bring every community back to its essential dispersal, to dissolve every tie [*lien*], beginning with that tie by which a body is *a* body. The background against which this Angel detaches the liberation of the subject from any relation of authority is nothing other than the ruin of relation in general.

Like the Terror as described by Hegel,[12] its politics is a politics of absolute freedom, that is to say, of death.[13] And since, when all is said and done, this Angel will associate only with these dismembered bodies, I will call it the *Cannibal Angel*.[14]

Unlike the Angel of imaginarisation, which I call the *Barbarian Angel*, the Cannibal Angel does not "delude" [*ne "leurre" pas*], it does not dispel angelic hope by raising it up to satisfy some bombastic nonsense, by replacing the negativity in which Great Politics proceeds with the positivity of a *content*. On the contrary, it liberates negation from any determinacy [*determinité*] to which it might be applied; with it, negation is the negation of *nothing* – pure negation.

If we now try to draw, from the possible political existence of such a mode of subjectivation, some sort of theoretical understanding, we must first accept that this understanding will have no prognostic, therapeutic, or practical value. All the same, it does offer one insight, one only (and it is moral, rather than political), but it is one of no small importance: the necessity of integrating *self-love* with what, in *La Véracité*, I described as "pathological duty."[15] For the first form of non-relation [*non-rapport*] is not between self and other but between self and self. If then the *realisation* of non-relation has cannibalism as its deadly and inevitable effect, one will be forbidden first of all from making a meal of one's own body [*c'est de son propre corps, d'abord, que l'on s'interdira de faire repas*]. Rousseau was perfectly right: pity and self-love are both specular affections, and one can share something of the suffering of others only inasmuch as one affirms a certain tenderness for oneself. Self-pity, self-esteem, admiration of oneself in the mirror – so many forms of narcissistic indulgence, but equally, of what Aristotle (certainly the better guide, here, than Plato) called self-sufficiency or self-love, of that *philautia* without which there can be no *philia*. Self-love is self-mastery, an agreement with oneself to which we are led by another self: what a blunder, Aristotle teaches us, ever to have said *eros*.[16]

But again, we can reach no further conclusion beyond this.

From the outset, by inquiring about an *appearance*, I have accepted that we must suspend judgement as regards its truth, and have set aside all responses of both principle and fact (including facts that seem to claim some generality). And as I come to a close I remain in this suspense, and am satisfied to remain so.

As far as matters of fact are concerned, of course, many rebellions, many "explodings" of Great Politics, took place well before philosophy began and they will no doubt continue to take place after it has run its course. It is not for philosophy either to embrace or to reject the intention [*voeu*] behind Great Politics – philosophy has nothing at all to say about it *immediately*, and it is not upon these manifestations that it operates but upon the *discourses* that exhibit them (discourses directed to this or that end, ends which have nothing in common with those of philosophy). Philosophy is content if it manages to index and deploy or put into motion these discourses in such a way as to multiply them – and the more it multiplies, the more contented it is.[17]

To be precise, this implies two separate points which, though they are certainly connected, for the sake of clarity I will distinguish as follows:

• If philosophy has nothing to say about Great Politics as such, this is simply because the one contradicts and excludes the other, and vice versa. We have often been urged to "have done with the political conception of the world," on the assumption that, by taking up philosophy we dismiss the hope that had inspired this conception. This, I believe, is to misunderstand the issue: what is at issue is not a matter of hope or despair, or of coming to terms with the way things are. It is a matter of changing the question, of asking no longer about the "failure" of Great Politics (for whatever reason, from whatever perspective) but about its *appearance*. This is the only aspect of the question that can be considered an object for philosophy. In other words: no political decision can be legitimately deduced from any philosophical position, and it would seem that the converse should be retained as a reliable criterion: any orientation of thought which presumes that political decisions might be directly concluded from it is an orientation that is foreign to philosophy.

• Philosophy is not a set (however tightly connected) of dogmatic propositions concerning certain great objects peculiar to it, but a system of indexations [*système d'indexations*] to which various statements are subjected – statements that come from elsewhere, that are produced by other discourses, however tenuous these might be.[18] What this means is that, although philosophy assuredly exists only on account of its systems, these systems are in no sense positivities but are rather machines for producing negation – first and foremost a negation applied to themselves. In terms borrowed from Lacan, I would say (no doubt without his approval) that philosophy only conforms to its concept if it always represents the "not-all" to the universal propositions upon which nonetheless it necessarily depends.

In saying this, I remain persuaded that every true philosophy endures, at each point of its development, the test of scepticism.

notes

1 I am grateful to Sam Gillespie for his help with this translation, and to Antoine Hatzenberger, Sarah Hirschmuller and Alberto Toscano for their characteristically careful reviews of earlier versions of the text. [Translator's note.]

2 "*Video meliora proboque, deteriora sequor*: I see and approve the better course, but I follow the worse." To be sure, examination of Ovid's famous maxim is harmful, as Leibniz demonstrated, for all ethical considerations (cf. Leibniz, *Theodicy* and *New Essays*). My own concern, however, above ethics and the remedies it proposes, beyond the sphere of conscience or consciousness [*la conscience*], of its mistakes and misfortunes, is with the "madness" that the ageing Kant, the Kant of *The End of All Things* (1794), finds haunting our highest resolutions. Along the same lines, Comte admits that he does not fear our bad inclinations so much as our propensity to pursue the good.

3 If the problem only takes shape when it relates an intention to its consequences, and vice versa, it will no doubt seem surprising that in my previous note I chose to refer its formulation to Kant – but the text in question turns on the interest of hope (the interest that compels recognition of the third question that reason addresses to itself), rather than on the practical interest of morality.

4 From this perspective, it is clear that an *immediate* summoning of the "death drive" must be understood as a naturalist response.

5 Kant, "An Old Question Raised Again: Is the Human Race Constantly Progressing?" in *Conflict of the Faculties*, part two [7: 79–94]; cf. Kant, *Idea for a Universal History with a Cosmopolitan Purpose* [8: 17–31 – the pagination here refers, as is customary, to the standard German edition of Kant]. The term "abderitist" implies smug, self-satisfied or static. Kant may have based the term on the name of Protagoras of Abdera or, more plausibly, may have adapted it from Christoph Wieland's 1774 satirical novel about the pettiness of provincial German life, *Die Geschichte der Abderiten*. See Rudolf Eisler, *Kant-Lexicon*, eds. Anne-Dominique Balmès and Pierre Osmo (Paris: Gallimard, 1994) 1. According to Bet Briggs, Wieland's novel was translated by Henry Christmas as *The Republic of Fools: Being the History of the State and People of Abdera in Thrace* (London: Allen, 1861). Cf. Briggs, "A Town Like Abdera," available online at <http://www.bikwil.zip.com.au/Vintage06/Abderites.html>. [Translator's note.]

6 The haste with which people rushed to conflate these questions (a haste to which I drew attention, at the time, in a number of texts) is what leads me to believe that the response to the problem that confused them must, in order to be convincing, include an anthropology as one of its moments. It was only by treating such an anthropology as a *moment*, however, that I went astray – for the empirical question, once clearly distinguished, obviously has its own pertinence, and for this reason a political anthropology of inverted rebellions [*des rébellions retournées*] remains highly desirable.

7 It would not be impossible, I think, to derive these modes from the procession of subjects that I outlined in my book *La Véracité*. But as things stand it seems simpler, and more convincing, and more economical, to refer to a doctrine whose power is already widely recognised.

8 Lardreau is referring to the late topological conception of the real, the symbolic and the imaginary (based on often cryptic applications of the "Borromean knot") that Lacan developed in his seminar of 1974–75, *Le Séminaire XXII: R.S.I.* (published in stages in the journal *Ornicar?*, nos. 2, 3, 4, 5 (1975)). [Translator's note.]

9 The French word *instance* is notoriously difficult to translate. In a psychoanalytic context it is usually translated as "agency" (Freud's *Instanz* – as in "the agency of the superego" or "the agency of censorship"), but readers should retain the resonance of its more general meanings: "authority" or "power," as well as "insistence." The title of Lacan's famous essay *L'Instance de la lettre dans l'inconscient*, for example, has been translated both as "The Agency of the Letter in the Unconscious" (by Alan Sheridan) and as "The Insistence of the Letter in the Unconscious" (by Jan Miel). Both the German *Instanz* and the French *instance* also have prominent juridical connotations, as in *tribunal d'instance* or *affaire en instance*. [Translator's note.]

10 Lardreau is referring to what is sometimes called Aristotle's theory of focal equivocation, the idea that various distinct uses of a word are nevertheless all "related to one [*pros hen*]" fundamental meaning. For instance, the word "healthy" can refer to something that leads to good health (like a healthy diet), to something that indicates good health (like a healthy appetite), or simply to the general condition of health (like a healthy person): Aristotle's point is that the first two meanings of the word are derived from the third. The same logic applies, famously, to the meaning of the word being:

> There are many senses in which a thing is said to be, but all refer to one starting-point; some things are said to be because they are substances, others because they are a process towards substance, or destructions or privations of qualities of substance, or productive or generative of substance, or of things which are relative to substance, or negations of some of these things or of substance itself. It is for this reason that we may say even of non-being that it *is* non-being. (Aristotle, *Metaphysics* 1003b1 in *The Complete Works of Aristotle*, ed. Jonathan Barnes (Princeton: Princeton UP, 1584) ii)

[Translator's note.]

11 I am referring, of course, to the formulation of the *Sophist*. [Cf. Plato, *Sophist*, 252e: "either all will blend, or none, or some will and some will not" – the phrase Lardreau uses here, *puissance de mélange*, is rendered in English versions of the *Sophist* in terms of "blending," "combining" or "participating with." (Translator's note.)] In fact, I would quite happily characterise the three letters with reference to the three hypotheses advanced in this dialogue: I, "everything can combine with everything"; R, "nothing can combine with nothing"; S, "something can combine with something." I say this on condition, however, that like the various hypotheses of the *Parmenides*, these three are all true in turn, according to the order of their presentation, and that the truth itself is nothing other than their entwining [*leur nouage*].

12 Lardreau is referring to Hegel's description of absolute freedom as the moment, associated with the Jacobin phase of the French Revolution, during which

> self-consciousness grasps the fact that its certainty of itself is the essence of all the spiritual "masses," or spheres, of the real as well as of the supersensible world, or conversely, that essence and actuality are consciousness's knowledge of itself [...]. It comes into existence in such a way that each individual consciousness raises itself out of its allotted sphere, no longer finds its essence and its work in this particular sphere, but grasps itself as the Notion of will, grasps all spheres as the essence of this will, and therefore can only realise itself in a work which is a work of the whole. In this absolute freedom, therefore, all social groups or classes which are the spiritual spheres into which the whole is articulated are abolished; the individual consciousness that belonged to any such sphere, and willed and fulfilled itself in it, has put aside its limitation; its purpose is the general purpose, its language universal law, its work the universal work [...]. In absolute freedom there was no reciprocal action between a consciousness that is immersed in the complexities of existence, or that sets itself specific aims and thoughts, and a valid external world, whether of reality or thought. (Hegel, *Phenomenology of Spirit*, trans. A.V. Miller (Oxford: Oxford UP, 1970) sects. 585–588, 594)

[Translator's note.]

13 Conversely, the watchword of imaginarisation is *Life* ("everything combining with everything …").

14 I am referring again to Kant here, in particular to his 1797 *Doctrine of Right* [*Rechtslehre*]. To be sure, what is at issue in this text concerns only the risks that accompany the directly sexual use of the other's body, but if it is true that every relation [*rapport*] is ultimately grounded in the sexual non-relation, so then the extension that I am giving to the concept here is not illegitimate. [Lardreau is thinking, of course, of Lacan's insistence that "there can be no sexual relationship [*il n'y a pas de rapport sexuel*]" (Lacan, *Le Séminaire XX: Encore* (Paris: Seuil, 1975) 17). (Translator's note.)]

15 To tell the truth, my own symptom, along with things that I still retained from my formative years, prevented me from accepting this necessity at the time.

16 Lardreau is referring to Aristotle, *Nicomachean Ethics* Books 8–11. [Translator's note.]

17 The French reads: "[*la philosophie*] *est contente si elle parvient à les faire tourner devant un système d'indexations qui les multiplie – et qui lui plaira d'autant mieux qu'il multiplie davantage.*" [Translator's note.]

18 In *L'Exercice différé de la philosophie* (1999), in order to account for a certain regime of the history of philosophy, I took on the task of showing how philosophy is sometimes able to treat its own statements as if they came from elsewhere.

works by lardreau

Les Cheveux d'epsilon. Paris: Mercure de France, 1966.

Le Singe d'or: essai sur le concept d'étape du marxisme. Paris: Mercure de France, 1973.

With Christian Jambet. *L'Ange. Ontologie de la révolution, tome 1: pour une cynégétique du semblant.* Paris: Grasset, 1976.

With Christian Jambet. *Le Monde, Réponse à la question: qu'est-ce que les droits de l'homme?* Paris: Grasset, 1978.

La Mort de Joseph Staline: bouffonnerie philosophique. Paris: Grasset, 1978.

With Georges Duby. *Dialogues.* Paris: Flammarion, 1980.

"Apocalypse et résurrection selon quelques textes syriaques." *Apocalypse et sens de l'histoire.* Ed. Jean-Louis Vieillard-Baron et al. Paris: Berg, 1983. 181–201.

Discours philosophique et discours spirituel: autour de la philosophie spirituelle de Philoxène de Mabboug. Paris: Seuil, 1985.

Fictions philosophiques et science-fiction: récréation philosophique. Arles: Actes Sud, 1988.

"Amour philosophique et amour spirituel." *Saint Bernard et la philosophie.* Ed. Rémi Brague. Paris: Presses Universitaires de France, 1993. 27–48.

La Véracité: essai d'une philosophie négative. Lagrasse: Verdier, 1993.

Présentation criminelle de quelques concepts majeurs de la philosophie: fantaisie pédagogique. Arles: Actes Sud, 1997.

L'Exercice différé de la philosophie: à l'occasion de Deleuze. Lagrasse: Verdier, 1999.

[Initially published as anonymous.] *Vive le matérialisme!* Lagrasse: Verdier, 2001.

Guy Lardreau
Lycée Carnot
16 Boulevard Thiers
21000 Dijon
France

Peter Hallward
French Department
King's College London
The Strand
London WC2R 2LS
UK
E-mail: peter.hallward@kcl.ac.uk

ANGELAKI
journal of the theoretical humanities
volume 8   number 2   august 2003

introduction

nick hanlon

Michel Henry taught philosophy for many years at the Université Paul Valéry – Montpellier III. His published work includes several novels (*L'Amour les yeux fermés* was awarded the Prix Renaudot in 1976), an analysis of Maine de Biran (1965), a two-volume study of Marx (1976), a book on the conceptual origins of psychoanalysis (1985), a book on Kandinsky (1988) and several books on Christianity (from 1996). His nine hundred page magnum opus, *The Essence of Manifestation*, was published in two volumes in 1963. Henry died in July 2002.

Henry is a phenomenologist first and foremost, and, in keeping with Husserl's teaching, his point of departure is the way things appear to and are experienced by the living subject. At the beginning of *The Essence of Manifestation* Henry describes his project as concerned with the meaning of the being of the self. This theme remains with him in one way or another throughout his work, as he attempts a reconceptualisation of the subject and its position in relation to phenomena in such a way as to overcome every variant of Cartesian dualism. In opposition to a broadly Cartesian or Kantian perspective, Henry conceives of manifestation in terms of the fundamental unity of subject and object: manifestation is an immanent relation of subject and "life." (Unlike Husserl, Henry distinguishes the term "life" with its existential associations of engagement and intensity from the more easily objectified or neutralised term "world.") In *The Essence of Manifestation* Henry proposes an ontology in which the subject is the absolute foundation of being, such that the experience of

michel henry

translated by nick hanlon

PHENOMENOLOGY OF LIFE

self is the very essence of the "Absolute." As with Heidegger's presentation of being as grounded in the (self-)interrogation of Dasein, Henry's subject is originary and primordial, but, rather more insistently than in Heidegger's conception of things, Henry's subject lives in dynamic reciprocity with the phenomena of life. The subject perceives such phenomena through receptive sensibility affected by mood, i.e. through "affectivity." In particular, Henry explores the experience of anguish in dialogue with Kierkegaard and the implications of mood entailed in Heidegger's key term *Befindlichkeit* (situatedness). In Henry's account being is thus not only "immanent" (i.e. immanent within the experience of one's self) but also experienced through affectivity, which is the essence of "ipse-

ISSN 0969-725X print/ISSN 1469-2899 online/03/020097-14 © 2003 Taylor & Francis Ltd and the Editors of *Angelaki*
DOI: 10.1080/0969725032000162602

ity," the indivisible identity of that which affects and that which is affected.

Henry reiterates the primacy of such living self-affection when he turns his attention to Marx and Freud. Against both the classical Marxist and Althusserian emphasis on the "pseudo-scientific" claims of dialectical materialism, Henry's *Marx: A Philosophy of Human Reality* (1976) is concerned with the fundamental conditions of human individuality, subjectivity and productivity. Henry reads Marx as a philosopher of living labour or creative praxis, of praxis considered, in both its existential intensity and complex social context, as the sole basis for all genuine value. Consequently, he downplays abstract concepts like productive forces or social class as merely derivative of "the subjective element of individual praxis, which alone founds value and accounts for the capitalist system,"[1] just as it inspires the quest for a communal socialism.

In *The Genealogy of Psychoanalysis* (1985) Henry again distinguishes living affectivity from its alienation in lifeless representation, as he charts the slow historical emergence, from Descartes to Freud, of the concept of the unconscious. In so far as this concept confirms the "radical immanence of auto-affection" (as it does, up to a point, in the affirmations of Schopenhauer and Nietzsche), it makes an essential contribution to an ontology of life. To the degree that psychoanalysis realises that "psyche's essence does not reside in the world's visible becoming or in what is ob-jected," so then it helps us to understand, among other things, anxiety as "the anxiety of life's inability to escape itself," or drive as "the principle of all activity."[2] On the other hand, in so far as the unconscious continues to be analysed in terms of representation or motivation (as it generally is, according to Henry, in Freudian psychoanalysis), i.e. in so far as the unconscious is reduced to a process that merely (albeit obscurely) registers and cathects certain objects and experiences of the world, so then it remains fully compatible with the fundamental operation of consciousness itself: the showing or seeing of that which appears in the world. *This* concept of the unconscious arises at the same time "and as the exact consequence" as that of consciousness in the broadly Cartesian

sense,[3] and it contributes to the same disastrous result: the dilution of living thought within the anaemic confines of representation.

Nowhere does Henry's lifelong distinction of life from world assume more dramatic form than in his first explicitly theological book, *I Am the Truth: Toward a Philosophy of Christianity* (1996). Christ figures here as nothing less than the original *Living*, the original instance of an eternal self-affecting and self-revealing Life forever independent of the world. Genuine life is "not possible in the world; living is possible only outside the world, where another Truth reigns"[4] – the other-worldly truth of Christianity. Christ is the Absolute in whom all living beings dwell, in so far as they are themselves incapable of accounting for their self-affection, which remains irreducible to any process that appears or evolves in the world, and thus irreducible to any philosophy of consciousness, no less than to any would-be "science" of life. In this, as in all of Henry's works, the primacy of affectivity manifests itself in and through the process of self-experiencing [*s'éprouver soi-même*], itself grounded in a sufficient (or divine) Self that experiences itself as the living of eternal self-revelation. Interest in such self-experience also implies, as you might expect, recognition of the primordial importance of the body, which has likewise remained one of Henry's most consistent concerns (from his first book *Philosophy and Phenomenology of the Body* (1965) to his last work *Incarnation: une philosophie de la chair* (2000)).

Above all, self-experience involves suffering and *pathos* which is coexistent with joy. The experience of suffering is ontologically primordial; it enables (through contrast and reciprocity) the experience of joy and constantly mediates our experience of self and phenomena. In section 70 of *The Essence of Manifestation* Henry cites the Christian slogan "Happy are those who suffer,"[5] a phrase to which he returns at the end of the present article. The phrase not only indicates the persistence of Henry's philosophical preoccupations but summarises in a single formula the way his ontology integrates the primacy of affectivity and corporeality, the co-constituency of suffering and joy, the self-reflexive character of life, just as it points towards the need for a reappraisal of Christian and, in particular, of Johannine thinking. It is no accident that the conclusion of Henry's last book is entitled "Beyond Phenomenology and Theology: The Johannine Archi-Intelligibility."

notes

1 Henry, *Marx: A Philosophy of Human Reality* 14.

2 Henry, *The Genealogy of Psychoanalysis* 285, 7, 298.

3 Ibid. 2.

4 Henry, *I Am the Truth: Toward a Philosophy of Christianity* 30.

5 Henry, *The Essence of Manifestation* 671.

phenomenology of life

michel henry

The phenomenology of life lies within the ambit of that great current of philosophical thinking which originated in Germany at the end of the nineteenth century with Edmund Husserl and that, via major thinkers such as Martin Heidegger and Max Scheler, continued throughout the whole of the twentieth century. It still remains very much alive today, notably in France.[1] I would like to show in which ways the phenomenology of life is a tributary of this movement of thought which is one of the most important in our culture, and in what ways it diverges from it.

The originality of phenomenology must be understood on the basis of the objective it has assigned itself. Whilst the other sciences study specific phenomena – physical, chemical, biological, juridical, social, economic, etc. – phenomenology explores what allows a phenomenon to be a phenomenon. Phenomenology investigates pure phenomenality as such. One can confer various names upon this pure phenomenality: pure manifestation, showing, unveiling, uncovering, appearing, revelation, or even a more traditional word: truth. As soon as the object of phenomenology is understood in its difference from the object of other sciences, a further distinction seems to impose itself: that of the phenomenon considered on the one hand in its particular content, and on the other hand in its phenomenality. Such is the distinction between that which shows itself, that which appears, and the fact of appearing, pure appearing as such. It is this difference that Heidegger formulates in his own way in paragraph 44 of *Being and Time* when he distinguishes truth in a secondary sense as that which is true, that which is unveiled, from, at a deeper level, the unveiling as such as "the most original phenomenon of truth [*das ursprünglichste Phänomen der Wahrheit*]."[2]

Another primary intuition of phenomenology is that appearing is more essential than being; it is only because it appears that a thing is able to be. To express this with Husserl, using a formula borrowed from the Marburg School (which I modify slightly): "Something is inasmuch as it appears [*Autant d'apparaître, autant d'être*]." I carry this precedence of phenomenology over ontology one step further by saying that it is only if the appearing appears in itself and as such that something, whatever it may be, can in turn appear, can show itself to us.

Despite these various points, however, the phenomenological presupposition of phenomenology still remains wholly indeterminate. The principles of phenomenology tell us that "something is inasmuch as it appears" and they urge us to go, to quote the famous slogan, "straight to the things themselves [*zu den Sachen selbst*]." But the meaning of these principles remains obscure, so long as we lack a clear definition of what is meant by the fact of appearing, by the concrete phenomenological mode according to which this pure appearing appears (i.e. the pure phenomenological matter, so to speak, in which phenomenality as such phenomenalises itself). Now, if one directs this question towards the founding texts of phenomenology one notices that behind the phenomenological indeterminacy of the principles of phenomenology, and owing to this same indeterminacy, a certain conception of phenomenality slips in, the very conception which initially presents itself to ordinary thought and which constitutes at the same time the oldest and least critical prejudice of traditional philosophy. This is the conception of phenomenality that is derived from the perception of objects in the world, which is to say, in the final reckoning, the appearing of the world itself.

The reader may not easily accept the idea that the founder of phenomenology, Edmund Husserl, confronted with the explicit question of "how" objects are given (*Gegenstände im Wie* – "objects in the how"),[3] answers: via the appearing of the world. Doesn't Husserl, in keeping with tradition, instead refer the principle of phenomenality to consciousness and thus to a type of "interiority"? However, we should not forget the essential definition of consciousness as intentionality. Understood as intentional, consciousness is nothing other than the movement through which it throws itself outside; its "substance" exhausts itself in this coming outside which produces phenomenality. The act of revealing in such a coming outside, in a setting at a distance, is what constitutes showing [*faire-voir*]. The possibility of vision resides in this setting at a distance of that which is placed in front of the seeing, and is thereby seen by it. Such is the phenomenological definition of the object: that which, placed in front, is rendered visible in this way. Appearing is here the appearing of the object in a double sense: in the sense that that which appears is the object, and also in the sense that since that which appears is the object, so then the mode of appearing at issue here is the mode of appearing peculiar to the object and that which renders it visible, i.e. this setting at a distance in which arises the visibility of all that which is susceptible of becoming visible for us.

At this point a further question cannot be avoided: how does the intentionality which shows or makes visible every thing reveal itself to itself? Could it be by directing a new intentionality upon itself? If so, can phenomenology avoid the bitter destiny of that classical philosophy of consciousness which finds itself bound in an endless regression, obliged to place a second consciousness behind the knowing consciousness (in our case a second intentionality behind the one that we are attempting to wrest from obscurity)? Or else does a mode of revelation exist other than the showing of intentionality, in which phenomenality would no longer be that of the outside? Phenomenology has no answer to this question. Thus a crisis of extreme gravity takes form in it which soon leads to aporia. The very possibility of phenomenality becomes problematic if the principle of phenomenality escapes its grasp. As we know, Husserl could only describe as "anonymous" that self which in the final instance is constitutive of the way things appear. It is with Heidegger that the appearing of the world is taken to its highest degree of elaboration. From section 7 of *Being and Time* the phenomenon is understood in the Greek sense – *phainomenon*, from the root *pha, phos*, which signifies light, so that appearing signifies coming into the light or into clarity, i.e. "that inside of which something can become visible or manifest in itself." The world is this ek-static horizon of

visibilisation inside of which every thing can become visible, and the second part of *Being and Time* declares explicitly that this "horizon" concerns exteriority, the "outside of self" as such. The world is identified here with temporality, and temporality is nothing other than "the originary 'outside of self' in and for itself [*Zeitlichkeit ist das ursprüngliche 'Außer-sich' an und für sich selbst*]."[4]

There are three decisive traits that characterise the appearing of the world. Their brief enumeration will serve as an introduction to the phenomenology of life itself, whose first thesis will be that no life can appear in the appearing of the world.

1. In so far as the appearing of the world consists in the "outside of self," in the coming outside of an Outside, so all that shows itself in it, shows itself outside, as exterior, as other, as different. *Exterior* because the structure in which it shows itself is that of exteriority; *other* because this ek-static structure is that of a primordial alterity (all that which is outside of me is other than me, all that which is outside of self is other than self); *different* because this Ek-stasis is identically a Difference, the operation which, opening up the divide of a distance, renders different everything to which this setting at a distance allows to appear – in the horizon of the world. Such an appearing turns away from itself with such a violence, it throws outside with such force (being itself nothing other than this originary expulsion of an Outside), that everything to which it gives appearance can never be anything other, effectively, than exterior in the dreadful sense of something which, placed outside, chased as it were from its true Residence, from its original Homeland, deprived of its ownmost possessions, finds itself from that point abandoned, without support, lost – prey to this abandonment from which Heidegger needed to deliver man once he had made of him, as "being-in-the-world," a being of this world and nothing more.

2. The appearing which unveils in the Difference of the world does not just render different all that which unveils itself in that fashion, it is in principle totally indifferent to it, it neither loves it nor desires it, and having no

affinity with it, it does not protect it in any way. As far as this appearing is concerned, it doesn't matter whether that which appears is a darkening sky or the equality of a circle's radii, a nanny-goat or a hydroplane, an image or a real thing, or even the formula that might contain the secret of the universe. Like the light of which Scripture speaks, which shines on the just as well as on the unjust, the appearing of the world illuminates everything that it illuminates in a terrifying neutrality, without distinguishing between things or persons. There are victims and torturers, charitable acts and genocides, rules and exceptions, and exactions, and wind, water, earth, and all this stands before us in the same way, in this ultimate manner of being which we express when we say "This is," "There is."

3. However, this indifference of the appearing of the world to that which it unveils in the Difference, which makes everything of it except that which a Father is for his Son, a brother for his brothers, a friend for his friends (a friend who knows everything that his friend knows, a brother who knows everything that his brothers know, and first and foremost the first among them: the First Born Son) – this indifference, we should say, hides a more radical destitution. The appearing of the world is not only indifferent to everything it unveils, it is incapable of conferring existence upon it. It is without doubt this incapacity of the appearing of the world to take account of that which unveils itself in it which explains its indifference towards it. Indifference and neutrality here mean powerlessness, from which they are derived. Heidegger, who first thought the concept of the world in its originary phenomenological signification as pure appearing, was quite aware of both this indifference (the anguish in which everything becomes indifferent) and this powerlessness. The unveiling unveils, uncovers, "opens," but does not create [macht nicht, öffnet]. This is how the ontological destitution of the appearing of the world reveals itself, as itself incapable of setting out reality.

Now this ontological destitution of the appearing of the world does not result from a peculiarly Heideggerian thesis: one finds it already in Kant's Critique of Pure Reason. Kant under-

stood what is at stake in the question of the world as phenomenological. This is why the Critique consists of an extremely rigorous description of the phenomenological structure of the world. The world is co-constituted through a priori forms of pure intuition, the intuition of space and of time, as well as through the categories of the understanding. "Forms of pure intuition" means pure ways of showing [faire-voir], considered in themselves, independently of the particular and contingent content (which is designated as "empirical") of that which they show on any given occasion. "A priori" means that these pure ways of showing precede all actual experience. Considered in terms more general than those of their specific characteristics (substance, causality, reciprocal action), the categories of understanding have the same fundamental phenomenological signification, that of belonging to showing and of rendering showing possible by assuring its unity. Now, the phenomenological structure of this unifying power is the same as that of the pure intuitions, it is a showing which consists in the fact of placing outside [poser dehors] that which becomes visible in this way. According to Kant's decisive affirmation, the forms of intuition and the categories of understanding are both representations. To represent in this sense is expressed in German as vor-stellen, which signifies very precisely "to place in front" [poser devant]. Now, what is important for us in all this, the recurrent thesis of the Critique, is that the phenomenological formation of the world in the conjoined and coherent action of these diverse "showings" is forever incapable, by itself, of setting out [poser] the reality which constitutes the concrete content of this world – in order to gain access to this reality, Kant was forced to have recourse to sensation.

But the appeal to sensation which can alone give access to reality hides within it an appeal to life, that is, to a radically different mode of appearing. Life is phenomenological through and through. It is neither a being [étant] nor a mode of being [être] of a being. This is not the life about which biology speaks. To tell the truth, modern biology no longer speaks about life. Since the Galilean revolution its object has narrowed to material processes compatible with those studied by physics. As François Jacob expresses it: "In today's laboratories one no longer enquires about life."[5]

The only life which exists is transcendental phenomenological life, the life which defines the originary mode of pure phenomenality to which henceforth, for the sake of clarity, we will reserve the name revelation. The revelation peculiar to life stands opposed point by point to the appearing of the world. Whereas the world unveils in the "outside of self," being only the "outside of self" as such, such that everything which it unveils is exterior, other, different, the first decisive trait of the revelation of life is that, because it carries no divide or gap within it and never differs from itself, it only ever reveals itself. Life reveals itself. Life is an auto-revelation. Auto-revelation, when it concerns life, thus means two things. On the one hand it is life which accomplishes the work of revelation, it is everything except a thing. On the other hand what it reveals is itself. Thus the opposition between that which appears and pure appearing, which had already been present in classical thought and which was then brought to the fore by phenomenology, disappears in the case of life. The revelation of life and that which reveals itself in it are as one.

Everywhere where there is life we encounter this extraordinary situation, which is discernible in each modality of life, even in the most humble of impressions. Take, for example, an experience of pain. Because in ordinary apprehension a pain is at first taken as a "physical pain," one attributed to part of the objective body, let us practice on it that reduction which retains only its painful character, the "painful as such," the purely affective element of suffering. This "pure" suffering "reveals itself to itself," which means that suffering alone allows us to know what suffering is, and that what is revealed in this revelation, which is the fact of suffering, is indeed precisely suffering. In this modality of our life the "outside of self" of the world might well be absent — a fact indicated by the lack of any divide that might separate suffering from itself, such that, driven back against itself, overwhelmed by its own weight, it is incapable of instituting any form of stepping-back from itself, a dimension of flight

thanks to which it might be possible for it to escape from itself and from that which was oppressive about its being. In the absence of any divide within suffering, the possibility of turning one's gaze upon it is ruled out. No one has ever seen their suffering, their anguish, or their joy. Suffering, like every modality of life, is invisible.

Invisible does not designate a dimension of unreality or illusion, some fantastical other world, but exactly the opposite. We have seen that it is the appearing of the *world* which, throwing every thing outside of itself, at the same time denudes it of its reality, reducing it to a series of exterior appearances into which it is impossible to penetrate because they have no "interior," each merely referring you to another one which is just as empty and devoid of content as itself, in this game of indefinite referrals which is the world. We have seen that, according to Heidegger, the appearing of the world is incapable of creating that which unveils itself in it. By contrast, each of the modalities of life is a reality — one that is abrupt, immediate, incontestable, insuperable. But as soon as I try to see this reality, it disappears. I am certainly able to form the image of my suffering, re-present it to myself, yet the fact remains that the reality of suffering never exists outside of itself. In the re-presentation of suffering I am only in the presence of a noematic unreality, of the signification "suffering." It is only when all distance is abolished, when suffering experiences itself as pure suffer*ing* and joy as pure enjoy*ing*, that we are dealing with actual suffering, that revelation and reality are as one.

This brings us to the third characteristic which opposes the revelation of life to the appearing of the world. Whereas the latter differs from every thing that it causes to show itself, in such a way that it is totally indifferent to every such thing, life, on the contrary, keeps within it that which it reveals, it resides inside, in every living being, as that which causes it to live and never leaves it for as long as it lives. This then is a new relationship, foreign to the world, peculiar and interior to life; we must now consider in itself the hitherto unthought relation between life and the living being, without which we can understand nothing of this living being that we are. Foreign to the world, acosmic, invisible, the relation of life to living being is a relation of absolute immanence. How could one conceive of a living being that did not carry life within it? But the question equally arises of knowing why there is a living being in life: why is no life possible that might be anonymous, impersonal, foreign to every individuality?

Now, no more than the question of immanence, the question of the relation of life to the living being is not a metaphysical one, an object of speculative constructions or of indefinite debates. It is a matter for phenomenology and more particularly for a phenomenology of life, of which it becomes the central question. It is also an originary question. It obliges us to go back to an absolute life, to the Life spoken of by John.

Absolute life is life which has the power to bring itself into life. Life "is" not, it happens and does not cease happening. This coming of life is its eternal reaching into itself, the process or trial [le procès] in which it gives itself to it*self*, crushes itself against itself, experiences itself [s'éprouve soi-même] and delights in itself, thus constantly producing its own essence, as far as this consists in this testing experience [épreuve] and delight in itself.[6] Now, no experience produces itself as experience or trial of it*self* if it does not generate in its very accomplishment the Ipseity whereby it is able to experience itself and delight in itself. As long as we are not speaking of the concept of life but of a real life, a phenomenologically actual life, then the Ipseity in which this real life comes into itself in experiencing itself is also one that is phenomenologically actual, it is a real Self, the First Living Self in which, experiencing itself, Life reveals itself to itself – its Word. Thus the process of Life's auto-generation is accomplished as the process of its auto-revelation, in such a way that the auto-revelation does not come at the end of this process but belongs to it and is consubstantial with it like an immanent condition of its effectuation. "In the beginning was the Word." There is no life without a living being, like this Self that all life carries in it in so far as it is this experience of self of which we are speaking. But equally there is no Self without this Life in which every Self is given in itself,

in such a way that outside of life no Self is possible.

However: doesn't this analysis of absolute life distance us from the phenomenology which seeks to confine itself to the concrete phenomena that we live through, does it not throw us back into speculation, if not into dogma or belief? Haven't we yielded to the "theological turn of French phenomenology"[7] denounced by Dominique Janicaud?

And yet are we not, we too, living beings? Living beings in the sense of a life which experiences itself, and not just a complex set of material processes which know nothing of themselves. Living beings which are themselves also living Selves. This strange analogy between the internal process of absolute life experiencing itself in the Self of the First Living Being and our own life revealing itself to itself in this singular Self that each of us is forever becomes less extraordinary than it seems at first sight if we first of all establish the distinction between them.

Our life is a finite life incapable of bringing itself into self. The Self that this life carries in it is itself a finite Self. As Husserl says in a manuscript of the 1930s: "I am not only for myself, but I am me [Ich bin nicht nur für mich, aber Ich bin Ich]." I am not only for myself, i.e. this individual appearing in the world, a thing among things, a man among men, who represents itself constantly to itself, always in a state of care for itself, who only busies itself with things and with others with a view to itself. In order to relate everything to oneself, one must first of all be this Self to whom everything is related, one must be able to say Ich bin Ich. But the point is that this Ich bin Ich is not at all originary. I am indeed myself, but I am not brought to myself in this me that I am. I am given to myself, but it is not me myself who gives me to me. A Self such as that of man, a living transcendental Self – such a Self is only ever to be found in the "Word of life" of the first letter of John, whom Paul described as "a First Born among many brothers" (Romans 8: 28–30). For we too are born of absolute Life. To be born does not mean to come into the world. Things appear for an instant in the light of the world before disappearing into it. Things are not "born." Birth concerns only living beings. And for these living beings, to be born means to come to be as one of these transcendental living Selves that each of us is. It is solely because we have first come into life that we are then able to come into the world.

In this way the nature of our transcendental birth becomes clear. How do we come into life? We come into life in so far as life comes in it*self* [*vient en soi*] and in the same way that life comes in itself. It is because absolute life comes into it*self* while experiencing itself in the ipseity of the First Living Self which is its Word that every man given to himself in the ipseity of this life comes into himself as a transcendental living Self. It is for this reason that every life, every transcendental phenomenological life, is marked at its heart with a radical and insurmountable individuality.

Here we should make an historical observation which is laden with repercussions for our time. Life has been notably absent from the Western philosophy inherited from Greece, which defines man through thought. When at the beginning of the nineteenth century life makes, with Schopenhauer, its great return to the European scene, it is a life stripped of individuality, anonymous, impersonal, savage, which will establish its rule not only over philosophy but over culture as a whole, conferring upon it its tragic and absurd character, clearing the way to brutal force, to violence, to nihilism.

The phenomenology of life is thus confronted with one last question. We said that in every living being life comes to pass as a Self which belongs to every life and to every determination of life. Thus there is no suffering which might be nobody's suffering. Because God is Life, one must effectively say with Meister Eckhart: "God engenders himself as myself [*Dieu s'engendre comme moi-même*]"[8] – an abyssal affirmation which suffices to dismiss all the various "crises of subject" of contemporary nihilism. However, since the latter not only conceives of life as anonymous but also as unconscious, so then, taken in once again by the Greek *phainomenon* which reserves manifestation to the light of exteriority, modernity proves incapable of grasping the invisible in its proper phenomenological positivity.

What does this phenomenological positivity consist in? Consider suffering once more. We said that suffering reveals suffering, but this proposition must be corrected. The auto-revelation of suffering which is accomplished in suffering cannot be the fact of suffering considered in its particular content, if it is true that it is accomplished just as well in joy, boredom, anguish or effort. It is in its affectivity in reality that anguish is revealed to itself, in this pathetic auto-impressionality which constitutes the flesh of this suffering as of every other modality of life.[9] This is the reason why these are all affective modalities. There is here, according to the inspired intuition of Maine de Biran, a "feeling of effort" such that it is only in the trouble of this effort or in its satisfaction that any form of action is possible, not as an objective displacement which is itself unconscious, but as an "I Can" experiencing itself, in and through its affectivity. Thus affectivity does not designate any particular sphere of our life, it penetrates and founds as a last resort the entire domain of action, of "work" and thus of economic phenomena, which consequently cannot be separated from the realm of human existence, as it is believed possible to do today.

In the same way, finally, there is a pathos of thought which explains the privilege accorded by classical philosophy to obviousness, to matters that seem self-evident. It is easy to recognise behind this privileging of the self-evident the reign of the visible which dominates the development of our culture, which remains a prisoner of Greek *theoria*. However, the fact is that thought, including rational thought, is only ever given to itself in the pathetic auto-revelation of life, and even Husserl himself, despite his effort to found phenomenological method upon the visibility of the self-evident, had to admit that "the consciousness which judges a mathematical 'state of things' is an impression."[10]

Against Husserl, then, let us acknowledge the decisive fact that all modalities of life, those of theoretical and cognitive thought no less than others, are affective at their root, and this is because the phenomenological matter in which pure phenomenality originally phenomenalises itself is an Archi-passibility; every "self-experi-

105

encing" only becomes possible through this Archi-passibility. In John's words, God is not only Life, he is Love. Thus an essential connection is set up between the pure fact of living and Affectivity.

If our various tonalities find their ultimate possibility in the essence of life, it follows in the first instance that they can never be explained solely from the worldly events that we interpret as their "motives" or "causes." We say: "a misfortune has occurred." This signifies that an objective event – accident, illness, bereavement – has produced a suffering to the point of being identified with it. Such an event, however dramatic it may be, can nonetheless only produce a feeling of suffering in a being that is susceptible to suffering, i.e. a living being given to itself in a life whose essence is Archi-passibility. Yet why should such a sentiment take on the form of this affective tonality rather than another? How can we fail to notice here that all the modalities of our life are divided up according to a decisive dichotomy between modalities lived as positive – impressions of pleasure or of happiness – and modalities said to be negative – impressions of pain or of sadness? As a result, our entire existence seems caught in an affective becoming which is not in the least bit indeterminate, ceaselessly oscillating between malaise and satisfaction, suffering and joy – with neutral tonalities like boredom or indifference presenting themselves as a sort of neutralisation of this primitive oscillation.

How, then, can this dichotomy be explained if it does not result merely from the events of the world, if instead we are determined to locate its ultimate condition within ourselves? We have replied to this question. In so far as the essence of "living" is "self-experiencing [s'éprouver soi-même]" in the immanence of a pathetic auto-affection without divide or distance vis-à-vis oneself, life is marked with a radical passivity towards itself, it is a suffering of oneself or a "self-suffering," a "self-enduring," a passivity stronger than all freedom and whose presence we have recognised in the most modest suffering which is incapable of escaping itself, driven back to itself in a primordial passion peculiar to every life and to every living being. It is only

because of this primitive "suffer*ing*" which belongs to every "self-experiencing" as the concrete phenomenological mode of its accomplishment that something like a "suffering" is possible.

In the accomplishment of this "self-suffering," however, life experiences itself, comes into it*self*, augments itself with its own content, delights in itself – it is enjoyment, it is joy. It is clear that these two originary and fundamental phenomenological tonalities, a pure "suffering" and a pure "enjoying," root themselves a priori in the "self-experiencing" which constitutes the essence of every conceivable life. In its turn, the dichotomy made manifest over the whole of our affective tonalities rests upon this division between the two fundamental phenomenological tonalities. But what is thereby revealed to us, at the same time as this most profound essence of life, is the a priori and transcendental possibility of the passing of all our tonalities each into each other. This continual slippage of our tonalities – whether it be a case of a continual transformation or of an abrupt change, of a "leap" – is itself also discernible in the concrete becoming of our quotidian existence. Such a becoming can sometimes seem absurd and incomprehensible when subjected to the vicissitudes of a contingent history or to the play of unconscious drives. Thus it was in the eyes of the poet Verlaine when, casting his gaze over the whole of his past existence, he wrote this disillusioned line: "Old good fortunes, old misfortunes, like a line of geese … [*Vieux bonheurs, vieux malheurs, comme une file d'oies …*]"[11]

This impression appears superficial, however, once we understand that this potential modification of our multiple modalities is inscribed in an originary possibility of the passage each into each other of the fundamental phenomenological tonalities belonging to the essence of life. And this is because pure suffering is the concrete phenomenological mode according to which the coming of life into itself accomplishes itself, its embracing of itself in pure enjoying and thus the possibility of every conceivable form of happiness and joy, something which in the final reckoning is never anything other than *joie de vivre*, the limitless happiness of existing.

Considered in their specific phenomenological content, suffering and joy are assuredly different, in the same way as are malaise and satisfaction, desire and gratification. It is even this difference, the will to substitute positive modalities for negative modalities, which most often determines action, and this from its most elementary forms (like the immediate impulse of every need to satisfy itself). However, despite their difference and sometimes their violent opposition, suffering and joy as well as their multiple modalisations are united in a more originary identity, which is that of the co-constituent suffer*ing* and enjoy*ing* of the essence of life and its ipseity.

In order to grasp this most originary identity, however, we must not lose sight of the finitude of our own life, we must perceive our life in its Foundation, i.e. no longer in that place where it seems to us that it experiences itself in a sort of psychological facticity always incapable of recognising itself, but instead where it is given to it*self* in the auto-donation of absolute life, in the place of our transcendental birth. Such was the inspired intuition of Kierkegaard when he understood that it is at the peak of his suffering, at the limit of his despair, that this despair inverts itself into beatitude, when, as he puts it, "the self plunges through its own transparency into the power which established it."[12]

From the Archi-passivity of absolute Life there further follows that most singular character of the human condition, which is being an incarnated existence. Because the latter is immediately interpreted as an existence in a body it refers us back to the question of the body which, like every fundamental question, refers us in its turn to a phenomenological foundation, that is, to a mode of appearing. Now, the mode of appearing which presents itself here as being evidently that of the body is the appearing of the world, and this in two senses. On the one hand, every body, whether it be our own body or any other body, shows itself to us in the world, taking its phenomenological properties from the phenomenological properties of the world, and first and foremost its very exteriority. However, this worldly body is not only "exterior," it is a body furnished with several sensual qualities.

This means that this body which is seen, touched, heard, etc. presupposes a second body, a transcendental body which feels it, which sees it, which touches it, which hears it, etc., thanks to the powers of its different senses. In the phenomenology of the twentieth century these powers are understood as so many intentionalities, in such a way that the transcendental body which constitutes the universe is an intentional body. It is in this second sense that *our* body is a body of the world, in this sense that it opens us to this world itself. The appearing upon which this opening to the world rests is the same as that in which the body-object of the philosophical tradition shows itself to us; it remains in both cases the "outside of self" as such. Only, as we have seen, the intentionality which causes every thing to be seen [*qui fait voir*] is incapable of bringing itself into phenomenality. The aporia upon which Husserlian phenomenology came to founder is repeated in respect of the body reduced to the intentional body. Each of these features of this transcendental body can only give us that which it gives – seeing, touching, hearing … – if it gives itself originally to itself in the giving that it accomplishes. An immanent auto-donation of this type only happens, however, in life, in its pathetic auto-revelation.

Only in this way can we overturn our conception of the body: when we understand that the appearing to which it is consigned is no longer that of the world, but precisely that of life. And this overturning consists precisely in the fact that this body which is ours differs completely from other bodies which people the universe, it is no longer a visible body but a flesh – an invisible flesh. For in so far as flesh finds its phenomenological foundation in life, it takes from this latter all of its phenomenological properties. It is characterised not only by acosmism and invisibility – which themselves suffice radically to distinguish flesh from the "body" of the philosophical tradition – but also by this fact, this small fact: that all flesh is the flesh of someone. All flesh is someone's, not just on account of a contingent liaison, but for this essential reason that since a Self is implicated in every auto-revelation of life, it erects itself in all flesh at the same time as life, in the very event which gives life to it*self* – in its transcendental birth. In every respect a tributary of life, flesh takes from this latter its own reality, this pure phenomenological matter of auto-impressionality which is indistinguishable from that of pathetic auto-affection. Flesh is very precisely the pure phenomenological matter of every genuine (i.e. radically immanent) auto-affection, in which life experiences itself pathetically. It is only because flesh is the phenomenological matter of auto-impressionality (which derives its possibility of auto-affection from life) that it finds itself constituting the reality of the whole of our impressions.

Our life, however, is a finite life.

Our finite life is only comprehensible on the basis of the infinite life in which it is given to it*self*. Just as our Self, incapable of bringing itself into itself, refers back to the First Living Self, to the Word in which absolute life reveals itself to itself, so too in the same way the auto-impressionality which renders possible every impression and every flesh presupposes the Archi-passibility of absolute life (i.e. the originary capacity to bring itself into itself in the mode of a pathetic phenomenological effectuation). It is only in this Archi-passibility that all flesh is passible, which is to say that it is possible in its turn – this flesh which is nothing other than that: the possibility of a finite life which draws its possibility from the Archi-passibility of infinite Life.

This is where the phenomenology of life can defend its claim that it is able to escape the domain of philosophical tradition. Is it not capable of illuminating certain decisive elements of our culture that belong to its non-Greek source, notably Judaeo-Christian spirituality? Precisely to the extent that all flesh is only given to it*self*, in the Archipassibility of life, the phenomenology of life unveils the singular link which establishes itself between the two initiatory declarations which mark the famous Prologue of John: "In the beginning was the Word," "And the Word was made flesh" (John 1: 1–14). We have already explained the first declaration, if it is true that no life is possible which does not imply in itself the Self in which it experiences itself. And if, coming now to the second expression, all flesh is only passible in the Archi-passibility of life in its Word, then the Incarnation of the Word ceases to seem absurd, as it seemed in the eyes of the Greeks. On the contrary, we must recognise between Word and flesh much more than an affinity – rather an identity of essence which is nothing other than that of absolute Life. As soon as flesh is given over to life, it ceases to be this objective body with its strange forms, with its incomprehensible sexual determination, apt to arouse our anguish, delivered to the world, indefinitely subjected to the question "why"? For as Meister Eckhart understood, life is without why. The flesh which carries in it the principle of its own revelation does not ask for any other authority to illuminate itself. When in its innocence each modality of our flesh experiences itself, when suffering says suffering and joy joy, it is Life that speaks in it, and nothing has power against its word.

This Archi-passibility beyond all passibility but present in it, immanent in all flesh as that which gives it to itself, beyond all sensible or intelligible evidence, what can it be called if not an Archi-intelligibility, an Archi-gnosis whose essence John described as the coming of absolute Life in its Word (before it makes possible the coming of the Word in a flesh similar to our own)? Thus Johannine Archi-intelligibility is implied everywhere that there is life, it reaches out even to these beings of flesh that we are, taking up in its incandescent Parousia our derisory sufferings and our hidden wounds, as it did the wounds of Christ on the cross. The more purely does each of our sufferings happen within us, the more each suffering is reduced to itself, to its phenomenological body of flesh, so the more strongly we experience in ourselves the limitless power which gives suffering to itself. And when this suffering reaches its limit point, in despair, then, as Kierkegaard puts it, "the self plunges through its own transparency into the power which established it," and the intoxication of life submerges us. Happy are those who suffer. In the Depth of its Night, our flesh is God. The Archignosis is the gnosis of the simple [*la gnose des simples*].

notes

1 "Phénoménologie de la vie" was first delivered as a lecture to the Munich Academy of Fine Arts, 14 November 2000. The French version of the text is available online at <http://www.philagora.net/philo-fac/henry-ph1>; *Angelaki* is grateful to Joseph and Joëlle Llapasset for permission to translate it. A month before he died in July 2002, Henry confirmed, in discussion with Joseph and Joëlle Llapasset, his belief that this article conveys the essence of his whole philosophical project. In the following translation I have chosen to adhere quite closely to the often dense French original, in particular so as to convey the effect of Henry's persistent use of reflexive constructions; readers should bear in mind the multiplicity of words used to refer to self or self-hood (*soi, se, Soi, soi-même, Ipséité, ipséité*). On occasion, when translating *soi*, I have italicised the "self" of "itself" (it*self*) to emphasise the sense of the reference to self in the French, which might be slightly obscured by a reading of "itself" as a primarily reflexive construction in English. [Translator's note.]

2 Martin Heidegger, *Sein und Zeit* (Halle: Niemeyer, 1941) 220–21.

3 Edmund Husserl, *Leçons pour une phénoménologie de la conscience intime du temps* (Paris: Presses Universitaires de France, 1964) 157.

4 Heidegger, *Sein und Zeit* 329.

5 François Jacob, *La Logique du vivant: une histoire de l'hérédité* (Paris: Gallimard, 1970) 320.

6 Picking up on the second meaning of *procès* (i.e. "trial," in the juridical sense), *épreuve* can mean trial, test, or experience of a hardship; *s'éprouver* means to feel or experience, but is also used in the sense of suffering or experiencing a hardship. The phrase "testing experience" is meant to convey this combination of meanings, since my rendering of *s'éprouver soi-même* as "experiencing itself" or "self-experiencing" otherwise loses the crucial sense of suffering or testing. [Translator's note.]

7 Dominique Janicaud, *Le Tournant théologique de la phénoménologie française* (Combas: L'Eclat, 1991).

8 Meister Eckhart, "Sermon no. 6" in *Traités et sermons* (Paris: Aubier, 1942) 146.

9 As Susan Emanuel (the translator of Henry's *I Am the Truth*) notes, Henry uses the term *pathé-*

henry

tique in its etymological sense, i.e. to refer not to an object that might arouse an emotion but to the person who undergoes that emotion, the person who is capable of suffering or feeling something ("Note on Terminology" in Henry, *I Am the Truth*). [Translator's note.]

10 Edmund Husserl, *Leçons* 124.

11 Paul Verlaine, "Ô vous, comme un qui boite au loin, Chagrins et Joies," *Sagesse* in *Oeuvres poétiques complètes*, eds. Yves-Gérard Le Dantec and Jacques Borel (Paris: Gallimard, "Pléiade," 1962) 247.

12 Søren Kierkegaard, *Traité du désespoir* (Paris: Gallimard, 1949) 64.

works by henry

Le Jeune Officier [novel]. Paris: Gallimard, 1954.

L'Essence de la manifestation. 1963. Paris: Presses Universitaires de France, 1990. *The Essence of Manifestation.* Trans. Girard Etzkorn. The Hague: Nijhoff, 1973.

Philosophie et phénoménologie du corps: essai sur l'ontologie biranienne. Paris: Presses Universitaires de France, 1965. *Philosophy and Phenomenology of the Body.* Trans. Girard Etzkorn. The Hague: Nijhoff, 1975.

L'Amour les yeux fermés [novel]. Paris: Gallimard, 1976.

Marx, 2 vols. I. *Une philosophie de la réalité;* II. *Une philosophie de l'économie.* Paris: Gallimard, 1976. *Marx: A Philosophy of Human Reality.* Trans. Kathleen McLaughlin; reworked and abbreviated by Michel Henry. Bloomington: Indiana UP, 1983.

Le Fils du roi [novel]. Paris: Gallimard, 1981.

Généalogie de la psychanalyse: le commencement perdu. Paris: Presses Universitaires de France, 1985. *The Genealogy of Psychoanalysis.* Trans. Douglas Brick with an introduction by François Roustang. Stanford: Stanford UP, 1993.

La Barbarie. Paris: Grasset, 1987.

Voir l'invisible: sur Kandinsky. Paris: Bourin, 1988.

Du communisme au capitalisme: théorie d'une catastrophe. Paris: Odile Jacob, 1990.

Phénoménologie matérielle. Paris: Presses Universitaires de France, 1990.

"The Critique of the Subject." *Who Comes after the Subject?* Ed. Eduardo Cadava et al. London: Routledge, 1991. 157–66.

"Narrer le pathos: entretien avec Michel Henry." *Revue des Sciences Humaines* 95.1 (1991): 49–65.

Le Cadavre indiscret [novel]. Paris: Albin Michel, 1996.

C'est moi la vérité: pour une philosophie du christian-isme. Paris: Seuil, 1996. *I Am the Truth: Toward a Philosophy of Christianity.* Trans. Susan Emanuel. Stanford: Stanford UP, 2003.

Incarnation: une philosophie de la chair. Paris: Seuil, 2000.

"Phénoménologie et langage." *Michel Henry: l'épreuve de la vie.* Ed. Alain David and Jean Greisch. Paris: Cerf, 2001.

Auto-donation: entretiens et conférences. Montpellier: Prétentaine, 2002.

Paroles du Christ. Paris: Seuil, 2002.

Nick Hanlon
Pembroke College
Cambridge CB2 1RF
UK
E-mail: nmh29@cam.ac.uk

journal of the theoretical humanities
volume 8   number 2   august 2003

introduction

peter hallward

Born in Rabat in 1937, a student of Althusser's at the École Normale Supérieure, Badiou taught philosophy at the University of Paris VIII (Vincennes/Saint Denis) from 1969 to 1999 before returning to the École Normale to take up Althusser's former position. Much of Badiou's life has been shaped by his dedication to the consequences of the May 1968 rebellion in Paris. A leading member of the *Union des jeunesses communistes de France (marxistes-léninistes)* in the 1960s, he remains with Sylvain Lazarus and Natacha Michel at the centre of *L'Organisation Politique*, an organisation dedicated, at a principled "distance from the state," to the pursuit of a "politics without party" – one concerned with direct popular intervention in a wide range of issues including immigration, labour and housing. He is the author of several novels and plays as well as more than a dozen philosophical works, of which the most important are *Being and Event* (1988), *Logiques des mondes* (forthcoming 2005) and *Théorie du sujet* (1982).

Very broadly speaking, Badiou seeks to link, on the one hand, a formal, axiomatic and egalitarian conception of thought (as opposed to any close association of thought with language, with the interpretation of meanings or the description of objects), with, on the other hand, a theory of militant and discontinuous innovation (as opposed to a theory of continuous change or a dialectical theory of mediation). The two principles connect, from time to time, in exceptional affirmative sequences through which an instance of pure conviction comes to acquire a universal validity. Such sequences are what Badiou calls

alain badiou

translated by bruno bosteels and alberto toscano

BEYOND FORMALISATION
an interview

"truths." Truths are affirmations to which in principle we can all actively *hold* true, in excess of our ability to prove that what we thereby affirm is correct or justified in any demonstrable sense. Truths are not to be confused with matters of knowledge or opinion, they are not subject to established criteria of adequation or verification. As Badiou explains in detail in his major work to date, *Being and Event*, truths are militant processes which, beginning from a specific time and place within a situation, pursue the step-by-step transformation of that situation in line with new forms of broadly egalitarian principles.

Badiou's most general goal can be described, in other words, as the effort to explore the potential for profound, universalisable innovation in any situation. Every such innovation can only

ISSN 0969-725X print/ISSN 1469-2899 online/03/020111-26 © 2003 Taylor & Francis Ltd and the Editors of *Angelaki*
DOI: 10.1080/0969725032000162611

begin with some sort of exceptional break with the status quo, an "event." Though events are ephemeral and leave no trace, what distinguishes an event from other incidents that might ordinarily take place in a situation is the fact that its implications, themselves illuminated by the consequences of previous events, make it impossible for those who affirm them to carry on as before. An event can occur at any time but not in just any place; events are located at the edge of whatever qualifies as "void" or indistinguishable in the situation, i.e. in that part of the situation where for literally fundamental reasons the prevailing forms of discernment and recognition cease to have any significant purchase. A truth then expands out of this "evental site" [*site événementiel*] in so far as it elicits the militant conviction of certain individuals who develop the revolutionary implications of the event, and by doing so constitute themselves as the subjects of its truth. A subject is thus anyone carried by his or her fidelity to the consequences, as rigorous as they are haphazard; the laborious, case-by-case application of these consequences will then serve to transform the entire way the situation organises and represents itself, in keeping with the implications of the event.

An ordinary individual or "some-one" only becomes a genuine subject (or part of a genuine collective subject) in so far as he or she is caught up in a radically transformative procedure of this kind. By the same token (for reasons sketched in Badiou's most accessible short work, *Ethics* (1993)), subjects only remain subjects in so far as their fidelity is in turn equipped to resist the various sorts of corruption it must inevitably face: fatigue, confusion and dogmatism. Every genuinely universal principle has its origin in an active and precisely situated *taking* of sides; every true affirmation of the universal interest begins as divisive, and persists without concern for the "ethical" coordination of opinions or differences. A subject, in short, is someone who continues to adhere to a cause whose ongoing implications relate indifferently to all members of the situation, and which thereby considers these members as elements of a properly indiscernible or "generic" collection.

Badiou distinguishes four general fields of truth, or four domains of subjectivation (which in turn operate as the four generic "conditions" of philosophy itself): politics, science, art and love. These are the only four fields in which a pure subjective commitment is possible, i.e. one indifferent to procedures of interpretation, representation or verification. Badiou provides his most concise overview of the generic procedures in his *Manifesto for Philosophy* (1989). True politics is a matter of collective mobilisation guided by a "general will" in something like Rousseau's sense, and not the business of bureaucratic administration or the socialised negotiation of interests or identities. Within the limits of the private sphere, genuine love begins in the wake of an unpredictable encounter that escapes the conventional representation of sexual roles, continues as a fidelity to the consequences of that encounter, and is sustained through an unrepresentable exposure to what Lacan famously described as the impossibility of a sexual relationship. True art and true science proceed in somewhat the same way, through a searching experimental fidelity to a line of enquiry opened up by a new discovery or break with tradition. Mathematics is then the most "truthful" component of science because, thanks to its strictly axiomatic foundation, it is the most firmly abstracted from any natural or objective mediation, the most removed from our habitual ways of thinking, and by the same token the most obviously indifferent to the identity of whoever comes to share in its articulation.

For the same reason, Badiou explains in the difficult opening meditations of *Being and Event*, mathematics is the only discourse suited to the literal articulation of pure being-as-being, or being considered without regard to being-this or being-that, being without reference to particular qualities or ways of being: being that simply *is*. More precisely, mathematics is the only discourse suited to the articulation of being as *pure multiplicity*, i.e. a multiplicity subtracted from any unity or unifying process. Only mathematics can think multiplicity considered without any constituent reference to unity. Why? Because the theoretical foundations of mathematics ensure that any unification, any consideration of something as one thing, must be thought as the *result* of an operation, the operation that treats or counts something as one; by the same token, these foundations oblige us to presume that whatever was thus counted, or unified, is itself not-one, or multiple.[1] A "situation," as Badiou defines it, is simply any instance of such a counting operation whereby a certain set of individuals or things are identified in some way as members of a coherent collection or set – think, for example, of the way in which citizens count and are counted in national situations, or the way employees count (or do not count) in economic situations, or how students count (or are discounted) in educational situations.

Pure multiplicity itself is a medium in which no decisive change or innovation is possible. Every truth must therefore begin with a break in the fabric of being-as-being – an event is precisely "that which is *not* being-as-being."[2] And as Sartre (Badiou's first and perhaps most influential mentor) understood with particular clarity, truly radical change can in a certain sense only proceed *ex nihilo*, i.e. from something that apparently counts as nothing, something whose being is indistinguishable from non-being, from something uncountable. Every situation includes some such uncountable or empty component: its *void*. In situations which count only property, wealth or consumption, for instance, human capacities which cannot be counted in such terms will remain empty or indiscernible as far as the situation is concerned; so too, within the ordinary routine of situation of parliamentary democracies, will popular political capacities whose expression is indifferent to the business of electoral representation. Marx conceives of the proletariat, to take the most obvious case, as the void of the developing capitalist situation. An event, then, will be something that takes place at the *edge* of its situation's void, within the orbit of that element that itself seems to have no attribute other than this void – that working class that "has nothing other than its chains," for instance. What Badiou's philosophy is designed to demonstrate, in short, is the coherence of processes of radical transformation that begin via an encounter with precisely that which appears as uncountable in a situation, and that continue as the development of ways of counting or grouping

badiou

the elements belonging to the situation according to no other criteria than the simple fact that they are all, equally and indistinctly, members of the situation.

As a result of the non-ontological status of the event, being and truth cannot be said in one and the same discourse. By consigning the tasks of ontology to mathematics, Badiou frees philosophy proper from its ultimate coordination with being (a coordination maintained in their different ways by Spinoza, Hegel, Heidegger and Deleuze). Any actively inventive philosophy, Badiou insists, is conditioned by the varied truth procedures operative in its time, rather than by an ultimately timeless mediation on being.

Badiou's own examples of such truth procedures are varied enough to include both St Paul's militant conception of an apostolic subjectivity that exists only through proclamation of an event (the resurrection of Christ) of universal import but of no recognisable or established significance, and the Jacobin or Bolshevik fidelity to revolutions that exceed, in their subjective power and generic scope, the various circumstances that contributed to their occurrence. Mallarmé, Schoenberg and Beckett figure prominently among the practitioners of a suitably subtractive or generic art, which is always an effort to devise new kinds of form at the very edge of what the situation considers monstrous or devoid of form. After Galileo and Descartes, Cantor and Cohen demonstrate what inventive scientific formalisation can achieve, at the limits of mathematical consistency.

In the end, every truth is founded only on the fundamental "inconsistency" that Badiou discerns as the exclusive and insubstantial being of any being – the generic being of all that *is* simply in so far as it is, but that is only *exceptionally* accessible, through the rare commitment of those who become subjects in the wake of its eventual exposure.

notes

I Very roughly speaking, the general stages of this argument run as follows: (i) being can be thought either in terms of the multiple or the one; (ii) the only coherent conception of being as one ultimately depends on some instance of the One either as transcendent limit (a One *beyond* being, or God) or as all-inclusive immanence (a cosmos or Nature); (iii) modernity, and in particular modern science, have demonstrated that God is dead, that Nature is not whole, and that the idea of a One-All is incoherent; (iv) therefore, if being can be thought at all, it must be thought as multiple rather than one; (v) only modern mathematics, as founded in axiomatic set theory, is genuinely capable of such thought. See Badiou, *L'Etre et l'événement*, mediations 1–8.

2 Badiou, *L'Etre et l'événement* 193.

beyond formalisation: an interview[1]

alain badiou

Peter Hallward: We'd like to start with some questions about the book you've just finished on the twentieth century, then talk about your current lecture series on aspects of the present historical moment, before finishing with a few points relating to your major work in progress, Logiques des mondes *[forthcoming].*

Starting then with The Century:[2] *what is your basic thesis in this book? In particular, can you explain the relationship between the "passion for the real"* [passion du réel] *you describe as characteristic of the truly inventive or innovative sequences of the last century, and the various programmes of radical formalisation that this passion inspired?*

Alain Badiou: I should begin by saying that my lectures on the twentieth century were devised in reaction to the mass of prevailing opinion, against various campaigns regarding the meaning of the last century. In France, the question of the twentieth century has been dominated – in the official record – by the ideas of totalitarianism, of the great massacres, of communism as crime, and the equation of communism with fascism. The twentieth century has been designated as the century of horror and mass crime. My lectures on the twentieth century sought to propose a different version of what happened – different, though not necessarily contrary as regards the facts. It is not a question of opposing facts with other facts, but of finding another path, an inroad or a way of thinking, so as to approach the century. This path had to be constructed. In order to do this, I sought out certain theses that the twentieth century proposed in the realm of thought – theses that would be compatible with the unfolding of the major political, artistic, and scientific experiments that have taken place in this century.

In the end, I identified as the possible centre of the century's experience something I've called

the passion for the real. What is this passion? It is the will to arrive – at all costs – at a real validation of one's hypotheses or programmes. This passion for the real is a voluntarism. It marks a break with the idea that history carries with it, in its own movement, the realisation of a certain number of promises, prophecies, or programmes. Rather, a real will is needed to *arrive* at the realisation of this promise or that programme. The nineteenth century was by and large the century of progress, of an idea of progress tied to a certain idea of history. The twentieth century was fundamentally a century of the real, of the will to the real [*la volonté de réel*]. A century in which it was necessary to have precise and practicable projects concerning the transformation of the world.

I then saw that this passion of the real – the idea that things had to take place, here and now, that they had to *come about*, to *realise* themselves – implied a whole series of other notions. For instance, the notion of a new humanity, or that of a total revolutionary overthrow of existing societies, or the creation of a new world, etc. And I saw that these consequences were themselves conditioned by a process of uninterrupted purification of the real. In order to arrive at the real, to produce it, a method was needed to eliminate the old world, to eliminate all the habits and things of old. In my view, a large part of the violence of the century, the extreme political cruelty that has dominated its first sixty years or so, is rooted in the conviction that ultimately no price is too high for an absolute beginning. If it is really a matter of founding a new world, then the price paid by the old world, even in the number of deaths or the quantity of suffering, becomes a relatively secondary question.

In this sense the relation to the real is not a matter of realism, but is instead expressed through a powerful will to formalisation. Indeed, it is a matter of attaining a radical simplification that would allow one to extract the kernel of the opposition between the new and the old in its purest form. One can only extract this kernel by proceeding through a series of extrications or disentanglements, through a series of axiomatic, formalising, and often brutal simplifications that allow one to operate this distinction without too many nuances or complications. Because if one re-establishes nuance or complexity, the pure idea of creation and novelty is in turn enfeebled.

The major consequence of my hypothesis is that there is no contradiction, but rather a relation of complementarity, between, on the one hand, the idea that the twentieth century was the century of the passion of the real, and, on the other, the obvious fact that the century's avant-gardes were fundamentally formal ones. The idea that the avant-gardes were concerned with creation in the domain of form is evident in the case of art, but if you think about it it's no less clear in politics. What was called Marxism-Leninism, for instance, when you look at it closely, is nothing but an extremely formalised view of Marxism itself. Today this type of stance is said to be "dogmatic," but in reality it was not lived or practised as a dogma or a belief. Rather, it was lived and practised as an effective process of formalisation. Needless to say, with regard to a large number of issues Leninism proceeded by way of extremely stark simplifications. But these simplifications should not be understood in terms of a stupid dogmatism. In the final analysis, they bear a great affinity to the paintings of Mondrian or Malevich, which are themselves projects that pursue radical simplifications of the project of painting.

You see, I tried to get a sense of the profound unity of the century's aesthetic adventure (understood as an adventure governed by formal abstraction and all its consequences, by defiguration [*défiguration*] and the consequences of defiguration) and the century's political adventure, which was that of a radical and revolutionary simplification guided by the idea of an absolute beginning. We could add that the movement of radical formalisation is equally dominant in the history of mathematics. The creation of modern algebra and general topology is situated in this same space of thought, and was inspired by the effort to begin the whole of mathematics all over again, by way of a complete formalisation.

P.H.: How then are we to understand the opacity, so to speak, introduced by the state appara- *tus (the police, the army) into this political project to formalise or simplify society, to make it transparent? Can this be dismissed as a merely contingent perversion of the communist project?*

A.B.: One day, someone should write a new history of the state in the twentieth century, a history that would not entirely subordinate the question to the opposition between democracy and totalitarianism, or between parliamentarism and bureaucracy. I believe that the twentieth century has indeed been the century of state power. But I also believe that the state itself really embodied, in the most extreme instances, something like the omni-potence of creation. We must understand where the *possibility* of these figures of the state comes from – for example, of states of the Stalinist type. It is obviously absurd to reduce these states to their extraordinary police function, a function which they certainly exerted. But we must enquire about the conditions of possibility of these functions. We know very well that a link must be found between the policing and dictatorial pressures, on the one hand, and, on the other, the general system of the subjective factors that made them possible. Everyone knows that in Russia as well as in the rest of the world, the Stalinist state was endowed with a real aura. It was not merely the sinister figure that we otherwise can and should associate with it. Where did this aura come from? I think that the state itself was experienced as the formalisation of absolute novelty, that it was itself an instance of formalisation and thereby also a violently simplified state as regards its operational capacity. Think of the general directives of these states, the five-year plans, the "great leaps forward," the powerful ideological campaigns. This formalising function, which was also one of purification [*épuration*][3] and simplification, is also perfectly evident in what was called the cult of personality, the extraordinary devotion accorded to the supreme leader. This is because this cult is nothing but another formal conviction. It comes down to the idea that the state should be able to present itself in the *simple* figure of a single will. To reduce the state to the figure of a charismatic leader is ultimately an effort related to the dialectic of singularity and universality: if the objectives of the state are formally universal, if they embody universal emancipation, then the state must itself be absolutely singular. In the end, this absolute singularity is simply the singularity of a single body, a single will, and a single leader. Thus, the dialectic between singularity and universality, considered with respect to an absolutely formal agency [*instance*], ends up – in a way that is consistent and not at all paradoxical – in such Stalinist or otherwise despotic figures of the state.

The problem is that there is obviously something mistaken in this line of reasoning. The truth is that there can never be any genuinely absolute beginning. Everything is ultimately a matter of procedure and labour; truths are always plural and never single or unique [*uniques*] even in their own particular domain, and so on. Consequently, state formalisation (and this will be true of the other formalisations as well) is prey to the real in a way that always partially differs from how it pretends to be. In other words, it differs from what it presents as its own absolute capacity without reserve, it differs from the absolutist character it attributes to its own inauguration, to the unhindered pursuit of its project; it differs in short, from the entire thematic of the resolute march towards socialism. This "march," in fact, doesn't exist. There is always only a localised becoming, irreducible to all totalisation, which in turn must be thought only as a singular point within this local becoming.

To my mind, this last remark is of great importance. The formalisation organised by the passion for the real leads to a kind of crushing of the local under the weight of the global. Each and every localisation of the procedure is immediately thought as an instance of the totality.

Such a relation to the real cannot be sustained indefinitely. Hence the massive inversion that progressively takes place, which shifts the terrain onto the side of non-transparency, secrecy, and hidden operations. Those who know what's really going on, those who have knowledge of the singularity of the situation, are supposed to keep quiet, and all the rest of it. Thus, little by little, a sort of general corrosion of the situation occurs

which, whilst announcing the absolute formal transparency of a grandiose project, is turned on its head and becomes an extremely defensive procedure. Everything that is locally produced seems at all times to threaten the aim of global transparency. Thus (and this is something very striking when you read serious studies of Stalinism, which are generally written by British scholars, or scholars from the USA, who have a less ideological relation to Stalinism than do the French or the Italians) the conviction held by the leaders of these revolutionary states is in fact nothing but the awareness of an absolute discrepancy between the situation and the means at their disposal. They themselves have the impression of being absolutely precarious figures. Any circumstance whatsoever gives them the impression that their own overthrow is imminent. On top of the police violence and the reciprocal surveillance of everyone by everyone, this subjectivity generates as its own guiding rule the circulation of lies and secrets, together with the non-revelation of what's really going on. But this rule can in turn be explained from the vantage point of the relation between the real and the formal, as well as of the relation between singularity and universality. That is to say, a universality that should remain local and prudent (as is always the case of true universality) is forced instead to bear an absolutely formal globality, and one is immediately obliged to refer this to an all-powerful singularity, to a will as inscrutable as God's – to take up a comparison that you [Peter] often draw between eventual absolutism and the theory of sovereignty.[4]

I wanted to clarify this entire matter by showing that in the political, aesthetic, and scientific adventures of the twentieth century we are not dealing with pathologies of gratuitous cruelty, or with some kind of historical sadism – a ridiculous hypothesis – but rather with significant intellectual operators [*opérateurs*]. That is why I adopted the method of always restricting myself as closely as possible to that which the century itself said about the century, so as to avoid getting caught in retrospection, in the tribunals of history or judgement. The twentieth century interrogated itself with particular intensity regarding its own nature, its own singularity. I wanted to remain very close to this interrogation, as well as to the intimate reasons of that which remains cloaked in shadow from the point of view of retrospective judgement – I mean the remarkable enthusiasm that surrounded all these developments. The widespread popular enthusiasm for communist politics, the creative enthusiasm of the artistic avant-gardes, the Promethean enthusiasm of the scientists ... To reduce this enthusiasm to the domain of the imaginary, to mere illusions, to misleading utopias, is to engage in a completely vacuous argument.

I find this argument just as weak and false, by the way, when it is used with reference to religion. Even today, it is an aberration to explain the subjective power of religion, at its highest moments, in terms of the logic of imaginary alienation. It is infinitely easier and more truthful to understand that there really is a genuine subjective dimension present in that which ultimately, in my own jargon, resembles a confusion between event and truth, i.e. something that reduces the considerable difficulties involved in maintaining fidelity to an event to a matter of pure insurrection. These difficulties require an infinite series of local inventions. It is always tempting (and moreover it is partially correct) to claim that these local inventions are anticipated by the primordial figure of the sequence, by the pure power of the pure event – for instance the figure of the revolution, in politics, and I think that we could prove the same holds in art and in the sciences. It is beyond doubt, for example, that the project of a complete formalisation of mathematics by Bourbaki in France, which in one respect led to something grandiose, at the same time also failed (if one must really speak of failure) as dramatically as did the construction of socialism in the USSR. It was something grandiose, which generated true enthusiasm and renovated mathematical thinking, but nevertheless it never proved possible to show that the actual development of mathematics was really *anticipated* by a stable axiomatic foundation. All the evidence points to the fact that the movement of mathematics also includes the need to modify the axioms, to transform them, to introduce new ones, and sometimes even to accept that the general position to which one adhered

had to be abandoned. No formalisation can claim to encompass the totality of the consequences of the event that it draws upon. However, the idea that it could be otherwise is not simply an illusion or an alienation. It is a powerful and creative subjective disposition, which brings to light new strata of the real.

I think the same is true of art. The various manifestos and new orientations proposed during the century sought to lead art back to the expression of its own conditions. The end of art was declared on the basis of an integral formalisation of art's own possibility. Everything that had to do with art's relation to empirical reality, to the contingency of representations, to imitation, was proclaimed to be nothing but a form of retardation [*arriération mentale*]. This whole movement was formidable, enlightening and creative. By and large, it has defined the century – but it could not anticipate the development of art for an indefinitely long time. In fact, the question today instead concerns the identification of formal conditions for a new realism.

Bruno Bosteels: To what extent does your own itinerary reflect a growing critical distance from this effort of the century? I am thinking in particular about your continuing debts to Maoism. At the height of the Cultural Revolution, the passion for the real was indeed exceptionally strong and often included an extremely violent tendency to purify the revolutionary attitude from all remnants of so-called revisionism – the tendency to annihilate the old and to develop the new. Does your current work on the twentieth century then amount to some kind of self-criticism in this regard? After all, you devote a central chapter in The Century *to the sequence of the Cultural Revolution and you seem to want to re-evaluate the significance of the famous idea that "One divides into two." To what extent does your conception of "subtraction," as opposed tb what you used to call "destruction," offer a genuinely alternative conception of radical innovation, subjective sacrifice, purification, and so on?*

A.B.: If I felt that I needed to make a self-criticism I would make one, but I don't think it's the case. Maoism really was an epic attempt, as Mao himself would have said, to re-launch the subjective process of the revolution. But this re-launching took place within the framework of categories inherited from Leninism and Stalinism, i.e. essentially within a figure of the party-state conceived as the only *formal* figure of power available. The idea of the Cultural Revolution was that the mass dynamics of the revolution were to be re-launched as a process of renovation, reform, and transformation of the party-state. Mao himself, however, observed that this was impossible. There are some texts of Mao's in which he accepts unequivocally that something in the Cultural Revolution did not work. The mobilisation of the masses, among the youth and the workers, was indeed immense. But it destroyed itself through divisions, factions and anarchic violence. The desperate preservation of the party-state framework in the midst of this storm finally led to its restoration in completely reactive conditions (the ubiquitous reintroduction of capitalist methods etc.). This is why we can define the Cultural Revolution as a saturation. It saturates the form of the party-state inherited from Lenin and from the Russian Revolution. The Cultural Revolution was an experiment at the farthest reaches of the truth procedure that had been initiated by the October Revolution.

Perhaps the issue needs to be considered on an even larger scale. The Cultural Revolution was perhaps also the last revolution. Between the October Revolution and the Cultural Revolution, or even between the French Revolution and the Cultural Revolution, there takes place a saturation of the category of revolution as a singular form of the relationship between mass movement and state power.

The word "Revolution" designates an historical form of the relation between politics and the state. This term first of all sets the relation politics/state – or politics/power – in a logic of antagonism, contradiction or civil war. In the second place, it sets this relation in a logic of sublation [*relève*], i.e. it aligns it with the project of a new state that would be entirely different: a revolutionary, republican state, the dictatorship of the proletariat, etc. It's this figure of the sublation of

the state by another state under the decisive pressure of the – popular, mass or class – historical actor which the word "Revolution" designates. Let's say that the Cultural Revolution constitutes the extreme limit of the age of revolutions.[5]

P.H.: And the turn to subtraction, as opposed to destruction, is part of this new, post-revolutionary orientation?

A.B.: For the time being I don't want to accord a metaphysical privilege to subtraction. I call "subtraction" that which, from within the previous sequence itself, as early as the start of the twentieth century, presents itself as a possible alternative path that differs from the dominant one. It's not just an idea that comes "after" antagonism and revolution. It's an idea that is dialectically articulated with those of antagonism, of the simplifying formalisation, of the absolute advent of the new, etc. Malevich's painting, for example, can be interpreted in two different ways. We could say that it expresses a destructive radicalism: starting out from a destruction of all figuration, Malevich allows the purely pictorial to arise in the form of an absolute beginning. But we might also say that, in fact, such painting finds its point of departure in what I've called the minimal difference, the minimal gap – for instance the gap between white and white – and that it draws considerable consequences from the capture of this minimal difference. These two interpretations do not contradict one another. There is something like an ideological decision involved here, one that gives priority to subtraction (or minimal difference) rather than to destruction (or antagonistic contradiction).

Is it really productive, today, to fix the determination of politics within the framework of a global antagonism? Can we, except in a completely abstract way, call upon a massive Two, a Two capable of structuring all situations: bourgeoisie against proletariat, or even republicans against aristocrats? Once again, I do not repudiate any of this, but it seems to me that we are obliged, at least for the moment (I also don't wish to anticipate the course of things), to consider the consequences of that which is given as a local difference, that is, to think and to act on *one* point, or at most a few. For instance, in terms of the organisation of workers without official residency papers [*prolétaires sans papiers*]. Or on the question of Palestine. Or on the "Western" and American aggressions against Serbia, against Afghanistan, against Iraq. And we must construct, on the basis of these points, an adequate political logic, without a preliminary formal guarantee that something like a contradiction within the totality necessarily structures this local differentiation. We can rely only on principles and we can only treat, on the basis of these principles, local situations in such a way as to pursue singular political processes within them. Based on this minimal, local, or punctual differentiation (or as the Lacanians would say, based on this point of the real) you will begin experiments to ascertain if the general system of consequences (that is, the political logic thought in terms of its results) is homogeneous or heterogeneous to the disposition of the state of your situation. Let's call "state logic" that which pretends to convey the meaning of the totality of the situation, and which therefore includes governments and ordinary "political" apparatuses, as well as the economy or legal system.

In Maoism itself there are elements of a subtractive type, if only because the revolutionary history of the liberated zones is different from the history of insurrections. Insurrectionism is the concentration in one point of a global deliberation; it is a certain relationship of the local and the global where you globally force the issue on one point. But, in the history of the Chinese Revolution, insurrectionism failed. The uprisings in Canton or in Shanghai were drowned in blood. The alternative logic proposed by Mao sets out a wholly different relationship between local confrontation and the situation as a whole. This is what Sylvain Lazarus has called the "dialectical" mode of politics. When you find yourself in Yenan for years, with a popular army and an independent administration, you do not stand in a metonymic relation to the global state of things. Yenan does not present the punctual test of strength in which the fate of global confrontation will be decided. You are

somewhere, a place in which you have managed to remain, perhaps a place to which you were eventually obliged to retreat, as in the case of the Long March. You were somewhere else, then you came here, and you have tried to preserve your strength by moving from one point to another. The temporality involved in this movement is not at all that of insurrection. The whole problem is that of endurance. This is what Mao calls "the prolonged war." So the Maoist experiment was different, and I'd say that something in the liberated zones was already rather more "subtractive" than antagonistic in the traditional sense of the term. In particular, I'm thinking of the idea of holding out on one point in such a way as to have the capacity to preserve your forces, without necessarily engaging them immediately in a global confrontation. Much the same could be said regarding Mao's quite remarkable idea of limiting an antagonism [*économiser l'antagonisme*]. Mao often repeated that it is better to treat all contradictions as if they were secondary ones, i.e. contradictions that operate in the midst of the people, rather than between the people and their enemy.

Now I think it's clear that these general ideas continue to exercise a real influence. Every interesting political experience today takes place along these lines. This is also the reason why the "planetary" demonstrations against globalisation, such as the one in Genoa, demonstrations whose model is clearly insurrectional (even if in them the insurrectional schema is considerably weakened), are absolutely archaic and sterile. All the more so to the extent that they congregate around the meetings of their adversary. What's the point of concentrating one's forces, not in the place decided according to the needs of a long-term and independent political strategy, but rather in precisely those places where governments and global banking institutions hold their economico-political ceremonies? Here is another subtractive imperative: never appear where you are most expected. Make sure that your own action is not undertaken on terrain decided by your adversary. It's also the case that the "anti-globalisation" movements dedicate themselves to a systemic and economicist identification of the adversary, which is already utterly misguided.

P.H.: I certainly see the strategic value in such a "guerrilla" approach to politics, one that asks what can be done here and now, with these particular people, these particular resources, etc. But how can we think such an approach together with Marx's basic insight, that each of these individual "points," as you describe them, are indeed structured by global, systematic processes of exploitation or domination?

A.B.: I'm not saying that we cannot think of each point as being determined by the global situation. But when we think of them that way we do nothing to enhance the strategic capacity of the point in question. We need to distinguish here between the analytical view of the situation and its political view. This distinction is of considerable importance. In approaching a singular point, one must always begin with its singularity. This does not mean that singularity is incompatible with a general analysis. However, it's not the general analysis that gives this singular point its political value, but rather the political deployment, experienced as a possibility, of its singularity. Today, for instance, we can always state that the world is polarised, that we should analyse the various manifestations of US sovereignty, the question of wars, the renewed forms of capital, etc. But all this doesn't determine anything effective in the field of politics. In my own philosophical vocabulary, I would say that these analyses are truthful [*véridiques*] but not true [*vraies*]. Consider the example of Chiapas. It's clear that, from the moment when it was constituted, this new arena of political activity could not be derived from any general analysis. If we stick to the general analysis, we can immediately and quite reasonably conclude that this attempt is destined to fail. Exactly in the same way, here in France those who devote themselves to global analysis conclude that it's necessary to participate in elections, that representative democracy must be upheld, because that is what the consensus deems to be the only acceptable space in which to negotiate political relations of force. The conclusion will thus be that any truly independent politics is impossible. *L'Organisation politique*, for example, is impossible.

Objective Marxist analysis is an excellent, even indispensable, practice but it's impossible to develop a politics of emancipation as a consequence of this analysis. Those who do so find themselves on the side of the totality and of its movement, hence on the side of the actually dominant power. To my mind, the "anti-globalisation" movements, or the Italian autonomists who follow the analyses of Toni Negri, for example, are only the most spectacular face of recent adaptations to domination. Their undifferentiated "movementism" integrates smoothly with the necessary adjustments of capital, and in my view does not constitute any really independent political space.

In order to treat a local situation in its political terms, that is, in its subjective terms, something more is needed than simply an understanding of the local derived from the general analysis. The subjectivation of a singular situation cannot be reduced to the idea that this situation is expressive of the totality.

This issue already sets Mao apart from Lenin. Or at least from what Lenin could still believe in abstract terms. When Lenin says that consciousness comes from outside, what he means is that the scientific knowledge of the inclusion of a particular situation in the general situation – in the situation of imperialism as the superior stage of capitalism – *creates* revolutionary consciousness. Today, I don't think (and already Mao and a few others had some insights here) that a reflexive and systematic Marxist analysis of the general distribution of capitalist and imperialist phenomena in the contemporary world constitutes a consciousness that is sufficiently subtracted, precisely, from this distribution.

P.H.: But is there a danger then that you might simply presuppose, in a less explicit way, the criteria that define a political situation, or the circumstances in which political subjectivation can take place? That you effectively treat each such singular point as if shaped by less precise (because less explicit) patterns of domination or inequality, and each mobilisation as inspired by a prescription that in each case is relatively predictable: the militant refusal of domination, or the subjective assertion of political equality?

beyond formalisation

That despite your professed interest in the singularity of a situation, you affirm a conception of political truth which is always formally, fundamentally, the same?

A.B.: For a philosopher, political thinking is always the same and it is always different. On the one hand, it's always the same because it's based on principles. Politics, like all active thought, is axiomatic. It's true that, in my conception of them, these axioms are relatively stable. They are always egalitarian axioms. Notwithstanding this axiomatic stability, in politics you have what we might call directives [*mots d'ordre*], which are singular inventions. The distinction between principles and directives is as essential in politics as the distinction in mathematics between the great axioms of a theory and its particular theorems. The directives express the way in which the principles, which are largely invariable, might become active in a situation. And their activity in the situation is also their transformation; they never simply stay the same. Just as we cannot maintain that the determination of political singularity is transitive to global analysis, it isn't simply transitive to axioms of the will or to strictly egalitarian maxims. I'm neither objectivist nor subjectivist with respect to these questions. In the end, what happens is the constitution of the situation *into a political situation* through the emergence of directives. When these emerge they also give some indication of the political capacity of the people in the situation.

Take the Palestinian situation, for example. We can say that this situation today is clearly defined: it is a colonial situation, perhaps even the last colonial situation. In this sense, it has a particular status: it figures as a sort of summary or consummation of a much larger sequence, the sequence of colonial occupations and the wars of liberation. This is also why the situation is so violent and so exemplary. From the point of view of subjective principles the situation is not especially complex. The axiom in question, in the end, is: "a country and a state for the Palestinians." On the other hand, as things stand today, what are the exact directives for this situation? To my mind this question is far more complicated, and this is one of the reasons for

the relative weakness of the Palestinians. This isn't a criticism (which would be ridiculous), it's an observation. Today, the actual directives that might be capable of really attracting a universal sympathy to the Palestinian cause are precarious or badly formulated. It's in this sense that the situation in Palestine is both a situation that is objectively and subjectively eminent and well-defined [*éminente et constituée*], and at the same time, politically speaking, it is a rather confused and weak situation.

B.B.: *Now that we are talking in terms of objective and subjective conditions, I'd like to ask you about your current understanding of dialectics. It's clear that in* Théorie du sujet *[1982] you maintain a broadly dialectical position, and as late as* Can Politics be Thought? *[1985] you suggest that terms such as "situation," "intervention," "fidelity" and so on, can lead to a renewal of dialectical thought.* Being and Event *[1988], however, seems to abandon or sidestep this tradition in favour of a strictly mathematical approach, even though you continue to speak of a "dialectic" of void and excess. Then again, in what I've had a chance to read of the first chapters of* Logiques des mondes, *you continue to measure your approach alongside, and against, Hegel's* Science of Logic, *in particular against Hegel's understanding of the negative. Through much of* The Century, *finally, your analysis is indebted to what Deleuze called "disjunctive synthesis." Much of the inventive force of the twentieth century would have privileged a type of non-dialectical solution: disjunctive resolutions of the relation, for example, between politics and history, between the subjective and the objective, between beginnings and ends, or between the real and its appearances. So where do you stand vis-à-vis the dialectic now? Would you say that the last century's penchant for disjunctive synthesis indicates a lasting exhaustion of dialectical thought? Or do the failures of the last century suggest that the dialectic is perhaps incomplete, or still unfulfilled, but not in principle over and done with?*

A.B.: That is a major question. You could almost say that my entire enterprise is one giant confrontation [*démêlé*] with the dialectic. That is why sometimes I declare myself a dialectician and write in defence of the great dialecticians (but I mean the French dialecticians,[6] which is not exactly the same as the Hegelian dialectic), while at other times I declare myself an anti-dialectician. You're absolutely right to perceive a certain confusion in this whole business.

First of all, I'd like to say that the nineteenth century was the great century of dialectics, in the ordinary sense of the term. Fundamentally, dialectics means the dialectics of progress. This is already the case with Hegel. In the end, we go towards the Absolute, however long it may take before we get there. And if negation does not exhaust itself, if negativity is creative and is not absorbed into itself, it is because it is pregnant with finality. The question of the labour of the negative is not simply the question of the efficacy of the negative; it is also the question of its *work*, in the sense of an artisan of History. This great nineteenth century dialectical tradition of thought allows us to think a sort of fusion between politics and history. Political subjectivity can feed on historical certainty. We might say – and in any case this has always been my conviction – that *The Communist Manifesto* is the great political text of the nineteenth century. It is the great text of that fundamental historical optimism which foresees, under the name of "communism," the triumph of generic humanity. It's well known that for Marx "proletariat" is the name for the historical agent of this triumph. And I remind you that in my own speculations, "generic" is the property of the True.

What happens at the beginning of the twentieth century? We go from the promise of a reconciliation or emancipation borne by history (which is the Marxist thesis) to the will, animated by the passion of the real, to force the issue, to accelerate the victory of the proletariat. We move to the Leninist idea according to which everything is still carried by history, of course, but where in the end what is decisive is precisely the decision, the organisation and the force of political will. As my friend Sylvain Lazarus has shown, we move from a consciousness organised by history to a consciousness organised by the party.

badiou

In the nineteenth century, both historicism and dialectical thinking (in the Hegelian sense) share a common destiny. Hegel's principal thesis was that "truth is the same as the history of truth," and this thesis endures through any number of materialist reversals and elaborations.

But what are the consequences for dialectics, when we arrive at the moment that recognises the supremacy of the political principle of organisation, the moment that celebrates the party as the source of political truth (a moment that is fully reached only with Stalin)? Which aspects of the dialectic are retained, which aspects are dropped? I think that what is retained is certainly the antagonism, and hence the negativity, but in a purely disjunctive sense: there is conflict, there is violence. What is preserved from history, and from its metaphor, is the figure of war. I'm perfectly prepared to say that Marxism in the twentieth century was, deep down, a Marxism of war, of class warfare. In nineteenth century Marxist thinking, this conception of class warfare was supported by the *general* figure of history. In the twentieth century, what is preserved and stressed is war as such. So what is retained from Hegelian finality, from the Absolute, in war? The idea of the ultimate war, the idea of a final war, a war that in a sense would itself be the Absolute. What happens, in the end, is that the Absolute no longer figures as the outcome of conflict. The Absolute as "goal": nobody has any experience of this, nobody seriously announces that this will come to pass. The Absolute is rather the idea of the final conflict, of the final struggle, very literally. The idea of a decisive war. The twentieth century presented itself to people's minds as the century that would bring the decisive war, the war to end all wars. It's in this sense that I speak of disjunctive synthesis. Instead of a figure of reconciliation, that is, a figure of the Absolute as synthesis, as that which absorbs all previous determinations, we have the presentation of the Absolute itself in the guise of war.

From this point of view I would like to reply to an objection that Bruno has often made to me. Don't I now have too pacified a view of things? Was I right to give up the central place of destruction? I would answer these questions as follows: I think that the idea that war is the absolute of subjectivity is now saturated, it is an idea that no longer has any political intensity. That's all I'm saying. I don't think that implacable conflict is a thing of the past, or that there will be no more wars. It's the idea of the war to end all wars that I criticise, because, in the end, in the field of politics, this idea was the last figure of the One. This idea, the idea of the "final struggle," indicates an inadequate acknowledgement of multiplicity. The ultimate war is the moment when the One takes possession of war, including war within the domain of the state. The Stalinist state was evidently a state of war, a militarised state, and this was also true at its very heart. It is one of the very few states that coldly decided to liquidate half of its military hierarchy. This is war against oneself. Why? Because here, in the end, the only instance of the absolute that one can take hold of is war. Such is the outcome, within dialectical thinking, of the passage from the historicist dialectic to the voluntaristic, partisan or party dialectic: self-immolation in the absolute of destruction.

This tendency, which is related to the intellectual transformations that took place at the beginning of the twentieth century, is not limited to so-called totalitarian politics. We could observe how, in the arts or sciences, there was also a passage from a constructive dialectic, one tied to the history of progress, to a dialectic of experimental immolation [brûlure expérimentale], of disjunction and destruction. This is why, in the end, the outcome of the experiment becomes indifferent. There is something in the century's thinking that says: "the process is more important than the product." In politics, this means that war is really more important than its result, that the class struggle is more important that its product, that the terrorist socialist state is more important than communism (which never arrives). The transition is itself interminable and, as a war-like transition, it is all that matters. We should recall Stalin's thesis, according to which the class struggle intensifies and becomes even more violent under socialism. This means that socialism, which was once anticipated as a peaceful outcome of the violent revolution, becomes in reality only one of several stages of conflict, and an even more violent stage than the previous one.

I think that today we need to learn what politics means in times of peace. Even if this politics is a politics of war. We need to invert the way we think about these questions. We must find a way to subordinate the politics of war to a subtractive understanding of politics, i.e. a politics that has no guarantee either in history or in the state. How can we understand emancipatory politics in terms other than those of the absolute of war? Mao, more than any other political thinker, was a military leader. Nevertheless Mao already sought to subordinate the absolute of war to something else. He considered that the principal tasks of the people's army were political. We too are experimenting with a politics that would not be entirely implicated with the question of power. Because it is the struggle for power that ends up leading revolutionaries to the absolutisation of war. What does it mean to construct, preserve and deploy one's forces, what does it mean to hold firm on one point, in the domain of peace? This is our main question, so long as no one forgets that when it's necessary to fight, we'll fight. You don't always have the choice.

P.H.: To what extent does your distance from dialectics, your determination to pursue a wholly affirmative conception of thought, push you towards an ultimately abstract conception of truth, or at least one whose subjective integrity is largely detached from the objective or concrete circumstances of its situation? In other words, just how radical is the process of subtraction? A thinker like Foucault (himself hardly a disciple of Hegel) works insistently towards an evacuation of all the things that fix or determine or specify the way people think or act in a situation, precisely by paying close attention to what he called the "microscopic" processes of its regulation or specification. By comparison, your conception of politics seems to leave very little scope for a dialectical relation with the historical or the social dimension.

A.B.: Abstraction is the foundation of all thought. However, the procedures of truth should not be reduced to abstraction. Yes, we start with the affirmation of a principle, with an axiomatic proposition. But the whole question is to know how and at what moment the axiom becomes the directive of a situation. It can do so only if something from the situation itself passes into it. It's obvious that a demand, for example, for the "unconditional regularisation of all workers without residency papers [*ouvriers sans-papiers*]" implies the existence of workers without papers, the pertinence of the question of their papers, the effect of certain governmental policies, etc. Above all, it's necessary that the *sans-papiers* themselves speak out about the situation, that they speak about it politically and not just by bearing witness to their own misery or misfortune. (It's time we recognised, by the way, that in politics misfortune does not exist.)

As for Foucault, I think that he completely underestimates the importance of separation [*la séparation*]. Among his disciples this tendency only gets worse. If there is now a convergence between "Foucauldianism" and "Negrism," if Agamben relies on Foucault, etc., it's because they all share the philosophical axiom that resistance is only the obverse of power. Resistance is coextensive with power itself. In particular, you begin thinking politics through consideration of the forms of power. I think that this is completely wrong. If you enter politics by thinking the forms of power then you will always end up with the state (in the general sense of the word) as your referent. Even the famous "multitudes," which is only a pedantic word for mass movements (and in particular petit-bourgeois mass movements) are thought as "constituent" *with regard* to domination. All this is only a historicism painted in fashionable hues. It's striking, moreover, that, besides Foucault, the philosophical sources for the "Negrist" current are to be found on the side of Spinoza and Deleuze. Both these thinkers are hostile to any form of the Two: they propose a metaphysical politics, a politics of the One, or what for me is a politics of the One. This is an anti-dialectical politics in the precise sense that it excludes negativity, and thus, in the end, the domain of the subject, or what for me is the subject. I am entirely opposed to the thesis according to which it is presumed possible, merely by isolating

(within the orbit of domination and control) that which has a constituent value, to create a space of liberty cut from the same cloth as that of the existing powers themselves. That which goes by the name "resistance," in this instance, is only a component of the progress of power itself. In its current form, the anti-globalisation movement is nothing other than a somewhat wild operator (and not even that wild, after all) of capitalist globalisation itself. In any case, it's not at all heterogeneous to it. It seeks to sketch out, for the imminent future, the new forms of comfort to be enjoyed by our planet's idle petite bourgeoisie.

B.B.: We were talking about some themes in Michael Hardt and Toni Negri's Empire *a few days ago. The most important of these is the reversibility between power and resistance, or between Empire and multitude – both appearing as a bloc, in a global and no doubt much too structural way, in a relation of immanent and thus anti-dialectical reciprocity. However, this relation of immanence explains that, in some way, Empire also always already means the power of the multitude. This imposes, then, merely a certain reading strategy, and perhaps it doesn't even allow for anything else. We remain, therefore, in spite of everything, in an interpretive, even hermeneutic approach. You've already analysed this in your book on Deleuze, in terms of the doctrine of the "double signature": every thing, for Deleuze, can be read both as an entity and in some sense as signalling being itself. With Negri and Hardt, this double signature is deployed in political terms. In an extremely seductive manner, especially for our times, dominated as they are by the homogeneity with no escape from the laws of the market and of war, it then becomes possible to read even a most brutal instance of domination by way of a sign of the very thing it represses, that is, the creativity and effervescence of the pure multitude, which for them in the end is nothing but the political, or politico-ontological name for Life. Is this how you would reply to the theses expounded in* Empire *by Hardt and Negri? Aren't there more profound affinities, for example, with your* On Metapolitics *[1998]?*

125

beyond formalisation

A.B.: In *The Communist Manifesto*, Marx already praised capitalism in an ambivalent way, based on a double reading. On the one hand, capitalism destroys all the moth-eaten figures of the old world, all the old feudal and sacred bonds.[7] In this sense, it is the violent creator of a new leverage point for generic humanity. On the other hand, the bourgeoisie is already organised in such a way as to maintain its domination; in this sense, it is the designated enemy of a new creative cycle, whose agent is the proletariat. Negri and his friends are desperately looking to re-establish this inaugural vision, in which the "multitudes" are both the result of capitalist atomisation and the new creative initiator of a "horizontal" modernity (networks, transversalities, "non-organisations," etc.). But all this amounts only to dreamy hallucination [*une rêverie hallucinée*]. Where is this "creative" capacity of the multitudes? All we've seen are very ordinary performances from the well-worn repertoire of petit-bourgeois mass movements, noisily laying claim to the right to enjoy without doing anything, while taking special care to avoid any form of discipline. Whereas we know that discipline, in all fields, is the key to truths. Without the least hesitation Marx would have recognised in Negri a backward romantic. I believe that deep down, what truly fascinates these "movementists" is capitalist activity itself, its flexibility and also its violence. They designate by "multitude" flexibility of a comparable sort, a predicate which their fictions attribute to "social movements." But today there is nothing to be gained from the category of movement. This is because this category is itself coupled to the logic of the state. It is the task of politics to construct new forms of discipline to replace the discipline of political parties, which are now saturated.

P.H.: Nevertheless, one of Foucault's fundamental ideas was precisely that the localisation of a possible break is always ramified, that it cannot be concentrated in a singular and exclusive point. In order adequately to think one such point – injustice in prisons, for example – you need to treat it precisely as an over-determined instance within a wider network. In this specific case, it's obviously a matter of understanding that the operation of punitive or disciplinary power is located, not only in this point which is the instance of the prison as such (itself a point that, as you well know, Foucault treated for some time in as "punctual," as focused, and as militant a fashion as you could wish for), but also in the general configuration of power at issue in the organisation of work, the education of children, the surveillance of public health, sexuality, etc. And he says this not so as to lose himself in the complexity of the network but, on the contrary, in order to analyse it in detail, to understand its effects, the better to clarify and undo it – and therefore very much in order to keep himself, to borrow from your vocabulary, at a distance from the normalising effects of power (since, unlike Deleuze, Foucault did not believe that you could ever escape absolutely from the networks of power). For example, I think that when you treat the question of the sans-papiers by considering the question of immigration along with the question of the organisation of work, you are in fact being quite faithful to Foucault.

A.B.: But the actual content of the political statements made by those who claim to be following in Foucault's footsteps does not localise this break [*la coupure*] anywhere. Of course, a given situation must be envisaged within an open space. There is a topology of situations, to which Foucault himself made important contributions. But in the end you need to find a way of crystallising the political break into differentiated statements. And these statements must concentrate the political rupture upon a single point. It is these statements or directives that are the bearers of discipline, in the sense that politics is nothing other than the constitution of the power of statements and the public exploration of their consequences. Now, "power" and "consequences" mean organisation, perseverance, unity and discipline. In politics, and likewise in art and in the sciences. It seems to me that the people I'm criticising here – let us call them the third generation of Foucauldians – abhor every crystallisation, and retreat to the idea that creative power will be "expressed" in the free unfolding of the multitudes. On this point, the organised logic of power is opposed to the expressive logic of power. Or perhaps you might say that axiomatic thought is opposed to descriptive thought. Plato against Aristotle.

P.H.: Can we move on now to look more closely at the way you propose to understand the "Images of the Present Time," to borrow the title of your current lecture series at the Collège International de la Philosophie? Has this new three-year series picked up where the previous series on the twentieth century left off?

A.B.: The lectures on the twentieth century aroused considerable interest. I decided that it was worth continuing the project by angling it towards the present time. Can we think the *present* philosophically? Can we reply to Hegel, who argued that philosophy always comes after the fact, that it recapitulates in the concept that which has already taken place?

For the moment, I'm guided by two main ideas. The first is that, in order to think the contemporary world in any fundamental way, it's necessary to take as your point of departure not the critique of capitalism but the critique of democracy. To separate thought from the dominant forms of ideology has always been one of philosophy's crucial tasks. Philosophy is useless if it doesn't allow us to criticise consensual and falsely self-evident ideas. Today it's easy to see that the consensual category is not at all that of liberal economics. In fact, lots of people are perfectly happy to criticise what Viviane Forrester, in a superficial and successful book, referred to as "the economic horror."[8] We are constantly being reminded of the cynicism of stock markets, the devastation of the planet, the famine in Africa, and so on. At the same time, this denunciation is in my view completely ineffective, precisely because it is an economico-objectivist one. The denunciation of objective mechanisms leads at best to reformist proposals of an entirely illusory nature. By contrast, no one is ready to criticise democracy. This is a real taboo, a genuine consensual fetish. Everywhere in the world, democracy is the true subjective principle – the rallying point – of liberal capital-

ism. So my first idea was to think about the role of the word "democracy" in the framework of a functional analysis: what exactly is its function, where is it situated, how does it operate as subjective fetish, etc. I've incorporated within this aspect of the project a careful re-reading of Plato's critique of democracy.

The second idea is the obverse of the first. It's a matter of identifying what I call contemporary nihilism; in other words, today's ordinary regime of subjectivity. I say that an ordinary subject, today, is nothing but a body facing the market. Who is the citizen of the market? This is a necessarily nihilistic figure, but it's a singular nihilism, a nihilism of enjoyment.

In the end, the goal is to clarify the coupling of nihilism and democracy as a politico-subjective configuration of the present time. Speaking in the terms of *Being and Event*, you could say that this coupling constitutes the "encyclopaedia" of the present time. It's what organises its regime of production, its institutions, its system of judgement and naming, its validations and counter-validations. Today, truth procedures involve finding a passage – which is always local, difficult, but creative – through the encyclopaedic coupling of democracy and nihilism.

Today's truth procedures will figure as "authoritarian" (because they must exceed democratic consensus) and affirmative (because they must exceed nihilistic subjectivity). This correlation of affirmation and authority is a particular characteristic of the present moment, because the encyclopaedia of this present is democratico-nihilistic. There have been times when things were different, of course, for example times in which nihilism figured as part of the cross to be borne by those who sought to proclaim a truth. This was the case, for example, during the end of the nineteenth century.

P.H.: Could you give us some examples of today's truth procedures?

A.B.: This is my project for next year: to identify the sequences that escape from the democratico-nihilistic encyclopaedia. For example, it's from this angle that I read your work on post-colonial literature.[9] I read it and ask myself: isn't there something here that anticipates, as a result of the postcolonial situation, something pertaining to affirmation and authority? And I think that other artistic examples can be found, in a certain return to musical constructivism, in the tentative experiments of contemporary writers trying to get past postmodernism, in the way some painters are now abandoning the formalism of the non-figurative, etc. I'm also very struck by the great debate in contemporary physics that sets those pursuing the axiomatic renewal of physics on the basis of a generalised doctrine of scalar transformations (and therefore an even more generalised relativity than the currently available version) against those who defend a configuration cobbled together from developments in quantum mechanics (a configuration which is extraordinarily sophisticated, but nonetheless trapped in a hopeless empiricism).

B.B.: Did your work on anti-philosophy – your lectures on Nietzsche, Wittgenstein, Lacan and Saint Paul, among others – prepare the ground for this analysis of our contemporary nihilism? Are anti-philosophy and nihilism part of the same configuration? What precise role does anti-philosophy play in the organisation of today's nihilism, as you describe it?

A.B.: The analysis of what I called anti-philosophy offered a sort of genealogy of this nihilism's dominant operators [*opérateurs*]. Although you certainly couldn't say that Lacan was a nihilist, and still less a democrat (in fact, you couldn't call Wittgenstein a democrat either, to say nothing of Nietzsche who was an overt anti-democrat), I nevertheless think that these anti-philosophers anticipated a fundamental trait of contemporary nihilism, namely the thesis that in the last instance there is nothing but bodies and language. I equate contemporary nihilism with a certain position of the body – in this sense, our nihilism is all the more in so far as it presents itself in the guise of a materialism. Such would be the materialism of democratic multiplicity, which is nothing but the multiplicity of bodies. Spinoza already proposed systematic arguments that work along these lines, which you still find among the theoreticians of the multi-

tude – even in Balibar. Everyone believes that the starting point is the multiplicity of bodies. We might say that this idea – that there is nothing but bodies and language – traverses all of contemporary anti-philosophy. Ever since Nietzsche, contemporary anti-philosophy wishes to have done with Platonism. But what is Platonism? Fundamentally, and this is why I always declare myself a Platonist, Platonism says that there is something other than bodies and language. There are truths, and a truth is neither a singular body (since it is generic) nor a phrase (since it punches a hole in the encyclopaedia of the situation).

The critical examination of anti-philosophy is already the examination of those who maintain that there is nothing but language and bodies. What I want to show is that, beneath its materialist surface, this thesis does nothing but prepare the way for the contemporary consensus, the democratico-nihilistic consensus. This is why in my seminar I presented a reading of Pierre Guyotat, in particular of the *Tombeau pour cinq cent mille soldats*.[10] Guyotat is the most radical writer of an atomistic vision of bodies. In the real [*réel*] of colonial war there is nothing but bodies and between these bodies there is only sexual attraction, which operates like a sort of deathly consumption. The only relief to be found in this universe is in linguistic sublimation. Let's say that for Guyotat, all there is are sexed bodies and the poem. Incidentally, this is precisely Lucretius' position, at least in the version that Jean-Claude Milner and Guy Lardreau are today trying to revitalise, the first explicitly against Plato (and against me), the other by cobbling together a "materialist" Plato (precisely in the sense of our nihilistic materialism).

Now it is indeed absolutely necessary to maintain that there is nothing but language and bodies if one wants subjects to be subjects of the market. Such a subject is someone who identifies him- or herself as a consumer, someone exposed to the market. The consumer can be rich or poor, accomplished or clumsy – it doesn't matter. The essential thing is that everybody stands before the market, whether or not one resents it or assents to it. But you can only reach this point and hold this position in so far as you are essentially a desiring body summoned by the general language of advertisement. The consumer is a body of (nihilistic) enjoyment submitted to a (democratic) linguistic injunction. The only obstacle to this injunction is the Idea, the intractable element of a truth. This is why the only truth of the pseudo-materialist thesis "there is nothing but bodies and language" lies in the presumption that every idea is useless. When all is said and done, the democratic imperative becomes: "Live without any Idea." Or if you prefer: "Buy your enjoyment."

P.H.: I'd like to conclude with some questions about the changes to your general system proposed in your forthcoming Logiques des mondes. Being and Event *obviously dealt with the question of being, among other things; with* Logiques des mondes *you are moving on to the question of appearing and appearance.[11] What is the relation between the one and the other? What is the relationship between being and what you present in terms of being-there?*

A.B.: We should start from the way *Being and Event* sets out its most basic category, the category of situation. In *Being and Event* there are two fundamental theses regarding being-as-being. First thesis: being is pure multiplicity, and so the science of being is mathematics, mathematics as they have developed over the course of history. Second thesis: a multiplicity is always presented in a situation. The concept of situation is designed to think being-as-being not only in its internal composition as pure multiplicity but also as having to be presented as the element of a multiplicity. The fundamental operator in the ontology of the multiple is *belonging* – $A \in B$, which reads "A belongs to B." Obviously this operator cannot be symmetrical (it does not have the same sense for A as it does for B). Multiplicity can be thought either as a constitutive element of another multiplicity, or else as a collecting together of other multiplicities (as its elements). This distinction does not have any great philosophical importance in *Being and Event* because that book remains on a very formal level. The only thing that needed to be axiomatised, via the axiom of foundation,

was the rule which ensures that the situation can never be an element of itself.

The question then of how we should think this particular dimension of being-as-being – the fact that being-as-being can be deployed as truth only to the extent that it belongs to a situation – remains absolutely open. It's this obligation to belong to a situation, the fact that every multiple-being must be localised, that I have decided to call "being-there." By treating such localisations as "worlds," what I'm trying to propose is a way of thinking being-there.

So – and now I'm getting to your question – it's clear that you cannot pass directly from being-as-being to being-there. Were I to pass from the one to the other by rational deduction I would simply be engaged in a reconstruction of Hegelianism. I would be drawing a figure of being-there directly from the being of multiplicity. Against this Hegelian inspiration, I assume the contingency of being-there. But, at the same time, I defend a variant of the thesis according to which it is of the essence of being to be-there. The two statements must be asserted together: being-there (or belonging to a world) pertains to the essence of being, but being-there cannot be drawn out or inferred from the essence of being. Every being is presented in a world, but no singular world can be drawn out from the system of multiplicities of which it is composed. It remains impossible to deduce the singularity of a world. But we can and must examine the conditions of possibility of being-there, the logic of worlds. The approach is more phenomenological, or critical, than is that of pure ontology. I'm trying to describe the laws under which appearance can be thought.

P.H.: If it's not possible to move smoothly from the one to the other, are there then two irreducibly distinct operations at work here? First, a being (or a multiplicity) is in so far as it belongs to another multiplicity, i.e. in so far as it is presented in a situation or set. And second, this same being then appears *in so far as it appears as part of a world (which is obviously a much larger notion than a set). Or do these two actions, belonging and appearing, overlap in some other sense?*

beyond formalisation

A.B.: With Hegel, I assume that it's of the essence of being to be there, and therefore that there is an intrinsic dimension of being that is engaged within appearance; but at the same time there is a contingency to this appearance, to this being-there-in-a-world. Our only access to being is in the form of being-there. Even when we think being-as-being in the field of mathematics we must recall that historically constituted mathematics is itself a world, and therefore a dimension of being-there. I hold absolutely to the thesis that figures expressly in *Being and Event*, that ontology is a situation. We can therefore say the following: *there are* only worlds [*il n'y a que des mondes*]. So what is a world? This is the question with which the book is concerned, at least in its first movement.

P.H.: One of the arguments that can be made against Being and Event *is that you simplify the actual mechanics of domination and specification – the mechanics conceived, for instance, in terms of hegemony by Gramsci, and in terms of power by Foucault – by referring them back to a single operation, the re-presentation performed by the state. Might a comparable argument be made against* Logiques des mondes, *that you now refer everything back to what you call the transcendental regime [*le transcendental*] of a world, which determines the relative intensity with which different things appear in a world? Isn't the whole question one of distinguishing and analysing the various processes that shape this transcendental regime? I can easily see the descriptive value of such an operator, but its explanatory value is less obvious.*

A.B.: Strictly speaking, the transcendental regime cannot be reduced to the measurement of degrees of intensity of appearance, even if these degrees constitute the basis for the ordering of appearance. The transcendental regime includes singular operations, like the conjunction or the envelope, along with immanent topologies, like the theory of points etc. The transcendental regime will account for two things that are formally essential. First, what does it mean to say that two entities appearing in a given world have

something in common? Second, how does it happen that a region of the world possesses a certain consistency? And what is this consistency? I answer these questions by means of what I believe to be a quite original theory of objects. This theory is not exclusively descriptive, it also accounts for *why* there is an object. That is, it accounts for why and how the One comes to be in the domain of appearance [*pourquoi et comment y-a-t-il de l'Un dans l'apparaître*]. This is why, in this book, I equate the laws of appearance with a logic. What is at stake is thinking consistency in general, the consistency of all that appears.

P.H.: What is the precise role that relation plays in your new conception of things? In Being and Event *you effectively exclude relations from the domain of being, or presentation, and tend to consider them exclusively from the perspective of the state, or of re-presentation.*

A.B.: Relation is defined very precisely in the *Logiques des mondes*. In pure being, there is only the multiple, and therefore relation is not [*la relation n'est pas*]. In the domain of appearing, on the contrary, there is relation, precisely in the sense that there is existence. I make a distinction between being and existence, inasmuch as existence is being in its specific intensity of appearing, being such as it appears "there," in *a* world. Relation is not between two beings, but relation exists between two existents. It is a fact of the world and not a fact of being.

P.H.: And what happens then when an event takes place? Does an event suspend the prevailing rules that govern the way things appear in a world?

A.B.: This is precisely the question I'm working on at the moment. I would like the theory of the event to be at once logical and ontological. I would like to maintain, if at all possible, the essential aspects of the ontological definition of the event. The essence of this definition is that the event is an un-founded multiplicity: it does not obey the axiom of foundation, because it is its own element, it belongs to itself. This is why, in *Being and Event*, I said that the event is an "ultra-One." I would also like to retain the theory of the event-site [*site événementiel*]: the event in some sense is always a surging forth of the site, or an insurrection of the site, which for a moment comes to belong to itself. But I would also like to introduce the idea that the event is a deregulation of the logic of the world, a transcendental dysfunction. An event modifies the rules of appearance. How? This is empirically attested by every genuine event: something whose value within the world was null or very weak attains, all of a sudden, in the event, a strong or even maximal intensity of existence. Within appearance, the core of the question of the event is really summed up by the idea that "we are nothing, let us be everything" (in the words of the *Internationale*). An element that prior to the event was indifferent, or even nonexistent, which did not appear, comes to appear. An existence – the political existence of the workers, for example – that the transcendental regime had measured as minimal, that was null from the vantage point of the world, all of a sudden turns out to have a maximal intensity. Therefore the event will conserve its ontological character as a surging forth of the site in a moment of self-belonging [*auto-appartenance*] and, at the same time, it will produce a brutal transformation of the regime of intensity, so as to allow that which was inexistent to come into existence.

P.H.: Will an event figure as maximally intense within the existing limits of its world, or will it appear above and beyond the pre-established maximum level of intensity?

A.B.: These are complicated technical details that to my mind do not really have important consequences. If *an* element finds itself absolutely modified in its transcendental degree of existence, then slowly but surely the transcendental regime in its entirety will no longer be able to maintain its rules. Everything will change: the comparisons of intensity in appearance, the existences involved, the possibility of relations, etc. There will be a rearrangement of the transcendental regime, and therefore, strictly speaking, a change of world.

The truth procedure itself will also receive a double status. I certainly aim to conserve its status as a generic production, its horizon of genericity. But, on the other hand, it will proceed to reconstruct – locally, to begin with – the whole set of rules by which things appear, in keeping with the fact that something that previously did not appear now must appear. Something that was invisible must now become visible. Therefore, a truth procedure will also consist in a rearrangement of transcendental correlations, around this passage from inexistence to existence. In particular, given that every object possesses its own inexistent aspect [*un inexistant propre*], if this inexistent aspect acquires a maximal value then another element will have to take its place. All of a sudden, the question of destruction reappears, ineluctably. It's in this sense that I hope to satisfy our friend Bruno with a synthesis of *Théorie du sujet* and *Being and Event*. I am obliged here to reintroduce the theme of destruction, whereas in *Being and Event* I thought I could make do with supplementation alone. In order for that which does not appear in a world suddenly to appear within it (and appear, most often, with the maximal value of appearance), there is a price to pay. Something else must disappear. In other words, something must die, or at least must die to the world in question.

For example, the moment that something like the proletariat comes to exist within politics, it is indeed necessary to accept the fact that something which prior to this irruption possessed prestige and intensity finds itself annulled or denied – for example, aristocratic values, bourgeois authority, the family, private property, etc. And by the same token, it's this element of new existential intensity – the proletariat – which will now mark all possible political subjectivities, at least for the duration of a certain sequence. Proletarian politics will be defined as that form of politics which assumes, or even produces, the consequences of this modification of intensity. Reactive politics, on the other hand, will be that which acts as if the old transcendental circumstances had themselves produced the consequences in question, as if the existential upsurge of the proletariat was of no consequence whatsoever.

In order to think through all of this, I will need a general theory of change in the domain of appearing. You will see that I distinguish between four types of change: modifications (which are consistent with the existing transcendental regime), weak singularities (or novelties with no strong existential consequences), strong singularities (which imply an important existential change but whose consequences remain measurable) and, finally, events (strong singularities whose consequences are virtually infinite).

B.B.: In your seminar dealing with the "The Axiomatic Theory of the Subject,"[12] you also anticipate a whole segment of Logiques des mondes *that will present a typology of various subjective figures, adding the reactive and obscure figures to that of fidelity, which was the only one considered in* Being and Event. *Concretely, what will be the consequences of this new configuration of things for your theory of the subject?*

A.B.: In *Being and Event* the theory of the subject is reduced to its name, in other words the subject is absolutely nothing more than the local dimension of a truth, a point of truth. Inasmuch as there is an active element to the subject it is to be found entirely in the process of forcing, as you yourself demonstrated in your contribution to the Bordeaux conference.[13] In *Logiques des mondes*, the fundamental notion of *consequence* is introduced – since we are in the realm of the transcendental, or of logic, we can give a rigorous meaning to the operator of consequence. But it will be necessary to locate differentially the subject within a wider virtuality, which I call the subjective space. It's not at all as it was in *Being and Event*, where all that's described is the truth procedure, where the subject is nothing but a finite fragment of this procedure. It was, I must admit, a compromise with modern notions concerning the finitude of human subjects, notions which I nevertheless try to oppose whenever I get the chance. Bruno made this objection, to which I am quite sensitive, very early on. All

in all, in *Being and Event* the subject is defined as a finite instance of the infinity of the True. What this means, in the end, is that one can only enter into the space of the subject as finite, under axioms of finitude, which is by no means a satisfactory solution.

Hegel's position has some advantages here. He maintains the possibility that the subject dialecticises the infinite in an immanent way; this constitutes the genuine theme of absolute knowledge. Leaving the anecdote about the end of history to one side, what's true in absolute knowledge is the idea that the finite can hold the infinite, that it's possible for the finite and the infinite not to figure as essentially disconnected. This was not exactly the case in *Being and Event*, where it's said rather that the infinite carries or bears the finite, that a truth carries the subject. We come back here to the question of dialectics: I'd like to develop a new dialectic, one that accepts that the distribution of truth and subject need not coincide with the distribution of infinite and finite.

My argument therefore is as follows. I demonstrate that the subject is identified by a type of marking, a post-eventral effect, whose system of operations is infinite. In other words, subjective capacity really is infinite, once the subject is constituted under the mark of the event. Why? Because subjective capacity amounts to drawing the consequences of a change, of a new situation, and if this change is eventral [*événementiel*] then its consequences are infinite.

In *Being and Event*, subjectivation ultimately fades away no less than does the event. Its status remains somewhat indeterminate, outside the thematics of the name of the event. But as Lyotard asked me from the beginning: isn't the naming of the event itself already fundamentally a form of subjectivation? And isn't there then a second subjectivation that is under the condition of the name fixed by the first subjectivation? Isn't the subject, as is often the case in philosophy, thereby presupposed by its very constitution?

I think that in my new arrangement the infinite capacity of subjects can be maintained in an immanent fashion, because the notion of consequence will be constantly bound to the subject him- or herself: this subject will need to have been specifically marked by the event in order really to participate in the labour of its consequences.

P.H.: What will the consequences of this be for your somewhat problematic theory of the unnameable?

A.B.: It's quite possible that the category of the unnameable may prove irrelevant. The theory of appearance provides all by itself the guarantee that every object of a world is marked (in its multiple composition) by an inexistent term. Since an event produces the intensification of an inexistence, at the cost of an inevitable price to be paid in terms of destruction, there is no need to limit the effects of this intensification. Once a price has been paid in the domain of the inexistent one cannot act as if this price has not indeed been paid. Disaster will no longer consist in wanting to name the unnameable at all costs, but rather in claiming that one can make something pass from inexistence to existence, in a given world, without paying any price. Ethics will consist instead in the assumption and evaluation of this price. In sum, I'm coming back to the maxim of the Chinese communists during the Cultural Revolution: "no construction without destruction." Ethics consists in applying this maxim with clarity, and with moderation. Of everything that comes into existence or comes to be constructed, we must ask: does it possess a universal value that might justify the particular destruction which its coming into existence demands?

P.H.: Can you describe how this might work more precisely? In the case of love, for instance, whose unnameable aspect was sexual pleasure: in what sense is such pleasure now directly accessible to the subject of love? And at what price, precisely?

A.B.: I'm not saying that the inexistent will take the place of the unnameable. I'm not saying that sexual desire will become inexistent. The perspective is a different one. The unnameable testified to a point, within the general field in

question, that remained inaccessible to the positivity of the true. These points of opacity, these resistances to the forcing of forms of knowledge, will always exist. But "unnameable" is not the right word. I've already done away with the moment of the naming of the event. In the procedure of love, it may happen that one is unable to draw all the consequences implied by an encounter (in such a way that the sexual factor might be entirely absorbed in these consequences). This does not mean that the sexual is unnameable. We are no longer in the logic of *names*, but in a logic of *consequences*. We will simply say that there are some things that are inconsequential, that some things do not enter into the field of consequences.

P.H.: Does a subject no longer run the risk, then, of perverting or totalising a truth, as you suggest in Ethics *[1993]?*

A.B.: The risk does not disappear. But it's no longer of the order of a forced nomination. Basically, by recognising the quasi-ontological category of the unnameable, I made concessions to the pervasive moralism of the 1980s and 1990s. I made concessions to the obsessive omnipresence of the problem of Evil. I no longer feel obliged to make such concessions. But neither do I wish to give up on the general idea of an ethic of truths. What corrupts a subject is the process of treating as a possible consequence of an event something that is not in fact a consequence. In brief, it's a matter of logical arrogance. For there's no reason why the possible consequences of a new intensity of existence should be identical to the totality of the world. To be honest, I have yet to work out these ethical questions in detail. The general idea is to substitute, for the overly moralising idea of a totality marked by an unnameable point, the idea (which is far more closely linked to the concrete practices of truth) of a field of consequences whose logic must be both reconstructed and respected. I'll be taking up these difficult questions in the final chapter of the *Logiques des mondes*.

notes

1 This interview was conducted by Bruno Bosteels and Peter Hallward in Paris on 2 July 2002.

2 Badiou, *Le Siècle/The Century* (2004).

3 *Epuration* means both purification and purging. [Translator's note.]

4 See Hallward, *Badiou: A Subject to Truth* (Minneapolis: U of Minnesota P, 2003) chapter 13.

5 For a more detailed account of Badiou's recent interpretation of the Cultural Revolution see his pamphlet *La Révolution culturelle: la dernière révolution?* (2002). [Translator's note.]

6 Badiou is referring here to a group of thinkers made up of Pascal, Rousseau, Mallarmé and Lacan. See his "Généaologie de la dialectique" in *Peut-on penser la politique?* 84–91. [Translator's note.]

7 Cf. Marx and Engels, *The Communist Manifesto*, trans. Samuel Moore (Harmondsworth: Penguin, 1967) 82.

8 Viviane Forrester, *L'Horreur économique* (Paris: Fayard, 1996).

9 Peter Hallward, *Absolutely Postcolonial: Writing between the Singular and the Specific* (Manchester: Manchester UP, 2001).

10 Pierre Guyotat, *Tombeau pour cinq cent mille soldats* (Paris: Gallimard, 1967); *Tomb for 500,000 Soldiers*, trans. Romain Slocombe (London: Creation, 2003).

11 The verb that Badiou always uses in this context, *apparaître* (to appear), is usually better translated as a noun (appearance, appearing); the most natural rendering is often "the domain of appearing." [Translator's note.]

12 Badiou's seminar at the Collège International de Philosophie was entitled, in the years from 1996 to 1998, *Théorie axiomatique du sujet*; the substance of this seminar will be incorporated into *Logiques des mondes*. [Translator's note.]

13 Badiou is referring to the conference on his work held in Bordeaux in October 1999. See Bruno Bosteels, "Vérité et forçage: Badiou avec Heidegger et Lacan" in *Alain Badiou: penser le multiple*, ed. Charles Ramond (Paris: L'Harmattan, 2002) 259–93. [Translator's note.]

works by badiou

Almagestes [novel]. Paris: Seuil, 1964.

"L'Autonomie du processus historique." *Cahiers Marxistes–Léninistes* 12/13 (1966): 77–89.

Portulans [novel]. Paris: Seuil, 1967.

"Le (Re)commencement du matérialisme dialectique." [Review of Althusser, *Pour Marx* and *Lire le Capital*.] *Critique* 240 (May 1967): 438–67.

"La Subversion infinitésimale." *Cahiers pour L'Analyse* 9 (1968): 118–37.

"Marque et manque: à propos du zéro." *Cahiers pour L'Analyse* 10 (1969): 150–73.

Le Concept de modèle. Introduction à une épistémologie matérialiste des mathématiques. Paris: Maspéro, 1972.

Théorie de la contradiction. Paris: Maspéro, 1975.

De l'idéologie. Paris: Maspéro, 1976.

L'Echarpe rouge [romanopéra]. Paris: Maspero, 1979.

Jean-Paul Sartre [pamphlet]. Paris: Potemkine, 1981.

Théorie du sujet. Paris: Seuil, 1982.

Peut-on penser la politique? Paris: Seuil, 1985. *Can Politics be Thought?* Trans. Bruno Bosteels. Durham, NC: Duke UP, 2004.

L'Etre et l'événement. Paris: Seuil, 1988. *Being and Event*. Trans. Oliver Feltham. London: Athlone, 2004.

"Dix-neuf réponses à beaucoup plus d''objections." *Cahiers du Collège Internationale de Philosophie* 8 (1989): 247–68.

Manifeste pour la philosophie. Paris: Seuil, 1989. *Manifesto for Philosophy*. Trans. Norman Madarasz. Albany: State U of New York P, 1999.

"D'un sujet enfin sans objet." *Cahiers Confrontations* 20 (1989): 13–22. "On a Finally Objectless Subject." Trans. Bruce Fink. *Who Comes after the Subject?* Ed. Eduardo Cadava et al. London: Routledge, 1991. 24–32.

"L'Entretien de Bruxelles." *Les Temps Modernes* 526 (1990): 1–26.

"Gilles Deleuze, *Le Pli: Leibniz et le baroque*" [Review essay]. *Annuaire philosophique 1988–1989*.

Paris: Seuil, 1990. 161–84. "Gilles Deleuze, *The Fold: Leibniz and the Baroque*." Trans. Thelma Sowley. *Gilles Deleuze: The Theatre of Philosophy*. Ed. Constantin Boundas and Dorothea Olkowski. New York: Columbia UP, 1994. 51–69.

Le Nombre et les nombres. Paris: Seuil, 1990.

Rhapsodie pour le théâtre. Paris: Le Spectateur français, 1990.

"Saisissement, dessaisie, fidélité" [on Sartre]. *Les Temps modernes* 531–533 (1990, 2 vols.). Vol. 1: 14–22.

D'un désastre obscur (droit, etat, politique). Paris: L'Aube, 1991. *Of an Obscure Disaster: On the End of the Truth of State*. Trans. Barbara P. Fulks. *lacanian ink* 22 (autumn 2003).

"L'Etre, l'événement et la militance." Interview conducted by Nicole-Edith Thévenin. *Futur Antérieur* 8 (1991): 13–23.

"L'Age des poètes." *La Politique des poètes. Pourquoi des poètes en temps de détresse*. Ed. Jacques Rancière. Paris: Albin Michel, 1992. 21–38.

Casser en deux l'histoire du monde? [Pamphlet on Nietzsche.] Paris: Le Perroquet, 1992.

Conditions. Paris: Seuil, 1992. Two chapters ("The (Re)turn of Philosophy *Itself*" and "Definition of Philosophy") are included in Madarasz's translation of the *Manifesto for Philosophy* (Albany: State U of New York P, 1999). Two other chapters ("Psychoanalysis and Philosophy" and "What is Love?") appeared in *Umbr(a)* 1 (Buffalo: State U of New York, 1996). "Philosophy and Art" and "Definition of Philosophy" are included in *Infinite Thought: Truth and the Return of Philosophy*. Ed. Justin Clemens and Oliver Feltham. London: Continuum, 2003.

"Les Lieux de la vérité." Interview conducted by Jacques Henri. *Art Press spécial: "20 ans: l'histoire continue." Hors série no. 13* (1992): 113–18.

Monde contemporain et désir de philosophie [pamphlet]. Reims: Cahier de Noria, no. 1, 1992. Trans. Justin Clemens and Oliver Feltham as "The Contemporary World and the Desire for Philosophy" in *Infinite Thought: Truth and the Return of Philosophy*. Ed. Justin Clemens and Oliver Feltham. London: Continuum, 2003.

"Le Statut philosophique du poème après Heidegger." *Penser après Heidegger*. Ed. Jacques Poulain and Wolfgang Schirmacher. Paris: L'Harmattan, 1992. 263–68.

badiou

L'Éthique: essai sur la conscience du mal. Paris: Hatier, 1993. *Ethics: An Essay on the Understanding of Evil*. Trans. Peter Hallward. London: Verso, 2001.

"Nous pouvons redéployer la philosophie." Interview conducted by Rober-Pol Droit. *Le Monde* 31 Aug. 1993: 2.

"Qu'est-ce que Louis Althusser entend par 'philosophie'?" *Politique et philosophie dans l'oeuvre de Louis Althusser*. Ed. Sylvain Lazarus. Paris: Presses Universitaires de France, 1993. 29–45.

Ahmed le subtil [theatre]. Arles: Actes Sud, 1994.

"Being by Numbers." Interview conducted by Lauren Sedofsky. *Artforum* 33.2 (1994): 84–87, 118, 123–24.

"Silence, solipsisme, sainteté: l'antiphilosophie de Wittgenstein." *BARCA! Poésie, Politique, Psychanalyse* 3 (1994): 13–53.

Ahmed se fâche, suivi par Ahmed philosophe [theatre]. Arles: Actes Sud, 1995.

Beckett: l'incrévable désir. Paris: Hachette, 1995. *On Beckett*. Ed., trans., and introduced by Alberto Toscano and Nina Power with Bruno Bosteels, with a foreword by Andrew Gibson. London: Clinamen, 2003. The translation includes "Etre, existence, pensée" from *Petit manuel d'inesthétique*, and "L'Ecriture du générique" from *Conditions*, as well as a brief piece from 1998 entitled "Ce qui arrive."

Citrouilles [theatre]. Arles: Actes Sud, 1995.

Calme bloc ici-bas [novel]. Paris: POL, 1997.

Gilles Deleuze: "La Clameur de l'Etre." Paris: Hachette, 1997. *Gilles Deleuze: The Clamor of Being*. Trans. Louise Burchill. Minneapolis: U of Minnesota P, 2000.

Saint Paul et la fondation de l'universalisme. Paris: Presses Universitaires de France, 1997. *Saint Paul: The Foundation of Universalism*. Trans. Ray Brassier. Stanford: Stanford UP, 2003.

Abrégé de métapolitique. Paris: Seuil, 1998. *On Metapolitics*. Trans. Jason Barker. London: Verso, 2004.

Court traité d'ontologie transitoire. Paris: Seuil, 1998. (Several chapters are translated in *Theoretical Writings*. By Alain Badiou. Ed. Ray Brassier and Alberto Toscano. London: Continuum, 2004.)

Petit manuel d'"inésthétique. Paris: Seuil, 1998. *Handbook of Inaesthetics*. Trans. Alberto Toscano. Stanford: Stanford UP, 2003.

"Politics and Philosophy." Interview conducted by Peter Hallward. *Angelaki* 3.3 (1998): 113–33.

"Considérations sur l'état actuel du cinéma." *L'Art du Cinéma* 24 (Mar. 1999): 7–22.

"Entretien avec Alain Badiou." Interview conducted by Nicolas Poirier. *Le Philosophoire* 9 (1999): 14–32.

"Les Langues de Wittgenstein." *Rue Descartes* 26 (Dec. 1999): 107–16.

"La Scène du deux." *De l'amour*. By Badiou et al. Paris: Flammarion, 1999. 177–90. "The Scene of Two." Trans. Barbara P. Fulks. *lacanian ink* 21 (spring 2003): 42–55.

"L'Existence et la mort." *Philosopher T2: les interrogations contemporaines, matériaux pour un enseignement*. Ed. Christian Delacampagne and Robert Maggiori. Paris: Fayard, 2000. 293–302. Trans. Alberto Toscano and Nina Power as "Existence and Death" in *Discourse: Journal for Theoretical Studies in Media and Culture*, 24.1 (2002): 63–73.

"Huit thèses sur l'universel." *Universel, singulier, sujet*. Ed. Jelica Sumic. Paris: Kimé, 2000. 11–20.

"Les Lieux de la philosophie." *Bleue: Littératures en Force* 1 (winter 2000): 120–25.

"Metaphysics and the Critique of Metaphysics." Trans. Alberto Toscano. *Pli* 10 (2000): 174–90.

"Théâtre et philosophie." *Frictions* 2 (spring 2000): 131–41.

"Un, multiple, multiplicité(s)" [on Deleuze]. *Multitudes* 1 (Mar. 2000): 195–211.

"Le Gardiennage du matin." *Jean-François Lyotard: l'exercice du différend*. Ed. Dolorès Lyotard et al. Paris: Presses Universitaires de France, 2001. 101–11.

"On Evil: An Interview with Alain Badiou." Interview conducted by Christoph Cox and Molly Whalen. *Cabinet* 5 (winter 2001): 69–74. Available online at <http://cabinetmagazine.org/issues/5/alainbadiou.php>.

"The Political as a Procedure of Truth." Trans. Barbara P. Fulks. *lacanian ink* 19 (fall 2001): 70–81.

"The Ethic of Truths: Construction and Potency." Trans. Thelma Sowley. *Pli* 12 (2002): 247–55.

"L'Investigation transcendantale." *Alain Badiou: penser le multiple*. Ed. Charles Ramond. Paris: L'Harmattan, 2002. 7–18.

La Révolution culturelle: la dernière révolution? [Pamphlet.] Paris: Les Conférences du Rouge-Gorge, 2002.

Circonstances I: Kosovo, 11 septembre, Chirac/Le Pen. Paris: Lignes & Manifestes/Léo Scheer, 2003.

La Commune de Paris: une déclaration politique sur la politique. Paris: Les Conférences du Rouge-Gorge, 2003.

Infinite Thought: Truth and the Return to Philosophy. Ed. Justin Clemens and Oliver Feltham. London: Continuum, 2003.

Le Siècle/The Century [bilingual ed.]. Trans. with a reply by Alberto Toscano. Paris: Seuil, 2004.

Theoretical Writings. Ed. Ray Brassier and Alberto Toscano. London: Continuum, 2004.

"Can Change be Thought? A Dialogue with Alain Badiou." Interview conducted by Bruno Bosteels. *Alain Badiou: Philosophy under Conditions*. Ed. Gabriel Riera. Albany: State U of New York P, forthcoming.

Logiques des mondes. Paris: Seuil, forthcoming 2005

Alain Badiou
École Normale Supérieure
45 rue d'Ulm
75230 Paris Cedex 05
France

Peter Hallward
French Department
King's College London
The Strand
London WC2R 2LS
UK
E-mail: peter.hallward@kcl.ac.uk

Bruno Bosteels
Department of Romance Studies
Morrill Hall
Cornell University
Ithaca, NY 14853
USA
E-mail: bb228@cornell.edu

Alberto Toscano
Sociology Department
Goldsmiths College, University of London
New Cross
London SE14 6NW
UK
E-mail: a.toscano@blueyonder.co.uk

ANGELAKI
journal of the theoretical humanities
volume 8   number 2   august 2003

introduction

diane morgan and peter hallward

Monique David-Ménard teaches philosophy at the Lycée Janson de Sailly and is directeur de recherches at the University of Paris VII – Denis Diderot (École Doctorale: Recherches en Psychanalyse); she is also vice-president of the Société de Psychanalyse Freudienne. David-Ménard's dual training as philosopher and psychoanalyst underlies many of the distinctive features of her work. Her books explore the complex relationships at work between philosophy and desire, between abstraction and the body, between logic and fantasy. Though she received a classical training in philosophy and epistemology, she has always approached the subject from an unorthodox perspective, one "derived from listening to the unconscious," and it has been clear from the beginning that her work was never going to fit easily with "the philosophy of the philosophers [...]. I work on all the things that go wrong in the relation between reason and the real." She recognises that there is always "something external to pure conceptuality that constantly underpins the conceptual work" of philosophy and that it seeks to conceal or repress – "without the struggle against fantasy," for example, "there would be no conceptual thought" as such.[1] She does not see the detection of such repressed "impurities" at the heart of philosophical abstraction in primarily destructive or critical terms: the *analysis* of such repression instead provides a way of tapping into philosophy's tense but creative negations, into its constitutive conflicts and exclusions.

David-Ménard's first book, *Hysteria from Freud to Lacan: Body and Language in Psychoanalysis* (1983) was motivated by an

monique david-ménard

translated by diane morgan

SEXUAL ALTERITY AND THE ALTERITY OF THE REAL FOR THOUGHT

interest in the way that "the field of the unconscious is resistant to the methodology of the history of science," by the effort to "try out the methods of the history of science in a domain where it looked as though they might not work."[2] The book reviews the way in which major psychoanalytic theories of hysteria conceive of the erogenous body, and deals in particular with the example of Freud's conception of conversion hysteria (i.e. the way mental disturbances or illnesses acquire bodily expression).

Meanwhile, inspired by Lacan's example, David-Ménard began to re-read the major texts of classical philosophy (Plato, Descartes, Kant, Hegel, Frege) in such a way as to underscore philosophy's agitated negotiations with its Other, with what lies at the limits of philosophy, with

ISSN 0969-725X print/ISSN 1469-2899 online/03/020137-14 © 2003 Taylor & Francis Ltd and the Editors of *Angelaki*
DOI: 10.1080/0969725032000162620

137

what defines philosophy and its limits – with what stretches philosophy to its limits. How does philosophy encounter and recognise that which is "heterogeneous to thought?" How does it cope with the "impasse of the real"? Her engagement with these questions culminated in the publication of *La Folie dans la raison pure: Kant lecteur de Swedenborg* (1990). The book takes its cue as much from Kant's early, precritical preoccupation with madness and other "maladies of the mind" as from the major concern of the critical project itself: reason's own propensity to become unreasonable, other to itself.[3] As is well known, Kant's aim in *The Critique of Pure Reason* is essentially negative – it is a matter of setting limits to reason, disciplining it, protecting it from speculative temptation, so as to prevent it from transgressing its own rationality. David-Ménard pays close attention to the various forms of such negation and negativity, in particular to that non-ontological and non-dialectical concept of negation that Kant names, as early as 1763, "real conflict." If Swedenborg's delirious speculation explores a world in which thought encounters nothing but itself, if it demonstrates the fate of any fully homogeneous (or utterly "rule-free") conception of thought, Kant's effort is precisely to stabilise the philosophical project through the very means whereby it both recognises and pacifies that "external" reality which itself remains forever irreducible to thought. In Kant's case, such stabilisation is achieved through the categories which mediate thought's exposure to actually existent "objects" of representation, where the object appears as constitutively heterogeneous to the subject. Philosophy only avoids delirium, in short, to the degree that it develops rational means of engaging with that which is heterogeneous to philosophy.

Generalising from this point, David-Ménard sees Kant as an exemplary instance of philosophy's wider concerns as a discipline, of its attempts to generate autonomous conceptual systems that allow it to define and justify its architectonic edifice against whatever might threaten to undermine its project(ion). In *Les Constructions de l'universel* (1997), she seeks to uncover the repressed role that fantasy plays in the elaboration of universal concepts. Universal

concepts (beginning with the most abstract examples – those which apply to "every human being" or "any variable" ...) are especially determined to erase any trace of the processes whereby they were constructed, processes that are invariably bound up with the sexuation and experience of those who construct and deploy them. "When we manage to pay attention to the means of transition between a fantasy and a concept, however, we are in a position to define a way of thinking not by its universality but by the process that detaches it from the drive that animates the thinker."[4] Though philosophy always seeks to devise ways of thinking that detach it from its subjective motivation, the logical organisation and generation of even the most abstract conceptual thought cannot be entirely separated from the drive to answer a question that remains forever unanswerable, forever caught up with the contingency of its experience, namely the question of what it means to be masculine or feminine.

Kant again provides a familiar example. His early view of women as motivated by the fickle play of pleasure and beauty rather than the inflexible invariance of principle is notorious:[5] according to David-Ménard, the strict universality of the moral law, which applies in a domain purged of all "pathological" interests, feelings, or desires, is bound up with Kant's fantasies about the inconstancy of women and, by extension, about the inconstancy of feeling in general (hence what she describes as his "melancholic" profile ...). The "universality" of pure practical reason is both built on and limited by the fantasy that it seeks to transcend. Picking up on Lacan's analysis of "Kant with Sade," David-Ménard goes on to show how, when the unconditional place occupied by the moral law (in Kant) is occupied instead by the unconditional pleasure of the libertine (in Sade), it brings to light the logic of a relation that remained hidden in practical philosophy. This is the relation between this unconditional function and the two universal series defined as "any desiring subject" and "any desirable object": in both cases the indifferent substitutability of the object (*any* object ...) figures, along with the particular experience of guilt that it engenders, as characteristic of a distinctly masculine form of desire. An alternative, feminine conception of renunciation relies on an alternative logic of substitution, one that rejects serial equivalence in favour of differential transitions that allow for a mediated passage from one object to another.[6] Lacan's own concept of sexual difference, she concludes, turns on the conjunction of a certain logic of the universal together with a masculine anthropology of desire.

David-Ménard's most recent and most accessible book, *Tout le plaisir est pour moi* (2000) reiterates the importance of the clinical practice of psychoanalysis for an understanding of the procedures of theoretical thought, the means by which it constructs itself and excludes that which it jettisons, converts, or displaces: its *contingency*. It is this contingency, the story that links a particular sequence of pleasure and suffering, a particular pattern of relations with others, that makes every individual unique. No individual can understand what motivates this sequence in isolation, not least since its development depends upon encounters with other people. What makes you *you*, in other words, is nothing other than that which escapes your grasp and opens you up to the others you meet. Because it has developed rational means of tracing such sequences in the distinctly "untheoretical" element in which they unfold (the element of pleasure and suffering, the element most anxiously activated in experiences of love, the element re-activated in processes of transference), psychoanalysis has emerged as the only discipline adequate to the irrational basis of our experience and desire.

notes

1 David-Ménard, "Critique of Pure Madness" 21–32.

2 David-Ménard, "Critique of Pure Madness" 21.

3 David-Ménard's translations into French of Kant's early essays *Essay on the Maladies of the Mind* and of *Observations on the Feeling of the Beautiful and the Sublime*, together with her substantial editorial introduction (1990), reinforce this emphasis on the dangerous hallucinations, illusions and speculative fantasies to which reason is exposed and confirm the centrality of such an enquiry for Kant's critical work.

4 David-Ménard, *Les Constructions de l'universel* 121.

5 "Women avoid evil not because it is wrong but because it is ugly [...]. Nothing in them is the result of duty, nothing of compulsion, nothing of obligation. Woman is intolerant of all commands and all morose constraint. They do something only because it pleases them [...]. I hardly believe that the fairer sex is capable of principles ..." (Kant, *Observations on the Feeling of the Beautiful and Sublime* quoted in David-Ménard, *Les Constructions de l'universel* 8).

6 David-Ménard, *Les Constructions de l'universel* 13, 18.

sexual alterity and the alterity of the real for thought[1]

monique david-ménard

Am Nebenmensch lernt der Mensch zu erkennen.[2]

Psychoanalysis is a practice, situated between therapy and culture, which intervenes in the sexuation of human beings. Feminine and masculine identities are not purely natural or biological facts, and nor are they simply social facts, as "gender" theories assume. They are, rather, constructed over the course of experiences that shape human singularities, experiences which shape the terrain upon which the insertion of human singularities into social realities is negotiated. Psychoanalysis, then, is not a philosophy. Nevertheless, the conceptual understanding of the modalities of its intervention does have implications for the ontological claims made by philosophy, for what is conventionally termed the universality of conceptual thought, for the logics and rhetorics of negation and for the problematic that links the contingent and the necessary.

This is the perspective I would like to clarify and put to the test, since it runs through the various axes of my work. These axes include: the plurality of approaches to the body, particularly when psychoanalysis is compared with neurobiology; the re-evaluation of what any particular philosophy constructs when it interesplices emotional interests with logic, when it takes – in each particular case – the articulation of concepts and fantasies as an index of what thought owes to the drives in dreams and symptoms, but also in art, and in forms of thought which claim to be universal.

In my book *Hysteria from Freud to Lacan: Body and Language in Psychoanalysis* (1983), I reflected upon the status of the body in psychoanalysis, noting how far removed it is from two Western traditions of thinking the body (those initiated by Aristotle and Descartes),

in order to make sense of what Freud calls the erogenous body and the drives. I was interested in the disagreement surrounding what the first psychoanalysts called the "psychosomatic," and wanted to gauge the divergence between two constructions of the body: the physiological and the instinctual. Since 1995 I have developed a new angle on this work by comparing psychoanalysis and neurobiology and I am currently pursuing that project within the context of the Centre d'Études du Vivant (University of Paris VII).

My book *La Folie dans la raison pure: Kant lecteur de Swedenborg* (1990) was concerned with understanding up to what point a philosophical system, in this case the transcendental theory of the object in the *Critique of Pure Reason*, can be understood as articulating a new logic of negation together with the fantasmatic encounter its author had with a mad thinker – Emanuel Swedenborg. I try to read the philosophical text as interweaving these two heterogeneous trajectories. To understand properly how this works we have to get away from the mistaken idea that Kant's writings on madness are no more than juvenilia, that they matter only in so far as they make some minor contribution to the systematic achievement of the three *Critiques*. This is why I wrote a substantial introduction to my translation of Kant's essay "On the Diseases of the Mind" (1764), which examined just how his subsequent essay "Dreams of a Spirit-Seer Elucidated by Dreams of Metaphysics" (1766) anticipates one of the central themes of the *Critique of Pure Reason* (1781). In the first *Critique*, the transcendental analytic and the transcendental dialectic are organised precisely as both a real conflict (the theory of the object) and as a dialectical conflict (the antinomy of pure reason). Because the former introduces a negative magnitude that is distinct from either an ontological negation or a logical contradiction, it allows us to understand how real objects are formed in knowledge. The second conflict, the dialectical conflict, shows how, in our reasoning about the world, thought misses the object because it fails to select the right use of the negative and reconcile it with the modality of existence. Such is the terrain of what

Kant calls the madness of reason [*Wahn*], whose mechanisms and logic he sets out to study in order to understand how the delirium of reason (which is characteristic of Leibnizian idealism) is both similar to and different from the delirium of Swedenborg (the prophet of other worlds). The very organisation of the first *Critique*, the way it opposes the dialectic to the analytic, its theory of modality, its idea of a critique of reason, the table of forms of "nothing" which follows the examination of the constitution of "something" ... – all of these decisive themes can then be explored in a new light. The main concern of this work was to understand, in a somewhat unusual way, what is involved in great philosophical thinking: in spite of its explicit claim to ground not only the idea of knowledge as a whole but also all of its own assertions, any great philosophy in fact owes the definition of its themes and its own field to the articulation of a *passion* (in Kant's case, the horror felt at the reading of Swedenborg's *Celestial Mysteries*) together with a logic of negation.

In *Les Constructions de l'universel* (1997), I tried to grasp the pertinence or impertinence of the concept of the universal when what is at issue is the understanding of how conceptual thought detaches itself from its author, and I compared, from this point of view, art, philosophy and the analysis of dreams. I also tried to evaluate the pertinence of Lacan's project of producing a logic of sexuation, and the degree of autonomy of such a project with respect to the internal ambiguities of the logical and philosophical concept of the universal. The great virtue of Lacan's attempt to describe the masculine and the feminine as different positions that might be written as functions which bring about the intervention of one unique and abstract term – the Phallus reduced to a letter – is that it encourages a non-essentialist conception of sexuation. However, Lacan does not carry his idea all the way through: because he thinks the relationship between the sexes in terms of a central function assigned to a single unique term (the Phallus), he is unable to situate the feminine elsewhere than at the edge of all symbolic elaborations of desire. From the conceptual point of view, he does not see that a logic of negation

reproduces the very confusion surrounding the philosophical concept of the universal which, ever since Kant, designates at one and the same time the universal quantity of subjects affected by the moral law or castration, the unconditional nature of the obligation which founds this law, and the indefinite seriality of "pathological" desires which are subjected to the law. Whether it be in the work of Kant, of Sade, or of Lacan, this syncretism of the universal seems to me to be linked to masculine fantasies concerning the a priori inscription of the absence of the objects of desire; it also concerns the experience of guilt, which is transformed into a relationship with "The Law."

We should try, therefore, to go back to this question of the differentiation of the feminine and the masculine and attempt, first of all, after setting theoretical prejudices aside, to understand the ordeals which instinctual objects undergo when they enter into a relation that Freud called, without sufficiently defining the term, "substitutability." To say that objects of drives are substitutable implies that they can be lost but it does not necessarily imply that they are indifferent, that is to say equivalent in the way they fulfil their function of veiling lack. My hypothesis is that it is precisely here that the masculine and the feminine are differentiated. The logic of the universal, even if clarified by hitherto unprecedented forms of negation, would never itself suffice to conceive this difference. It is crucial, then, that we re-open the question of the relationship between the theoretical constructs and the clinical practice of psychoanalysis.

This is why, in *Tout le plaisir est pour moi* (2000), I try to give an account of what is involved in the way psychoanalysts think and operate. What concepts do they rely on in their daily work? Which philosophical debates – debates which may well otherwise be of great epistemological interest – can they now, after a hundred years of psychoanalytical theory and practice, afford to sidestep or ignore? How do psychoanalysts create a space of thought in which their clinical experience might fit with the theoretical notions they have appropriated?

The concepts which I find indispensable for clarifying my own practice of psychoanalysis are as follows: the drives, pleasure, unpleasure, anxiety, repetition and transference. It seems to me that it is advisable to retain the etymological meaning of "symbolic" in order to understand both the formation of symptoms and the vicissitudes of drives whose objects are not so much lacking or indifferent as they are inadequate to the satisfaction that they organise.

Over the course of these four books I have put into practice a philosophy of contingency: the contingency of the relation between discourses which apprehend the "same" object, and the contingency of the real for any thought which seeks to approach it by means of a practice or a knowledge. This is what I would now like to develop.

I the forms of the contingent

Something is contingent if it might not have been. In Aristotle's ontology, contingency is opposed to necessity. Something is necessary, precisely, if it cannot not have been. Such necessity takes two mutually reinforcing forms. In the first place, even if being can be said in a number of different ways, philosophy consists in reducing, through the univocity of a single discourse, these multiple forms of being to a fundamental analogy that traverses their diversity. Every region of being becomes intelligible when the philosopher grasps it by measuring it with concepts of power and action, by thinking its mode of being in terms of the specific way that some indeterminate material falls under the effect of a form, a form which then determines the qualities that this matter can have. In the second place, according to this way of thinking being, chance figures merely as the limit of the determination that might be attributed to a being. A single discourse thus gathers up the apparent disparity of what is and arranges it in terms of the unity of the common measure supplied by the concepts of matter and form. Science, then, only concerns itself with necessity – and this applies even when philosophy comes to think about transformation or becoming, and measures each being against the actualisation of which it is capable. The unity of a discourse that runs through all the forms of being and the impossibility of ontological chance are part and parcel of the same configuration of thought.

By contrast, contemporary forms of thought may be characterised as the exploration of a coherent counterpoint to Aristotle's ontology: the real is now to be grasped at the articulation of several discourses which, far from linking up via a fundamental analogy, instead signal its existence thanks to an inter-discursive discordance, a discordance which varies in describable ways from instance to instance. The discordance that can be detected in this way between the various discourses concerned with what first appears as one and the same region of the real is precisely an indicator, in the operation of thought, of the effectivity of this real – the real thus forces thought to approach it in these disparate ways.

What I would like to explore here is the relation of mutual implication between the fact, on the one hand, that although thought remains adequate to the intelligible aspects of the real, the real appears to thought as essentially contingent, and, on the other hand, the fact that the real can be grasped as real only at the jagged intersection of several disciplines of thought. The real is precisely that which may be grasped at the intersection of several discourses and practices that lack any single common model but which do not, for all that, exist in a relation of simple juxtaposition or contradiction.

Consider the following examples.

In *Madness and Civilisation* Michel Foucault analyses what he calls "the great confinement." He postulates that a real change in the status of madness took place at a point that articulates together two different registers of historical reality: the administrative measure which consisted in locking up libertines, the unemployed, and the mad in the former (now obsolete) leper-houses, does not share a common logic with the reasons which led Descartes to conceive the relation between reason and madness in a new and mutually exclusive way. If there really was a "great confinement," it is precisely because what this expression denotes can only be located in the articulation of a series of discourses or circumstances, a series that cannot be considered (along the lines proposed by Antoine Augustin Cournot) in terms of a divergence within an otherwise homogeneous conception of causality – it would be more accurate to say that what is involved are indeed heterogeneous processes which nevertheless intersect at a point which determines a real.

The second example is that of the body in the articulation of the biological and of the instinctual, as it has been conceptualised since Freud. We know that Freud discovered what was peculiar to the forms of hysterical paralysis by differentiating them from the forms of motor organic paralysis (whose symptoms could be understood in terms of the structure of the nervous system). The reality of these hysterical disturbances was only established through a different construction of the body, which Freud initially called the erogenous body, before he settled on his conception of the drives; this other construction crossed over with the notion of body based on the physiology of the nervous system, all the while remaining incompatible with it. Of course, there is certainly a contiguity between the biological body and the instinctual body. The clinician knows that it is the "same" parts of the body that serve, on the one hand, to maintain physiological exchanges with the organism's environment, that on the other hand constitute the zones upon which the relations of the pre-verbal child or infant [*infans*] with other humans inscribe the various marks and letters, which in turn provide the basis upon which certain configurations of pleasures, unpleasures and anxieties will come to shape the fantasies of that infant. If there is a reality of the body, it is because what we call "the body" exists through the articulation of these two disciplines, which do not share a common language. We will never be able to reduce the instinctual body to the biological body or vice versa, since the reality of the body can only be approached as that which obliges the construction of these heterogeneous disciplines. These disciplines can never be unified, and the real to which they relate can only be conceived in so far as we give up trying to think of it as the *analogon* of the two disciplines that determine it.

So what we have are two negative propositions – in the first case, that what we call unrea-

son is that real which emerges from the articulation of an administrative measure and a philosophical text which nevertheless have no common model or referent; in the second case, that "what we call 'the body' exists through the articulation of these two disciplines which do not share a common language." But this negation – the negation involved in not having a common measure – refers back in fact to positive procedures of accessing a real, given that the real figures as correlative to the disjunctive relationship of the discourses that apprehend it. The negative formulations used here only point to the fact that such a method always distances itself from a determination of the real as the *analogon* of those plural discourses which apprehend it: the real is there where analogical appearance can be criticised as an illusion, thanks to this divergence of disciplines which are able to come to terms with their exclusive partiality.

II the real and truth in freud and kant

It goes without saying that if the real is that which induces a describable disarticulation of the discourses and practices which apprehend it, truth can no longer be defined in terms of the adequacy with which a concept fits an object. The truth of a knowledge that links practices and discourses is, on the contrary, the regulated and determinable inadequation of multiple concepts to their real. If we might call "disarticulation" the relation of the divergent discourses that concern or invest [*investissent*] the same object, and "inadequation" the persistent heterogeneity of the object with respect to the concept that allows it to be grasped, then naturally there will be a relation between the disarticulation of these discourses and the regulated inadequation which characterises the relationship of the discursive to the real. With respect to one of these two aspects of the matter, i.e. renunciation of the idea that truth entails adequation of concept to object, Kant is often rightly considered as an important precursor. After all, what is the idea of the transcendental synthesis at work in the judgements of knowledge, other than a way of bringing to light the heterogeneity between that which is

sexual alterity

sensed or intuited and that which is conceived? Kant recognises this heterogeneity as the precondition for knowledge, and the schematism regulates it without abolishing it. Indeed, there is a passage in the *Critique of Pure Reason* in which Kant even says that the transcendental synthesis itself offers an indication that the real is different from the operation that determines it by its categories, such that, henceforth, we can no longer simply define truth in terms of the adequation of concept and object.

When he came to establish the metaphysical site of his way of thinking, Kant identifies it as both a "transcendental idealism" and an "empirical realism." These terms mean that it is precisely because space and time are not properties of things that we are entitled to say that objects in space are real and are different from the representation that apprehends them. In order to establish this point, Kant reflects upon the difference between two experiences involving time, experiences which are both very simple and imaginary. When you scan a building with your eyes, the act by which you perceive it is successive, but the object itself exists as something simultaneous. This is proved by the fact that our gaze is able to scan the building from bottom to top or from top to bottom, but an essential property of the object is that it remains indifferent to the spatio-temporal variation of the subjective synthesis that apprehends it. On the other hand, when I scan the movement of a boat, the subjective synthesis which permits me to follow this movement is always successive and I am *not* free to perceive the movement of the boat back to front, contrary to what was the case with the house. I am able to think the reality of the boat and of the house because they lend different kinds of temporality not so much to the subjective synthesis that apprehends them as to what we might be tempted to call, with Husserl, the noematic correlation of this subjective synthesis. But Kant is not Husserl. Kant is determined to remain a metaphysician; he has no reason to "suspend the thesis of the world." Quite the contrary, analysis of the relationship between the transcendental syntheses and their objects provides the means to "refute idealism." He refutes idealism by situating the contingency of

the real at the centre of the transcendental synthesis that apprehends it.

We should not let more recent conceptions of time and space allow us to forget that Kant understood them in non-relativist terms. The important point to remember is that he grounds his metaphysical position, which he calls empirical realism, in a meditation on the difference between, or rather on, the *heterogeneity* of the real in relation to the thought which grasps it. And this heterogeneity is determined in the comparison of two transcendental syntheses. What is real for Kant is that which makes the perceiving of a house and the perceiving of a moving boat, as far as their subjective apprehension is concerned, fundamentally different. However, Kant was only able to arrive at this philosophical perspective through an encounter with the risk that, by defining itself as idealism, thought might become almost identical to delirium, a delirium similar to Swedenborg's. Far from devaluing Kantian thought, this "bad encounter," this contingent event, shows rather how contingency "affects" philosophy, even when the latter defines itself as foundational and transcendental.

Amongst the disciplines that only intermittently interconnect or intercept, and that allow for a real to be grasped as that which corresponds to this intermittent interception of thought, there are two that are especially important for me: psychoanalysis and philosophy. What's interesting about psychoanalysis is not just the way it forces us to rethink the relationship between fantasy and the concept, the way it leads us to recognise fantasy as one of the anthropological preconditions that helps determine the perspective or opening up of a conceptual construct. Rather, the philosophical interest of psychoanalysis is that it radicalises this disruption of the relations between the contingent and the necessary. It does this in two ways in particular:

1. Since there is no masculine essence, no feminine essence, since the masculine and the feminine are not determined in any necessary or essential way, so then psychoanalysis applies itself to thinking the necessity of a difference whose own content is itself contingent. Sexual

144

difference must be sought in all dimensions of existence (social, psychological, intellectual), but it can never be found. And this question without an answer leaves its mark on everything else: social determinations, systems of thought, symbolic roles, etc. All thinking is traversed by the inescapable requirement to give this difference a content, content which will always be borrowed. The paradox is as follows. On the one hand, the thinking through which human subjects seek to construct an identity as sexed beings, that is to say, their fantasies, are necessary, i.e. they cannot not be. Yet, on the other hand, in their content, they cannot find any guarantee in being. They can no more find it in socio-historical constructs than they can find it in some "nature." Even if the anatomical difference between the sexes intervenes as one form of the raw material with which each human subject imagines his or her place as a sexed being, it is not this difference that lends structure to the symbolic devices by which that peculiar kind of non-being known as human sexuality inscribes itself in our actions and in our thoughts.

2. Because of the specificity of the empirical field it explores, psychoanalysis deals with a particularly clear instance of the intertwining of contingency and of necessity. It is through the aleatory contingency of our amorous encounters that the necessity of our configurations of alterity plays itself out, i.e. those configurations that have shaped both the structure of our desires and the forms of our identification with certain traits coming from the Other. The "aleatory" quality of amorous encounters should be understood not simply in terms of what we commonly call "chance encounters," but as a result of the fact that what is attractive about those who arouse our passions refers to those aspects of ourselves that remain unknown to us, and that escape our grasp in a manner which is anything but haphazard. These unknown aspects constitute us but we have no direct access to them. We only discover them as ours – often in situations of revolt and contestation – because it is this particular "object" and not another which arouses our passion. The effect of contingency turns here upon the way that a certain revelation of yourself

can only come from the other, the other who crystallises that aspect of yourself that eludes you.

The contingent aspect of this configuration is introduced, then, by the objects we encounter; its necessary aspect (though it is the same phenomenon) emerges through the letters [lettres] which summarise the ways we identify with the Other, i.e. the impact of alterity upon us.

This is a point that Freud had already made very clearly, and Lacan developed it: the identificatory traits which singularise human beings are letters. As I explained earlier, in their materiality these letters are the marks of our relationship with the other, marks which produce, in ways that are always unique for every human being, the erogeneity of the body. As letters, they are also what drive a human subject (who is always prey to pleasure, unpleasure and anxiety) to formulate ways of thinking what it means for him or her to be a man or a woman, given that there can be no answering this question in terms of an essence or form of being. Over the course of a psychoanalytic treatment, points of identity are established between what is said during the sessions and what is activated in the transference between patient and analyst. What such analysis can then decipher, through the repetition of someone's dreams, amorous encounters and ways of thinking, is the arrangement of those traits coming from the Other that structure the way this person lives, thinks and acts. Psychoanalysis offers a way of getting to grips with a necessity constitutive of this person but that he or she cannot master. A necessity that we do not master but that constitutes us all the same.

The first and second aspects of the contingency at work here are linked. The access we have to ourselves in so far as "our selves" elude us follows a path through this domain of non-being where we seek to define ourselves as a man or as a woman – that is to say, in the domain of fantasy. Contingency takes on several forms here. It affects the aleatory character of sexual amorous encounters which, thanks to certain unpredictable details, reactivate the structure of the objects that cause or provoke our desire. It affects the double-sided quality of the letter, the letter that comes from the other, which is both erogenous and signifying. And, finally, contingency ensures that sexuation cannot be located in the order of being. But by the same token, such contingency ensures that we are all necessarily launched upon a fantasmatic quest in search of the masculine and the feminine, a quest through which the uniqueness of each human being is formed. And again, the contingent ups and downs of desires are themselves inscribed in the necessity of those identifications with the traits of the Other that constitute us and that figure as the object, if not of a science, then at least of a knowledge.

Now Freud makes an explicit link between a theory of knowledge (a knowledge compatible with the notion of a regulated and *determinable* inadequation of concept and of object) and the theory of desire (where desire is determined as the haphazard encounter in other human beings of that which escapes the subject in the structure of his desires). This Freudian philosophy can be summarised in two sentences, taken from sections 17 and 18 of the *Project for a Scientific Psychology*. "For this reason it is in relation to a fellow human being that a human being learns to cognise [*apprend à connaître*]." And: "What we call *Things* are residues which evade judgement." The real is that which eludes the judgements and practices that aim to assimilate it.

We might compare, with respect to this point, Freud's formulations with those of Lacan when he reads Freud's *Project* in *Seminars* II and VII. Lacan distinguishes between the real and reality. By contrast, in his *Project* Freud did not separate the real from reality: even when they bear on an inanimate real object, all judgements of knowledge are constructed "in relation to the Other," that is to say, "in relation to a fellow human being [*am Nebenmensch*]." This Other can be partially assimilated by thought and, in the Aristotelian logic to which Freud refers, following Brentano's lead, this assimilation consists in the relation of predicates to a logical subject. In the sample statement "S is P, Q, and R," the letters "P, Q, R" represent what the subject of knowledge can assimilate of what he is trying to know, i.e. those qualities of the object with which he can identify in the very process of identifying

them. But the logical subject itself, precisely when considered as the stable core of an object to be known, remains both strange to and a stranger for the thought that seeks to know it. The real is that with respect to which knowledge fails. The very permanence of the logical subject (i.e. of the Aristotelian substance) is a thing of uncanny strangeness, and even this subject is caught up with the obscure face of the Other. So there is no reason, therefore, to distinguish as radically as Lacan does between *connaissance* and *savoir*, or between knowledge of the Real and knowledge of reality. Perhaps, then, there is some relationship between contingency such as it is experienced, under its various guises, in the regional field of psychoanalysis, and the contingency by which modern notions of science and truth are affected.

III negations in clinical practice and the philosophy of negation

The revaluation of philosophical notions or principles which psychoanalysis urges us to make is not centred exclusively, of course, on the question of contingency. The practice of psychoanalysis also invites us to be attentive to the manner in which analysands use all forms of grammatical, stylistic, and logical negation to transform the organisation of their drives.

The logician Frege was interested in "thoughts without owners" or bearers, i.e. thoughts that were not borne or carried by any identifiable thinker [*pensées sans porteur*].[3] During these same years, the 1920s, Freud became interested in negation because this logical and grammatical operator seemed to him to characterise the manner in which subjects "carry their thoughts [*porte ses pensées*]," so to speak. To deny the content of a thought in an instance of judgement is to distance yourself from an instinctual movement which inhabits you, since the person who speaks in this way constitutes herself as a subject on the basis of the knowledge that she has of this very movement. It might seem that to distance yourself is simply a form of refusal. But things are more complex than this. For this rejection of something in yourself that takes the form of the knowledge that you have of it is not an absolute rejection. There are worse things, in the life of a soul, than mere negation. Something more destructive is possible, for oneself and for the other, namely the radical expulsion of whatever hurts us, such that the hurtful thing figures as utterly outside us, as something hostile by its very nature. Something that will not be allowed to touch or concern us in any sense. What Freud calls, at the end of his text, "the negativism displayed by so many psychotics," relates to behaviour whose linguistic manifestation entails intolerance of any sort of compromise, including precisely that compromise with the "bad" enabled by ordinary forms of negation. To exclude, to say "no" to everything, is to enclose oneself in an absolute refusal of the world. Such refusal can take the form of mutism or of a paranoid delirium – in either case the little word "no" has no role to play. By contrast, denial or repudiation (*nier ou denier*, according to the first French translations of *Verneinung*) does entail a certain recognition of that which has been abolished, even as it wordlessly rejects it out into the external darkness. "Now you'll think I mean to say something insulting, but really I've no such intention" – such is the structure of the example Freud uses in order to emphasise the creative aspect of recourse to language. This recourse genuinely forms the subject when he or she knows how to use the word "no" in such a way that it envelops and makes apparent in a determinate way that which was rejected. Psychotics, on the other hand – those who say "no" systematically, those who say no to everything – do not enter into that play with what they are rejecting that negation makes possible.

In presenting negation in this way, by bringing together in a short-circuit the beginning and the end of Freud's text, I have deliberately skipped over the question of the logical dimension of judgement. It is as Brentano's pupil that Freud deals with this question. But at the same time, what he has to say about negation comes from elsewhere: from a reflection on the proximity and the difference between external reality understood as that which has been excluded from oneself, and the power that language has, thanks to negation, to reintroduce the excluded as the

object of knowledge. This reintroduction does not entail acceptance of what has been excluded, but it makes it possible for us to move beyond the claim of "not wishing to know anything about it," a claim so radical that it cannot even be said.

In order for the mechanism of negation to work, the subject must be capable of misrecognising a content by attributing it to an other: "you are going to think that … but no, it is not the case!" Or alternatively, what is bad is what the other holds in his or her possession. In other words, Freud's way of thinking this problem turns on the problematic of alterity, rather than on an ontology. Negation does not relate to non-being, but to the violence carried out against oneself and against the other. If this has anything to do with the logic of judgement as debated by Husserl and Frege, it is in so far as the connections and disconnections effected by the copula at the centre of affirmative and negative judgements (respectively) are among the acts that structure the drives. And there is another basis for this rapprochement, namely the Freudian idea about the real as being that which you exclude from yourself because it is so bad that you do not want to have anything to do with it. In the light of this idea, the question of the fold between being and discourse (the question which logic deals with by distinguishing attributive from existential judgements) can be treated in a new way: an element of the real can only ever be grasped against its will, as a defensive or unwilling body [*ce n'est jamais qu'à son corps défendant qu'on saisit un élément de réel*]. It is this body, which defends itself in and from thinking, that organises the *Verneinung*. Negation is not a relation to non-being, it relates to the difference between being excluded and existing. We might well ask whether there can still be any common denominator to the philosophical approach to the question of being, the logical approach to the question of existence, and the psychoanalytical approach to the real. These divergences may come to light through enquiry into the nature of judgement.

We need to take stock, therefore, of the articulation linking the question of negation in psychoanalysis and contingency.

In this context, negation needs to be considered from within the illusions proper to the domain of fantasies, that is to say, proper to the traces left within us of our first experiences of satisfaction (experiences which knew nothing of the difference between desire and reality).

Consequently, as Freud emphasised in relation to one of the examples cited here, the function of the words "no" and "not" should be analysed within the framework of a problematic of hallucinations, illusions and beliefs, in so far as these are elaborated in the grammar, the style, and even (as Freud said) in the *logic* of thought.

These points should be taken as so many hypotheses needing to be put to the test by the clinical practice of psychoanalysis: up to what point might we describe the history of sexuation of a human being, the formation of sexed identities, the organisation of fantasies which try to give a content to the feminine and to the masculine, and so on, in light of the way that a subject tries to come to terms with certain experiences, certain dangers or threats, certain indications of the limits to his omnipotence?

The ways that Freud and Kant think about negation, or rather negations, coincide in another sense as well. This plural form – negations – reminds us that *Verneinung* is not the only means recognised by psychoanalysis of reaching a compromise with whatever attacks or threatens the soul, *die Seele*. As is well known, Freud differentiated between psychosis, neurosis and perversion as three ways of getting around the limitations imposed by the distinction between the sexes and the existence of death. Psychosis is an absolute rejection or *Verwerfung* of that which is inassimilable – Lacan translates this process as "foreclosure." Perversion is a denial or disavowal, *Verleugnung*, of the inassimilable. As we have seen, the *Verneinung* of neurosis negates whatever is disturbing. In all three forms of experience, the form that negation or denial takes produces, in turn, its own forms of certainty and belief and hence its own ways of relating to different sorts of reality.

We are entitled to be surprised to find, at work in Kant's reflections on the illusions or the

delirium [*Wahn*] that haunt human thought when it reasons about the relation of thought to external reality, the same kind of distinction as the one Freud develops in order to characterise the various forms of negation at issue in what is known as castration. Consider, for instance, the text from the first edition of *The Critique of Pure Reason* entitled "The Paralogism of Idealism." In this text, Kant establishes the reality of objects in space. He does not proceed by way of demonstration, however; instead, he criticises from within their own logic the various metaphysical positions that try to deny the reality of objects in space. In order to distinguish dogmatic idealism (Berkeley) from problematic idealism (Descartes) he uses two distinct terms: "The dogmatic idealist would the one who *denies* [*leugnet*] the existence of matter; the sceptical idealist the one who *doubts* [*bezweifelt*] matter's existence because he considers such existence to be unprovable."[4] These two metaphysical theses are explicitly presented as beliefs [*Glauben*] from which we have to extricate ourselves by means other than those of demonstration or proof. What is wrong with both these theses is precisely the way they assume that the relation of thought to the real can be treated as an object of proof. Kant's strategy is thus to escape from these beliefs by placing "beyond doubt" the reality of objects in space, once the reality of these objects has been understood as external or outside as far as our own representation is concerned, rather than as being in some sense external in itself.

The implications of this text are considerable, as they establish two decisive points at one and the same time. On the one hand, they characterise metaphysical theses as beliefs forged by negations. On the other hand, since the philosopher agrees to work his way through these illusions in order to find a way out of them, Kant's text effectively presents his own metaphysical position as a certain type of belief, a position that is acceptable in so far as it succeeds in exposing the source and logic of those illusions. It is precisely this critique of illusions which underpins the truth of a transcendental idealism combined with an empirical realism. Kant's text multiplies the terms that describe what thought can accept [*annehmen*], admit [*gelten lassen*] and allow [*gestehen*] as real – in each case, the important thing is to validate the testimony [*Zeugnis*] of perception by understanding the transcendental conditions under which it is produced, rather than indulging in delirious speculation on the supposed necessity of proving the existence of external objects. This idea that we cannot proceed directly by successive demonstrations or proofs towards establishing the nature of reality, this idea that it is necessary to make our way through the lures of illusions (illusions that are themselves so many misplaced negations) in order eventually to arrive at the proper play of the negative [*le juste jeu du négatif*] – this idea allows us to reflect on what might become, based on this interconnection of Kant and Freud, a new way of thinking the indirect relationship we sustain with reality (a relation sustained precisely via the forms of negation that we have at our disposal).

It will be clear, I hope, from the peregrinations of my own reflections as they proceed through the chiasmus that organises the relations between philosophy and psychoanalysis, that there is no one sovereign discipline capable of grounding the status of the other, any more than there could be a metalanguage capable of rising above or internalising the various fields of thought it might encounter. Such, it seems to me, is the status of contemporary thought, and such are the themes that I wish to develop in the coming years.

notes

1 Monique David-Ménard kindly wrote this article in response to *Angelaki*'s request for a general overview of the main themes of her work to date. I'm grateful to David Macey for his helpful review of an earlier version of this translation. [Translator's note.]

2 "It is in relation to a fellow human being that a human being learns to cognise" (Sigmund Freud, *Project for a Scientific Psychology* [1895] in *The Standard Edition of the Complete Psychological Works of Sigmund Freud*, ed. and trans. James Strachey, vol. 1 (London: Hogarth, 1953) 331).

3 Frege concludes, for instance, that "the thought we have expressed in the Pythagorean theorem is timelessly true, true independently of whether anyone takes it to be true. It needs no owner" (Gottlob Frege, "Thought" in *The Frege Reader: Selected Philosophical Writings*, ed. Michael Beaney (Oxford: Blackwell, 1997) 337; see also Frege, "Negation," ibid. 346ff.). [Editor's note: I am grateful to Damian Veal for drawing my attention to these passages.]

4 Kant, *Critique of Pure Reason*, trans. Werner S. Pluhar (Indianapolis: Hackett, 1996) A377.

works by david-ménard

"Lacanians against Lacan." Trans. Brian Massumi. *Social Text* 6 (autumn 1982): 86–111.

L'Hystérique entre Freud et Lacan: corps et langage en psychanalyse. Paris: Éditions Universitaires, 1983. *Hysteria from Freud to Lacan: Body and Language in Psychoanalysis.* Trans. Catherine Porter with a foreword by Ned Lukacher. Ithaca: Cornell UP, 1989.

(Ed.). *Les Identifications: confrontation de la clinique et de la théorie de Freud à Lacan.* Paris: Denoël, 1987.

(Ed. and trans.). *Essai sur les maladies de la tête. Observations sur le sentiment du beau et du sublime.* By Immanuel Kant. Paris: Flammarion, 1990. The introduction to this edition appears in translation as "Kant's *An Essay on the Maladies of the Mind* and *Observations on the Feeling of the Beautiful and the Sublime*." Trans. Alison Ross. *Hypatia* 15.4 (2000): 77–98.

La Folie dans la raison pure: Kant lecteur de Swedenborg. Paris: Vrin, 1990.

With Geneviève Fraisse et Michel Tort. *L'Exercice du savoir et la différence des sexes.* Paris: L'Harmattan, 1991.

With Judith Feher-Gurewich and Michel Tort (eds.). *Lacan avec la psychanalyse américaine.* Paris: Denoël, 1996. *The Subject and the Self: Lacan and American Psychoanalysis.* Ed. Judith Feher-Gurewich and Michel Tort. Northvall, NJ: Jason Aronson, 1996.

Les Constructions de l'universel: psychanalyse, philosophie. Paris: Presses Universitaires de France, 1997.

"Kant, the Law, and Desire." Trans. Leslie Lykes de Galbert. *Feminist Interpretations of Immanuel*

Kant. Ed. Robin May Schott. University Park, PA: Pennsylvania State UP, 1997.

(Ed.). "Singularité dans la psychanalyse, singularité de la psychanalyse." Special issue of *Rue Descartes* 22 (1998).

"Must One Seek the Universal in Beauty?" *Umbr(a)* 1 (summer 1999): 45–60.

"Critique of Pure Madness." Interview conducted by Penelope Deutscher. *Women's Philosophy Review* 24 (2000): 19–33.

"La Différence des sexes a-t-elle changé?" *La Différence des sexes est-elle visible? Les Hommes et les femmes au cinéma.* Ed. Jacques Aumont. Paris: Cinémathèque Française, 2000.

"D'une femme à l'autre, qu'est-ce qui fait la différence?" *De la différence des sexes entre les femmes.* Ed. Dominique Lecourt. Paris: Presses Universitaires de France, 2000.

"La Pluralité des disciplines, une stratégie de pensée a-ontologique." *Universel, singulier, sujet.* Ed. Jelica Sumic. Paris: Kimé, 2000.

Tout le plaisir est pour moi: la psychanalyse aujour-d'hui. Paris: Hachette, 2000.

"La Négation comme sortie de l'ontologie." *Revue de Métaphysique et de Morale* 2 (June 2001): 59–67.

"Processus stationnaire et vitesse infinie dans les cures de patients psychotiques." *Le Temps du désespoir.* Ed. Jacques André. Paris: Presses Universitaires de France, 2002.

"Sexualité." *Dictionnaire d'histoire et de philosophie de la médecine.* Ed. Dominique Lecourt. Paris: Presses Universitaires de France, 2003.

Monique David-Ménard
Laboratoire de psychopathologie fondamentale et psychanalyse
Université de Paris VII (Denis Diderot)
2 Place de Jussieu
75005 Paris
France

Peter Hallward
French Department
King's College London
The Strand
London WC2R 2LS
UK
E-mail: peter.hallward@kcl.ac.uk

Diane Morgan
School of Cultural Studies
University College Northampton
Park Campus
Northampton NN2 7AL
UK

ANGELAKI
journal of the theoretical humanities
volume 8   number 2   august 2003

introduction

sean gaston

Born in 1952, Bernard Stiegler teaches philosophy at the Université de Compiègne, where in 1992 he founded the research unit Connaissances, Organisations et Systèmes Techniques (COSTECH). He was the director of the Institut National de l'Audiovisuel (INA) from 1996 to 1999 and is currently the director of the Institut de Recherche et Coordination Acoustique/Musique (IRCAM). Asked at a conference in April 2003 how he became a philosopher, Stiegler revealed that he became one while serving a five-year prison sentence (1978–83) for a series of bank robberies. In a short autobiographical work, *Passer à l'acte* (2003), he describes how, encouraged by the late Gérard Granel, he spent most of these years intensively reading philosophy. Granel also suggested that he write to Derrida. After leaving prison, Stiegler studied with Derrida, received his doctorate from the École des Hautes Études en Sciences Sociales, and began teaching at the Collège International de Philosophie.

Stiegler is preoccupied with the questions of technics and time. He is in the midst of writing a remarkable project that has an almost Proustian scale: three volumes of *La Technique et le temps* have so far been published: *I La Faute d'Épiméthée* (1994); *II La Désorientation* (1996); *III Le Temps du cinéma et la question du mal-être* (2001), and two more are promised (*IV Symboles et diaboles ou la guerre des esprits*; *V Le Défaut qu'il faut*). Stiegler has also published *Échographies de la télévision* (1996), a "live" recording of an interview with Derrida. Stiegler concludes *Échographies* with an essay on Barthes' analysis of the "this-has-been"

bernard stiegler

translated by sean gaston

TECHNICS OF DECISION

an interview

["*ça-a-été*"] in photography in relation to new digital technology. A short work, *Aimer, s'aimer, nous aimer*, dealing with the question of self-esteem and the recent case of Richard Durn (who in 2002 shot and killed several people in Nanterre), is due out later this year.

For Stiegler, the technical is more than the tool, more than the machine: it involves the *invention* of the human. Life is always already reliant on technics. Technics make the transmission of the past and the anticipation of the future possible. Without technics there can be no memory, no heritage, no adoption, no invention. Technics give us time. Underlying Stiegler's re-examination of technics is an original fault, default, or lack of origin (*le défaut*

ISSN 0969-725X print/ISSN 1469-2899 online/03/020151-18 © 2003 Taylor & Francis Ltd and the Editors of *Angelaki*
DOI: 10.1080/0969725032000162639

d'origine) that makes technics and prostheses necessary. Like Derrida's notion of the supplement of the origin (an always necessary addition – to give the illusion of a full plenitude or self-sufficiency – that displaces, replaces and re-marks a fundamental lack, void or abyss), an original fault or default suggests that there can be no "origin" no "beginning," no "inside" without exteriorisation and differentiation, without the artifice of technics. From the start, a "default" – and the reliance on technics – is always necessary: *un défaut qu'il faut.* In "Derrida and Technology" (2002), Stiegler situates Derrida's thought "within the context of an unprecedented development in technology" and argues that deconstruction is first and foremost a "thinking of technics."[1]

In *La Technique et le temps I*, Stiegler attempts to extricate the technical from its traditional determination in such metaphysical oppositions as dynamic/mechanic, human/technical, subject/object, nature/culture, inside/outside, etc. Through readings of André Leroi-Gourhan, Gilbert Simondon and Heidegger, Stiegler identifies the history of technics as "the evolution of the living by other means than life."[2] Stiegler sees in Heidegger's analysis of the clock a repetition of the traditional attitude towards calculation and measurement as the attempt to "program the unprogrammable." In contrast to Heidegger's ambivalent view of technics, Stiegler argues that it is the "pro-grammatic" that registers the already-there in the "form of the *not-yet*," "a past that is not mine (that I have not lived, but without which my past is nothing)." *Dasein* is "pros-thetic," "pro-posing and pro-jecting itself outside of itself, in front of itself": technics as temporalisation.[3]

La Technique et le temps II is dominated by the question of memory and industrialisation. There can be no memory without an initial forgetting, an original default. Memory requires prosthetic supplements. Turning to Bergson, Husserl and Barthes, Stiegler traces the creation and transformation of memory through the technics of writing and the development of industrial temporal objects (photography, recorded music, radio, cinema, television).[4] The advent of recorded sounds and images reveals that an *identical* repetition must – like the original forgetting or default that produces memory – be received each time as a modification, as a difference. These industrial temporal objects register the flux of time as an already-there that produces a not-yet. Stiegler argues that memory as technics challenges the Husserlian opposition of primary retention (perception) and secondary retention (imagination). Consciousness is indicative of a *distinction* between perception and imagination that cannot be reduced to an *opposition*. Living reality does not exhaust consciousness, which is haunted by fictions and phantasms of the passing of time, of our own passing.[5]

In *La Technique et le temps III* Stiegler develops the intricate relationship between consciousness and new industrial temporal objects by raising "the question of Kant" and turning to the politics of hyperindustrialisation, mass media, global telecommunications and the Internet. Through a reading of the *Critique of Pure Reason* Stiegler argues that consciousness has "an essentially cinemato-graphic structure," employing prosthetic processes of selection, montage, contraction and projection. Like cinema, consciousness relies on the constant adoption of an unlived past and the projection of an unlived future. Stiegler discerns in the difficulties that arise from the Kantian opposition of perception to imagination and of the image to the schemata the need for an inherently cinematographic "'a priori' prosthetic synthesis." For Stiegler, it is because consciousness *is* cinema (adoption and projection) that Hollywood and "THE AMERICAN WAY OF LIFE" has had – and is having – such a dramatic effect on consciousness and belief.[6] The hegemony of Hollywood, only compounded by the simultaneous watching of live events by hundreds of millions of people and the domination of the Internet, threatens a mass manipulation and mass synchronisation of individual (diachronic) consciousness. Industrial control and globalisation have created a new opposition between the synchronic and the diachronic, and provoked a crisis of social decomposition, entropy and spiritual disorientation that demands an urgent and radical critique.

notes

1 Stiegler, "Derrida and Technology" 238–39. For differing accounts of Stiegler's reading of Derrida, see Geoffrey Bennington, "Emergencies," *Oxford Literary Review* 18 (1996) 175–216, and John Lechte, "The Who and the What of Writing in the Electronic Age," *Oxford Literary Review* 21 (1999): 135–60.

2 Stiegler, *Technics and Time 1* 135.

3 Stiegler, *Technics and Time 1* 225–26, 232–34, 270.

4 With their constant references to past volumes and promise of future volumes to come, the books that make up *La Technique et le temps* themselves have the performative quality of "temporal objects" that register the flux of time.

5 See also Stiegler, *Le Temps du cinéma* 36–49.

6 See Stiegler, *Le Temps du cinéma* 35, 217, 130.

technics of decision:
an interview[1]

bernard stiegler

Peter Hallward: At the beginning of the first volume of La Technique et le temps *you say that philosophy has repressed the question of technics [*la technique*]. Why did this happen? Is it mainly a result of the association of* tekhnē *with sophistry, i.e. with the corrupt manipulation of knowledge? Or does this repression stem from the orientation of philosophy, after the poem of Parmenides, towards the being of being – an orientation that leads it down the path of the eternal, of that which neither changes nor evolves?*

Bernard Stiegler: I think that it is both and that they cannot be separated. In *La Technique et le temps I*, I first address this problem with respect to the question of sophistry, but I finish the work by returning to the Heideggerian question of being, since Heidegger both asks and fails to ask the question of technics. The question of this repression of technics is linked to the fact that, strictly speaking, philosophy, in other words the thought of Plato (what I call philosophy in the strict sense is metaphysics, defined first of all as a post-tragic discourse, and thus one that denies mortality), constituted itself in opposition to sophistry defined as the technical use of the *logos*. This is how I respond to your question in the first volume.

At the same time, however, I think the problem goes deeper than this. *Before Plato*, what is at stake in Parmenides' question of Being (which to my mind still belongs to the tragic epoch)? It would take too long to explain what I mean by tragic here – let's say it refers to the pre-Socratic epoch, an epoch where the immortality of the soul is not yet recognised as a principle. This is what I call tragic: Greek thought that does not yet reason from within a framework that presumes the immortality of the soul, but on the contrary, that takes as its essential starting point mortality and the fact that mortality is ineluctable, that there is no horizon beyond

death. This certainly does not mean that the dead do not return: spirits do indeed return (and the whole problematic, for example, of Antigone rests on this), but that does not mean that they are immortal. What is involved is quite different. They are ghosts [*revenances*]. And they are ghosts that transmit an inheritance – the inheritance comes from a "spirit" ["*esprit*"] that crosses generations along with the spirits (in the plural) that bear and convey it.

We need to ask then: where does Parmenides come from, the *spirit* of Parmenides, that is, the *question of being*? Parmenides' thought inscribes itself in the same vein as that opened by Thales, by Solon and by the Seven Sages – people who are at once thinkers, poets and politicians, founders of cities, as one says, and even founders of the idea of the city. Thales had written the laws of his city, had been a geometer, had set out the first discourse on *phusis*. My thesis is that all these problems, which arise with Thales, fundamentally proceed from the appearance of a *techno-logy*, in this case a technique of writing. A technique appears, that of linear writing, that radically transforms the way all spirits transmit and are transmitted from generation to generation, and the way spirit transmits itself from generation to generation through them – but this time as a unified spirit, precisely through the unification of language enabled by literalisation. It is this mnemotechnics that makes possible the writing of laws, the founding of cities, the construction of geometric reasoning (Thales embodies the origin of geometry), the practice of philosophy. It involves a massive transformation of the social group that raises a thousand questions. It overturns, for example, the relation to tradition, to spirits, and, more precisely, the articulation between the city and religion, the relation between the profane and the sacred, the place of the clans inside the city-states or territories [*demes*], and so on. It raises, in short, questions that are not entirely foreign to what we are experiencing today, on a global scale, with respect to contemporary forms of technology (however novel our current situation might otherwise be).

The sophists, denounced by philosophy as mere technicians of the logos, are a by-product of this situation. From the seventh century BCE the city appears and straightaway transforms itself, because it is essentially a process of transformation. The city is always in transformation, but I believe that its initial period of foundation/transformation, between the seventh and fifth centuries, has specific characteristics that remain unclear to this day, in particular as regards their consequences for the genesis of philosophy itself. This initial period of foundation/transformation, during which everything changes completely, is very rapid – it lasts about 150 years. These years are witness to a process which in a short time gives birth to sophistry – the arrival of the *grammatists*, the masters of letters, of writing, who are the predecessors of the sophists. The sophists then go on systematically to develop a technique of language that quickly acquires a critical dimension, in so far as this technique of developed language will in turn engender a moral crisis.

P.H.: It's not an essentially oral technique, a technique of speaking well?

B.S.: Certainly not. And this is precisely what Plato denounces: they always manage to speak well, he says, but they learn everything by heart, by means of this techno-logical "hypomnesis" that is logography, the preliminary writing out of speeches. It is because writing exists that the sophists can learn the apparently "oral" technique of language that is rhetorical construction. And this knowledge is not reducible to the arts of the story teller, it is of an entirely other nature, even if Plato also denounces, elsewhere, those who make up stories and fables – even if it is quite clear that Plato, when he mocks the rhapsode in *Ion*, makes a direct connection between the poets (who as you know will be condemned in the *Republic* as mere imitators and tellers of tales) and the sophists. He will conclude that essentially the same thing is at stake in both cases, in both the *tekhnē* of the poet, or of the rhapsode, and the *tekhnē* of the sophist. They work along the same lines in the same vein, the same grain of falsehoods. Sophists, poets, are only liars, *that is to say, technicians.*

So to conclude my answer to your question, I would say that the question of technics, considered in this way and as the object of repression, is a question that emerges *with* and *by* its denunciation by Plato. But it is a question that emerges also and above all as a *denial*, and in this sense therefore as *a kind of forgetting*. It's a paradoxical situation, since what Plato denounces in technics is precisely its power of forgetting. The canonical text here is *Phaedrus*.

But, at the same time, the question of technics that I'm trying to explore appears well *before* Plato, and appears first of all as the *question of transformation and becoming [devenir]* (raised by the economic crisis associated with the development of navigation, money, and thousands of other new technics that appear at that time) in the Greek cities. This is how I see it. And it is not simply a question of technics, but also and above all of *mnemo*technics, that is to say of technics of the future, in its capacity profoundly to transform the conditions of being together, the terms of the law, the rules of life, etc.

P.H.: Let's try to isolate the domain of temporality, since the question of memory of the past obviously arises well before the invention of writing. Are you saying that temporality as such is linked in an original way to technics, such that we distinguish it in principle from the experience of the living? Or is there "before" this a temporality of the living as living, a temporality of life considered without reference to technics?

B.S.: As far as I am concerned, one can speak of at least three kinds of temporality. There is physical temporality, in other words, what we call entropy, the degradation of matter, the expansion of the universe – personally, I never call this temporality, I call this *becoming [le devenir]*. Then there is the temporality of the living, which as you know is a negentropic temporality, that is to say a temporality that fights against disorder and which already involves a *différance* with an "a," as Jacques Derrida defines it, that is to say a structure that attempts to differ from and to defer [*différer*] entropy, that fights against entropy. This is life. And there is a third tempo-

155

rality, the one that people generally call human temporality. But I don't like to call it human, because I think that it is an anthropocentric determination. I call it *technics*. It is a temporality within which a living being, in particular the one that we call man, is constituted in relation to the temporality of a technics which is itself a technical development or becoming, which is the main dimension of becoming for human beings. The technical object only exists within a technical system that develops with the living in a situation that both extends and breaks with the living, in so far as mortals, from the beginning – and this is what is related in the myth of Prometheus and Epimetheus, in Plato's *Protagoras* 320d ff. – are not predestined to be what they are. Mortals are *prosthetic*, that is to say they are endowed with artefacts and are capable of altering the artefacts which they adopt. In this sense, they are not doomed to a predestination, they "have to be" what they are, they are destined to *decision*, that is, to time understood in this sense, which is not that of life. The myth tells us about the singularity of this time, which calls upon *dikē* [justice] and *aido* [modesty, respect].[2]

Let me recall this myth very briefly. One day Zeus says to Prometheus: the time is come to bring into this world the non-immortals, those who are not immortal. Zeus gives him qualities, *dunameis*, powers and clay: he gives him forms and matter and the responsibility to distribute the qualities. But Prometheus leaves it to his twin brother to act in his place. Epimetheus hands out all the qualities, but forgets to keep one for that mortal being we call man: there remains enough matter "to bring him into the world," but there are no more qualities. On account of this *lack of quality* [*à défaut de qualité*], Prometheus is obliged to go and steal the technics that permit the invention and fabrication of artefacts, that enable the adoption of all qualities. Prometheus steals fire from the home of Hephaestus, the lame blacksmith god.

In this sense, the mortal is a being by default, a being marked by its own original flaw or lack, that is to say afflicted with an original handicap[3] – one received from a god who is himself handicapped – and for which he has need

of prostheses to supplement this original flaw, or more exactly to defer (and differ from) it [*le différer*]. For this flaw cannot be *made good*, the lack can never be *filled*; the problem that then arises is that mortals cannot agree on how to use this impotent power of the artefact. The artefact brings disorder (*eris*, *polemos*). Consequently, mortals fight each other and destroy themselves. They are put in charge of their own fate, but nothing tells them what this fate is, because the lack [*défaut*] of origin is also a lack of purpose or end. It is in this way that technics *constitutes* the *problem* of *decision* – and this problem, and its experience, is what I call time (in the third sense of the word), that is a time that is neither the becoming of the universe, nor the negentropy that fights against the becoming-entropic of the universe, i.e. life. This third meaning requires a decision, it calls for a capacity to make a difference, a capacity imposed by the lack of origin, by our original default. The feeling for such a difference, which arises from this "*différance*," is what Hermes, sent by Zeus, then brings to mortals as a double feeling of *dikē* and *aido*.

P.H.: From this perspective, is Heidegger your main philosophical adversary, despite the care with which you read his work, in so far as he wants to think this moment of indetermination (this opening up of a space of imminent decision, the prelude to any possible resolution, etc.) at an essential distance from the question of technics?

B.S.: For me, Heidegger is not an adversary. In any case, I do not have philosophical adversaries. It is *in* Heidegger that I have investigated everything that I'm telling you about, and obviously, it is also against him. There is a saying, *un mot d'esprit*, that you may know. The actor and film director Sacha Guitry said "I am against women, right up against them [*je suis contre les femmes, tout contre*]." "I am against them," because I am not a woman and I am "right up against them," because I love what I am not and the very fact that I am not that. As far as I'm concerned, one can only have a dialogue with a philosopher in so far as one is "against this philosopher, right up against him": you are very close to him, but to be *close* to him, you must not be him. Ok. This is what I mean about Heidegger and the same applies to my relation with Plato, even with Derrida.

Now, to answer your question, it is true that in *The Fault of Epimetheus*, my dialectical interlocutor, in the old (Greek) sense of the word, the interlocutor that I speak against or contra-dict, is indeed Heidegger. Heidegger is my interlocutor because in the twentieth century he is the one (though there is also Simondon) who has done the most to advance the thought of temporality that I have just spoken about, the third temporality. And at the same time he thought this temporality both along with technics and against technics in a very traditional Platonic sense. After Marx, the greatest thinker of technics is Heidegger, but in a way – and this is particularly apt – *by default* [*par défaut*]. But I am, of course, speaking to you about something that is a *negative* for Heidegger. The way I read Heidegger is obviously not the way that Heidegger would read himself. In effect, I consider – and it is a possibility that Heidegger himself opens when he discusses Kant – that the way Heidegger reads Heidegger is not the best way to read Heidegger.

In *Being and Time* (but I am also thinking, for example, of *Identity and Difference*) Heidegger suggests that the temporality of what he calls *Dasein* is originally technical, when he says that to be a temporal being in the sense of *having to be* [*d'avoir à être*], i.e. in the sense of *existing*, is to be in a world. He describes this world as constituting what he calls the structure of reference [*renvoi*].[4] And he explains what this structure of reference is by analysing the latch of a door.[5] He shows that the door refers to something else which refers to something different and that this forms a horizon of *significance* – but in doing this he describes what in the history of technics is called a technical system. He shows that the material world, the world of useful objects, of tools, utensils, equipment, supports a structure of finality – within which develops what he calls *Besorgen*, concern [*préoccupation*], which, as he conceives it, is fundamentally a relation to death. For this relation to death to be able to exist this whole structure must be there.

stiegler

Heidegger is the first thinker after Marx to insist so forcefully – certainly from a completely different perspective – that existence is constituted by an original technicity. This, incidentally, is what Hubert Dreyfus has both understood so well and so badly (I say badly because in a rather poor text published in French in the *Cahier de l'Herne* devoted to Heidegger, he reproaches Heidegger for having "technicised being" – in other words he *denounces* what is properly *revolutionary* in Heidegger's work).[6]

The difference or disagreement [*différend*] that I have with Heidegger concerns what he says about the temporality that he calls original, authentic, proper, *eigentlich*. This is the temporality of the relation to death, of being-toward-death, and I fully ascribe to such an analysis. But he adds that in *Besorgen*, in concern, I am always already concealing my relation to death, hiding it, and that is why technics, which is the horizon of the temporality of concern, reduces the indeterminacy of time to a calculation and therefore to a determination. As a result, technics regains the same status that it had in Plato, namely the status of that which obscures the true relation to *aletheia*, to *Eigentlichkeit*. And there is an enormous contradiction here – because there is at the same time a great difference between Heidegger and Plato. The origin of *Dasein*, of time, is what Heidegger calls worldhood [*mondanéité*], which is also a lack of origin or original flaw, that is to say a *facticity* [*facticité*]. Worldhood is fundamentally and necessarily the structure of reference, and the structure of reference is what he calls the world of tools, of technics, of concern. Heidegger says that this structure of reference conditions the constitution of worldhood, but at the same time he says that authentic temporality is the temporality of being for death that frees itself from concern. In other words, he attempts to make good the original fault – which is itself *the worst of faults*, and the basis of a formidable *political* adventure.[7]

What I have attempted to show against Heidegger – and in this case it is *truly against*, my reasoning proceeds alongside his, right up against his – concerns this *structure of inheritance* that he describes, starting from the analysis of the world as the world of objects, which forms, at the heart of the system of referring, what he calls the already-there of historicality, of *Geschichtlichkeit*. I inherit the world (the world of objects) precisely as a *history*. As *Dasein*, I am someone whose past has *always already gone ahead* of me. This is what section 6 of *Being and Time* says. As you know, he says that the past does not follow *Dasein*, but on the contrary it "always already goes ahead of it." This means that I am an heir, that fundamentally my past is not *my* past: it is the past of a culture that I inherit, the past of those spirits I mentioned a moment ago, the past of the dead. I am always already haunted by the dead, through the objects that they leave to me, mostly anonymously. This is what I found most interesting in Heidegger, but it is also the most dangerous aspect of his thought because, politically, it leads to the romantico-national-socialism that has made so many people detest Heidegger, with good reason, unfortunately. Or at least with good reason on this point which, of course, has many other regrettable consequences for other aspects of Heidegger's thought – but many of those who detest him on account of this also wrongly believe that they are entitled not to read him, and so their hatred turns good reason into bad. Now, I believe that this terrifying political outcome is made possible *precisely* because Heidegger does not raise the question *here* of the actual conditions of this inheritance, inasmuch as they are already inscribed in its original technicity. It is on this point, in sections 76, 77, 80 and 81 of *Being and Time*, that Heidegger is faced with a dilemma, hesitates, and comes down on the wrong side of the question.

Before developing this point further, I'd like to go back to the analyses of *The Fault of Epimetheus* – which might first seem anthropological, if not biological, but this is obviously not my position. I'm not interested in what we call "man" but in *temporality*, temporality that, as a form of life, has to decide what it is to become (and it so happens that this form of life is still called man today). Even when man is finished, when he belongs to the past, this form of life may well continue on, becoming ever more complex – and perhaps man is *already* finished. But if there is something profoundly *necessary* in man it is

precisely his fundamental anxiety, in so far as this *opens up possibilities* – and in the end, perhaps this is what accounts for the fact that the question of his possible end always remains, from the beginning and throughout the course of his life, an open question. If I do not in fact wish for the disappearance of man, it is because I do not wish for the disappearance of this opening of possibilities that results from this always open experience of the possible end. I certainly don't want to be turned into a homeostatic machine, let's put it that way (and this also is certainly a possibility). But I am already and have always been constituted by my relation to the *mēkhanē* and, through it, to all possible machines. It was around four million years ago, according to the dating of Leroi-Gourhan (since reduced to 2.8 million years ago), that a new form of life appeared, one supported by prostheses. In a certain way, this is what the myth of Prometheus and Epimetheus describes. This living being that we call man and that this myth more soberly designates as *mortal* (that is to say: the being who anticipates his own end and his *difference* from the *immortals*, from whom he receives, albeit by theft, his power, his fire, that is to say *tekhnē* and all its possibilities, and who therefore endures, in the ordeal of non-predestination that results from this, the experience of a difference marking his origin, which is thus essentially the difference between the sacred and the profane) is a being that, to survive, requires non-living organs. These non-living organs – eye-glasses, houses, clothes, sharpened flints, etc., absolutely everything that Heidegger describes as constituting the system of reference and significance: worldhood – make up a set of entities that I characterise as inorganic (artificial) yet organised (articulated).

Now, by manufacturing these artefacts – for example, in order to cut meat, to cut down trees, to work materials, to fight – this new form of life creates a new basis for memory. Every living sexual being is constituted by two kinds of memory which, since August Weismann, have been called germinal and somatic – the genetic memory of the species preserved in DNA, and the somatic, individual memory preserved in an organism's nervous system. Now, with what

Leroi-Gourhan calls the process of exteriorisation there appeared around three million years ago a third form of memory: *technical* memory that enables the transmission of the individual experience of people from generation to generation, something inconceivable in animality. This experience of individuals inherited by other individuals is what I call *the world*, the world inasmuch as it is always *inhabited by spirits*.

P.H.: You think temporality along with its technical conditions – temporality understood as the opening in which one decides something, where one creates the unpredictable, the new. Is this the main source of your criticism of Heidegger? That although he recognises that such an open space depends on these conditions, despite everything he confines it to the really *decisive moments of anguish, resolution, etc. This tendency is even stronger in Sartre: the decision takes place in the emptiness of pure consciousness, in the absence of any prosthesis. But doesn't a viable theory of decision need to find some* way of thinking such an experience of evacuation or emptiness, this moment devoid of all determination *– and so in a sense devoid of any subject, in the usual meaning of the term? And which then (as Badiou likes to suggest) might not even have a place "in" temporality as such, since a genuine decision configures a new experience of time in its wake.*

B.S.: As for your first question: it is this and many other things that constitute my disagreement with Heidegger – but *in* Heidegger. The first thing that I dispute in Heidegger is the opposition between the determinate and indeterminate that he establishes and assumes as self-evident. He says that concern, *Besorgen*, always seeks to *determine* the indeterminate, i.e. to determine the indetermination that constitutes my ignorance of the time and manner of my death, whereas in fact the when and the how of death are structurally indeterminable. According to Heidegger, what makes me absolutely unique is that I am caught up in an original relation to my own death, that I do not know when or how it will occur. And this ignorance, which is a non-knowledge, is structural: the knowledge of death

is from the start the knowledge of an ignorance. Using my own vocabulary, I would say that here one experiences, from the beginning and at an elemental level, the feeling of a lack of origin or original default [*défaut d'origine*], along with its inverse, the default or *lack of an end* [*défaut de la fin*]. Being in absolute ignorance of the how and the when of my death, I am plunged into an absolute indetermination, which means that I cannot give responsibility for my own life to another because this other does not know the end any more than I do. (By "end" I mean both the limit or conclusion, and the meaning or direction, and thus the content, of my life, which is only determined after the fact and too late, once my death has occurred and I am no longer there to live, and which will always have remained indeterminate for me: my end is an event that will only "happen" to me in my absence, by default.)

But when I *flee from* my own life, I tend to determine this indetermination in reference to what Heidegger calls the "they," *das Man*: I tend to give myself over to others and to abandon my indetermination to them, by adopting gregarious forms of behaviour – along with all the conventional and stereotypical ways of behaving in the face of the indeterminate, of fleeing from the anguish that also always constitutes this indetermination. This is the refusal to assume what Heidegger calls isolation, solitude, loneliness, and it is also the Sartrean moment. Heidegger *opposes* this – this solitary determination – to indetermination.

Now, and here I am coming to your second question, I believe that this opposition is extremely superficial, *because what makes indetermination possible is precisely determination.* The principle of individuation, which is the concretisation of indetermination, can operate all the more vigorously – as happens, for example, with the proliferation of individual interpretations of a text – the more the literal and public establishment of such a text, the most unequivocal determination possible of its identity, enables each of its readers (all of whom will thus have read the same text in the same form, written in an absolutely identical way) to read it differently, in relation to his or her own indetermination.

Each reader then acts as the carrier and "opener" of a still greater indetermination of readers (that the text affects in so far as it intensifies their singularity). In each case, every individual indetermination opens up in and through the general indeterminacy of meaning, an indeterminacy which all the more effectively guarantees and exhibits the determination of significations (it is essential to distinguish, here, between signification, which is determinate, and meaning, which is indeterminate). I am sure everyone has noticed that if you read the same text three times in your life, three different readings happen each time: faced by the determined identity of the text (the web of significations), we have an especially acute experience of our indetermination, which is also to say of our temporality. It is only starting from this moment that we truly experience the ordeal of indetermination. That is in fact why during the age of alphabetic writing the figure of the citizen appears who is above all a singular individual [*une singularité*], the affirmation of singularity in the collective. On the basis of the identical text on which is written the common law, each citizen has the experience of the *strangeness* of this identity which, each time that it is brought into play, produces a difference. What Heidegger neglects in the relation between determinate and indeterminate is the question of the difference *in* repetition. And this opposition of determination to indetermination that we find in Heidegger is a typically metaphysical opposition.

Your question, however, concerns decision, and there is decision, strictly speaking, when there is *epoché*. I use the word *epoché* in several senses at once – in the sense of the Stoics, in the sense of Husserl and even in the sense of Heidegger. With the Stoics, *epoché* is decision as the interruption of a flow, an arrest or halt that issues a judgment – and in French *arrêt* remains a word for legal judgment. In Husserl, it is a method: the phenomenological method whereby our experience of the world (the thesis that there is a world) is suspended, i.e. whereby we suspend our ordinary preoccupation with particular objects so as to reflect instead on the pure operations of consciousness. In Heidegger, it punctuates the history of being, being is essentially history, and this history is the history of the epochs of being as a succession of suspensions. In this respect, there is a big problem in Heidegger. Heidegger had written *Being and Time* – and a whole series of works that are always, directly or not, readings of Kant, in particular *Being and Time* and *Kant and the Problem of Metaphysics*, but also the *Phenomenological Interpretation of Kant's Critique of Pure Reason*. However, in 1927, Heidegger had not managed to finish *Being and Time*: he had published it unfinished, announcing a second part which would never actually appear. Now, what finally did appear, in 1935, was the *Introduction to Metaphysics*. And this is a complete change of discourse, in which it is no longer essentially a question of *Dasein* – and, above all, there is no longer any question of an existential analytic.

From that point on, Heidegger devotes himself instead to a history of being. In other words, he is torn between two paths that are antagonistic in some respects, but whose critical synthesis seems possible in principle. On the one hand, he tries to think the existential analytic of the individual: he fails. On the other hand, he attempts to think the history of Western being, that is to say the history of the *globality* of the history of the West – which leaves us wondering what happened to the endeavour of the existential analytic, which seems in some ways to have disappeared before its status has been clarified. What is extremely problematic in all this is that the years between 1927 and 1935 are marked, of course, by the National Socialist episode. So there are a lot of reasons to investigate that which brings together or on the contrary distances these two paths. In my opinion, the essential factors (which serve to explain the hesitations and the sort of secret rift which, after all, separates 1935 from 1927) are already at issue in sections 73 to 77 of *Being and Time*, where Heidegger tries to return to the question of original temporality through the analysis of what he calls "antiquities," where he speaks of *Weltgeschichtlichkeit*. This world-historicality stems from the objective and material traces that I receive from the world, and the question is whether these must be taken into account in the constitution of original temporality. If, for example, I go to a museum, I can see and study antiquities: does this *constitute*, as something inherited, as something already-there, my original temporality? I believe that Heidegger really hesitates here, that he *truly* asks himself this question. But he eventually decides no, it doesn't.

Now, and here I am finally getting back to your question, this "decision" is an enormous problem – it is even a catastrophe, which will lead him to *oppose* the "they," on the one hand, and the "I" on the other. It implies that a decision is produced absolutely outside of any collectivity, a decision which is essentially solitary, one made in the solitude of being-towards-death. To this I would object, first of all, that it makes absolutely inconceivable and unthinkable the *problem* of immortality, which is nevertheless a constituent aspect of metaphysics – one of the great limits of Heidegger's existential analytic is the way it relies, unconditionally, an a priori thanatology which implies that once I am dead, *nothing* more can happen. Now this is not true: *my whole life is dedicated to or overdetermined by that which comes after-my-death*, which is also to say by the births to come. It's only in this way, at least, that my life can be liveable. Everything that precedes my death is only of little interest, when all is said and done, compared with that which will survive it – or rather, it is only of any real interest in terms of that which will survive it. Fundamentally, today, in this epoch that is at present ours, the one in which we are trying to live, and which is a-theological, totally profane if not totally profaned, there is something that persists above and beyond any becoming-profane, which ensures that no one says nor above all thinks: "After me, the flood [*Aprés moi, le déluge*]." Certainly, corporate capitalism says this, that is to say *signifies this as a process*. But no one, and not even a capitalist (*as a person*), no one on the planet says or would dare say to himself: "Right, let's take full advantage of things, let's exploit our resources as much as we can, and in fifty years there will be nothing left – but we couldn't care less about this, since in any case we will not be here anymore." No one dares say this because

we cannot not think that after us there is and there will be something else. This is why we always already live in the after-me, in the after-us, always and fundamentally – even if the *they* tends, on the contrary, to live in the denial of such a destiny, in denial of the fact that *it is precisely this: destiny*. This is why we write books: everything that we *do*, we do essentially according to this above-and-beyond. And it is here that Heidegger is greatly mistaken, because he imagines that concern is exclusively dedicated to the struggle against death. Whereas to my mind what he calls concern, *Besorgen*, and what I (after Marx) would also simply call labour or work, is also, beyond the mere activity that survival requires, the will to *be*, that is to say to exist, to be in the sense of ex-isting, and therefore, of *marking, leaving a trace.*

It is because he opposes concern and "resoluteness" that Heidegger objects to the original articulation of the "I" and of the "we." I am devoting a large part of my current work to the study of this original articulation of the I and the we, and to the historical forms through which its transformation proceeds. Simondon, in his *L'Individuation physique et collective*, tries to avoid opposing the I and the we. The I *in* the we is what it means to be we as singularity – which is also to say, as the exception. The I can only be an exception. I can only be as an exception in the sense that I exempt myself from the we. I am not the we, and yet I am nothing outside the we: I am a figure of the we, a projection of the we that is always in some sense in excess of this we. This is what I call an instance or *occurring* of the we. I have found some similar ideas in Badiou, in his little book on ethics.[8]

All of this relates to what Simondon calls individuation, and to what a moment ago I called *epoché*, suspension, inasmuch as this is a process of inadequation. *I* individuate, I individuate myself [*je m'individue*]: I am always already and continuously in the midst of individuating. I am structurally incomplete (this is also what Heidegger says) and I seek to individuate myself, i.e. to collect and to complete myself, but at the same time I also try to defer [*différer*] my completion since my completion is my death, the end of individuation. To use

Derrida's terms, I am caught up in *différance*, if you like.

Now this structure only affects me to the extent that it *also* affects the group to which I belong. The process of individuation does not only proceed at the level of individual minds, a social entity is also a process of individuation at the level of a *group*. And a group can only individuate itself if it is composed of individuals who are themselves individuating in and against the group, at one and the same time in excess of the group and as its highest expression, who mark the process that is set in motion by the inadequation of the individual to the group and vice versa. The I and the we are inadequate to themselves (incomplete, evolving) precisely in so far as they are both inadequate to but also inseparable from each other. They are in a state of co-individuation, and I only individuate myself to the degree that I participate in this way in the individuation of the group, no less than in my own individuation. This signifies that my individuation can only be as effective as is my socialisation. But the latter can take a lot of time: belonging constitutes itself here as difference, that is to say as *différance* – as time. And there is co-individuation in so far as the I shares with the we a pre-individual milieu [*milieu*]: I is an heir (the we is always older than the I). Which brings us back again to the already-there of Heidegger. With this difference, perhaps – that the we of which I speak here is also always already younger than the I.

P.H.: Could Heidegger agree with you here, up to a point, since the "they" is not static but something that changes and evolves over time?

B.S.: No, because the "they [*das Man*]" for Heidegger is precisely the collapse of individuation. This is the whole problem, and it's a result of the fact that Heidegger confuses or at least does not distinguish the we and the they. I believe that the lack of such a distinction is also the reason why he abandons the historicality of *Dasein* when he undertakes, from 1935, the interpretation of the history of being, a history that he will attempt to rethink precisely as the individuation of being. At this point it is indeed *being* that individuates itself as such, as far as Heidegger is concerned. But the problem is that he doesn't really maintain a relation with the existential analytic. He goes back and forth: sometimes he comes down on the side of the "we" (which is not at all the same thing as the "they") as historical being; at other times he comes down on the side of the "I" as solitary *Dasein* – even if, undoubtedly, *Dasein*, as the heir of an already-there, always tends towards a we. But the problem is to figure out how the two join together – and this is what Heidegger fails to do. That is why there is no politics in Heidegger, because politics is precisely this: to join the "I" and the "we." Isn't this what *Antigone* tells us?

Now, all of this proceeds through inadequation, and inadequation proceeds through technics. Because human beings, or existential beings, or beings who deal with decision – the decision of their temporality – are continuously called into question by the development of technics which overtake them. Technics simultaneously give them access to the already-there (i.e. join the I to the we) and form what I call the retentional mechanism of their pre-individual background. When I say that technics overtake mortals, I am relying on Marx as well as on Leroi-Gourhan and Gille, and also on Simondon:[9] people form technical objects but these objects, because they themselves form a dynamic system, go on to overtake their makers. Objects form a *system* because no technical object is ever thinkable in isolation – for example, in the tape recorder that you're using to record this interview there is a cassette, which is of no use without the tape recorder, which itself is of no use without the microphone, and so on: technics is essentially a system of references [*renvois*], just like the system of the world that Heidegger analyses in *Being and Time*. And such systems are *dynamic*, meaning that they are always marked by particular tendencies. It is Leroi-Gourhan who develops the concept of technical tendency, and he owes the notion to Bergson. There are also concepts of tendency, or of force, in Freud and in Nietzsche. And a tendency only exists along with a counter-tendency – such as, for example, pleasure and reality in Freud. The human, or what we call human, is essentially a negotiation between tendencies. What matters is to understand how these tendencies combine, to describe the conditions of such combinations, to describe how they make the *connectivity* of a social fabric possible. To understand and to describe this connectivity is to struggle against the always imminent possibility of a decomposition of tendencies, against an archi-tendency, if I might put it this way, towards decomposition.

A human society is always based on a technical system – what Marx calls a system of production. A society puts this technical system to work, but at some point it no longer provides the expected results – for example because it has enabled a social transformation in relation to which it "disadjusts" itself. This disadjustment then induces a dynamic exogenous to the system, one that may in turn come up against a dynamic endogenous to the system itself. For example, the steam engine enables the production of better steel which enables the production of more effective machines and this constitutes a positive retroactive loop, which progresses until the machine reaches an optimal performance and then declines. And in the end this changes the technical system. The result of these dynamics is a process of technical evolution that regularly leads to a transformation of the very laws of the system and so produces a boomerang effect, such that the system itself then impacts upon society as excess, disadjustment, inadequation, etc. Or again: mnemotechnics, in so far as it gives me access to the already-there, for example in the literal form of a text, thereby opens me, on the basis of this literality, to the meaning of the text [*l'esprit de la lettre*] which is essentially indeterminate precisely to the extent that confirmation of the literal text ensures the permanence of textual significations (according to the logic that we looked at a moment ago). Technics (as mnemotechnics) here constitutes my indeterminacy, that is to say my inadequacy to myself, precisely as determination. And the point is that everything related to a problem of decision proceeds through a structure of this kind, as dynamic coupling.

P.H.: Automobiles are invented and developed, they impact on the organisation of towns; this

then forces change in the organisation of work, of social life, and so on ...

B.S.: For example. But one can also understand this more radically and more "constitutively." Let's say, for example, that one night I write the sentence: "it is dark." I then reread this sentence twelve hours later and I say to myself: hang on, it's not dark, it's light. I have entered into the dialectic. What is to be done here? Why does Hegel attempt to introduce "sense certainty" into the dialectic through this thematic of writing? It's certainly not a coincidence. That which makes consciousness be self-consciousness (i.e. consciousness that is conscious of contradiction with itself) is the fact that consciousness is capable of externalising itself. This is why Hegel is the first thinker of exteriority, the great thinker of exteriority. And it's upon this principle that Marx founds the whole of his reinvestment of the dialectic, as in *The German Ideology*. He takes up Hegel's problematic of exteriorisation from the materialist point of view – but the great invention in this is exteriorisation. I write "it is dark" and when I read it twelve hours later it is light. There is therefore a contradiction between times, the time of the consciousness when I wrote this and the time of the consciousness when I read it. But as for me, I have the same consciousness: my consciousness is therefore put in crisis. It is *always* in the play of exteriority that decisions are made. Questions which call for decisions arise only like this: they always go through exteriority, they are induced and led, more or less palpably, by exteriorisation. For example, Cézanne's decision: to see the mountain is to show it. Seeing is therefore painting: I do not see without painting, Cézanne says to us, but this painting is a decision as to how I "see." The visible is not what informs the eye, but what the eye uses to *make* or do something. Now, this action is in the final analysis an inscription, an exteriorisation which constitutes the interior, which means that interiority does not precede exteriority or vice versa. It is above all because he has formulated this question like no one else before him that Derrida is very important.

Furthermore, this question of decision is always that of knowing how *I* join myself to the group. I am only who I am in so far as I am in relation to a group. How is it that I am called Stiegler, when I live in France? This means that I have at least one Germanic grandparent. I am an heir, but in quite a complex way: I speak French, I consider myself French, while both my grandfathers have German names (Trautmann and Stiegler). And yet I say that I am French, heir of the *sans-culottes*, of the French Revolution, of the language of French literature, of Descartes, Proust, Mallarmé, Queneau, Char and Blanchot. I cannot escape this. Later, it may be that I'll want to escape this, to declare that the national domain does not interest me, does not concern me. But can I then avoid being taken into the structure of another group, if only by default [*par défaut*]? I might, for example, join up with a more tribal group, perhaps a sort of network, or else something more nomadic, perhaps through the Internet, if not by the much older and more common path of an international journal – when I speak of Heidegger, for instance, you know who this is, we can communicate because we are part of the same group, in the end: the group of readers of philosophy. In this sense we are talking about the same things. Now, what constitutes these groups, each time, these groups which in each case are the theatre of every possible decision, is still and always exteriority.

P.H.: Ok – even if our capacity to communicate has an effectively transcendental or quasi-transcendental status (as Habermas, Chomsky and Pinker might say, each in their own way), this capacity can only actualise itself within a group of more or less specific interlocutors. Your perspective accords very well, it seems to me, with the dynamic coordination of the I and the we described by Deleuze, which proceeds through the ceaseless invention of assemblages and machines that increase our collective power. But does that which opens us up to sharing (linguistic sharing, in this case) itself depend on a preliminary belonging? And, on the other hand, even if I am not an "I" before I communicate with others, isn't it necessary to distinguish the I of communication (the I with the you, the I which is part of a we) from the I of a genuine

decision? Does decisive action restrict itself to the differentiation of an I amongst a we? Everyday communication clearly discourages any decision: why then must the decision depend, in general, on a sort of communication? Isn't the act of decision indifferent to these particular conditions of possibility, at least?

B.S.: I think that what you call the transcendental in Chomsky is not at all transcendental, in fact – on the contrary, it's just a form of scientistic naturalism. I don't believe that language is a competence shared by humanity and registered in biological equipment: I believe that language is first an *incompetence*, the sense of a flaw or lack [*défaut*], a default of language and of pronunciation that marks the diversity of idioms – and this is what Babel means. That human beings have the neurological possibility of speaking a language is an obvious fact, a platitude, but I do not believe that it consists of "rules," and, above all, if they have not learnt it culturally they will never learn it. Moreover, I believe that this neurological competence is the same as that used to coordinate acts of manufacturing, of technical production: it is the competence of exteriorisation, which, as Leroi-Gourhan recognised well before Chomsky, clearly requires a level of suitable cortical and subcortical organisation. Now, this competence is nothing other than the mark of a lack or default of quality. A language is an *echo* of this lack or default, and this echo is essentially learnt and received from preceding generations, that is to say from the preceding "we." At the same time, I absolutely do not believe that there are universal rules of language. I have always found this fanciful, and what's more, very ethnocentric. It is at once ethnocentric and metaphysical. As Sylvain Auroux has shown, with its project of general grammar the West has enslaved the evolution of exotic idioms, imposing on them a grammatical model which has either obliterated or profoundly altered them.[10] Through its religious missions, which have completed the grammatisation of all vernaculars, the West has truly waged a spiritual war – one that I examine in the book that I am now writing, *Symboles et diaboles, ou la guerre des esprits*.

I don't believe that there is an original generative syntax from which I could beget all the linguistic formulae of the entire world. This cognitivist point of view misses the heart of the problem, which is that "language" is always already diachronic, which means that it is always already idiomatic. In other words, there is no "language": it does not exist, because only *languages* exist, including the various ways of speaking "the" French language. If I wanted to describe "the" French language, I'd take a tape recorder like the one you're using now and I'd record and sample lots of people who speak French. I'd go to Marseilles, to Lille, to Paris, to Strasbourg, to Ajaccio, to Brussels, to Canada, to the West Indies, to the Ivory Coast, to Mali, etc. And by doing so I would record as many different French languages. Of course, they understand each other, they understand each other up to the point where they stop understanding each other – and *therefore* they have something to say. For this is precisely the problem of speech: if they understood each other completely they would have absolutely no need to talk. We talk because we do not understand each other, but at the same time we only talk when we understand each other, a little, that is to say because we *believe* in the possibility of understanding each other. But this is an endless possibility on which, when we talk, we *wager* that what we say will make sense, that it will be significant, that it will not be in-significant.

The question here concerns idiom, and I will return to it through the question of the exception, which is also the question of invention. And this is my way of returning to your own question:

1. I do not believe that the I can in any way precede the we; on the contrary, it is the already-there of a we that makes the individuation of the I possible.

2. Nor do I believe that it is a matter here of communication, strictly speaking: the relation of the I to the we is not so much a communication as a signification [*signifiance*], i.e. a non-insignificance – or if you prefer, an idiomatic invention.

For signification does not depend on communication, any more than does idiomatic inven-

tion. "Communication" assumes that I already know what I want to say before saying it. This does happen sometimes, of course. But in idiomatic invention, in signification – of which poetry is the form par excellence – what I want to say is constituted *by* the way in which I say it, and this is then no longer simply a matter of communication.

Having said that, I am not speaking here in the name of the transcendental (any more than I am taking refuge in the empirical): my reasoning is "a-transcendental," in the sense in which Bataille spoke "a-theologically." Bataille owes the a-theological form of thought to a theological history of thought: he comes after theology, but in the sense that he comes *from* theology. The after of theology is completely overdetermined by theology. In a sense you could describe me as an a-transcendental philosopher: I consider that everything that precedes me in philosophy proceeds from what we call the transcendental, but at the same time I believe that I belong to an era that challenges the difference between what is transcendental and what is empirical, an era that says that this difference is not relevant. And I think that this is because, technics being at once empirical and constitutive, we can no longer be satisfied with the old distinction between transcendental and empirical. We are confronted, in other words, by a new question about difference: how to *invent difference*, that is to say to *make* a difference, beyond the difference between the empirical and the transcendental that is ruined by the constitutive dimension of technics? But at the same time, *all* the questions that interest us have been *given* to us by the transcendental tradition, and once the constitutive dimension of technics has been taken on board, all these questions remain intact. It is necessary to re-examine them just as the transcendental manner of questioning bequeaths them to us, but by inventing another way of answering them, which is not at all empiricist or naturalistic.

I can only speak a language if the language that I speak is absolutely unique in the world. This is why you came to speak to me, to interview me: because you think that what I have to say can only be said by me. There are some people who no longer speak at all in their own name: these are people who live in poverty, people who are manipulated and alienated by the media. They are the outcome of the last stage of the war of spirits [*guerre des esprits*] (which is also a war of minds, and the whole question concerns the way we understand this link between spirit and mind), which not only reduces the idiomatic diversity of exotic speech to nil but also tends to destroy the diachronicity of consciousness itself, through the imposition of statements and ways of speaking produced by marketing and the information and communication industries. This stage of the war of spirits is that of the industrial production of symbols, which leads to their inversion into what I call *diaboles* (because their expressions are insignificant): what's at stake here is an *ecology of the mind* [*écologie de l'esprit*]. The ruin of the mind causes the annihilation of the I and the we in the they.

In order for someone to signify, two apparently contradictory things must happen. On the one hand, speakers make use of the rules that they share with others: if you understand me, it's because you understand French grammar. But all of these rules are implemented in the service of an *irregular* construction. And it's an *absolute* irregularity – for example, *the* French language does *not exist*. The French language does not exist, but each time we speak, we try to invent it: this is what I call the structure of invention. In other words, *the French language, which does not exist, consists.* This insistent consistency is what ties the I to the we.

In order that I can speak to you, we must be able to synchronise with each other, to share the rules that we have in common. This sharing makes up what Saussure calls a synchronic period of language. But inside this synchrony there is a diachrony: each speaker is radically diachronic, and here again we encounter the problem of time. The speaker can only speak in a time which is absolutely his own, but he speaks *for* synchrony, that is to say for the "we": to register the speaker in the "we." In other words, it is not necessary to oppose the exceptional to the banal, or diachrony to synchrony. Diachrony and synchrony must continuously work together

in order for signification to take place. Today, in the age of the information and communication industry, that is to say the age of the industrial production of symbols that have as their essential purpose *the synchronisation of consciousnesses by nullifying their diachrony* (by adapting them to mass markets, by subjecting them to standardised models of behaviour), synchrony and diachrony oppose each other and fall apart, decompose. This *decomposition of the symbolic* is literally *diabolical*: it generates disconnection, that is to say, the *decomposition of the social* itself.

notes

I This interview was conducted in Paris on 28 June 2002. I have used Macquarrie and Robinson's translation of *Being and Time* as my guide in rendering Stiegler's Heideggerian terms into English (Heidegger, *Being and Time*, trans. John Macquarrie and Edward Robinson (New York: Harper, 1962)). I would like to thank Viviane de Charrière for her invaluable help and wise advice. [Translator's note.]

2 Cf. Stiegler, *Technics and Time I* 200–01.

3 The French reads: "*En ce sens, le mortel est un être par défaut, un être marqué d'un défaut d'origine, c'est à dire plongé dans un handicap d'origine ...*" *Etre par défaut* connotes the phrase *condamner par défaut* (to condemn someone in their absence), as well as the usual meanings of *défaut*: absence, lack, failure, fault, flaw, defect, and so on. There is no longer any one English word that conveys these various connotations, but since Stiegler uses the term *défaut* as an effectively technical term it seems important to translate it literally, at least much of the time. Here and elsewhere *défaut d'origine* could be more naturally translated either as "original flaw" or as "lack of an origin," but in order to preserve the effect of Stiegler's usage we will occasionally translate is as "original default." In such cases the reader should remember the (now archaic) connotations of failure, want, and absence in dated expressions like "for default of" or "in default of," as well as the more familiar implication of phrases like "to win by default." As in other deconstructive contexts, one effect of the phrase is to blur the difference between an

original and a pre-original condition. Collins and Beardsworth, confronted with the same problem, generally translate *défaut* as "de-fault" (see Stiegler, *Technics and Time I* 280, n. 12). Jennifer Bajorek translates *défaut d'origine* as "original lack or lack of origin" (Stiegler, *Echographies* 173, n. 10). [Editor's note.]

4 Cf. Heidegger, *Being and Time*, sect. 17. Macquarrie and Robinson translate Heidegger's *Verweisung, verweisen* (and its cognates *anweisen* and *zuweisen*) as "the phenomenon of *reference* or *assignment*" (*Being and Time* 107). [Translator's note.]

5 Cf. Heidegger, *Being and Time* 96.

6 Hubert Dreyfus, "De la *technè* à la technique: le statut ambigu de l'ustensilité dans *Être et temps*" in *Cahier de l'Herne: Martin Heidegger*, ed. Michel Haar (Paris: L'Herne, 1983) 285–303.

7 The French reads: "*Autrement dit il tente de combler le défaut d'origine – comble du défaut, comme on dit en français, qui est aussi une redoutable aventure politique.*" [Translator's note].

8 Alain Badiou, *Ethics: An Essay on the Understanding of Evil*, trans. Peter Hallward (London: Verso, 2001).

9 See, in particular, André Leroi-Gourhan, *Évolution et techniques*, 2 vols. (Paris: Albin Michel, 1943–45); Leroi-Gourhan, *Prehistoric Man* (New York: Philosophical Library, 1957); Leroi-Gourhan, *Gesture and Speech* (Cambridge, MA: MIT P, 1993); Bertrand Gille, *History of Techniques* (New York: Gordon, 1986); Gilbert Simondon, *L'Individuation psychique et collective* (Paris: Aubier, 1989); Simondon, *Du mode d'existence des objets techniques* (Paris: Aubier, 2001).

10 Cf. Sylvain Auroux, *La Révolution technologique de la grammatisation: introduction à l'histoire des sciences du langage* (Liège: Mardaga, 1994); Auroux (ed.), *Le Développement de la grammaire occidentale: histoire des idées linguistiques*, vol. 2. (Liège: Mardaga, 1989); Auroux, *La Raison, le langage et les normes* (Paris: Presses Universitaires de France, 1998).

works by stiegler

"L'Effondrement techno-logique du temps, *les machines virtuelles.*" *Traverses* 44–45 (1988).

"La Culture de l'écran: la lecture assistée par ordinateur." *Les Nouveaux outils du savoir.* Ed. Pierre Chambat and Pierre Lévy. Paris: Descartes, 1991.

"Leroi-Gourhan, part maudite de l'anthropologie." *Les Nouvelles de l'Archéologie* 48–49 (1992): 23–30.

"Questioning Technology and Time." *Tekhnema* 1 (1993).

La Technique et le temps I: la faute d'Épiméthée. Paris: Galilée, 1994. *Technics and Time I: The Fault of Epimetheus.* Trans. Richard Beardsworth and George Collins. Stanford: Stanford UP, 1998.

"Machines à écrire et machines à penser." *Genesis* 5 (1994): 25–49.

"Ce qui fait défaut." *Césure* 54 (1995).

"Etre là-bas: phénoménologie et orientation." *Alter* 4 (1996): 263–77.

"L'Image discrète." *Échographies de la télévision: entretiens filmés.* By Bernard Stiegler and Jacques Derrida. Paris: Galilée, 1996. "The Discrete Image." *Echographies of Television: Filmed Interviews.* Trans. Jennifer Bajorek. Cambridge: Polity, 2002. 145–63.

"Persephone, Oedipus, Epimetheus." *Tekhnema* 3 (1996). Available online at <http://tekhnema.free.fr/3editorial.htm>.

La Technique et le temps II: la désorientation. Paris: Galilée, 1996.

"Les Bouleversements de l'audiovisuel dans le monde" (3 Oct. 1997). Available online at <http://www.amafrance-ma.org/archives/image/image06.htm>.

"La Convergence ou la mort ..." *Libération* 13 Mar. 1998: 4.

"Temps, technique et individuation dans l'oeuvre de Simondon." *Intellectica* 26–27 (1998).

"Time of Cinema: On the 'New World' and 'Cultural Exception.'" *Tekhnema* 4 (1998).

"L'Hyperindustrialisation de la culture et le temps des attrape-nigauds. Manifeste pour une écologie de l'esprit." *Art Press* hors série 2 (Nov. 1999). Available online at <http://www.artpress.com/Pages/hors-serie/Internet/extmenu-inter.html>.

"Une Synchronie généralisee." *Libération* 11 Sept. 1999: 47.

"Le Temps des attrape-nigauds: 'Rapido,' l'assommoir contemporain." *Le Monde Diplomatique* Aug. 2000: 28. Available online at <http://www.monde-diplomatique.fr/2000/08/STIEGLER/14126>.

Note prospective sur l'évolution des conditions d'aménagement du territoire dans le contexte de la société de l'information et dans le domaine culturel [2000]. Published online at <http://www.atica.pm.gouv.fr/dossiers/documents/schema/culture.doc>.

"Derrida and Technology: Fidelity at the Limits of Deconstruction and the Prosthesis of Faith." *Jacques Derrida and the Humanities: A Critical Reader.* Ed. Tom Cohen. Trans. Richard Beardsworth. Cambridge: Cambridge UP, 2002. 238–70.

La Technique et le temps III: le temps du cinéma et la question du mal être. Paris: Galilée, 2001. (Chapter 4 has been translated by Stefan Herbrechter as "Our Ailing Educational Institutions: The Global Mnemotechnical System" in *Culture Machine* 5 (Mar. 2003). Available online at <http://culturemachine.tees.ac.uk/Articles/Stiegler.htm>.)

"Entretien avec Bernard Stiegler." Conducted by Bruno Serrou. *Res Musica* 4 June 2002. Available online at <http://www.resmusica.com/aff_article.php3?art=123>.

"Nous nous acheminons vers un monde trans-esthetique." *Libération* 3 June 2002: 39.

"La Philosophie dans le studio." *L'Humanité* 17 June 2002. Available online at <http://www.humanite.presse.fr/journal/2002-06-17/2002-06-17-35707>.

"Transcendental Imagination in a Thousand Points." Trans. George Collins. *New Formations* 46 (2002): 7–22.

Aimer, s'aimer, nous aimer. Paris: Galilée, 2003.

Passer à l'acte. Paris: Galilée, 2003.

Bernard Stiegler
IRCAM
1 place Igor Stravinsky
75004 Paris
France

Peter Hallward
French Department
King's College London
The Strand
London WC2R 2LS
UK
E-mail: peter.hallward@kcl.ac.uk

Sean Gaston
81 Godstow Road
Wolvercote
Oxford OX2 8PE
UK
E-mail: elan-gaston@carsean.demon.co.uk

journal of the theoretical humanities
volume 8   number 2   august 2003

introduction

ray brassier

François Laruelle, born in 1937, is Professor of Contemporary Philosophy at the University of Paris X (Nanterre), where he has taught since 1967. He is a prolific writer whose output is notable both for its quantity and its reputation for difficulty. Apart from the sixteen books he has published since 1971 – beginning with *Phénomène et différence* (1971) and including *Machines textuelles* (1976), *Les Philosophies de la différence* (1986), *Principes de la non-philosophie* (1996) and most recently *Le Christ futur* (2002) – there has also been a constant stream of essays and "experimental texts,"[1] only a fraction of which have been published, and at least two complete treatises that remain unpublished or perhaps unpublishable, given their gargantuan heft (both are over six hundred pages long) and hair-raising conceptual severity.[2]

Severity, or an adamantine density of conceptual abstraction, is a hallmark of Laruelle's writing, one that has elicited charges of "obscurantism" against him and encouraged some to dismiss him as a wilful *provocateur* or even to accuse him of something akin to "terrorism"[3] (presumably theoretical). But the austere abstraction of Laruelle's writing is a function of its ambition: to elaborate a transcendental theory of philosophy in which the latter is reduced to the status of a mere empirical material. This is not a meta-philosophical conceit, Laruelle insists. He distinguishes between philosophy and theory, and hence between a meta-philosophical philosophy of philosophy and his own attempt to construct a non-philosophical *theory* of philosophy. According to Laruelle, the meta-philosophical dimension is intrinsic to the inherently

françois laruelle

translated by ray brassier

WHAT CAN NON-PHILOSOPHY DO?

reflexive nature of philosophical thought, so that every philosophy worthy of the name harbours a philosophy of philosophy. But what is required, Laruelle argues, is not more reflection but *less*, so that a non-philosophical theory of philosophy will not be "an intensified reduplication of philosophy," a meta-philosophy, but rather its "simplification." The intrinsically reflexive or specular nature of philosophical thought makes of philosophy a practice of interpretation rather than a theory: "Philosophy is interpretation at a global level because it is infinite repetition and self-reference, overview and contemplation of the world."[4]

Instead of a philosophy of philosophy, then, Laruelle proposes a non-reflexive and hence *non-philosophical* theory capable of *explaining* –

ISSN 0969-725X print/ISSN 1469-2899 online/03/020169-21 © 2003 Taylor & Francis Ltd and the Editors of *Angelaki*
DOI: 10.1080/0969725032000162648

rather than reflecting or interpreting – the reflexive mechanisms of philosophy in terms that are themselves irreducible to philosophy's own specular logic. For Laruelle, theoretical *explanation* – of the kind exemplified by scientific theory – requires a heterogeneity between *explanans* and *explanandum* and is importantly distinct from philosophical *speculation*, which invariably includes mechanisms of interpretation and evaluation (whether explicitly as in Nietzsche, Heidegger and Deleuze, or implicitly as in Kant, Hegel and Husserl); mechanisms that necessitate a structural isomorphy between speculation and whatever is "speculated." Against the speculative narcissism of philosophy, for which every phenomenon functions as a mirror through which philosophy can conduct its own interminable self-interpretation, Laruelle proposes a non-philosophical theory that simultaneously explains philosophy and releases phenomena from their subordination to philosophical interpretation.

This preoccupation with achieving a theoretical mastery of the logic of philosophy is already apparent in Laruelle's early work, which he now classifies under the heading "Philosophy I" (1971–81). The latter finds its initial impetus in a prolonged and systematic engagement with the "philosophies of difference": Nietzsche, Heidegger, Derrida and Deleuze. It is in the wake of this engagement that Laruelle claims to have identified a structural invariant governing the logic of philosophy as such; an invariant at once more universal and more all-encompassing than the logic of metaphysics, representation or ontotheology. This is the logic of philosophical decision *as* difference (a logic that *includes* the deconstruction of metaphysics and the dismantling of representation). In *Les Philosophies de la différence* (1986), Laruelle argues that Nietzsche, Heidegger, Derrida and Deleuze do not so much undermine the authority of the Greek logos as reinforce it by exemplifying its underlying structure: the structure of philosophical decision as a dyad or difference that simultaneously includes *and* excludes its own identity as a supplementary third term. Thus, the structure of philosophical decision is a fractional structure comprising 2/3 or 3/2 terms. In the former case, the 2 qua difference between x and y is divided by the 3 as identity *of* that difference, but an identity that has to be added on to it as its necessary supplement in order to constitute it. In the latter case, the 3 qua supplement of identity added on to x and y is divided by the 2 as their difference, which has to be subtracted from their identity in order to constitute it. Nietzsche and Deleuze exemplify the former schema; Heidegger and Derrida the latter.

Laruelle concludes that philosophy, from Heraclitus to Heidegger, Derrida and Deleuze, has only ever exploited identity in order to think being qua difference. Even when it laid claim to the supremacy of the self-identical Notion, as in Hegel, philosophy surreptitiously privileged difference, for the Hegelian "identity of identity and difference" is nothing but their difference as absolute contradiction or self-relating negativity. In the final analysis, being is just a synonym for difference and expressions such as "ontological difference," "differential ontology" and even "philosophy of difference" are all ultimately pleonasms. Hence it should come as no surprise that the re-invigoration of ontology in twentieth-century European philosophy goes hand in hand with a renewed preoccupation with difference and an attempt to "deconstruct" identity; nor that the "identity" deconstructed by the philosophies of difference is little more than a paltry shadow cast by ontological difference. Moreover, by pushing this differential mechanism of the Greek logos to its ultimate limit, the philosophies of difference expose the fundamental parameters of philosophical decision as consisting in a set of variations on the Parmenidean theme of the identity-in-difference of thought and being. Thus, it is decision as identity-in-difference of *logos* and *phusis*, thought and being, that reveals the idealism inherent in every philosophy, even if it calls itself "materialist," because it consists in an interpretative practice of thought that already presupposes a reciprocity – albeit a complex, differential one – between thought and the real. Hence the charge of "idealism" that has often been levelled at philosophy by Laruelle.

Having uncovered the structure of decision as the invariant governing the possibilities of philosophising, Laruelle, in *Philosophie et non-philosophie* (1989), proposes to suspend the authority of philosophy through a non-decisional or non-philosophical thinking in order to explore new, previously unenvisageable conceptual possibilities – much as non-Euclidean geometries began exploring previously inconceivable geometries once they suspended Euclid's fifth axiom about parallel lines. The key to the possibility of this suspension lies in the discovery that identity as radical immanence or what Laruelle calls "the One-in-One" has *already* effected this radical or unilateral separation between itself and the decisional dyad with regard to which identity is both a supplement and a deficit. Identity qua radical immanence is not some ineffable abstraction which the non-philosopher has to strive to attain: it is the element he or she is already concretely operating from, the "cause-of-the-last-instance" that is already determining his or her thinking. It is the identity of man as "the One without being." But man's identity as radical immanence is an identity-without-unity or ontological consistency; an identity that has already set aside or suspended the pertinence of ontological difference as decision or co-constitution of identity and difference.[5] The point, Laruelle insists, is not to get out of philosophy but to realise that you were never in it in the first place; to liberate yourself from the intrinsically philosophical hallucination that you need to be liberated from philosophy:

> The point is not to engender non-philosophical effects within philosophy, which would still be to presuppose philosophy's uncircumventable validity. It is to install thought from the outset within the space of the universal opening as such, the space of the opening as essence rather than as mere event, attribute or alterity. The point is to install thought within the space of an opening that no longer needs to be brought about by means of constitutive operations such as those of overturning or displacement; an opening that has always already been brought about by the One and is simply its correlate.[6]

Accordingly, unlike the space of philosophical or decisional thinking, whose parameters are shaped by the structure of decision as differential synthesis or One-of-the-dyad (where the One is simultaneously added to and subtracted from the dyad), the space of non-philosophical or non-decisional thinking is shaped by what Laruelle calls the "unilaterality" whereby the One is separate from the dyad without the dyad being separate from the One. Thus, whereas the logic of philosophical decision consists in dyadic synthesis (+ or − One), the logic of non-decisional or non-philosophical thinking consists in *unilateralisation*: dyadic synthesis is converted into a "unilateral duality" where the One as identity without synthesis determines decision as a duality that is also without synthesis. This conversion of decisional synthesis into unilateral duality is what Laruelle calls "determination-in-the-last-instance" or, more recently, "cloning." Laruelle provides an exhaustive analysis of the logic of unilateralisation, as well as of the non-philosophical "cloning" of philosophy to which it gives rise, in *Principes de la non-philosophie* (1996), which he regards as his most important book to date and in which the concepts, procedures and operations specific to non-philosophy attain their full realisation. This is also the book in which Laruelle tries to explain the (highly complex) nature of the shift in his thinking from "Philosophie II" (1981–92) to "Philosophie III" (1995 to the present).

Following the systematic presentation of non-philosophical method in *Principes*, Laruelle has, in subsequent work, tried to "apply" this method to various philosophical materials in a manner consonant with non-philosophy's explicitly experimental ethos. Thus, *Éthique de l'étranger* (2000) proposes a "non-ethical" treatment of Platonist, Kantian and Levinasian accounts of the ethical, while *Introduction au non-marxisme* (2000) delineates a "non-Marxist" reading of Marx. Most recently, 2002's *Le Christ futur* is an exercise in "non-Christian heresy" organised around the concept of a Christ-subject who effectuates an unenvisageable future "other than" the world's.

notes

1 Examples of these can be found in *La Décision Philosophique*, the journal edited by Laruelle between 1987 and 1989.

2   Laruelle, *Économie générale des effets d'être* (1974), and *Matière et phénomène* (1976).

3 See, for example, the interviews with Laruelle conducted by Jacques Derrida, Sarah Kofman, Philippe Lacoue-Labarthe and Jean-Luc Nancy, and included as appendices to Laruelle's *Le Déclin de l'écriture* (1977). Laruelle responds to the charge of "terrorism" in a debate with Derrida that took place in 1986 at the Collège International de Philosophie, published as "Controverse sur la possibilité d'une science de la philosophie" in *La Décision Philosophique* 5 (1988): 63–76.

4 See below, Laruelle, "What Can Non-Philosophy Do?" 184–85.

5 "The One's radical autonomy, its real indifference with regard to being and to thought [...] invalidates a fundamental thesis of ontology: that of the convertibility between the One and being [...]. It also limits the putatively primary pertinence of the thesis of another convertibility: that of the *ontological difference* between being and beings" (Laruelle, *Principes de la non-philosophie* 24).

6 Laruelle, *Philosophie et non-philosophie* 32.

what can non-philosophy do?

françois laruelle

I the infinite end of philosophy

Our contemporary situation is, as ever, complex. It harbours numerous contrasts. But one of its most telling characteristics is that of a bustling philosophical activity that masks a fundamental indifference to philosophy. Were we to set aside those distortions that are a function of historical perspective, we would see that this situation is perfectly normal, but a superficial awareness or consciousness of this phenomenon is particularly acute at the present time. Is this indicative of a lack of interest? A lack of purpose? Indifference? Unlike their predecessors, who were directly preoccupied with philosophy itself, modern philosophers have tended to be more preoccupied with their relation to philosophy as it is mediated across historical distance. We no longer practise philosophy naively and spontaneously from within itself, as though it were a second nature or a habitat. Kant shattered this spontaneity and bequeathed to us a new problem: that of the *use* of philosophy. What are we to do with metaphysics from now on? It is as though we have been burdened with a suffocating legacy – we have inherited scraps that we do not know what to do with. Are we supposed to reprocess or even recycle these scraps of thought? Is it a question of the ecology of thought – a thought that no longer knows how to dispose of its products? There is something of this in our legacy and in our overburdened memory. But why does modern man formulate the problem of his legacy by wondering how to manage something that sometimes appears as a shortage and at other times as a surplus? Perhaps it is necessary to reformulate the problem of our relation to the tradition and begin by putting the latter to one side. Is it then a question of the "end of philosophy"?

But is not the expression "end of philosophy" or "end of metaphysics" part of this same cumbersome legacy? Let us use the expression "without-philosophy" instead, but only on condition that we ascribe the lack or absence of philosophy to man now understood as "man-in-person," and that we re-examine these problems according to this new angle. To understand this change in problematic, we have to go back to the essential origins of philosophy.

"End of philosophy" is a philosophical expression not only by virtue of its formulation but also through its meaning and as a matter of principle. It expresses philosophy in its ultimate possibility – winding around itself, gathering itself and withdrawing from thought. Philosophy encloses itself, consummates itself as a form of technique, leaving behind an empty space for a new experience of thought. Heidegger and Derrida have added certain important nuances to this schema. But it still has to be understood as expressing the essence of philosophy: an auto-positional essence indefinitely closing on itself, whilst missing or exceeding itself by a difference intrinsic to that identity, so that it never fully achieves either a perfect closure or a perfect opening. This is not to say that auto-positioning or auto-beginning always fails, or fails as a matter of principle. It fails only to the same degree as it succeeds because this structure – specular in nature – is divided by a difference or alterity that remains subordinated to its identity, the whole forming a dyadic/triadic structure that is equally and simultaneously open and closed.

It may be that this structure is never manifested in a pure state within the history of philosophy, that it is always somewhat unbalanced depending on whether the emphasis is on identity or alterity. Nevertheless, it forms the principal core, the minimal invariant that must be presupposed as operative in any doctrine of a philosophical or systematic type. This core defines philosophy as a "theoreticist idealism" or "idealist theoreticism." This is not the name of a particular doctrine but another name for the essence of philosophy as such. In other words, every philosophy, however it comes to be realised, is bound to a specularity that it mistakes for the real, bound to a primacy and priority of theory as reflection of that real – the two together constituting "speculation." Different doctrines may vary this structure but they "economise" philosophy's presence and absence in such a way that its absence remains intrinsic to its continuous presence. It is always philosophical mastery that decides – without deciding – about philosophy's end: for example (since we are talking about speculation) about its overcoming or internalising *Aufhebung*.

The unitary and sufficient presupposition which is intrinsic to philosophy's self-relation (and which fuelled theoreticist idealism from the Greeks to Hegel) was merely somewhat weakened by the various kinds of deconstruction when they began to acknowledge that philosophy's auto-closure was simultaneously enabled and hindered by an alterity – but an alterity that they in turn continued to presuppose as sufficient or absolute, rather than as a radical alterity or alterity in-person. This amounted to yet another division (albeit one that was now uneven) between philosophy and an alterity that is partially extra-philosophical yet that continues to ratify philosophy's basic sufficiency. The latter is precisely what an anonymous alterity of this kind is incapable of revoking.

II the real or identity-in-person

Non-philosophy is not a return to identity or to its primacy in the wake of twentieth-century philosophy's orgy of alterity and difference. It is not some sort of reaction. Perhaps it is another identity altogether that is at issue here. Identity-in-person has never yet been attained. Identity has only ever been aimed at as though it were homologous with an object, one that might be used for various ends. Philosophical thought is directed towards identity intentionally, via transcendence as *epekeina* rather than as *meta*. Thus, it is obliged to make certain corrective adjustments in that practice of objectivation. Identity becomes the object of desire rather than of knowledge; it conditions the latter without falling under it, etc. *Nevertheless, it remains inseparable from transcendence as deployed through the* meta, *from eidetic Being – as though it constituted an uneven half tacked on to this transcendence.* Whence the fact that the *epekeina*, which is absolute transcendence, remains relatively dependent upon the *meta*, which is relative transcendence. Like desire,

philosophy is ambitious, it is the enjoyment of the absolutely other; but the weakness of the absolute resides in its point of departure and in its process, which consists in an absolutisation of experience.

Non-philosophy is founded in another experience of identity. It conceives of identity precisely as that to which it is impossible to direct thought towards intentionally – whether as object or horizon. It conceives of identity as something that cannot be attained via transcendence. This is identity-in-person, the One in flesh and blood, which does not tolerate either internal transcendence or external, operational transcendence. It is not the object of a construction or of a philosophical desire deployed within the realm of what is operationally intuitable. It is the philosopher, not just philosophy, who is from the outset (albeit not definitively) put out of play as a *deus ex machina*. This is why non-philosophy simulates philosophy in its beginning, but does so through a different gesture. Philosophy begins and remains within itself, within its own immanence, by presupposing itself – but in such a way as to be capable of minimising and reintegrating its own presuppositions, which are gathered up in transcendence. The immanence of philosophy is complex, split into two: it is at once thematic and functional, requiring various gestures of transcendence or presupposition, but ones that can ultimately be minimised and reintegrated, or that are already directly amenable to integration (Hegel). This is characteristic of the auto-encompassing style of philosophy.

By way of contrast, although non-philosophy also begins in immanence and remains within it, it does not take the form of a self-encompassing movement in which identity merely functions to close or seal the circle. In non-philosophy, identity as such is no longer a function of anything else. No matter how much a functional identity simulates the real, or engenders real effects, it invariably dissolves in the only available reality: the reality of the system as the meta-stable, self-encompassing reality of philosophical desire. The question, then, is whether it is enough to restrict oneself to the construction – and thereby to the deconstruction – of a system of philosophical desire; or whether – in complete contrast – we should try to elaborate a theory of it instead. Let us continue our analysis.

III the transcendental or the separated middle: a theory of alterity

Identity-in-person is a primary name. There are others, such as man-in-person. Once it has been rigorously defined, rather than given over to the realm of unitary, metaphysical or anthropological generality; once it has been axiomatically determined rather than presupposed through vague theses or statements, what we are calling "man" as identity is so in-consistent, so devoid of essence as to constitute *a hole in nothingness itself, not just in being*. It is a blind-spot for philosophical auto-reflection, which now assumes the mantle of nothingness, now being, or shifts from one to the other. The concept of auto-reflection applies equally to the most ancient philosophies as to modern ones. It is indicative of theoreticist idealism and speculation as the essence of philosophical systems. Yet not only is the One-in-One foreign to all ontological or linguistic consistency, it is also foreign to all inconsistency. It is the without-consistency. Man-in-person or identity can be defined, in terms that are homologous with the simultaneously excluded and included middle that systematically opens and closes philosophy, as the *identity-without-middle* or better still as *the separated middle*, which is neither included nor excluded, neither consistent nor inconsistent, etc. It is neither of these two predicates as opposed to one another or as synthesised into a third term. In other words, no set of dyadic philosophical predicates is appropriate to "man-in-person" – which is not to say the latter is "ineffable," as is objected by philosophers who assume that to state something about x or y is to attribute a predicate to a subject and thereby to affect the real through language. The separated middle is neither included nor excluded ... but not because it is both at once, in the manner of a philosophical synthesis. It is *separated* ... from inclusion and exclusion as such, separated from the kind of relation involved in those dualities with which thought traditionally operates. It is a rule of philosophy that the "neither ... nor ...," which

appears to exclude predicates from the real, actually reintroduces them into it by assuring us that it is "at once" one and the other, with the obvious proviso that this double negation be included within the final result. In non-philosophy, however, the "neither ... nor ..." is definitive from the outset because it expresses the being-separated proper to identity, or to the separated-in-person.

In other words, this being-separated, which we will later refer to as the *other than ...*, is not an attribute of identity, analytically or synthetically contained within the latter. Rather, it is its transcendental aspect, which as real is invisible. This transcendental aspect is not a *property* of identity but is instead the very same thing as identity, or the function of *relation to ...* which identity is always able to assume. Nevertheless, it is only in so far as it is real or immanent that identity can constitute a transcendental alterity, rather than the other way round. It may seem strange to think identity as the middle but this is an example of a philosophical necessity – in this instance, the way in which identity regularly functions as the third fundamental term in philosophy – being reconfigured non-philosophically.

How are we to conceive of this transcendental alterity that is proper to the real as identity-in-person? Let us consider for a moment dialectical identity as that which differentiates itself from itself, becomes other than itself, etc. Alterity affects it or belongs to its complex essence even if it is surmounted or overcome by identity. Identity is at once a "subordinate part" and the whole, while alterity is a subordinate part of the whole, the two together forming a continuous plane, or something susceptible to further dialecticisation. Let us suppose now that instead of finding alterity at the heart of identity, one encountered there only identity itself – identity as the flesh of the One itself rather than as the remainder of a gesture of abstraction. Such abstraction would reduce identity to something still less than an envelope, something that is not even a topological plane or pure surface but more like a logically formalised term or symbol. Yet identity-in-person is not a symbol but an identity whose own identity constitutes its phenomenon, its "flesh." Real identity is impoverished, impoverished to an extent that is unimaginable for philosophy, but it is not impoverished because all alterity has been abstracted from it or because it has been stripped bare through a process of alienation. It is indeed articulated through a symbol, and its effects are in turn articulated through a play of symbols, but to confuse the real with its symbol is precisely the mistake of theoreticist idealism and the root of all philosophical illusion.

This confusion begins when, without one's noticing it, identity-in-person is spontaneously imagined to be a bare term, a pure signifier devoid of signification. In fact, identity-in-person has no need of signification and is not of the order of the signifier. The real is not just what is impossible for the symbol; it is of an entirely other order and capable of determining a sign as symbol. This is enough to distinguish non-philosophy from psychoanalysis. Identity did not undergo the "linguistic turn" and nor does the symbol when it is determined by identity. There is a sense in which identity-in-person is the real-transcendental cause − rather than the condition of possibility − of symbolisation in a way that precludes the assumption that symbols are given ready-made, or provided via a symbolising givenness. In other words, any philosophical coupling of terms directed at the One, or even at being, may be used to name real identity, provided those terms undergo a symbolic abstraction (but one that bears only on the symbol and not also on the real). As for the real itself, it is already abstract without there having been an operation of abstraction.

Having nothing but its own being-manifest − which is not even an essence − as content, identity cannot, strictly speaking, act or exert a direct positive causality. Since it is without essence, it can be neither active nor passive − no more so than it can be both at once, as though to compensate for this supposed deficiency. It is incapable of functioning as motor for a dialectic. It is "negative" rather than negational; a non-sufficient cause, rather than one that is sufficient and essential. Yet this quasi-sterility, this neutrality without return or compensation, in no way prevents it from taking into account or "cloning" philosophy as a reduced datum or material. This

taking into account does not cause it to exit from itself; it does not constrain it to act. It is separated without that separation eating into it or affecting its essence. At the same time, since this being-separated directly expresses identity or radical immanence, it is brought forth, so to speak, by the vision-in-One as the latter takes into account what is offered by philosophy. Immanent knowledge is *other than* … philosophical. We must replace Levinas' *otherwise than*, which is still anonymous and pertains to absolute transcendence, with *other than* …: an adjective rather than an adverb, but one that has been raised to the status of a primary name for the real or man-in-person.

Of course, philosophy also invokes a One-Other as the object that provides the supreme instance of absolute transcendence or *epekeina*. But there the situation is complicated by the fact that the nature of this object is still that of the philosophical combination in its topological form as infinite, self-enclosed Moebius strip. The radical One, by way of contrast, is initially in-One without the Other belonging to it. Consequently, it is Other only to the extent to which it is Other-in-Other or Other than … In philosophy, the combinatory structure or system continues to predominate so that philosophy can only posit the One-Other as a term in the guise of something that remains an "ideological" artefact: an effect or result that has been abstracted from the process through which it was produced. In non-philosophy, on the contrary, the One as such is not subordinated to any thing or structure because it is genuinely independent and has no need of such support. But at the same time the One is the Other-in-Other, which by virtue of this fact also acquires a radical autonomy. We could say that, as in philosophy, the Other is still first, but that it no longer has any primacy. Alternatively, and more precisely, we could say that primacy and priority always go hand in hand, but that in philosophy they are actually subordinated to a combinatory structure which is the true locus of power and independence; one that secretly enjoys a kind of hyper-primacy and is deployed in the realm of operational transcendence. In non-philosophy, however, the One-Other subsists without being subordinated in an idealist fashion to the syntax of this operational transcendence and its combinatory economy. Both primacy and priority are shorn of the equivocal, self-doubling nature which is characteristic of speculative identity. Primacy and priority go together but as the real that is also capable of assuming the function of transcendental or other than … for philosophy. They go together as the real that is independent but that is also primary.

Rather than dividing and doubling the One-Other by itself, or infinitely multiplying it, non-philosophy simplifies it. In philosophy, the One is never purely and simply "One," unless it is a mere symbol, as it is in the principle of identity, in which it is already doubled by itself. Philosophy invariably doubles and multiplies it, as in the neo-Platonists' hierarchy of Ones, or the more or less mediated identity of (difference and) identity. It is imperative not to confuse the One of philosophy, which is the *One (of the) One*, with the One of non-philosophy, which is the One-in-One or the One-in-person, the One in flesh and blood. Is the latter also multiplied, either by itself or by being divided? Or does it amount to an impoverishment, an abstraction-subtraction, a One − 1? The expression "One-in-One" or "vision-in-One" indicates the absence of any operation that would define the latter; the fact that it is not inscribed within an operational space or more powerful structure; its immanence *in* itself rather than *to* anything else; its naked simplicity as never either exceeding or lacking, because it is the only measure required, but one that is never a self-measurement, one that measures nothing as long as there is nothing to measure.

IV producing a programme of existence

If there is a non-philosophical programme, it consists in appropriating philosophy or the world (in a broadened sense of the term).

Why does non-philosophy invariably appear in the form of a programme or a project, one that irritates people because it never seems to be realised? The answer is that, although it has nothing to do with a programme in its essential or practical aspect, its inessential aspect (which is precisely the philosophical aspect non-philosophy assumes through its "material") makes it appear as though it does. This programmatic appearance is unavoidable but it is no more than an appearance, in other words, something we will call a programme-without-programming or at the very least a programme for de-programming. What matters is knowing whether or not it will be possible to overcome this appearance and to acknowledge it as such. What follows explores part of this programme, guided by the theme of non-philosophical practice and what it is capable of, with regard to philosophy but also in the eyes of philosophy.

Why a "non-philosophy"? Philosophy is so varied, so fickle that it has already criticised itself in an infinite variety of ways, already exhibited such a degree of metamorphic plasticity as to disqualify any attempt to reduce it to a single invariant of thought. Was there any point in trying to do so? The question "what *is* non-philosophy?" must be replaced by the question about what it can and cannot *do*. To ask what it can do is already to acknowledge that its capacities are not unlimited. This question is partly Spinozist: no one knows what a body can do. It is partly Kantian: circumscribe philosophy's illusory power, the power of reason or the faculties, and do not extend its sufficiency in the shape of another philosophy. It is also partly Marxist: how much of philosophy can be transformed through practice, how much of it can be withdrawn from its "ideological" use? And finally, it is also partly Wittgensteinian: how can one limit philosophical language through its proper use?

But these apparent philosophical proximities and family resemblances are only valid up to a point. That point is called the real – determination-in-the-last-instance, the unilateral duality, etc. – which is to say, all of non-philosophy in-person. In other words, these kinds of comparisons are devoid of meaning, or at best profoundly misleading, because non-philosophy is "performative" and exhausts itself as an immanent practice rather than as a programme.

The answer to the question "what are we to do with philosophy?" must already have been given in the form of the question "what can non-philosophy do?" The latter provides a rigorous formulation of the former by delineating a space within which it can enjoy a certain pertinence without being allowed to get carried away with itself. It was Heidegger who unleashed the absurd delirium of "total questioning." But his work is seldom read right through to the end, to the point where the primacy of the question is overturned in favour of a primacy of the answer. We can radicalise him and affirm the primacy of the answer over questions, which we will characterise as merely "primary" and as pertaining to the beginning but not to the real. Conversely, however, the answer cannot be primary in some dogmatic sense, it can only impose or determine a way of answering.

Non-philosophy is usually interrogated about its efficacy, about what it can achieve in terms of *effects*. "What are the politics of non-philosophy?" "What are its ethical consequences?" Without realising it, such questions harbour a whole host of assumptions and prejudices, which is not to say that we have an excuse for ignoring them. But it is important that we not allow ourselves to be intimidated by these kinds of questions or objections. They are only valid for philosophy, they reiterate its bad habits in order to reassure it. This way of formulating questions imposes a double limitation. On the one hand, it assumes a linear and above all unitary causality in terms of causes and effects that are ultimately reversible and "Euclidean" (one cause, one effect). This is to assume a form of empiricism: causality is specified through the nature of its effects, a regional nature that is carved out from the world. What would a "non-Euclidean" action be like? One that acted upon the world as such, rather than on part of it or on a sector of philosophy? This is a problem that involves a change in methods and objectives, a change in the nature of the object, rather than a mere change in scale or the choice of another region traced from an already given section of the world. The entire theory of causality will have to be transformed in its meaning and bearing relative to philosophy. There may well be political as well as other kinds of effects of non-philosophy, but does this justify such a crude formulation of the question?

In this regard, it was Marxism that first cast suspicion on any attempt to provide a slightly more nuanced analysis of the political problem by encouraging the belief that such attempts secretly sought to obscure the class struggle. Yet it is not clear whether non-philosophy can be appraised in terms of a "programme," or whether it consummates itself in something like a programme. In this regard, on the contrary, the Marxist notion of class struggle paved the way for an acknowledgement of the fact that politics has a real content, albeit one which is not political according to superficial, factual criteria. Similarly, just as man does not produce his existence but his means of existence, *he does not produce his political existence or nature but his means of political existence*. If he can wage class struggle through politics, he can "wage politics" through the class struggle. Which is why a slightly more rigorous (and probably already "non-Marxist") understanding of Marx's formula requires us to effect a unilateral distinction between the political struggle and a struggle that is constitutive of its subjects, a struggle whose universality envelops a possible but non-necessary reference (unless it be the general necessity of referring to a material) to politics or any other worldly activity. This is the way in which subjects produce themselves as means (organons) of political existence.

Marx's formula is thus in need of urgent rectification, the better to maximise its novelty and scope: *man-in-person is given as the real presupposition on the basis of which subjects produce themselves as means of existence with the participation of their political existence in the world.* Consequently, we should distinguish between (1) man-in-person as the real presupposition whose nature has never been either political or anything else; (2) the political existence of subjects in the world; and finally, (3) the subject proper as "means of existence" – a subject whose rigorous, quasi-mathematical formulation clearly marks it out as an organon constituted with the aid of that against which it struggles, i.e. existence. The aim of this "dualysis" of Marx's formula is to lay low the theoreticist idealism of philosophy, which levels out in a unitary continuum man-in-person and his duality as subject, together with the existence in terms of which this structure is interpreted whenever the question of political action, or of other effects, is raised. Thus, we interpret "class-struggle" as a struggle that is constitutive of subjects (but not of man-in-man), but in a way that reinserts it into the apparatus as an articulatory hinge, instead of placing it either at the centre or the periphery. Of course, struggle constitutes the essence of subjects and finds support in the *existence of classes* but it cannot be reduced to the latter. It is as subjects that humans become indistinguishable from classes, but this is precisely so as to be better able to distinguish themselves from classes. Whence this corollary: humans do not produce their non-philosophical existence or essence, but only a programme that functions as a means of their existence.

Non-philosophy needs to be resituated in the context of the struggle against philosophy – or at least against philosophy understood as theoreticist idealism, which transcends any particular philosophical position and prevents the elaboration of a unified theory of philosophy and (for example) politics. It should not be circumscribed from the outset within the narrow ambit of "politics" [*la-politique*] in the restricted sense, which encourages all sorts of illusion. As we shall see, it is the transcendental yet practical dimension of non-philosophy that accounts for the erroneous or spontaneously philosophical character of the demand that it have political or other effects within the contemporary situation. For the real problem is not how to intervene in the world of philosophy, such as it supposedly subsists in-itself, or how to transform it from within. The problem is how to use philosophy so as to effect a real transformation of the subject in such a way as to allow it to break the spell of its bewitchment by the world and enable it to constitute itself through a certain struggle with the latter. The goal is not to effect a specular doubling or duplication of the world, thereby reinforcing its grip, but to elaborate a new order, that of the radical subjectivity of the Stranger as subject who is in-struggle by definition. Thus, what had been an aporia for philosophy, but also partially for Marxism – the possibility of man's alienation in the world (an alienation that is now merely partial and only involves the Stranger-subject, not man's essence-without-essence), along with

the corresponding possibility of man's dis-alienation – is finally resolved here. The unilateral duality of man and the world-subject or Stranger-subject finally resolves this aporia.

V practice of theory

The question now is whether practice can have any meaning other than as a purely theoretical practice. The economy of theory and practice harbours all sorts of traps for the unwary because it is intra-philosophical and follows the classic distinctions, distinctions that comprise both division *and* identity, and that give rise to self-encompassing indecisions and hesitations between theory and practice – exchanges and ambiguities, mutual trespasses and territorial disputes, oppositions and contradictions. This kind of distribution pertains not only to philosophy but also to experience, injecting it with its vicious circles and interminable debates. The solutions proposed by philosophy are well known so we will not go over them here. They have been a staple of philosophy from Plato to Marx and beyond.

Non-philosophy introduces order into this combinatory confusion, but not in a philosophical manner. It does not oppose its own practice (which is theoretical) to philosophical theory, as though the former were at last the true transformative practice while the latter remained a merely contemplative theory. There is no question of reiterating the kind of intra-philosophical distinctions that Marxism popularised through the use of opposition and contradiction. Here, once again, the unilateral duality governs the relation to philosophy and it does not reshuffle philosophical distinctions but instead "simplifies" them by suspending a redundant postulate, a suspension that allows us to attain a radical universality. This is why we speak of practice being "of" or "in" theory: far from being opposed to it, practice is able to determine in-the-last-instance the philosophical forms of theory and their combination with empirical practice. To determine-in-the-last-instance is to posit the real-transcendental identity of a subject who is structured like a *mixture* (rather than a combination) of the theoretical stance and the practical stance, but in such a way that neither stance trespasses upon the other's terrain. The unilateral duality is the practical essence that must be pitted against philosophy's theoreticist idealism. But it is certainly not opposed to theory, implying rather a simplifying concentrate of philosophical combinations. Where philosophy mixes theory and practice according to the invariant of combination, non-philosophy associates them without synthesis or analysis, without a mediating term. The transcendental identity or essence of the subject is not a mediating agency or third term countable within the same operational space as the duality of the combination. The subject's transcendental identity provides the reason why non-philosophy can be an identity *for* ... philosophy, which is to say, its "dualysis." Although the subject is radically identical in its essence, it can only concretely effectuate identity with the aid of a variety of philosophical solutions that delineate the contours of the world, which the subject accompanies and which continuously fill out its non-saturated being.

Ultimately, then, identity as cause of practice is commensurate with its non-consistency. Practice is the only stance that is heterogeneous to every other activity because it is univocal for all of them, give or take their determination-in-the-last-instance. But here it is practice in theory and relative to it, because theory is the only practice of first science, which is constituted by the stances of science and philosophy.

VI transforming the site of transformation

Non-philosophy transforms materials but these materials are both taken from the world *and* possess the general form of the world. Yet the philosophical requirement of efficacy postulates a universal site for philosophy in the world. Here we encounter an initial assumption that expresses a unitary and levelling conception of action, which is supposed to affect only one region of experience and to exhaust itself in it. This quasi-universal empiricism of action and practice is philosophically self-evident: it seems obvious that all production consists in transforming a material while staying on the same level as it, remaining content with distending the general convertibility of the realms implicated in practice. Even when structured by Difference as such, rather than merely specific differences as in Marxism, practices are still not heterogeneous enough to exceed the world, to which they return once the latter has been given its widest possible definition, which is precisely in terms of Difference and its alterity.

By way of contrast, if practice is conceived in terms of unilateral duality, which is the syntax proper to the strict immanence of the real as other than ... the world, this non-representative causality of determination-in-the-last-instance presupposes a radical distinction between the order of reality and the order of syntax, so that neither one of these encompasses the other. Once it has been founded upon a non-agency or non-realm like the real, the conception of agencies, realms or orders eliminates every facile dialectic, no matter how deeply entrenched in representation. It institutes a transformation of the material as production of a new agency that cannot be ultimately reabsorbed into that material, an agency that does not consummate itself within the order of the world. The subject produced in this way is one that emerges beyond the world but who nevertheless continues to refer to the world as a form of necessary yet secondary and entirely occasional causality. Such is the transcendence specific to the subject in so far as it stands beyond all philosophical transcendence, not so much through an excess of hyperbolic transcendence as through an immanent grasp or cloning of the latter. Cloning is an operation of radical immanence in so far as it takes on a transcendental relation to a given datum that has the form of the world, transforming that datum into a material by virtue of the very fact that it is *other than* ... it. Because the agency of the subject exists-(as a)-Stranger, the site of production remains distinct from the world, announcing itself (among other things) as the future-in-person, utopia-in-person, or the transcendental city of multitudes. Thus, practice first transforms the very site of the world's transformation and effects what we might legitimately call its "radical" displacement.

If we want to formulate correctly the question of the effects of non-philosophy, we must have "exited" from the world without first having had to enter into it in order to leave it. We have to think according to the real – which does not mean without the world – rather than according to the world. Non-philosophy is entirely oriented towards the future, and, more fundamentally, it is entirely oriented towards a utopia of the real. It is produced as the *identity* of transformation and chooses to abandon not the world as such but rather the site of the world. It is a new way of relating to things-according-to the world, one that no longer considers them in terms of the previous ways of relating to entities within the horizon of the world as something simply presupposed. If things are inseparable from the world it is not on account of philosophical desire but because the world functions as their a priori mode of givenness, such that it is the site of their transformation that has to change.

As a result, there will be a change in the meaning and scope of alienation and appropriation. They no longer pertain to man in general in his anthropological essence but only to the subject conceived on the basis of man-in-person, who is neither alienable nor inalienable and too inconsistent to be circumscribed in terms of this antinomy. What alienates the subject is a system of transcendental hallucination and illusion that obviously goes unnoticed, but which the subject has to notice and whose spell he has to shake off, without being able simply to destroy it, in order to constitute himself as such or as subject *for* the world. To believe that the world can be treated in the same way as an object in the world, that it gives rise to the same kinds of illusion, would simply be a philosophical delusion. The proper distinction is not so much between world and entity as between the world supposedly subsisting in-itself (within an operational transcendence) and the world as reduced or delivered from its sufficiency. Consequently, the distinction is not so much between the world and another realm of practice in-itself, or between the world and a transcendent realm of practice, but between two ways of relating to the world, one governed by the world, the other determined-according-to the real. The heterogeneity between

the subject-agency and the site of production is not traced from transcendence in general but rather articulated in terms of the kind of scission proper to determination-in-the-last-instance, which is the scission between a transcendence which is assumed to be in-itself and a transcendence-in-radical immanence.

When we say that intervention does not operate upon the world, this is too vague and equivocal a formulation, since there is a sense in which the world is also employed for the auto-constitution of the subject. What we mean is that intervention does not operate "upon (the illusion of) the world in itself," which is acknowledged but not destroyed. The hallucination and illusion continue to subsist for themselves: although they are acknowledged or identified, they continue to enjoy *for themselves* the capacity to re-engender the *absolute belief* in the world, a belief that persists as such. It is only for the subject that they are acknowledged and that the world can also be used or dismembered. The world is two faces in one: belief and pretension on the one hand, a material for constituting the subject on the other.

VII an immanent practice against the exception of thought

One initial consequence of the foregoing considerations is that of the simultaneously objectivist and ideal character of action and its effects. Since philosophical thought is oriented towards transcendence, the structure of philosophy requires it to describe ideal or idealised situations and to legislate about the world in a detached, contemplative manner without implicating itself in its own discourse, or rather by exempting itself from it. Philosophical thought cumulates the negative effects of a mode of objectivity that is indifferent both to its objects and to its own reabsorption into a unitary circuit. This is a consequence of philosophical thought's tendency towards "objectivation" and its pernicious mode of "attachment" to the object; it follows from objectivation as a mode of objectivity that takes up a position of survey or overview relative to its object and ultimately evaporates into contemplation. Philosophy can only distinguish between enunciation and enunciability (which it conflates with the enunciated) or between objectivation and objectivity (which it conflates with the objectified) in a weak, unitary fashion – even more so perhaps than other forms of thought – that fails to constitute them as rigorously heterogeneous orders.

Although an explicit philosophy of practice seems to be free of this idealising tendency and seems to take on board the gravity of action, by using the term "practice" it too perpetuates the unitary conflation between ideal practical objectivity and action upon the world. It protects the former, which formulates the meaning and worth of things – what is good and bad, true or false for the world – from the latter. And with regard to itself, the philosophy of practice believes that it has achieved something sufficient but also something superior by setting out the aforementioned distinction, which makes of it an exception to the world and allows it to enunciate laws, norms and essences without itself falling under them, since it instantiates their "higher" form. Philosophy begins by putting itself on the same level or plane as the world, but this is only so as to raise itself above it and present itself as the true and authentic form of science, art, truth, ethics, etc., in such a way as to end up turning itself into an exception and instituting its exception as the absolute that rules and consummates its own (seemingly democratic) primary combination with the world. If philosophy is intrinsically political, as is so often but so glibly maintained, it is intrinsically anti-democratic.

The entire theory of philosophy's practice, causality, effects and efficacy is vitiated by this exceptional status that philosophy ascribes to its own thought, by its ulterior motivation, its cunning which is not cunning, etc. Can we introduce seriousness and work into thought in place and instead of the pathos of seriousness and gravity which has made it so light-headed? Can we put practice into theory rather than just inserting practice "in theory"? Can we, ultimately, turn the thought of commitment into a commitment of thought? We are obviously assuming that in this current context mere inversion would be useless (which is to say philosophical), and that

this kind of operation should be supplanted by others capable of transforming philosophy ...

Superficially, the problem consists in channelling philosophical effects upon the world into the realm of thought as such. For example: how can "democracy" also be attributed to the thought that attributes it to social life? How can philosophical enunciation finally be rendered democratic rather than merely functioning as a universal instance of legitimation while exempting both itself and the philosopher? The spontaneous solution to this problem would be to say that thought should be affected by its object or affect itself with its object. But this would be to reiterate the philosophical circle as auto-affection and would merely invert philosophy's primacy over politics and democracy. Marx would have seen in such a move a typically philosophical contortion or "somersault," one that reinforces philosophy's dialectical games and dissolves practice, as well as the democracy that is supposed to accompany it, in the vicious circle whereby everything becomes philosophy in so far as philosophy is affected by everything. The principle governing such a somersault is quite simple. Philosophical dualities, in which one term invariably enjoys a supplement of alterity and unity relative to the other, can be inverted and overturned because of this supplement, so that democracy becomes disseminated into philosophy and vice versa but always to the ultimate benefit of philosophy.

The principle behind the non-philosophical solution consists in exploiting the power of identity (which is un-convertible) rather than the power of philosophical duality (which is convertible). In order to eliminate division, difference and their quasi-dialectical games, what must be given – but without an act of giving – is an identity that is performative, or better still, that is performed without an act of performance, and that thereby contains the identity of thought, on the one hand, and those practical consequences that thought habitually enunciates or programmes for the world, on the other. Of course, such an identity cannot really "contain" two apparently – or at least philosophically – opposed entities such as these. In other words, it will "contain" them only "in-the-last-instance," not as real parts, which would divide identity once again. But identity must be the determination of the now transcendental identity of thought and practice as forever inseparable. Determination-in-the-last-instance and cloning ensure the radical interlocking of thought and practice. We will call "unified theory" this transcendental but determined identity of thought and practice, of knowledge and the consequences of action, which have now been withdrawn from the law of the world and the exception of philosophy. And we will require of every enterprise which claims to be non-philosophical that it take charge of, rather than merely internalise conceptually, all those effects and ideals it presumes to impose upon the world or what it calls the world.

Thus, the dilemma of theory and practice is resolved in a determination or *performation-in-the-last-instance* (rather than the performativity traced from its linguistic form) of theory as practice. Moreover, the universality of practice is not tied to the specific positivity of its cause, which is without-consistency. Practice finds its freedom and universality not in nothingness (which no doubt would already suffice to liberate it) but in man-in-person as without-consistency.

VIII can we intervene in the world?

The question of the political (or ethical) consequences of non-philosophy is usually badly formulated because it is formulated philosophically. Whenever it tries to think practice, philosophy postulates that it is possible to intervene in the world – "intervene" as philosophy understands it, obviously. What does such intervention mean when it applies to non-philosophy? Can an operation of the philosophical type apply only to things of the world?

Philosophy supposes, rightly or wrongly, that it has effects upon reality and it expects the same of non-philosophy. Wrongly perhaps, because what philosophy calls "reality" is in any case a concept – attenuated at worst, elaborate at best – of the world. Through this concept, philosophy projects *a reality in itself, which is to say, one that has been constructed in the realm of operational transcendence,* within which it claims to

intervene, and in terms of which it gauges all possible intervention. But the real content of philosophy, once the illusion of the in-itself has been bracketed, is this very correlation between itself and the world. In any case, it is within *this* experience that non-philosophy can "intervene," and not in the philosophical concept of experience itself (which is too narrow and devised too much in the manner of a projection). We can universalise Kant's distinction between judgments of perception and judgments of experience and posit that our object is no longer the judgment of perception, whose role the philosophy of reality now plays for us, but the judgment of experience, i.e. the affirmation of existence as such, in terms of which philosophy-in-person, or philosophy as form of the world, presents itself. Philosophical intervention is itself highly problematic within the confines of a reality that is alternately anticipated and projected, forgotten and desired; it is both ahead of and lagging behind the conjuncture, "in the midst of" experience and its combinations but without getting to grips with the identity of the conjuncture, whose significance escapes it.

Philosophy projects its operation of division and re-appropriation onto a diverse variety of things, objects and sensations through the intermediary of a schema which seems to be primarily derived from language and, in the order of so-called regional forms of knowledge, science. The latter provides it with forms of knowledge that philosophy abstracts from their process of production and which it uses to fill out its own universal, necessary structures, which combine difference and identity but are empty and so have to be filled. Thus, philosophy grafts itself onto experience and claims to intervene within it on the basis of an identification and confusion of the very orders it requires. Philosophy is a long-suffering desire for the real, to which it aspires but only so as to be able to construct or reaffirm itself in its own proper, consistent order – an order structured by those transcendentals which function like an absolute metaphor for experience.

Every intervention in philosophy, which is to say, every intervention upon its objects, remains intra-philosophical, caught up in philosophy's self-encompassing structure. Every such intervention, consequently, remains in the world. But in so far as every practice of this type remains subsumed beneath the law of self-positioning and its pretensions, so then (*from the point of view of non-philosophy*) it continues to postulate a philosophy or a world "in itself." The world as in-itself or self-encompassing is the source of antinomies that only non-philosophy can identify and suspend.

Given these conditions, it is difficult to maintain that philosophy *transforms* the world. It *is* the world or attaches itself to regional representations as the very "dimension" of the world. It "transforms" regional representations in an ideal-real or representational (in the enlarged sense we have given this term) modality, regional representations that it appropriates and from which it extracts a surplus value of meaning and empirical (but also transcendental or transformed empirical) content. Philosophical intervention consists in adding and subtracting philosophy, as the form of the world, to and from things. It consists in interpretation.

So what can non-philosophy hope to achieve with regard to the world itself? The non-philosophical operation is quite different from the philosophical version; it no longer comprises the combination of division and identity but instead radical identity and hence unilateral duality. The result is a gain in simplicity and minimality. Non-philosophy does not project itself onto things but solicits them necessarily and says so without trying to hide the fact in the manner that philosophy sometimes does. On the other hand, it clones subjects from philosophy, and here again cloning is the reduced or minimal form, the real core of philosophical projection. As for its object, this is now the world or the philosophy-form as such, rather than things. Consequently, non-philosophy is not an intensified reduplication of philosophy, a meta-philosophy, but rather its "simplification." It does not represent a change in scale with respect to philosophy, as though the structure of the latter was maintained for smaller elements. It is the "same" structure but in a more concentrated, more focused form – it is withdrawn from identity as merely desired and brought to the level of iden-

tity as performed. It is a non-unity rather than a meta-unity. The gesture is one of universalisation, of simplification in the number of postulates. This simplification, which is achieved through the suspension of a certain postulate (that of the reciprocal determination of thought and the real), is capable of producing an explanation of philosophy *in so far as it can be explained and in the terms in which it can.* As in philosophy, there is a practical gain at the level of theory, but a theory that is wholly different from the philosophical kind.

IX interpretation, transformation, determination-in-the-last-instance

How does all this affect the duality of interpretation and transformation (Marx) once this duality has been reconceived according to the primacy of practice, and once practice has been prised free from philosophical difference and determined according to the real? Philosophy is interpretation at a global level because it is infinite repetition and self-reference, overview and contemplation of the world in the narrow sense presupposed by philosophy. Yet it also comprises a transcendental recursion, relating through itself to experience, which it does not so much dominate in the manner of a transcendent religious heaven as "transform" or help "constitute." But is constitution equivalent to transformation as defined by an immanent performative practice?

Philosophy, as we have already observed, is not wholly devoid of operations, but these operations – such as overturning and displacement, to say nothing of more specular ones such as hermeneutics, or auto-specular ones such as the dialectic – not only operate at the heart of representations, they also operate with these representations: combining them, analysing them, deconstructing them, dialecticising them. Philosophy programmes a transformation of the world, but one which is ideal, objectified, incapable of getting an effective grip on it; one that achieves something akin to an effect only by adding to or subtracting from what is given (conceived now as a representation) new and equally ideal determinations that double then redouble it, simplifying or even deconstructing it without really transforming it. Throughout its practice, twentieth-century philosophy has admitted and shown – but only ever under its breath, so to speak, without ever "truly" being aware of it (thereby demonstrating the extent to which its practice remains ideal) – that it has only ever worked with representations, with the *logos*, which is to say with metaphysics, even as it tried to criticise or deconstruct the latter. Such philosophy remains under the jurisdiction of philosophical tradition and submits to the authority of its tribunal. *Genuine transformation does not consist in playing a game (whether at the level of language, of practice, or of the world) with representation, but rather in determining the latter through a radically un-representable agency or instance – more precisely, through a without-representation that allows itself to be thought by means of representations which have been reduced to the status of philosophically inert material.*

Since the world has now been enlarged to include all possible philosophical thought, it is likewise necessary to enlarge the concept of representation and relate it to an agency or instance that has to function like a "last instance" for it, rather than an "ulterior instance," a world-behind-the-scenes or thing-in-itself. Every instance of thought that is left to itself and not determined by a without-representation-of-the-last-instance is a representation in this widened sense of the term. To put it another way: we will call "representation" every presentation that refers back to itself through a transcendental recursion that, although capable of criticising, deconstructing or modifying presentation, cannot determine it in-(the)-real.

As for non-philosophy, it uses these representations, which are by definition its only material, but so as to confer upon them a new condition relative to their philosophical condition as *combinations*. We call this new condition a "mixture" because it is the transcendental identity of a duality of philosophical representations and (for example) scientific or artistic operations that are delivered from their subsumption by philosophy. This is a duality without an operation of synthesis or analysis.

laruelle

X a transcendental practice

A genuinely transformative practice must answer to several conditions. Among other things, it must be genuinely practical, which is to say *real by virtue of its cause*, in order not to become confused with globally ideal representations. It must also be capable of relating immanently or transcendentally, rather than externally or in an empirico-idealist fashion, to these representations. It is often and erroneously imagined that practice is opposed to idealism but above all opposed to philosophy's transcendental dimension. This is because philosophy lives off those divisions and hierarchies through which primacy and priority are linked together, and because the transcendental approach has traditionally been idealist, whereas it is in fact that aspect of the real which is "other than ..."

Consequently, it is the philosophical apparatus as a whole which must be completely overhauled, practically transformed, so as to give back to practice its immanent force. Once the transcendental is determined by the real, as is the case in non-philosophy, it changes its status, it no longer represents the apex of an ontological hierarchy but rather a function which the real may or may not assume. Since practice is indissociable from the syntax of unilateral duality that follows from the real, it is indissociable from the real's transcendental function. Practical effects and transcendental function are identical for the real; they are possible functions of it that become effectuated once the world is taken into account for itself or solicits the real and the latter "responds" to that solicitation – on account of the world's being-given-in-the-real – with a transcendental practice.

Far from being a crude primary activity, or an idealist activity taken from the world (as is the case, for philosophical reasons, with Fichte), practice is the transcendental essence of the subject in so far as the latter is now distinguished from the world, which the subject uses as an occasion or material. This is why practice consists in transforming or dualysing representations and ceases to be an "activity" grafted onto these representations and controlling them both from within and from without. Practice is transcendental through its real immanent root, which renders it radically heterogeneous to all representation. But this heterogeneity does not prevent it from being transcendental or effectuated by those representations that make up the world. Like the real, practice is immanent, but there is nothing to prevent it from relating to representations or from being sufficiently heterogeneous to these representations to be able to transform them. Obviously, in spite of its origin in the real, the transcendental is not valid for supposedly absolute representations or for the world in so far as it is supposed to be in itself, but only for the world-form or for the philosophy-form as a priori form of the world. Like practice, the transcendental pertains to this a priori form rather than to objects or to the world-object as sufficient reality.

XI the pragmatic appropriation of philosophy

"Man is universally predestined to philosophy just as philosophy has man as its destination" – this is the fundamental postulate of philosophy: that philosophy and man are reciprocally convertible on condition of a certain labour, education or ascesis. In order to render this postulate credible, in order to put it into practice and ensure its dominion over man, philosophy claims to define man by means of some circular duality (e.g. as a rational, linguistic or religious animal), a duality that is ultimately unitary and encompassing (man as the metaphysical animal). This begs the question by simply presupposing an interface between philosophy and man in the form of his philosophical definition, which is always an exclusive, unitary definition. It is a package deal: a definition of man is possible provided it is philosophical and posits the convertibility between a putative human essence and its attributes. "Man" becomes a combination of all sorts of essences and properties, depending on the doctrine in question: a generality in which what should have been distinguished non-philosophically – man's non-philosophical essence – is instead conflated with an infinitely nuanced definition that encapsulates an entire philosoph-

ical system. In order to think man, or to think him in a manner adequate to his being, a distinction must cut across "man" as generality. But in order to avoid begging the question and so as to render the distinction rigorous, it should no longer coincide with any of those philosophical "differences" (of degree, kind, form, writing, affect or will). We will leave behind these aporias and the politics of the philosophical subjection of humans by positing the following axioms:

1. "Man," "ego," "subject," "human(s)" are no longer concepts but primary names posed in axioms.

2. Primary names are terms extracted from philosophy but abstracted from their naive intuitive horizon, from the world of metaphysical objects and representations. Their signifying base serves as a support for an alternative logic, an alternative organisation of thought which we will call "non-philosophy."

3. Non-philosophical thought and its theoretical practice is determined by its object, which we will designate by the symbol "man-in-man" ("in-man" for short, or even "man" when the context precludes misunderstanding). Such thought is not derived or received from some external or philosophical source, and it has the power to abstract philosophical terms from the realm of meaning within which they normally function.

4. The "object" of non-philosophy, and that which determines it, is its cause: "man-in-man."

5. Man-in-man is not a concept or unitary entity. It is not amenable to definition: it is posited through real-transcendental axioms.

Posited in this way, the human is no longer a unitary generality, a conflation of the concept with the real object, of the attribute with the "essence." On the one hand, this is the *in-man* as real rather than ideal cause, as the real rather than a reason or even the principle of reason. On the other hand, this is a *subject* in a new sense because the real is no longer the absolute subject of philosophy or even the classical subject; it is now ascribed to the in-man alone. The subject is no longer the real or something that co-operates with the real but rather an operation exercised upon the world or upon philosophy and constituting itself through that exercise. But the relation to the world and the supposedly essential relation to philosophy is no longer attributed to the human cause. For the expression "man-in-man" means that the latter is without a determining essence, without consistency; dispossessed of nothingness as much as being, dispossessed of substance as much as presence-to-itself. Of course this distinction is no longer a difference, which is to say a unitary structure, a more or less asymmetrical convertibility between cause and subject. The latter are *radically but not absolutely* distinct. The in-man is radically autonomous because man can only be found in-man rather than in philosophy or the world. But the subject is in an altogether more complex and more interesting situation. It is not between the in-man and the world, as though it constituted their (once more divided) in-between or their difference, or a duality of two substances. It is the *indivisible clone* produced on the basis of the world under the influence of the in-man. This is not some new version of man as microcosm who is convertible with the macrocosm, give or take a difference in scale. The subject registers the minimum of relationality that philosophy imposes upon the in-man but also the clone-form that the latter imposes upon philosophy. Yet although they are the asymmetrical cooperation of distinct roles, the cause and the subject are not juxtaposed. Since man and the subject are identical in-man or in-the-last-instance, the subject enjoys a relative autonomy which he gains from that of philosophy so that he is not entirely indistinguishable from the in-man. We say that he is determined-in-the-last-instance by the in-man.

In so far as he is posited in this "ultimate" fashion through a theoretical act we call a "primary ultimation," man no longer has a privileged or essential affinity with philosophy. Instead, he receives it as a realm of (no doubt "fundamental") objects, as the universal and necessary form of the world. Non-philosophy proposes to examine the fundamental structures of this a priori world-form while at the same time using it with a view to providing its theoretical explanation. Man is no longer a concept or even the object of a concept and, being devoid of essence, he cannot be *essentially*

destined to a philosophical activity which now interests him only in the context of a practice in which he is a *subject-for-philosophy*. Humans are without-philosophy – not just men without qualities but men who are primarily without essence, yet all the more *destined-for-the-world or philosophy without having decided or willed it*. Philosophy has always wanted us and we have been obliged to consent to it – but have we ever wanted philosophy?

The critique of the philosophical "end" of philosophy and of its sufficiency in foreseeing and deciding its own death leads back to man-in-person, not to man in so far as he is capable of lack of interest, lack of purpose, or indifference. This is not a void that one describes in the hope of shoring up by returning to or reactivating a past of which we have been disinherited. We call "appropriation of philosophy" the theory of philosophy carried out on the basis of the real-transcendental indifference that philosophy itself effectuates. What is radically poor in essence and in philosophy remains radically poor throughout this appropriation whereby philosophy is cloned as what is proper to man-in-person. Appropriation has none of the bulimic or anorexic traits of re-appropriation: it is what is poor in philosophy as such that takes the latter into consideration and strips it of its sufficiency. It is by virtue of this poverty that the human relation to philosophy takes the form of a pragmatics determined in-the-last-instance rather than an auto-pragmatics. To abandon the end of philosophy to metaphysics alone, to repeat the gesture of self-positing in a nihilist mode and turn it into a gesture of self-repudiation is to fail to see that this end still harbours a sense-of-the-last-instance for man-in-man – but this is precisely a non-philosophical or *other than ... philosophical* sense. With the end of philosophy, it becomes easier to see the extent to which philosophy exerts its "grip" on the radical human subject. Consequently, the hypothesis of men-without-philosophy means that the latter is not an attribute and that our transcendental and contingent relation to it is brought forth with man-in-person and effectuated by philosophy itself as material [*comme matériau*]. It is a question of restoring or rather giving to philosophy a utopian and uchronic force that it has deprived itself of – or that it has been deprived of as a result of man-in-person's being-foreclosed.

Non-philosophy is a programme for appropriating philosophy itself as necessary relation to the world, since our "experience" is the world as such. Non-philosophical cognition does not relate to the world as an entity or to entities in the world (as objects or forms of knowledge): it is transcendental and exposes the reality of a cognition that relates to philosophy as the world's a priori form, as "knowledge" or "existence" of the world.

works by laruelle

Philosophy I

Phénomène et différence: essai sur l'ontologie de Ravaisson. Paris: Klincksieck, 1971.

"Le Style di-phallique de Jacques Derrida." *Critique* 334 (1975): 320–39.

Machines textuelles. Déconstruction et libido d'écriture. Paris: Seuil, 1976.

"La Scène du vomi ou comment ça se détraque dans la théorie." *Critique* 347 (1976): 418–43.

Le Déclin de l'écriture. Paris: Aubier-Flammarion, 1977.

Nietzsche contre Heidegger: thèses pour une politique nietzschéenne. Paris: Payot, 1977.

Au-delà du principe de pouvoir. Paris: Payot, 1978.

"Au delà du pouvoir. Le concept transcendantal de la diaspora." *Textes pour Emmanuel Levinas*. Ed. François Laruelle. Paris: Jean-Michel Place, 1980. 111–25.

"Homo ex machina." *Revue Philosophique de la France et de l'Étranger* 105 (1980): 325–42.

"Irrécusable, irrecevable: un éssai de presentation." *Textes pour Emmanuel Levinas*. Ed. François Laruelle. Paris: Jean-Michel Place, 1980. 7–14.

"Réflexions sur le sens de la finitude dans la *Critique de la Raison Pure*." *Revue Internationale de Philosophie* 35 (1981): 269–83.

Philosophy II

Le Principe de minorité. Paris: Aubier-Montaigne, 1981.

"Comment 'sortir' de Heidegger et de la différence en general." *Heidegger (Exercice de la patience). Cahiers de Philosophie* 3–4. Paris: Obsidiane, 1982.

Une Biographie de l'homme ordinaire: des autorités et des minorités. Paris: Aubier, 1985.

Les Philosophies de la différence. Introduction critique. Paris: Presses Universitaires de France, 1986.

"Abrégé d'une science humaine de la philosophie." *La Décision Philosophique* 3 (1987): 105–11.

"Biographie de solitude." *La Décision Philosophique* 3 (1987): 101–04.

"Exercice sur Péguy: 'une philosophie qui ne vient pas faute éternellement.'" *La Décision Philosophique* 3 (1987): 119–24.

"Octonaire de la suffisance philosophique." *La Décision Philosophique* 3 (1987): 113–17.

"Théorèmes de la bonne nouvelle." *La Décision Philosophique* 1 (1987): 86–94.

"Variations sur un thème de Heidegger." *La Décision Philosophique* 1 (1987): 86–94.

"La Vérité selon Hermès: théorèmes sur le secret et la communication." *Analecta Husserliana* 22 (1987): 397–401.

"Controverse sur la possibilité d'une science de la philosophie." [Debate with Jacques Derrida.] *La Décision Philosophique* 5 (1988): 63–76.

"Lettre à Deleuze." *La Décision Philosophique* 5 (1988): 101–05.

"Du Noir Univers dans les fondations humaines de la couleur." *La Décision Philosophique* 5 (1988): 107–12.

"Variations Leibniz." *La Décision Philosophique* 5 (1988): 113–24.

"Biographie de l'oeil." *La Décision Philosophique* 7 (1989): 93–104.

"Ce que l'Un voit dans l'Un." *La Décision Philosophique* 7 (1989): 115–21.

"Le Concept d'analyse généralisée ou de 'non-analyse.'" *Revue Internationale de Philosophie* 43 (1989): 506–24.

"Marges et limites de la métaphysique." *Encyclopédie Philosophique Universelle.* Ed. André Jacob. Vol. I. Paris: Presses Universitaires de France, 1989. 71–80.

"La Méthode transcendantale." *Encyclopédie Philosophique Universelle.* Ed. André Jacob. Vol. I. Paris: Presses Universitaires de France, 1989. 693–700.

"Mon Parmenide." *La Décision Philosophique* 7 (1989): 105–14.

Philosophie et non-philosophie. Liège: Mardaga, 1989.

"La Cause de l'homme: juste un individu." *Analecta Husserliana* 29 (1990): 49–56.

"L'Appel et le phénomène." [Response to Jean-Luc Marion's "Réduction et donation."] *Revue de Métaphysique et de Morale* 1991.1 (1991): 27–41.

"La Science des phénomènes et la critique de la décision phénoménologique." *Analecta Husserliana* 34 (1991): 115–27.

En tant qu'un: la "non-philosophie" expliquée aux philosophes. Paris: Aubier, 1991.

Théorie des identités: fractalité généralisée et philosophie artificielle. Paris: Presses Universitaires de France, 1992.

Philosophy III

"Réponse à Deleuze." *La Non-Philosophie des contemporains. Althusser, Badiou, Deleuze, Derrida, Fichte, Kojève, Husserl, Russell, Sartre, Wittgenstein.* By Laruelle et al. Paris: Kimé, 1995. 49–78.

Théorie des étrangers: science des hommes, démocratie, non-psychanalyse. Paris: Kimé, 1995.

Principes de la non-philosophie. Paris: Presses Universitaires de France, 1996.

"Qu'est-ce que la non-philosophie?" *Initiation à la pensée de François Laruelle.* By Juan-Diego Blanco. Paris: L'Harmattan, 1997. 13–64.

(Ed.). *Dictionnaire de la non-philosophie.* Paris: Kimé, 1998.

"De la non-philosophie comme hérésie." *Discipline hérétique.* By Laruelle et al. Paris: Kimé, 1998. 7–23.

"A Summary of Non-Philosophy." Trans. Ray Brassier. *Pli* (1999): 138–48.

"Alien-sans-aliénation. Programme pour une philo-fiction." *Philosophie et science-fiction.* Ed. Gilbert Hottois. Paris: Vrin, 2000. 145–56.

Le Christ futur: une leçon d'hérésie. Paris: Exils, 2002.

Éthique de l'étranger. Du crime contre l'humanité. Paris: Kimé, 2000.

"Identity and Event." Trans. Ray Brassier. *Pli* 9 (2000): 174–89.

Introduction au non-marxisme. Paris: Presses Universitaires de France, 2000.

François Laruelle
Université Paris X – Nanterre
200, avenue de la République
92001 Nanterre
France

Ray Brassier
Department of Philosophy
University of Middlesex
White Hart Lane
London N17 8HR
UK
E-mail: r.brassier@mdx.ac.uk

journal of the theoretical humanities
volume 8   number 2   august 2003

introduction

peter hallward

Jacques Rancière retired from teaching philosophy at the University of Paris VIII (Saint-Denis) in 2002. In most of his otherwise varied projects he seeks to overturn all imposed forms of classification or distinction, to subvert all norms of representation that might allow for the stable differentiation of one class of person or experience from another (workers from intellectuals, masters from followers, the articulate from the inarticulate, the artistic from the non-artistic, etc.). As a general rule, Rancière believes that "it is in the moments when the real world wavers and seems to reel into mere appearance, more than in the slow accumulation of day-to-day experiences, that it becomes possible to form a judgement about the world."[1]

As a student at the École Normale Supérieure in the 1960s, Rancière was influenced by Althusser and wrote an important section of *Reading Capital* in which, like Althusser, he distinguished between the necessarily deluded experience of social agents and the quasi-scientific authority of theory (exclusively able to grasp, for instance, the mechanics of production or commodification). It is hardly an exaggeration to say that everything else Rancière has written rejects this distinction and all its implications. Outraged by Althusser's distance from the political mobilisations during and after 1968, and suspicious of the ever-widening gap between theory and reality he found in the work of his fellow *soixante-huitards*, Rancière published a spectacular critique of his former teacher in 1974. Turning instead to Foucault for methodological inspiration, Rancière founded the journal *Les Révoltes Logiques* in 1975,

jacques rancière

translated by forbes morlock

POLITICS AND AESTHETICS
an interview

dedicated to recasting the relation between work and philosophy, or proletarians and intellectuals, in such a way as to block any prescriptive appropriation or representation of the former by the latter.

Like Foucault, Rancière has applied the work of de-normalisation or de-classification on a number of successive though overlapping fronts, which for the sake of analysis might be distinguished as philosophical, pedagogical, historiographical, political, sociological, and aesthetic.

Rancière's general argument with philosophy, most substantially stated in *Le Philosophe et ses pauvres* (1983), concerns its inaugural attempt to distinguish people capable of genuine thought from others who, entirely defined by their economic occupation, are presumed to lack the

ISSN 0969-725X print/ISSN 1469-2899 online/03/020191-21 © 2003 Taylor & Francis Ltd and the Editors of *Angelaki*
DOI: 10.1080/0969725032000162657

ability, time and leisure required for thought. The paradigm here is Plato's division of society into functional orders (artisans, warriors, rulers), such that slaves, or shoemakers, for instance, are forever banished from the domain of philosophy. To each type of person, one allotted task: labour, war, or thought. Hence the importance of excluding those who, by seeking to imitate a type other than their own, threaten to cross these functional lines. Rancière finds echoes of both this division and this exclusion in the work of Marx, Sartre and Bourdieu.

In pedagogical terms, Rancière's argument (in *The Ignorant Schoolmaster*, 1987) targets any attempt to conceive of education in terms of the generalised classification of children, i.e. in terms of a process that leads them from initial postures of submission and docility *towards* relative security precisely in so far as they come to accept their suitably sanctioned place. Inspired by the maverick example of Joseph Jacotot (1770–1840), Rancière's guiding pedagogical principle is that "all people are virtually capable of understanding what others have done and understood [...]. Equality is not a goal to be attained but a point of departure, a supposition to be maintained in all circumstances."[2] Everyone has the same intelligence; what varies is the will and opportunity to exercise it. On the basis of this supposition, superior knowledge ceases to be a necessary qualification of the teacher, just as the process of "explication" (with its attendant metaphors that distinguish children as slow or quick, that conceive of educational time in terms of progress, training and qualification) is exposed as the dominant "myth of pedagogy."

When Rancière turns to the writing of history, it is in order to expose the way historians from Michelet to Braudel have likewise presented a picture of the world in which each individual is set in their appropriate place, in which any particular voice becomes audible in so far as it articulates the logic associated with that place. In Michelet's histories, in keeping with a principle that still dominates the discipline as a whole, "everything has a meaning to the degree that every speech production is assignable to the legitimate expression of a place: the earth that shapes men, the sea on which their exchanges take place, the everyday objects in which their relations can be read ..."[3] What is banished from this territorialising conception of history is the very possibility of heresy (heresy understood as the dis-placing of the speaker and dis-aggregation of the community[4]), in particular that modern "democratic heresy" incarnated by the arrival upon the historical stage of a popular voice that refuses any clear assignation of place, the voice of the masses of people who both labour *and* think – a voice noticeably absent, Rancière observes, from the *Annales*-inspired conception of history.

It is precisely this heretical conception of political speech that informs Rancière's most programmatic work to date: *Disagreement* (1995). The supervision of places and functions is the business of what Rancière calls the "police"; a *political* sequence begins, then, when this supervision is interrupted so as to allow a properly anarchic disruption of function and place, a sweeping de-classification of speech. The democratic voice is the voice of those who reject the prevailing social distribution of roles, who refuse the way a society shares out power and authority, the voice of "floating subjects that deregulate all representations of places and portions."[5]

Applied in sociological terms, Rancière's subversion of classes and norms applies as much to Marxist attempts to squeeze the complexity of workers' experience into the theory-certified simplicity of the proletariat as it does to nostalgic attempts to preserve a "traditional" working class identity. *The Nights of Labor* (1981), Rancière's first (and still most) substantial book, a record and analysis of proletarian intellectual life in the 1830s and 1840s, undercuts any effort "to preserve popular, plebeian or proletarian purity" and, in the absence left by the disappearance of *the* authentic working class, clears a space for the emergence of unauthorised combinations and inventions – transposed utopias, reappropriations of literary forms, worker-run newspapers and nocturnal poetry societies, trans-occupational associations, etc.[6] The workers recorded by Rancière complain less about material hardship and more about the predetermined quality of lives framed by rigid social hierarchy. "Perhaps the truly dangerous classes," he concludes, "were not so much the uncivilised ones thought to undermine society from below but rather the migrants who move at the borders between classes – individuals and groups who develop capabilities of no direct use for the improvement of their material lives, and which might in fact make them despise material concerns."[7]

It is only a small if not imperceptible shift from here to an interest in the attempt, which Rancière names the "aesthetic revolution," to move from a rule-bound conception of art preoccupied with matching any given object with its appropriate form of representation (the basis for a secure distinction of art from non-art) to a regime of art which, in the absence of representational norms, embraces the endless confusion of art and non-art.[8] In this aesthetic regime (whose origins Rancière traces to Schiller, first and foremost), genuine art is what indistinguishes, in newly creative ways and with the resources peculiar to a specific artistic practice, art and the other of art – examples include Balzac's application of epic modes of description to the banalities of everyday life, or Flaubert's extension of an aristocratic conception of style to a "democratic" equality of subjects, or Mallarmé's blending of the most subtle movements of syntax with a general "reframing of the human abode." Rather than the author of a purely intransitive or hermetic discourse, Mallarmé figures here as the writer who conceives of poetry as *both* the purest possible expression of language and as caught up in the rituals of private, collective and industrial life (in the tiny movements of a dancer, the fluttering of a fan, the fireworks of Bastille Day, and so on, all part of that celebration of the ordinary which comes to replace "the forlorn ceremonies of throne and religion").[9] Orthodox modernism, by contrast, in its determination to restore a strict barrier between (non-representational) art and non-art, can only figure here as complicit in the perpetual attempt to restore traditional hierarchies, to return things to their officially authorised place, to squash the insurgent promise of democracy.

notes

1 Jacques Rancière, *Nights of Labor* 19.

2 Rancière, *Le Maître ignorant* 9, 229.

3 Rancière, *Names of History* 65. "Michelet invents the art of making the poor speak by keeping them silent, of making them speak as silent people," in so far as only the historian or analyst is able to understand their words. Only the historian is able to let the dead rest peacefully in the tomb to which their garrulous silence confines them (62–63).

4 In Le Roy Ladurie's celebrated book *Montaillou* (1975), for example, the historian's "object is not heresy but the village that gives it a place." The result effectively repeats the inquisitorial gesture: "the historian suppresses heresy by giving it roots" (Rancière, *Names of History* 73).

5 Rancière, *Disagreement* 99–100.

6 Rancière, *Nights of Labor* x, 10.

7 Rancière, "Good Times or Pleasures at the Barriers" (1978) 50.

8 "In the aesthetic regime of art, art is art to the extent that it is something other than art" (Rancière, "The Aesthetic Revolution and its Outcomes" 137 – this article offers a compressed summary of aspects of the longer analyses that Rancière has undertaken in his books *Mallarmé* (1996), *La Chair des mots* (1998), *La Parole muette* (1998) and *Le Partage du sensible* (2000)).

9 Rancière, "The Aesthetic Revolution and its Outcomes" 140.

politics and aesthetics: an interview[1]

jacques rancière

Peter Hallward: One of your constant concerns has been to analyse and condemn any posture of mastery, particularly theoretical, pedagogical, "academic" mastery. So may I ask why you started teaching? How did you first get involved with education?

Jacques Rancière: I became involved almost unwittingly, when I went through the École Normale Supérieure (ENS), which was set up to train teachers. I am, in the first instance, a student. I am one of those people who is a perpetual student and whose professional fate, as a consequence, is to teach others. "Teaching" obviously implies a certain position of mastery, "researcher" implies in some way a position of knowledge, "teacher-researcher" implies the idea of the teacher adapting a position of institutional mastery to one of mastery based on knowledge.

At the outset, I was immersed in an Althusserian milieu, and consequently marked by its idea of forms of authority linked specifically to knowledge. But I was also caught up in the whole period of 1968, which threw into question the connection between positions of mastery and knowledge. I went through it all with the mentality of a researcher: I thought of myself, above all, as someone who did research and let others know about his research. Which meant, for example, that as a teacher I always resisted divisions into levels (advanced, intermediate, etc.). At the University of Paris VIII, where I have taught for most of my career, there were no levels in the philosophy department and I have always tried hard to maintain this lack of division into levels. In my courses I often have people of all different levels, in the belief that each student does what he or she can do and wants to do with what I say.

P.H.: I suppose you must have made your initial decision to take up teaching and research path

at about the age of fifteen or sixteen: did you grow up in a milieu where this option was encouraged?

J.R.: As a child, I wanted to go to the ENS because I wanted to be an archaeologist. But by the time I got into the ENS I'd lost that sense of vocation. It has to be said, too, that this was a time when, for people like me, there wasn't really much of a choice: you were good in either arts or sciences. And if you were good in arts, you aimed for what was considered the best in the field, which is to say, the ENS. That, rather than any vocation to teach, is how I ended up there.

P.H.: And your initial collaboration with Althusser, was it a true conversion or the result of a theoretical interest? What happened at that point?

J.R.: Several things happened. First, there was my interest in Marxism, which was not at all part of the world I'd been brought up in. For people like me, our interest in Marxism before Althusser had to follow some slightly unorthodox paths. The people who had written books on Marx, the authorities on Marx at the time, were priests like Father Calvez, who had written a hefty book on Marx's thought, or people like Sartre. So, I arrived at Marxism with a sort of Marxian corpus which was hardly that of someone from the communist tradition, but which did provide access to Marx at a time when he didn't have a university presence and when theory was not very developed within the French Communist Party.

In relation to all that, Althusser represented a break. People told me about him when I first entered the ENS: they said he was brilliant. He really did offer a way of breaking with the Marxist humanist milieu in which we had been learning about Marx at the time. So, of course, I was enthusiastic, because Althusser was seductive, and I was working against myself in a way, because following Althusser's thinking meant breaking with the sort of Marxism that I had known, that I was getting to know, and with those forms of thought that did not share its sort of theoretical engagement.

P.H.: Would it be too simple to say that Althusser was a teacher, whereas Sartre was something else – not a researcher or a teacher, but a writer or an intellectual, I guess?

J.R.: I don't know if you can say "teacher." In the end, Althusser taught relatively little. His words seduced us, but they were those of certain written texts as much as anything oral. He was like the priest of a religion of Marxist rigour, or of the return to the text. It wasn't really the rigour of his teaching that appealed so much as an enthusiasm for his declaration that there was virgin ground to be opened up. His project to read *Capital* was a little like that: the completely naive idea that we were pioneers, that no one had really read Marx before and that we were going to start to read him.

So there were two sides to our relation with Althusser. There was, first of all, a sense of going off on an adventure: for the seminar on *Capital*, I was supposed to talk, to explain to people the rationality of *Capital*, when I still hadn't read the book. So I rushed about, rushed to start reading the various volumes of *Capital*, in order to be able to talk to others about them. There was this adventurous side, but there was something else as well: our roles as pioneers put us in a position of authority, it gave us the authority of those who know, and it instituted a sort of authority of theory, of those who have knowledge, in the midst of a political eclecticism. Thus, there was an adventurous side and a dogmatic side to it all, and they came together: the adventure in theory was at the same time dogmatism in theory.

P.H.: It's the role of the pioneer you've held on to. Did your break with Althusser take place during the events of May 1968? What happened exactly?

J.R.: For me, the key moment wasn't the events of May 1968, which I watched from a certain distance, but rather the creation of Paris VIII. With the creation of a philosophy department full of Althusserians, we had to decide what we were going to do. It was then I realised that Althusser stood for a certain power of the professor, the professor of Marxism who was so distant from

what we had seen taking place in the student and other social movements it was almost laughable. At the time, what really made me react was a programme for the department put together by Etienne Balibar, a programme to teach people theoretical practice as it should be taught. I came out rather violently against this programme, and from that point began a whole retrospective reflection on the dogmatism of theory and on the position of scholarly knowledge we had adopted.

That's more or less how things started for me, not with the shock of 1968 but with the aftershock. Which is to say, with the creation of an institution, an institution where we were, in one sense, the masters. It was a matter of knowing what we were going to do with it, how we were going to manage this institutional mastery, if we were going to identify it with the transmission of science or not.

P.H.: How did that work at Paris VIII? How did you bring the rather anarchic side of egalitarian teaching together with the institutional necessity of granting degrees, verifying qualifications, etc.?

J.R.: At the time, I had thought very little about an alternative pedagogical practice. I had more or less given up on philosophy, the teaching of philosophy, and academic practice. What seemed important was direct political practice, so for a time I stopped reflecting on and thinking of myself as creating a new pedagogical practice or a new type of knowledge. This was linked to the fact that the diploma in philosophy at Paris VIII was quickly invalidated. We no longer gave national diplomas, so we were no longer bound by the criteria needed to award them. For a good while, then, I was absolutely uninterested in rethinking pedagogy: I was thinking, first, of militant practice and then, when that was thrown into question, of my practice as a researcher. For years my main activity was consulting archives and going to the Bibliothèque Nationale. My investment in the practice of teaching was fairly limited.

P.H.: Did your courses continue more or less as usual, that is, as lectures?

J.R.: Not entirely. It varied: there were lectures, but there were also courses which took the form of conversations and interventions.

P.H.: La Leçon d'Althusser *[1974] insists on the urgency of the time, a time full of possibilities, when it was still possible to present Marxism as a way of thinking an imminent victory. When you started to work on the nineteenth century and on proletarian thinking in the 1830s and 1840s, was that partly to compensate for philosophical defeat in the present?*

J.R.: I don't think so. In the beginning, mine was a fairly naive approach: to try to understand what the words "workers' movement," "class consciousness," "workers' thought," and so on really meant, and what they concealed. Basically, it was clear that the Marxism we had learned at school and had seen practised by Marxist organisations was a long way from the reality of forms of struggle and forms of consciousness. I wanted to construct a genealogy of that difference.

P.H.: *A difference that begins in the moment just before Marx?*

J.R.: What I wanted to do, starting out from the present, from 1968 (and from what had been proved inappropriate not only by Althusserianism and the Communist Party but also by the movements of the Left more generally), was to rewrite the genealogy of the previous century and a half. In particular, I wanted to return to the moment of Marxism's birth to try to mark the difference between Marxism and what could have been an alternative workers' tradition. This project soon swerved off course. Initially it was a matter of searching for genuine forms of workers' thinking, a genuine workers' movement. In relation to Marxism, then, mine was a rather identitarian perspective. But the more I worked the more I realised that what was at issue was precisely a form of movement that broke with the very idea of an identitarian movement. Being a "worker" wasn't in the first instance a condition reflected in forms of consciousness or action; it was a form of symbolisation, the arrangement of a certain set of state-ments or utterances. I became interested in reconstituting the world that made these utter-ances [*énonciations*] possible.

P.H.: *Many of your contemporaries abandoned Marxism rather quickly, having come to the conclusion that the proletariat – as the univer-sal subject of an eventually singular history, the class that incarnates the dissolution of class – seemed to lead more or less directly to the Gulag. You, on the other hand, continued to reflect on the proletariat in its singularity, but by resituating it in an historical sequence that seemed better able to anticipate the risks of dogmatism and dictatorship. It was still a ques-tion of a universal singularity, but a singular-ity in some sense absent from itself, a deferred, differentiated singularity.*

J.R.: In the end, what interested me was a double movement, the movement of singularisation and its opposite. On the one hand, there was a move-ment away from the properties that characterised the worker's being and the forms of statement that were supposed to go along with that condi-tion. On the other hand, this withdrawal itself created forms of universalisation, forms of symbolisation which also constituted the positiv-ity of a figure. What interested me was always this play between negativation and positivation. I was interested in thinking it through as an impossible identification, since the intellectual revolution in question here was, in the first instance, a work of disidentification. The prole-tarians of the 1830s were people seeking to constitute themselves as speaking beings, as thinking beings in their own right. But this effort to break down the barrier between those who think and those who don't came to constitute a sort of shared symbolic system, a system forever threatened by new positivation. As a result, you could no longer say that there had been an authentic workers' movement somewhere, one that had managed to escape all forms of positi-vation and deterioration.

I wanted to show that these forms of subjecti-vation or disidentification were always at risk of falling into an identitarian positivation, whether that was a corporative conception of class or the glorious body of a community of producers. It wasn't a matter of opposing a true proletariat to some corporatist degeneration or to the Marxists' proletariat; rather, I wanted to show how the figure of subjectivation itself was constantly unstable, constantly caught between the work of symbolic disincorporation and the constitution of new bodies.

P.H.: Sometimes you present political practice as a sort of ex nihilo *innovation, almost like the constitution of a new world, even if the world in question is extremely fragile, uncertain, ephemeral. Don't you need to consider political innovation alongside the development of its conditions of possibility? I mean, for instance, on the political side of things, the role played by civic institutions and state organisations, the public space opened up, in Athens, in France, by the invention of democratic institutions (that is, the sort of factors you generally relegate to the sphere of the* police, *as opposed to the sphere of* politics*). And on the linguistic side of things, I'm thinking of some sort of preliminary equality of competences, a basic sharing of the symbolic domain. Such might be the objection of someone working in the Habermasian tradition. In short, which comes first: the people or the citizen?*

J.R.: I don't know if you can say that one of those comes before the other, because so many of these things work retroactively. There is an inscription of citizenship because there is a movement which forces this inscription, but this movement to force inscription almost always refers back to some sort of *pre-inscription*. Men who are free and equal in their rights are always supposed already to exist in order that their existence can be proclaimed and their legal inscription enforced. I would say, though, that this equality or legal freedom produces nothing in itself. It exists only in so far as it defines a possibility, in so far as there is an effective movement which can grasp it and bring it into existence retroactively.

For me the question of a return to origins is hopeless. If we take modern democracy, it is clear it works by recourse to an earlier inscrip-

tion. There is always an earlier inscription, be it 1789, the American or English Revolution, Christianity, or the ancient city-state; as a result, the question of origins doesn't really come up. As to the origin of origins, you can conceive it in different ways: it could be an originary anthropology of the political, but I know I don't have the means or tools to think of it this way. It could be a transcendental condition, but, for me, this transcendental condition can work only as a process of retroactive demonstration. I don't have any answers as to real, actual origins, and I don't think you can set out something like a transcendental condition for there being people in general.

P.H.: Nonetheless, you insist on an equality that exists once people speak, once they say to themselves they are equal as people who speak. Doesn't this equality, however, establish at the very same time the conditions of an inequality between people who speak more or less well? An abstract equality between players taking part in the same game and following the same rules always exists, but obviously that doesn't stop there being winners and losers. Is it a matter of a real equality or some sort of inclusion presupposed by participation in the game (which, in the end, is less a matter of equality than of formal similarity)?

J.R.: It isn't a formal similarity. Rather, it is the necessity of some minimal equality of competence in order for the game to be playable. As I said when I went back to Joseph Jacotot [discussed in detail in *The Ignorant Schoolmaster* (1987)] in *Disagreement* (1995): for an order to be transmitted and executed there has to be a minimal level of linguistic equality. This is the problem that troubles Aristotle: slaves need to understand what they are told. Aristotle gets around it by saying that the slave participates in language by understanding it but not possessing it. He discerns a kind of hard kernel in the *possession* of language, which he opposes to its simple use. But what is this possession, this *hexis*, which he opposes to the simple fact of understanding? He never explains it.

197

I don't have an irenic understanding of language as some sort of common patrimony which allows everyone to be equal. I'm just saying that language games, and especially language games that institute forms of dependence, presume a minimal equality of competence in order that inequality itself can operate. That's all I'm saying. And I say this not to ground equality but to show, rather, how this equality only ever functions polemically. If it is a transcendental category, its only substance lies in the acts which make manifest its effectiveness.

P.H.: Isn't there a quasi-transcendental or at least transhistorical aspect to your idea that the political actor, the universal actor, is always to be found on the side of those who aren't accounted for in the organisation of society? Politics as you conceive it always concerns the mobilisation of those who aren't included in the social totality, who constitute a part of society which groups those who belong to no identifiable social part (or who have no particular share [part] of society) and who thus establish themselves as the incarnation of the universal interest. The examples you give (Athenian democracy, 1789, proletarian singularity, etc.), are they thus examples of a more general rule: that politics only happens when the excluded are able to affirm themselves in universal terms? What leads you to believe that this remains the rule in today's and tomorrow's political conflicts? It's difficult to imagine a genuine conception of the universal in the USA today, for example, when people are so caught up in the conflict between the abstract power of the market and various communitarian and identitarian movements.

J.R.: It isn't a question of belief so much as of defining the political. There are clearly all sorts of government and many different modes of domination and management. If "politics" has a meaning, and a meaning that applies to everything we seek to elaborate as specifically political, for me its meaning is just this: there is a whole that constitutes itself other than as a collection of existing parts. For me, this is the only condition under which we can speak of poli-

tics. Which doesn't stop there being states, communities, and collectivities, all of which operate according to their different logics. But we must distinguish this very specific form, where the capacity for power is attributed to those who have no *particular* ability to exercise it, where the accounting of the whole is dissociated from any organic conception, from the generality of forms of assembly, government, and domination.

I think that the USA is indeed a barely political community. This doesn't mean that there aren't conflicts. But there is a whole structured system of being together which is not only thought but also massively practised in terms of belonging or membership (perhaps founded on sub-memberships), in terms of properties and rights attached to memberships, and so on. For me, all this defines an ethical rather than a political conception of community. This conception doesn't necessarily have disastrous consequences, even though it seems to in the USA today. I see it as a question of definition: a community is political when it authorises forms of subjectivation for the uncounted, for those unaccounted for. This needn't imply a visible category which identifies itself as "the excluded" and which wants to identify the community with itself – in that case we'd be back in ethics. I am simply saying that when there is a properly political symbolising of the community, then this, in the last instance, is where it lies. Inequality first takes effect as a miscounting or misaccounting, an inequality of the community to itself.

Now as to the question: is politics still possible today? I would say that politics is always possible, there is no reason for it to be impossible. But is politics actually imminent? Here, obviously, I share your sadness, if not your pessimism, about the current state of public affairs.

P.H.: There has often been, for instance, in the anti-colonial struggles, in the struggle for civil rights in the USA, a universalist moment, as you conceive it. This moment rarely lasts, however, and many Americans might say that under the circumstances there were good reasons to replace Martin Luther King with Malcolm X – in short, that in the reality of the struggle a choice had to be made: to adopt some sort of militant particularism or accept the effective end of the struggle.

J.R.: I wouldn't claim to advise American political movements, especially those that took place in the past. I think that we are always ambiguously placed, at constant risk of being coercively pinned down. Either you are taken in by a universal that is someone else's, that is, you trust some idea of citizenship and equality as it operates in a society that in fact denies you these things, or you feel you must radically denounce the gap between idea and fact, usually by recourse to some identitarian logic. At this point, though, whatever you manage to achieve comes because you show yourself to belong to this identity. It's very difficult, but I think that politics consists of refusing this dilemma and putting the universal under stress. Politics involves pushing both others' universal and one's own particularity to the point where each comes to contradict itself. It turns on the possibility of connecting the symbolic violence of a separation with a reclaiming of universality. The double risk of what goes by the name of liberalism still remains: on the one hand, submission to the universal as formulated by those who dominate; on the other hand, confinement within an identitarian perspective in those instances where the functioning of this universal is interrupted. No movement has really managed to avoid both risks altogether.

P.H.: Does your idea of democracy presuppose democracy as it is supposed to have existed for several centuries, that is, where the place of power is in principle empty, such that it might be occupied, at least occasionally, by exceptional figures of universal interest?

J.R.: I don't think the place of power is empty. Unlike Claude Lefort, I don't tie democracy to the theme of an empty place of power. Democracy is first and foremost neither a form of power nor a form of the emptiness of power, that is, a form of *symbolising* political power.

For me, democracy isn't a form of power but the very existence of the political (in so far as politics is distinct from knowing who has the right to occupy power or how power should be occupied), precisely because it defines a paradoxical power – one that doesn't allow anyone legitimately to claim a place on the basis of his or her competences. Democracy is, first of all, a practice, which means that the very same institutions of power may or may not be accompanied by a democratic life. The same forms of parliamentary powers, the same institutional frameworks can either give rise to a democratic life, that is, a subjectivation of the gap between two ways of counting or accounting for the community, or operate simply as instruments for the reproduction of an oligarchic power.

P.H.: It isn't first and foremost a question of power? This is Slavoj Žižek's objection, when he reads you (briefly) in his The Ticklish Subject *[1999]: that you posit unrealistic, impossibly ideal conditions for political practice, and as a result end up just keeping your hands clean. How might we organise a true popular mobilisation without recourse to power, the party, authority, etc.?*

J.R.: I'm not saying you need absolutely no power. I'm not preaching spontaneity as against organisation. Forms of organisation and relations of authority are always being set up. The fact that I don't much care for the practices of power and the forms of thought they engender is a secondary, personal concern. The central problem is theoretical. Politics may well have to do with powers and their implementation, but that doesn't mean that politics and power are one and the same. The essential point is that politics cannot be defined simply as the organisation of a community. Nor can it be defined as the occupation of the place of government, which isn't to say that this place doesn't exist or doesn't have to be occupied. It is the peculiar tendency of what I call the police to confuse these things. Politics is always an alternative to any police order, regardless of both the forms of power the former must develop and the latter's organisation, form or value.

P.H.: But, leaving aside the business of government, how are we to think the organisation of political authority in this sense? What sorts of organisation enable the insurrection of the excluded or the militant mobilisation of universal interest? It's obvious you're not a party thinker. But how are we to pursue a politics without party which will, nevertheless, remain a militant politics? Is this something that needs to be reinvented within each political episode?

J.R.: I don't think there are rules for good militant organisation. If there were, we'd already have applied them and we'd certainly be further along than we are at the moment. All I can define are forms of perception, forms of utterance. As to how these are then taken up by organisations, I must admit that I've never been able to endure any one of them for very long, but I know I have nothing better to propose.

P.H.: Towards the end of Disagreement, *I think, you say there was a genuine political movement in France at the time of the Algerian war, a subversive movement, that was clearly different from the movements of generalised "sympathy" which developed around the recent conflicts in Bosnia, Rwanda, and Timor. Can you see the beginnings of a new movement of this type, against the aggressor, in some currents of anti-American and anti-globalisation thinking?*

J.R.: That is difficult to define today. It's easy to see that people are inspired by the dream of a political movement that would define itself in opposition to the domination of *international* capitalism. In reality, though, no political movement has yet defined itself against international capital. To this point they have been defined within national frameworks, or as relations between distinct peoples and their national states, or possibly as three-way relations, as was the case with Algeria and with the anti-imperialist struggles more generally. In such cases the national stage split on the international stage and allowed the uncounted to be accounted for. This three-way game, this *political* cause of the other, seems impossible today. The anti-globalisation movements want to take on capital as world government directly. But capital is precisely a government that isn't one: it isn't a state, and it doesn't recognise any "people" inside or outside it who might serve as its point of reference or offer themselves for subjectivation. The idea of the multitude proposed by Negri and Hardt is a direct response to this absence of points at which political subjectivation might take hold. In the end, their idea rests on the transposition of a Marxian economic schema by which the forces of production break through the external framework of the relations of production. Capital escapes all political holds. The vast demonstrations of recent years have, in fact, sought to force it onto the political stage through the institutional or policing instruments by which it operates.

The idea of a direct relation between the multitude and empire seems to me to bypass the problem of constituting a global political stage. I'm not sure that we will ever attain a directly political form of anti-capitalist struggle. I don't think there can be an anti-imperialist politics which isn't mediated by relations to states, bringing into play an inside and an outside. It's easy to sense the difficulties that the anti-globalisation movements and their theorists have when it comes to current forms of imperialism – for example, with American politics after 11 September. It's clear that the rules of the game are being mixed up today. At the time of the big anti-imperialist movements against the Vietnam War, for instance, we had a clear sense of who was the aggressor and who was under attack; we could play on the obvious contradiction between internal democratic discourse and external imperialist aggression. Again, when the USA supported such and such a dictatorship in the name of the struggle against communism, we could demonstrate the discrepancy between the declared struggle for democracy and the reality of supporting dictatorships. What has characterised the whole period after 11 September, however, has been the erasure of these signs of contradiction. The war in Afghanistan was presented directly as a war of good against evil. The contradictions between inside and outside, like those between words and deeds, have disappeared in favour of a general moralising of political life. The global reign of the economy is accompanied by a global reign of morality, in which it is harder for political action to find its stakes.

P.H.: So, for you, national mediation remains essential and effective for the moment?

J.R.: I think national mediation remains effective, yes, because it's there that the relation between a structure of inclusion and what it excludes plays itself out. If lots of things are happening around those "without" – particularly around immigrants "without papers [*sans-papiers*]" – it is because the example of those without papers exposes the contradiction between affirming free circulation in a world without borders and the practices of keeping borders under surveillance and defining groups of people who cannot cross them. So, I think there are specific scenes of contradiction in confining some people while allowing others to circulate freely, but not one great nomadic movement of the multitude against empire or one overarching relation between the system and its peripheries.

P.H.: A last question on politics. You say that "the essential work of politics is the configuration of its own space. It is to get the world of its subjects and its operations to be seen."[2] You want to distinguish all political action – every instance of dissensus – from what you call the domain of the police, the domain of social coordination, the government, etc. But don't we have to think of politics in relation to all the various ways that social inequality is structured, in relation, for example, to education, the organisation of urban life, conditions of employment, economic power, etc.?

J.R.: There I think you're attributing to me an idea that isn't mine but Badiou's. I think that it is indeed possible to define what is specific to politics, and in such a way as to separate political practice and the ideas of political community from all forms of negotiation between the interests of social groups. That's why I say that the political isn't the social. But I'd also say that the "social" as an historical configuration isn't some sort of shameful empirical magma – situational,

state-controlled, and so on (rather as Badiou imagines it) – which the political act would escape from. On the contrary, I think that the social is a complex domain, that what we call the social is a sort of mixture where the policing logics which determine how things are to be distributed or shared out among social groups encounter the various ways of configuring the common space which throw these same distributions into question. What we call "social benefits" are not only forms of redistributing national income; they are always also ways of reconfiguring what is shared or common. In the end, everything in politics turns on the distribution of spaces. What are these places? How do they function? Why are they there? Who can occupy them? For me, political action always acts upon the social as the litigious distribution of places and roles. It is always a matter of knowing who is qualified to say what a particular place is and what is done in it.

So, I think that politics constantly emerges from questions traditionally thought of as social, that politics runs through labour movements and strikes, as well as around educational questions. You could say that the great political movements in France over the last twenty years have been connected with social questions, those of school and university, the status of employees, the *sans-papiers* or the unemployed – all fundamentally questions we might call social. But what does social mean? It means that what is at stake in institutional problems relating to school or nationality, or in problems arising around the distribution of work and wealth (employment or social benefits), is really the configuring of what is shared or common. I'm thinking, for example, of the movements in France that grew up around university selection in 1986, or around pensions and social benefits in the autumn of 1995. The battle over selection reminded us that the school and university system is not simply an instrument of "training" or "reproduction"; it is also the institution by which a society signifies to itself the meaning of the community that institutes it. In the same way, questions relating to pensions, health, and social security not only concern what are referred to as employees' privileges and rights but also engage with the idea of the configuration of the common sphere. Whether healthcare and pensions operate by a system of redistribution and solidarity, or through individual private insurance, doesn't just concern the privileges that employees may have acquired at any historical moment: it touches on the configuring of the common sphere. Within any so-called social negotiation there is always negotiation over what the community holds as common.

P.H.: You quote Hannah Arendt from time to time: do you feel close to her conception of politics, politics as a place of negotiation, a place of performances and appearances (rather than timeless essences), of the vita activa *valued above the pretensions of theory, philosophy, and the* vita contemplativa*?*

J.R.: Let's say there's some ground for agreement, coupled with a very strong disagreement (a disagreement which is also a reaction against the dominant uses and interpretations of her work today). The basis of agreement is that politics is a matter of appearance [*apparence*], a matter of constituting a common stage or acting out common scenes rather than governing common interests. That said, in Hannah Arendt this fundamental affirmation is linked to the idea that the political stage is blurred or cluttered by the claims of the social – I'm thinking of what she has to say about the French Revolution and the role of pity, where compassion for the "needy" clouds the purity of the political scene. To my mind this just returns us to some of the most traditional preconceptions about there being two distinct sorts of life: one able to play the political game of appearance and the other supposedly devoted to the sole reality of reproducing life. Her conception of political appearance simply mirrors the traditional (that is, Platonic) opposition, which reserves the legitimate use of appearance for one form of life alone. For me, by contrast, the appearance of the *demos* shatters any division between those who are deemed able and those who are not. Her opposition between the political and the social returns us to the old oppositions in Greek philosophy between men of leisure and men of necessity, the latter being

men whose needs exclude them from the domain of appearance and, hence, from politics.

A significant part of what I've managed to write about politics is a response to Hannah Arendt's use, in *On Revolution*, of John Adams's little phrase, that the misfortune of the poor lies in their being unseen. She says that such an idea could only have occurred to someone who was already a participant in the distinction of political life, that it cannot be shared by the poor in question, because they do not realise they are not seen – so a demand for visibility has no meaning for them. However, all my work on workers' emancipation showed that the most prominent of the claims put forward by the workers and the poor was precisely the claim to visibility, a will to enter the political realm of appearance, the affirmation of a capacity for appearance. Hannah Arendt remains a prisoner of the tautology by which those who "cannot" think a thing do not think it. As I understand it, though, politics begins exactly when those who "cannot" do something show that in fact they can. That is the theoretical differend. As for practice, Arendt's distinction between the political and the social has been widely used (during the events of December 1995 to justify governmental policies, for example). "Liberals" and "republicans" keep on reciting their Hannah Arendt to show that politics – which is to say, the state and the government – is above social pettiness, a realm of common collective interests that transcends corporate egoisms.

P.H.: Michelet figures prominently in your The Names of History *[1992]. Did his conception of history as the history of collective liberty, of a people becoming conscious of itself, the story of a hitherto silent people's entry into speech, inspire you in one way or another? And what is Michelet's relation, say, to the egalitarian thought of a Jacotot (as you describe it in* The Ignorant Schoolmaster*)?*

J.R.: I wanted, above all, to show how Michelet had invented a new form of mastery, one based on anonymous collective speech. It's the Romantic thesis of a speech that is supposed to come from below in opposition to the dominant, noisy voices of the day. But Michelet never lets this speech from below actually be spoken, in its own terms. He converts the speech of revolutionary assemblies into a kind of discourse of the earth: a discourse of the fields or the city, of rural harvests or the mud in the streets, the silent word of truth as opposed to the actual words of speakers. What I tried to explain was the constitution of this paradigm of the silent masses (as distinct from the noisy people), the poetico-political paradigm of a great anonymous, unconscious thought expressing itself not through people's words but through their silence, which then becomes a scientific paradigm in history and sociology. This wordless speech is something completely different from Jacotot and his affirmation of the capacity to speak of those who "don't know how," that is, his presupposition and verification of the equality of intelligences.

There are two ways of thinking equality. It can be thought in terms of intellectual emancipation founded on the idea of man as a "literary animal" – an idea of equality as a capacity to be verified by *anybody*. Or it can be thought in terms of the indifferentiation of a collective speech, a great anonymous voice – the idea that speech is everywhere, that there is speech written on things, some voice of reality itself which speaks better than any uttered word. This second idea begins in literature, in Victor Hugo's speech of the sewer that says everything, and in Michelet's voice of the mud or the harvest. Later, this poetic paradigm becomes a scientific one.

The obvious problem is that these two paradigms, these two ways of thinking the equality of the nameless, which are opposed in theory, keep mixing in practice, so that discourses of emancipation continually interweave the ability to speak demonstrated by anyone at all together with the silent power of the collective.

P.H.: This is perhaps a good moment to move on to questions of aesthetics. Your book on Mallarmé *came out in 1996, followed by* La Parole muette *in 1998. Since then you seem to have been working mainly on topics relating to art, literature, and aesthetics. Why the shift in interest? Was it something foreseen, something you had been anticipating?*

J.R.: I've never had a programme for the future, have never programmed my future projects. So, I've never imagined my work developing from politics to aesthetics, especially since it has always sought to blur boundaries. What I wanted to show when I wrote *Nights of Labor* [1981] was that a so-called political and social movement was also an intellectual and aesthetic one, a way of reconfiguring the frameworks of the visible and the thinkable. In the same way, in *Disagreement* I tried to show how politics is an aesthetic matter, a reconfiguration of the way we share out or divide places and times, speech and silence, the visible and the invisible. My personal interests have most often drawn me to literature and cinema, certainly more than to questions of so-called political science, which in themselves have never interested me very much. And if I was able to write on workers' history it was because I always had in mind a whole play of literary references, because I saw workers' texts through a number of models offered by literature, and because I developed a mode of writing and composition that allowed me to break, in practice, with the politics implicit in the traditional way of treating "workers' speech," as the *expression* of a condition. For me, the elaboration of a philosophical discourse or a theoretical scene is always also the putting into practice of a certain poetics.

So, for me, there has never been a move from politics to aesthetics. Take the *Mallarmé* book, for example: what was the core of my interest in Mallarmé? Something like a community of scene [*de scène*]. The two prose poems in which Mallarmé stages the poet's relation to the proletarian interested me initially because they replayed in a new way scenes that had already been acted out between proletarians and utopians. Even the relation between day and night in Mallarmé (which is generally understood through the themes of nocturnal anxiety and purity) reminded me strongly of why I had spoken of the *nights* of labour – not on account of workers' misfortune, but in recognition of the fact that they annex the night, the time of rest, and thereby break the order of time which keeps them confined to a certain place. All this has always been absolutely connected for me, whether I take it as the aesthetics inherent in politics or the politics inherent in writing. Before *Mallarmé*, before *La Parole muette*, even before *Disagreement*, I led a seminar over several years on the politics of writing – that is, not on "how to write politics" but on "what is properly political in writing." The work on Michelet was about the birth of a certain way of writing history. Does writing translate properties and transmit knowledge, or does it itself constitute an act, a way of configuring and dividing the shared domain of the sensible? These questions have continued to interest me.

This politics of writing is, then, something completely different from the questions of representation by which politics and aesthetics are generally linked. Knowing how writers represent women, workers, and foreigners has never really interested me. My interest has always been in writing as a way of cutting up the universal singular. I'm thinking, for example, of Flaubert's declarations, such as "I am interested less in the ragged than in the lice who feed on them," which suppose a whole idea of the relation between the population of a novel and a social population (or the people in a political sense), and which posit a literary "equality" on a level that is no longer the one used to debate political equality. In its own way, literature too introduces a dissensus and a miscounting which are not those of political action. I am interested in the relation between the two, rather than, say, the various forms of "bias" in the representation of social categories in Flaubert. I began to reflect on these things via the question of writing history, and this reflection grew into the work on the politics of literature.

Then, on account of my work on history and the writing of history, I happened to be asked by people in the arts to apply my analyses to their fields and problems – both in cinema, in which I've always had a personal interest (my first substantial text on cinema, for example, dealt with the relation between the "aesthetic" and the "social" in Rossellini's *Europe 51*), and in other, less familiar fields (I was asked to speak, for example, "in my own way" about history for the exhibition *Face à l'histoire* organised by the Centre Pompidou in 1997). This last invitation

gave me the opportunity to work on the question of contemporary art, a topic that had not interested me up to then.

So there is a constant aesthetic core in everything I do, even if I only began to speak of literature explicitly at a particular moment, having addressed it until then through questions of history and what one might call the forms of workers' literary appropriations. Then came requests for me to speak on topics about which I had no real competence. After what I had done, people thought I should have things to say about contemporary art, for example. I didn't know a lot about it, but I wanted to respond to the challenge, because it was a chance to learn something new, and to learn how to talk about it.

P.H.: Is there a conceptual parallel between the status of literature as you describe it in the wake of the Romantic revolution – on the one hand, the writing of everything, a systematic, encyclopaedic, even geological, literature in the manner of Cuvier and Balzac, and, on the other hand, a literature of nothing, a writing which ultimately refers only to itself[3] – and the status of politics? As if they were both efforts to connect everything and nothing, exclusion and the universal?

J.R.: There is no direct link between the two, but they both refer back to the same kernel of meaning. It is the ancient fictional or dramatic "plot," the same organic, Aristotelian idea of the work that bursts either from a profusion of things and signs or from the rarefaction of events and senses. Broadly, literature as a regime of writing defines itself in the period after the Revolution not simply as another way of writing, another way of conceiving of the art of writing, but also as a whole mode of interpreting society and the place of speech in it. Literature defines itself around an idea of speech that somehow exceeds the simple figure of the speaker. It defines itself around the idea that there is speech [*parole*] everywhere, and that what speaks in a poem is not necessarily what any speaking intention has put into it. This is all the legacy of Vico. Either that or there is language [*langage*] everywhere, which is Balzac's position. There is something like a vast poem everywhere, which is the poem that society itself writes by both uttering and hiding itself in a multitude of signs.

Or, if you take the Flaubertian perspective, the "book about nothing" comes to replace the lost totality. In fact, this is still Schiller's idea of "naive" (as opposed to "sentimental") poetry as the poem of a world (an idea with colossal force whose effects are still with us), an unconscious or "involuntary" poem for which we must produce an equivalent in the inverse form of a work that relates only to itself. The lost totality rediscovers itself on the side of nothing, but we must look at what this nothing means. Flaubert invents a sort of atomic micrology which is supposed to pulverise the democratic population. At the same time, he contributes to what we could call an aesthetic of equal intensities – opposed to the hierarchies of the representative tradition – which is the aesthetic he addresses to Madame Bovary even as he condemns her. There is a conflictual complicity between the fictional population and the social world that this literature addresses. Flaubert writes "against" Madame Bovary and the "democratic" confusion of art and life, but, at the same time, he writes from the "democratic" point of view which affirms the equality of subjects and intensities. It is this tension that interests me. Literature invents itself as another way of talking about the things politicians talk about.

P.H.: For some time now, most aesthetic thinkers have emphasised the importance of modernism and the avant-garde. Among your contemporaries, you are one of the few to pay more attention to Romanticism and to the nineteenth century more generally. For you, the answers to many of the questions that aesthetics asks are still to be found in Schiller, Kant, and Balzac. What is the key to what you call the "aesthetic revolution"?[4] And how do you understand modernism?

J.R.: What is the kernel of the aesthetic revolution? First of all, negatively, it means the ruin of any art defined as a set of systematisable practices with clear rules. It means the ruin of any art where art's dignity is defined by the dignity of its

subjects – in the end, the ruin of the whole hierarchical conception of art which places tragedy above comedy and history painting above genre painting, etc. To begin with, then, the aesthetic revolution is the idea that everything is material for art, so that art is no longer governed by its subject, by what it speaks of: art can show and speak of everything in the same manner. In this sense, the aesthetic revolution is an extension to infinity of the realm of language, of poetry.

It is the affirmation that poems are everywhere, that paintings are everywhere. So, it is also the development of a whole series of forms of perception which allow us to see the beautiful everywhere. This implies a great anonymisation of the beautiful (Mallarmé's "ordinary" splendour). I think this is the real kernel: the idea of equality and anonymity. At this point, the ideal of art becomes the conjunction of artistic will and the beauty or poeticity that is in some sense immanent in everything, or that can be uncovered everywhere.

That is what you find all through the fiction of the nineteenth century, but it's at work in the poetry too. For example, it's what Benjamin isolated in Baudelaire, but it's something much broader than that too. It implies a sort of exploding of genre and, in particular, that great mixing of literature and painting which dominates both literature and painting in the nineteenth century. It is this blending of literature and painting, pure and applied art, art for art's sake and art within life, which will later be opposed by the whole modernist doxa that asserts the growing autonomy of the various arts.

The entire modernist ideology is constructed on the completely simplistic image of a great anti-representational rupture: at a certain moment, supposedly, nobody represents any more, nobody copies models, art applies its own efforts to its own materials, and in the process each form of art becomes autonomous. Obviously all this falls apart in the 1960s and 1970s, in what some will see as the betrayal of modernism. I think, though, that modernism is an ideology of art elaborated completely retrospectively. "Modernists" are always trying to think Mallarmé and the pure poem, abstract painting, pure painting, or Schoenberg and a music that would no longer be expressive, etc. But if you look at how this came about, you realise that all the so-called movements to define a pure art were in fact completely mixed up with all sorts of other preoccupations – architectural, social, religious, political, and so on. The whole paradox of an aesthetic regime of art is that art defines itself by its very identity with non-art. You cannot understand people like Malevich, Mondrian or Schoenberg if you don't remember that their "pure" art is inscribed in the midst of questions regarding synaesthesia, the construction of an individual or collective setting for life, utopias of community, new forms of spirituality, etc. The modernist doxa is constructed exactly at the point when the slightly confused mixture of political and artistic rationalities begins to come apart.

Remarkably, modernism – that is, the conception of modern art as the art of autonomy – was largely invented by Marxists. Why? Because it was a case of proving that, even if the social revolution had been confiscated, in art the purity of a rupture had been maintained, and with it the promise of emancipation. I'm racing through all this, but I do think that this is what lies behind Adorno or Greenberg: a way of defining art's radicality by the radicality of its separation, that is, a way of separating art radically from politics in order to preserve its political potential. Afterwards, this complicated dialectic is effaced in the simplistic dogma of modern art as the art of autonomy. Obviously, this dogma does not survive for very long in the face of the reality of artistic practices, and when it collapses, people start saying "Modernity is falling apart." But it hasn't: what has fallen apart is just a very partial and belated interpretation of what I call the aesthetic mode of art.

P.H.: For you, then, is it a matter of maintaining the contradictory relations of the aesthetic regime, of continuing in the difficult dialectic of whole and nothing, of the controlled inscription of a generalised speech (an anonymous beauty, as you put it) and the vacillation of an ultimately silent discourse which affirms its own unconsciousness and lack of identity? You seek to continue in that tradition, rather than

swing in the opposite direction, towards the postmodern, for example, or the post-whatever?

J.R.: I don't really believe in any great historical break between the modern and the postmodern. There aren't many solid identifying features of an art that would be postmodern. How exactly are you going to define postmodernism? By the return of figuration? But that is only a part of it. By the mixing of genres? But that is much older. For me, if you want to think about breaks, it's important first of all to understand the continuities – to understand, for example, that modern art was not born, as we still believe, in a simple and radical break with the realist tradition. The categories which allow us to think modern art were entirely elaborated in the modes of focusing perception that were first imposed by the realist novel: indifference to subject, close-ups, the primacy of detail and tone. It was often novelists – like the Goncourts, for example – who as art critics reconfigured the logic of visibility in the field of painting (which was still very much figurative), valorising the pictorial material over its subject. Painting was seen in a new way, one that abstracted its subject, before painters themselves abandoned figuration.

To take another example: installation is one of the central forms of contemporary art. But you will find an extraordinary passage in Zola's *Le Ventre de Paris* – a completely mad book from 1874, a great hymn to poetry, and to great modern poetry in particular. Now, what is this great modern poetry? And what is the great monument of the nineteenth century? Les Halles [the central markets] in Paris. Zola installs his painter, Claude Lantier – the impressionist painter as he sees him, a painter in search of modern beauty – in this monument of modernity. At one point, Lantier explains that his most beautiful work wasn't a painting. Rather, he created his masterpiece the day he redid his cousin the butcher's window display. He describes this display, how he arranged the blood sausages, dried sausages, turkeys, and hams. Still with Zola, in *Au Bonheur des dames* you also have the department store as a work of modern art, with the capitalist, Octave Mouret, as the great poet of modernity, the poet of commodity installation. At that time, then, no one made installations, but an indecision between the art of the canvas and the art of display can already be marked. An art that has only developed in the last twenty or thirty years had, in some sense, already found its thought and its visibility. The "modern" solitude of art has always also been its non-solitude.

P.H.: But what if you take a hard modernist like Rothko, whose last paintings revolve around blackness, the absence of all figuration, all "application"?

J.R.: Sure, but that was an idea of modern*ism*, and, in any case, we know that it wasn't an idea of pure painting, since at the time Rothko was becoming more and more mystical. Of course, you can cite painters who fit into the exemplary configuration of modernism as it was constructed, most notably, by Greenberg. But, in the end, what is this configuration? A short sequence of abstract art done at a particular moment by artists with roots in other traditions, notably surrealism. You absolutely cannot reduce modern art to this short sequence of abstract painting. Modern art is also constructivism, surrealism, Dadaism, or what have you – all forms of art with roots in Romantic thinking about the relation between art and life. I do not like modernism as a concept, because it seeks to identify an entire regime of art with a few particular manifestations that it presents as exemplary, interprets in an extraordinarily restrictive way, and links to an absolutely uncritical idea of historical time.

P.H.: Moving on now to my last questions, which are mostly about the immediate intellectual context of your work. I was struck by your reading of Freud, or rather your literary recontextualising of Freud's work in L'Inconscient esthétique *[2001]. Can you generalise your position a little, to incorporate Lacan, for example – Lacan as a thinker who insists on the primacy of speech, precisely, on the equality and essential anonymity of all speech phenomena, on the importance of listening to speech qua speech, etc.?*

J.R.: I won't say very much about Lacan, because I still really don't know what to think of him or, rather, what to do with his thought. For me, the problem with Lacan is that he seemed to hover between several rationalities. When my generation got to know him, it was the time of the primacy of the signifier, the great structuralist moment, which in my view had no important consequences at the level of aesthetics. What became visible in Lacan's subsequent work, though, was a whole other legacy, the surrealist legacy of Bataille and all those movements in the 1930s which wanted in their own way to rethink relations between aesthetics and politics – a whole way of thinking the obscure rationality of thought that was not dependent on the Freudian logic of the symptom (itself still linked to an Aristotelian poetics of history as causal agency). Lacan, in this sense, is a lot closer to Romantic poetics than Freud is. Where Freud deciphers, Lacan turns to the silent words that remain silent, those ultimate blocks of nonsense which can either become emblems of an absolute freedom (à la Breton) or embody the accursed share, the opaque residue impenetrable to sense (à la Bataille). For me, that is ultimately the difference Lacan brings.

This difference shows up clearly in the uses Freud and Lacan make of Sophocles. Freud obviously constructs everything around the figure of Oedipus, around the link between incestuous desire as an object and an Enlightenment notion of rationality (the path of interpretation reconstituting the causal chain). Lacan, on the other hand, turns more and more to Antigone, whose desire does not lend itself to interpretation, who wants only to maintain a stubborn fidelity to the powers below, who, in short, wants only death. I'm thinking here of Lacan taking up Antigone at the time of the Baader-Meinhof gang, to show that she has nothing to do with the icon of "human rights in the face of power" that she is always made out to be, but is in fact closer to Ulrike Meinhof and the radicality of those German terrorists. The regime of signification in which Lacan constructs Antigone is a lot closer to what one might call aesthetic reason than the one Freud uses. The latter reconstitutes classical causalities, where Antigone as Lacan reconstructs her is closer to those half-obscure figures of the Romantic and realist periods.

P.H.: Is there a risk that your idea of silent speech might lead eventually to silence pure and simple? Were you ever tempted by the mystical tendency that runs through the work of Bataille, precisely, and to some extent in the writings of Blanchot, Foucault and Deleuze, for example?

J.R.: I've never been very receptive to either Blanchot and Bataille or to what the following generation – Foucault, Derrida, Deleuze – made of them. It all struck me as very opaque. Rather, I became sensitive to the question through the whole problematic of the will in the nineteenth century. In nineteenth-century literature, let's say from Balzac to Zola – not forgetting Strindberg, Ibsen, and what happens in Dostoyevsky and Tolstoy – there is a long train of thought that either challenges the will or carries it on to some final disaster. Thinking through the death drive begins not just with stories of the will exacerbated (as with Vautrin) or annihilated (as with Oblomov) but also with the very logic of the regime of writing proper to literature, its way of untying the representative knot connecting action, will, and meaning. At the heart of the aesthetic regime of art there is an idea that the highest effort of the will is to identify itself with the highest point of its abdication. So, there is something like a race towards nothingness, which is always represented either as the hero's experience or identified as the force which runs through writing itself. I have found the theme of the self-destructive will, which is generally thought to belong to Schopenhauer and nihilism in the strict sense, throughout the literature of the nineteenth century. And I have been rereading Freud's texts in this light, telling myself that it is really this he is measuring himself against. I myself have no inclination towards a mysticism of silence, but I do feel very deeply the link between a whole regime of writing and the desertion of a certain idea of meaning, between the privilege of "silent speech" and the dramaturgy of a self-annihilating will.

P.H.: Your own writing is often heavily ironic, motivated by a sort of dynamic indignation, as if the weight of history and silence has forced you into a constant movement. Is this part of your resistance to that nihilism?

J.R.: I'd say that, broadly speaking, it is less a specific resistance to the death drive than part of a strategy of writing which tries to put uncertainty back into statements. On the one hand, it's a matter of introducing some give or play into dogmatic statements. On the other, you can only contest the assurance of people with knowledge by undoing the way they construct their other: the one who does not know, the ignorant or naive one. That is why I wanted to give the discourse of workers' emancipation its share of play, of doubt about what it says. I wanted to shatter the image of the naive believer in a land of milk and honey, to show that workers' utopian discourse always also knows at a certain point that it is an illusory and ironic discourse, which does not entirely believe what it says. The problem is to challenge the distribution of roles. And that concerns the status of my own assertions as well. I have tried to offer them as *probable* assertions, to avoid a certain affirmative, categorical style which I know is elsewhere encouraged in philosophy, but which I have never been able to assimilate.

P.H.: How do you situate yourself in terms of your contemporaries? Your interest in writing and the deferral of certainties seems to align you, up to a point, with Derrida; on the other hand, your interest in axiomatic equality and exceptional configurations of universality reminds me of Badiou. But it's hard to imagine two more different conceptions of thought!

J.R.: Those are not quite the markers by which I would define myself. I have read Derrida with interest but from a certain distance, from a slightly out-of-kilter perspective. (If I too, in my own way, have tried to reread the *Phaedrus*, it has been in order to find at work in that text not the *pharmakon* or *dissemination* but a sharing out of the modes of speech homologous to the sharing out of the destinies of souls and bodies – in short, a politics of writing.) If, among the thinkers of my generation, there was one I was quite close to at one point, it was Foucault. Something of Foucault's archaeological project – the will to think the conditions of possibility of such and such a form of statement or such and such an object's constitution – has stuck with me. As to Badiou, there are doubtless certain similarities: a shared fidelity to a common history, a similar way of thinking politics by separating it from state practice, the question of power, and the tradition of political philosophy. But there is also in Badiou this affirmative posture oriented towards eternity which I absolutely cannot identify with. His idea of absolute disconnection or unrelation, his idea of an event that stands out sharply against the situation, his idea of the quasi-miraculous force of the eventual statement[5] – these are ideas I absolutely cannot share.

P.H.: To close, what are you working on now? What are your plans for the future?

J.R.: I have no great project. I'm still working on questions around the aesthetic regime of art, the relation between aesthetics and politics, what you could call the politics of literature. I've now accumulated masses of material on the topic which I don't quite know what to do with. I have enough material for a five-volume summa on the aesthetic regime of art, but no desire to write it. So I am trying to find forms of writing that allow me to make a few points about what is at stake in thinking the aesthetic regime of art – forms that, through significant objects and angles, allow me to say as much as possible in as little space as possible. I suppose my idea of research is indissociable from the invention of a way of writing.

notes

1 This interview was conducted in Paris on 29 August 2002.

2 Rancière, "Eleven Theses on Politics" (Dec. 1996), available online at <http://www.zrc-sazu.si/www/fi/aktual96/ranciere.htm>.

3 See, in particular, Rancière, *La Parole muette* 14, 88–89.

4 See, in particular, Rancière, "The Aesthetic Revolution and its Outcomes" (2002).

5 What Badiou calls an "eventual statement" is one that emerges in the wake of an event, where an event is defined as something that makes it impossible for those who recognise it to carry on as before – for example, in the wake of an encounter with another person, the statement "I love you." [Editor's note.]

works by rancière

"Le Concept de critique et la critique de l'économie politique des *Manuscrits de 1844* au *Capital*." *Lire le capital.* By Louis Althusser, Pierre Macherey, Etienne Balibar and Roger Establet. 2 Vols. Paris: Maspero, 1965. Vol. 1, 93–210. "The Concept of 'Critique' and the 'Critique of Political Economy' (From the *Manuscripts* of 1844 to *Capital*)." *Ideology, Method and Marx: Essays from Economy and Society.* Ed. Ali Rattansi. London: Routledge, 1989. 74–180.

La Leçon d'Althusser. Paris: Gallimard, 1974. Chapter 6 has been translated by Martin Jordin as "On the Theory of Ideology (The Politics of Althusser)." *Radical Philosophy* 7 (spring 1974): 2–15. Reprinted in *Radical Philosophy Reader.* Ed. Roy Edgley and Richard Osborne. London: Verso, 1985. 101–36.

With Patrick Vauday. "En Allant à l'expo. L'ouvrier, sa femme et les machines." *Révoltes Logiques* 1 (1975): 5–22. "Going to the Expo: The Worker, His Wife and Machines." *Voices of the People.* Ed. Adrian Rifkin and Roger Thomas. London: Routledge, 1988. 23–44.

With Alain Faure (eds.). *La Parole ouvrière 1830–1851: textes rassemblés et présentés.* Paris: Union générale d'éditions, 1976.

"Le Bon Temps ou la barrière des plaisirs." *Révoltes Logiques* 7 (1978): 25–66. "Good Times or Pleasures at the Barriers." Trans. John Moore. *Voices of the People.* Ed. Adrian Rifkin and Roger Thomas. London: Routledge, 1988. 45–94.

"'*Le Social*': The Lost Tradition in French Labour History." *People's History and Socialist Theory.* Ed. Raphael Samuel. London: Routledge, 1980. 267–72.

politics and aesthetics

La Nuit des prolétaires: archives du rêve ouvrier. Paris: Fayard, 1981. *The Nights of Labor: The Workers' Dream in Nineteenth-Century France.* Trans. John Drury with an introduction by Donald Reid. Philadelphia: Temple UP, 1989.

"The Myth of the Artisan: Critical Reflections on a Social Category." 1983. Trans. David H. Lake and Cynthia J. Koepp. *Working in France: Representations, Meanings, Organization, and Practice.* Ed. Steven Laurence Kaplan and Cynthia J. Koepp. Ithaca: Cornell UP, 1986. 317–34.

Le Philosophe et ses pauvres. Paris: Fayard, 1983. *The Philosopher and His Poor.* Trans. John Drury, Corinne Oster and Andrew Parker. Ed. with an introduction by Andrew Parker. Durham, NC: Duke UP, 2004.

(Ed.). *Le Philosophe plébéien.* By Gabriel Gauny. Paris: La Découverte/Maspero, 1983.

With the Collectif "Révoltes logiques." *L'Empire du sociologue.* Paris: La Découverte, 1984.

"Entretien avec Jacques Rancière." Interview conducted by Edmond El Maleh. *Entretiens avec "Le Monde" I. Philosophies.* Ed. Christian Delacampagne. Paris: La Découverte/Le Monde, 1984. 158–66.

With the Collectif "Révoltes logiques." *Esthétiques du peuple.* Paris: La Découverte, 1985.

"La Visite du peuple. Entretien avec Jacques Rancière." Conducted by Serge Le Péron and Charles Tesson. *Cahiers de Cinéma* 371–372 (May 1985): 106–11.

"Nous qui sommes si critiques ..." *La Grève des philosophes: école et philosophie.* By Jacques Derrida et al. Paris: Osiris, 1986. 110–21.

Le Maître ignorant: cinq leçons sur l'émancipation intellectuelle. Paris: Fayard, 1987. *The Ignorant Schoolmaster: Five Lessons in Intellectual Emancipation.* Trans. with an introduction by Kristin Ross. Stanford: Stanford UP, 1991.

"After What." 1988. Trans. Christina Davis. *Who Comes after the Subject?* Ed. Eduardo Cadava et al. London: Routledge, 1991. 246–52.

"Réponse à Alain Badiou: *L'Être et l'évènement.*" *Cahiers du Collège International de Philosophie* 8 (Oct. 1989): 211–25.

Aux bords du politique. Paris: Osiris, 1990. Enlarged 2nd ed. Paris: La Fabrique, 1998. *On the Shores of Politics.* Trans. Liz Heron. London: Verso, 1995.

Courts Voyages au pays du peuple. Paris: Seuil, 1990. *Short Voyages to the Land of the People.* Trans. James B. Swenson. Stanford: Stanford UP, 2003.

Les Mots de l'histoire: essai de poétique du savoir [subsequent editions: *Les Noms de l'histoire*]. Paris: Seuil, 1992. *The Names of History: On the Poetics of Knowledge.* Trans. Hassan Melehy with a foreword by Hayden White. Minneapolis: U of Minnesota P, 1994.

"Overlegitimation." Trans. Kristin Ross. *Social Text* 31–32 (1992): 252–57.

"Politics, Identification, and Subjectivization." *October* 61 (summer 1992): 58–64.

"Préface." *La Politique des poètes. Pourquoi des poètes en temps de détresse?* Ed. Jacques Rancière. Paris: Albin Michel, 1992. 9–18.

"Préface: la pensée du non-retour." *La Raison nomade.* By Jean Borreil. Ed. Christine Buci-Glucksmann et al. Paris: Payot, 1993. 9–18.

"Discovering New Worlds: Politics of Travel and Metaphors of Space." *Travellers' Tales: Narratives of Home and Displacement.* Ed. George Robertson et al. London: Routledge, 1994. 29–37.

"Post-Democracy, Politics and Philosophy: An Interview with Jacques Rancière." Trans. Kate Nash. *Angelaki* 1.3 (1994): 171–78.

La Mésentente: politique et philosophie. Paris: Galilée, 1995. *Disagreement: Politics and Philosophy.* Trans. Julie Rose. Minneapolis: U of Minnesota P, 1999.

"The Archaeomodern Turn." *Walter Benjamin and the Demands of History.* Ed. Michael P. Sternberg. Ithaca: Cornell UP, 1996: 24–40.

"Eleven Theses on Politics." Lecture given at Ljubljana, 4 December 1996. Synopsis available online at <http://www.zrc-sazu.si/www/fi/aktual196/ranciere.htm>.

Mallarmé: la politique de la sirène. Paris: Hachette, 1996.

"Democracy Means Equality." Trans. David Macey. *Radical Philosophy* 82 (Mar. 1997): 29–36.

"Casser l'opposition des mots et des choses." Interview conducted by Robert Maggiori. *Libération* 5233 (5 Mar. 1998): 3.

La Chair des mots: politiques de l'écriture. Paris: Galilée, 1998.

"Existe-t-il une esthétique deleuzienne?" *Gilles Deleuze: une vie philosophique.* Ed. Eric Alliez. Le Plessis-Robinson: Institut Synthélabo pour le progrès de la connaissance, 1998. 525–36.

La Parole muette: essai sur les contradictions de la littérature. Paris: Hachette, 1998.

"Biopolitique ou politique? Entretien avec Jacques Rancière." Interview conducted by Eric Alliez. *Multitudes* 1 (Mar. 2000). Available online at <http://multitudes.samizdat.net/article.php3?id_article=210>.

"Dissenting Words: A Conversation with Jacques Rancière." Interview conducted by Davide Panagia. Trans. Davide Panagia. *Diacritics* 30.2 (2000): 113–26.

Le Partage du sensible: esthétique et politique. Paris: La Fabrique, 2000.

"What Aesthetics Can Mean." Trans. Brian Holmes. *From an Aesthetic Point of View: Philosophy, Art and the Senses.* Ed. Peter Osborne. London: Serpent's Tail, 2000. 13–33.

"Entretien avec Jacques Rancière." Interview conducted by Sophie Charlin et al. *Balthazar* 4 (summer 2001). Available online at <http:/perso.club-internet.fr/cyrilbg/ranciere.html>.

"Entretien avec Jacques Rancière." Interview conducted by Nicolas Poirier. *Le Philosophoire* 13 (winter 2001): 7–20.

La Fable cinématographique. Paris: Seuil, 2001.

L'Inconscient esthétique. Paris: Galilée, 2001.

"The Aesthetic Revolution and its Outcomes: Emplotments of Autonomy and Heteronomy." *New Left Review* 14 (Apr. 2002): 133–51.

"Jacques Rancière: le cinéma, art continué." Interview conducted by Stéphane Bouquet and Jean-Marc Lalanne. *Cahiers du Cinéma* 567 (Apr. 2002): 56–63.

Jacques Rancière
c/o Éditions Galilée
9, rue Linné
75005 Paris
France

Peter Hallward
French Department
King's College London
The Strand
London WC2R 2LS
UK
E-mail: peter.hallward@kcl.ac.uk

Forbes Morlock
Syracuse University London Centre
24 Kensington Park Gardens
London W11 2QU
UK
E-mail: forbes.helix@btopenworld.com

journal of the theoretical humanities
volume 8   number 2   august 2003

introduction

alistair swiffen and peter hallward

Born in Toulouse in 1946, Daniel Bensaïd teaches philosophy at the University of Paris VIII (Saint-Denis) and is editor of the review *Contre Temps*. He is a leading figure in one of France's two main Trotskyist groups, the *Ligue Communiste Révolutionnaire*, which he helped found in the immediate aftermath of May 1968. He has also long been active in Latin American politics, particularly in Brazil.

Bensaïd's primary concerns include the theory and practice of militant politics, popular revolutionary traditions, the subversive potential of messianic conceptions of history, the contemporary significance of Marx and Marxism, and the organisation of today's anti-capitalist movement. Much of Bensaïd's work seeks to inspire effective resistance to the ongoing subordination of social existence to the law of the market. Determined to avoid the excesses of both voluntarism and passivity, he persists in a conception of politics that links necessity and contingency, event and historicity, analysis and commitment. His major work to date, *Marx for our Times* (1995), is an unorthodox revival and application of the analytical resources offered by Marx's critique of political economy, framed as a major theoretical assault on the ongoing "privatisation of the world."[1]

Rather more insistently than most Western Marxists, Bensaïd's most fundamental principle is a version of the famous eleventh thesis on Feuerbach: it is not enough "merely to interpret the world; the point is to change it."[2] Bensaïd's project is at all levels bound up with the search for practical alternatives to the perpetual reign of capital and commodity fetishism. The collapse of

daniel bensaïd

translated by alistair swiffen

THE MOLE AND THE LOCOMOTIVE

Stalinism and the dissolution of the Soviet Union have made this search both more hopeful (it is no longer necessary to fight a war on two fronts) and more desperate (in an age dominated by various versions of the end of history if not the end of politics *tout court*). His recent pamphlet *Les Irréductibles* offers a succinct overview of the principles that now inform this search. In a context marked by the achievements and limitations of the new social movements of the 1980s and 1990s, by the recent mobilisation of groups of people defined as "without" (without residency papers, without housing, without employment, and so on), by the more immediately international dimension of both capitalism and the opposition to capitalism, Bensaïd discerns five general theorems that might guide sustain-

ISSN 0969-725X print/ISSN 1469-2899 online/03/020213-14 © 2003 Taylor & Francis Ltd and the Editors of *Angelaki*
DOI: 10.1080/0969725032000162666

able resistance to the status quo. (i) Class struggle is irreducible to communitarian conceptions
of identity and belonging. (ii) Politics is irreducible to ethics and aesthetics. (iii) Imperialism
has not simply dissolved in the supposedly
painless progress of market-driven globalisation.
(iv) The fate of communism is independent of
Stalinism and the bureaucratic inertia of the
former socialist states. (v) The future of rational
critique is independent of the pseudo-resistant
sterility of postmodernism and indifferent to the
prevailing emphasis on anodyne diversity,
ephemeral fragmentation and inconsequential
disenchantment.[3]

Unsurprisingly, Bensaïd has resisted the neo-
liberal turn in both French philosophy and politics ever since it began. His first publications
were devoted to May 1968, the French student
movement and the Portuguese revolution of
1975; pursuing a long argument with those
"repentant" former *soixante-huitards* become
nouveaux philosophes, his *Mai si!* (1988, co-
written with Alain Krivine) continues to call for
the renewal of revolutionary struggle in the spirit
of May. Bensaïd exposed the conceptual incoher-
ence of "third way" politics decades before the
label was invented, and opposed from its incep-
tion that retreat to the "centre left" initiated by
Mitterrand and Rocard and completed so spec-
tacularly by Jospin.[4]

Although many philosophers over the past
decade or so have retained a reference to Marx as
a critic of capitalism (Derrida's *Spectres of Marx*
(1993) is perhaps the most familiar example),
Bensaïd is one of the very few who persist in a
reading of Marx as the prophet of communism.
Marx for our Times (1995) marks the culmination of a long effort to free Marxism from its
disastrous conflation with Stalinism on the one
hand and positivism or scientism on the other.
Retrospectively illuminated by the militant principles of Gramsci and Benjamin, Bensaïd's Marx
is first and foremost a revolutionary thinker, a
philosopher of active political intervention. Like
Benjamin, his overriding concern is to think the
emancipatory potential that suddenly appears
in moments of crisis and emergency. Bensaïd's
critical project, then, is directed against the most
dangerous ways such potential might be

minimised or disarmed. In particular, he seeks to
preserve Marxism from either its reduction to a
form of science (an empirical sociology or a
mathematised economics) or its incorporation
into a linear or teleological version of history,
one driven by a crudely mechanical progression
towards the inevitable triumph of socialism.

Bensaïd organises the otherwise eclectic material of his book into three parts, corresponding to
the principal aspects of this fundamental critical
gesture. In the first, the "Critique of Historical
Reason," he affirms a disruptive conception of
time against the determinisms defended by
orthodox and analytic versions of Marxism:

> punctuated by events, history no longer
> possesses the meaningful unity of a universal
> History governed by an alliance between order
> and progress. From its fractures issues a
> vortex of cycles and spirals, revolutions and
> restorations [...], a world of explosions, cata-
> clysms and crises, whose contradictions are
> resolved in the violence of decisiveness.[5]

Marx figures here as a philosopher of disjunctive
and non-linear time, of a temporality in which
any given era is never quite in step with itself, in
which "ancient times, long-past times and recent
times still work anachronistically upon the
dimensions of the present."[6] Part two, the
"Critique of Sociological Reason," is a defence of
the political and subjective (or "anti-sociologi-
cal") primacy of class struggle against its reduction to "the inert domain of pure objectivity."[7]
The third and final part, the "Critique of
Scientific Positivism," is as much an attack on
one conception of science (positivist, detached,
exact, lifeless, etc.) as the celebration of another
(philosophical, chaotic, heterogeneous, disconcerting, etc.): "in a breathless quest for the living
organism, where conceptual order constantly
comes undone in carnal disorder, Marx's science
continually mingles synchrony and diachrony,
the universality of structure and the singularity
of history."[8]

This disruptive conception of Marxism has its
roots in Bensaïd's rejection, as a student, of
Althusser's structuralist reading of Marx.
Dissatisfied with Althusser's inability to cope
with unpredictable events and interventions, for

inspiration he turned instead to Lucien Goldmann's meditations on Pascal.[9] Bensaïd's watchful but unshakable historical optimism might be traced, in the end, to his own version of the logic which justifies Pascal's famous wager on the existence of God – precisely because the outcome is irreducible to the logic of deduction and proof, there is nothing to lose and everything to gain by putting your faith in the contingent future of communist revolution.[10] By the same token, such faith in the future is best sustained by a conception of the present which sees it as haunted by a revolutionary past. In his *Walter Benjamin, sentinelle messianique* (1990), Bensaïd recognises Benjamin (together with Charles Péguy) as the primary source for his acute awareness of the living resonance of bygone struggles. It is this awareness which informs Bensaïd's celebration of the legacy of Joan of Arc and his "alternative bicentenary commemoration" of the French Revolution, one that dwells on the *sans-culottes'* conception of a directly empowering practice of politics.[11] In each case, the effort to transform the world is motivated by a rational wager or "logical revolt," a secular wager free of any trace of transcendence.

Bensaïd's interest in Péguy and Benjamin, reinforced by his admiration for Benjamin's most significant recent French reader, Françoise Proust, has led him to reflect at length on the difference between utopian and messianic thought. Utopia is more subject to closure, more definite in its content, and thus more susceptible to disappointment than a messianism which trusts in the open indeterminacy of history and relies upon the fragile resilience of hope. In *Résistances* (2001), Bensaïd seeks to renew the revolutionary potential of messianism in a critical confrontation with the twin dangers of utopian escapism and cynical determinism. "The Mole and the Locomotive" is a translation of the introduction to this book, which is Bensaïd's most substantial study of contemporary philosophy to date. The remainder of *Résistances* is made up of critical reviews of what he identifies as four of the most important (and most ambiguous) recent interventions to offer some inspiration for the renewal of a secular messianism – the work of Althusser, Derrida, Badiou and Negri.

In order to lend more substance to his introduction, it may be worth briefly anticipating Bensaïd's conclusions here.

Bensaïd acknowledges that it is too easy to portray Althusser as a structuralist who leaves no space for individual agency in historical developments. He condemns Althusser's reluctance to distance himself unequivocally from Stalin and is critical of his inflated emphasis on the autonomy of science, of his dismissal of matters of experience and struggle, and of his increasingly desperate effort to locate a decisive epistemological break, in Marx's work, between a scientific orientation and a merely ideological concern for alienation. Nevertheless, he applauds Althusser's later efforts to reconcile a notion of history as a "process without a subject" together with the contingency of encounters and situations, such that individual engagement in specific political situations begins to appear productive of historical change (rather than the other way around). The result is a failed but provocative attempt to rethink the relation of chance and necessity within a Marxist conception of history.

Bensaïd likewise finds much to praise in the unsettling and elusive optimism that inspires Derrida's *Spectres of Marx* (1993). Again broadly in keeping with Benjamin's conception of things, Derrida differentiates messianic experience from (abstract, resigned, deferential) utopianism, and associates the former with a concrete, optimistic and immediate effort to disrupt the status quo in the name of justice. Though not themselves revolutionary in Bensaïd's sense of the word, Derrida's "spectres" haunt the prevailing order of things and may allow the spirit of communism to inspire steps towards future revolution. Derrida's aversion to presence and the present, however, his reluctance to embrace what he describes as Marx's version of "onto-theology," coupled with his own aversion to organised communism and his belief that class conflict is essentially a thing of the past, seem to combine to consign the revolutionary project to a sort of permanent uncertainty and indecision.

The opposite problem, in a sense, undermines Badiou's post-Maoist revival of the category of the subject. Bensaïd is understandably sympa-

thetic to Badiou's engaged and militant conception of politics, but believes that it fails to pay
sufficient attention to matters of historical conti-
nuity and political organisation. Badiou is overly
dependent on an abrupt, if not "miraculous,"
conception of transformative events as the
primary source of political and philosophical
inspiration, and his conception of the subject
involves little more than the *repetition* of
Pascal's wager. His conception of politics undertaken at a principled distance from history and
the state, his affirmation of a "politics without
party," threatens to deprive organised politics of
its material force.

If Badiou is overly reliant upon the exceptional
discontinuity of events, Bensaïd reads Negri as
overly reconciled to historical inevitability, to the
supposedly ineluctable movement of history
towards the triumph of communism. Bensaïd is
more directly involved in the organisation of
concrete political resistance than Negri. But he
also has much in common with Negri, not least
with the latter's careful attempt, in his works
from the 1970s and more recently in
Insurgencies, to devise a theory of political
subjectivity that links a neo-Leninist emphasis on
organisation and decision with an analysis of the
changing material configurations of exploitation,
class composition and surplus extraction based on
Marx's *Grundrisse*.[12] Roughly speaking, what
Negri calls "constitutive power" – creative
potency (*puissance* or *potentia*), the power to
create new situations, as distinct from power
(*pouvoir* or *potestas*) as actually exercised within
an already constituted situation – takes modern
political shape as the growing collective capacity
to make history rather than simply endure it. In
Empire (2000), Negri and his collaborator
Michael Hardt examine the ways in which the
contemporary form of constituted or "sovereign"
power has progressively escaped the limitations of
the nation-state and become a truly global, truly
deterritorialised force, itself ultimately a (repres-
sive) reaction to an equally mobile, equally
transnational version of popular constituent
power – the power of the "multitude."[13] In the
form of empire, capitalism tends progressively to
purge itself of all anachronistic forms of mediation and transcendence and so prepare the way

for a frontal struggle with communism. Bensaïd
is uneasy, however, about the effectively absolute
quality of certain aspects of constituent power,
and about what he sees as Negri's relative disinterest in the strategic, institutional and organisa-
tional factors that might enable the newly global
potential for insurgency to become an actual reality. Since constituent power is itself the dynamic
principle behind historical change, since it is
resistant to oppression as a matter of course, and
since it realises itself as uninterrupted "permanent revolution,"[14] Negri sometimes seems to
anticipate communist victory as virtually auto-
matic or as latent in the very nature of things.
Bensaïd concludes that, in the end, Negri's quasi-
"Franciscan" orientation is inadequate to the task
of inspiring a viable version of genuine democracy and democratic empowerment.

notes

1 Bensaïd, "Preface to the English Edition," *Marx for our Times* xv.

2 Marx, *Theses on Feuerbach* XI.

3 Bensaïd, *Les Irréductibles* (2001).

4 See, for instance, Bensaïd, *L'Anti-Rocard* (1980) and *Lionel, qu'as-tu fait de notre victoire?* (1998; in 1966, Bensaïd was expelled from the French Communist Party for refusing to support Mitterrand's presidential campaign). More recent pamphlets have attacked French complicity in the new imperialist interventions in the Gulf, Kosovo and Afghanistan (*Les Irréductibles* (2001); *Le Nouvel Internationalisme contre les guerres impériales et la privatisation du monde* (2003)).

5 Bensaïd, *Marx for our Times* 69, 90.

6 Bensaïd, *La Discordance des temps* 346–47.

7 Bensaïd, *Marx for our Times* 101. "Classes do not exist as separable entities, but only in the dialectic of their struggle. They do not disappear when the more vital or conscious forms of struggle die down. Heterogeneous and uneven, consciousness is inherent in the conflict that commences with the sale of labour-power and resistance to exploitation – and is unceasing" (118).

8 Bensaïd, *Marx for our Times* 204. In the tenth chapter of the book, "Choreographies of Chaos,"

Bensaïd associates Marx's project with the pioneering development of those "sciences of transformation" that, later formalised as chaos theory and systems theory, would begin to analyse not "factual certainties but probabilities, choices, and bifurcations, […], instability and disequilibrium," and so on (288; see especially 295–300).

9 Lucien Goldmann, *The Hidden God: A Study of Tragic Vision in the Pensées of Pascal and the Tragedies of Racine*, trans. Philip Thody (New York: Humanities, 1964). Bensaïd studied under Jean-Toussaint Desanti and Henri Lefebvre: his choice of topic for his Masters' dissertation ("Lenin's Notion of Revolutionary Crisis," submitted in 1968) already gives a good indication of his priorities, and of his distance from the structuralist orientation prevalent at the time.

10 See, in particular, Bensaïd, *Le Pari mélancolique* (1997).

11 Bensaïd, *Jeanne, de guerre lasse* (1991); Bensaïd, *Moi, la Révolution* (1989).

12 Antonio Negri, *Insurgencies: Constituent Power and the Modern State* (Minneapolis: U of Minnesota P, 1999).

13 Antonio Negri and Michael Hardt, *Empire* (Cambridge, MA: Harvard UP, 2000).

14 Bensaïd, *Résistances* 204 (quoting Negri, *Insurgencies*).

the mole and the locomotive[1]

daniel bensaïd

> Well said, old mole! canst work i' the earth so
> fast?
> A worthy pioner!
>   *Shakespeare*, Hamlet *I:5*

Our old friend is short-sighted. He is a haemophiliac as well. Doubly infirm and doubly fragile. And yet, patiently, obstinately, from tunnel to passage, he cheerfully continues his mole's progress towards his next invasion.

The nineteenth century experienced history as an arrow pointing in the direction of progress. The Destiny of the ancients and divine Providence bowed down before the prosaic activity of a modern human species, which produced and reproduced the conditions of its own improbable existence. This sharpened sense of historical development was born of a long, slow movement of secularisation. Heavenly miracles were lost among earthly contingencies. Rather than illuminated by the past, the future now offered justification for the present. Events no longer seemed miraculous. Where before they had been sacred, now they were profane.

The railway, the steamship, the telegraph all contributed to a feeling that history was speeding up and that distances were getting shorter, as if humanity had built up enough speed to break free. It was the era of revolutions.

There was the revolution in transport and travel: in scarcely a quarter of a century, between 1850 and 1875, the great railway companies, the Reuter's agency and the Cook agency all emerged. The rotary press multiplied circulation figures. From now on it would be possible to travel around the world in eighty days. That hero of modernity, the explorer, heralded the air-conditioned exoticism of the tour operators.

There was the revolution in materials: with the triumph of the railway came the reign of coal, of glass and of steel, of crystal palaces and metallic cathedrals. High-speed transport, architectural transformations, the engineering of public health, altered the face of the city and transformed its relation to the suburbs.

There was a revolution in knowledge: the theory of evolution and developments in geology changed the place of man in natural history. The first murmurings of ecology explored the subtle metabolic interaction between society and its environment. Thermodynamics opened up new perspectives in energy control. The blossoming of statistics furnished calculating reason with an instrument for quantification and measurement.

There was a revolution in production: the "age of capital" saw the furious circulation of investments and commodities, their accelerated turnover, the great universal exhibitions, mass production, and the beginnings of mass consumption with the opening of the first department stores. It was also a time of frenzy on the stock exchange, of speculation in real estate, of fortunes quickly made and just as quickly lost, of scandals, of affairs, of crashing bankruptcies, the time of the Pereires, the Saccards, the Rothschilds and the Boucicauts. And it was the era of empires and colonial divisions, when armies carved up territories and continents.

There was a revolution in working practices and social relations: mechanised industry usurped the workshop. The modern proletariat of the factories and the cities took over from the artisan class of tailors, joiners, cobblers, weavers. From 1851 to 1873, this growth in capitalist globalisation gave birth to a new workers' movement, which gained notoriety in 1864 with the creation of the International Working Men's Association.

This prodigious quarter of a century also saw the industrialisation of the arms trade, foreshadowing the "slaughter industry" and total war. It was the era of the social crime, "which does not seem like murder, because there is no murderer to be seen, because the victim's death appears natural, but which is no less a murder."[2] Between Edgar Allan Poe and Arthur Conan Doyle, the appearance of detective fiction, the development of rational modes of enquiry, and the scientific refinement of detection methods sum up the mindset of this period with its urban "mysteries": the loot passes from one hand to another, and all trace of the guilty party is lost in the anonymity of the crowd.

The railway was the perfect symbol and emblem of this rush towards technology and profit. Launched into a conquest of the future along the tracks of progress, these revolutions appeared to be the roaring locomotives of history!

The last quarter of the twentieth century offers a number of analogies with the third quarter of the nineteenth century, albeit on a completely different scale. Telecommunications, satellites and the Internet are the contemporary equivalents of the telegraph and the railway. New sources of energy, biotechnologies and transformations in working practices are revolutionising production in their turn. Industrial manufacturing techniques increasingly make consumption a mass phenomenon. The development of credit and of mass marketing lubricates the circulation of capital. The result is a new gold rush (in the field of computers), a fusion of the upper echelons of the state with the financial elites, and relentless speculation with all its attendant Mafia scandals and spectacular bankruptcies.

The new era of capitalist globalisation is seeing the commodification of the world and a generalised fetishism. The time has come for a seismic overturning of national and international boundaries, for new forces of imperial domination which are armed right up to the stars. Yet the dream of this twilight era has already ceased to be one of infinite progress and great historical promises. Condemned to go round in circles on the wheel of fortune, our social imagination withdraws from history and, from Kubrick to Spielberg, escapes into space. The weight of defeats and disasters reduces every event to a dusty powder of minor news items, of sound bites which are skipped over just as soon as they are received, of ephemeral fashions and of faddish anecdotes.

This world in decline, prey to the inconsolable desolation of a faithless religiosity, of a commercialised spirituality, of an individualism without individuality, prey to the standardisation of differences and to the formatting of opinions, no longer enjoys either "magnificent sunrises" or

triumphant dawns. It is as if the catastrophes and disappointments of the past century have exhausted all sense of history and destroyed any experience of the event, leaving only the mirages of a pulverised present.

This eclipse of the future imperils tradition, which is now seized by the conformism of remembrance commemorations. The past, notes Paul Ricoeur in *La Mémoire, l'histoire, l'oubli*, is no longer recounted so as to set us a task, but rather so as to institute a "piety of memory," a devout remembrance and a conventional notion of right-thinking.[3] This fetishism of memory claims to steer away from collective amnesia an era condemned to the snapshots of an eternal present.

Detached from any creative perspective, critical recollection turns to tired-out ritual. It loses the "unfailing consciousness of everything which has not come to pass."[4] The postmodern labyrinth is thus unaware of "the dark crossroads" where "the dead return, bringing new announcements." History, which is no longer "pushed towards the status of legend," no longer appears to be "illuminated by an internal light," contained "in the wealth of witnesses who look forward to the Revolution and the Apocalypse." It crumbles into a dust of images or into the scattered pieces of a puzzle which no longer fits together.

The train of progress has been derailed. In the saga of the railway, sinister cattle trucks have eclipsed the iron horse. Already for Walter Benjamin, revolution was no longer comparable to a race won by an invincible machine, but rather to an alarm signal, fired so as to interrupt its mad race towards catastrophe.

That said, just as the reed outlives the oak, so the mole prevails over the locomotive. Though he looks tired, our old friend is still digging away. The eclipse of the event has not put an end to the hidden work of resistance which discreetly, when everything seems asleep, prepares the way for new rebellions. Just as the Victorian era's "growth without development" gave rise to the First International, just as the muted social war exploded in the uprising of the Communards, so too are new contradictions brewing in the great transformations of the present time.

However limited they might seem, the marginal conspiracies and plots active at any given moment are also fermenting the great rages of days to come. They herald new outpourings. They are the place of that "hard-fought advance" Ernst Bloch speaks of, "a peregrination, a ramble, full of tragic disturbances, seething, blistered with fissures, explosions, isolated engagements."[5] It is a stubborn advance made up of irreconcilable resistances, well-directed ramblings along tunnels which seem to lead nowhere and yet which open up into daylight, into an astonishing, blinding light.

Thus the underground heresies of the Flagellants, the Dolcinians and other Beguines paved the way for the likes of Thomas Münzer (1490–1525) to appear with his "apocalyptic propaganda calling for action," before his execution sealed the lasting alliance between the reformed priest and the country squire. After the egalitarian revolt of the Levellers, the great fear of the propertied classes cemented the puritan holy alliance between the bourgeoisie and aristocracy of England. After the creative upheaval of the French Revolution came Thermidor's period of restoration. After the great hope of the October Revolution followed the time of bureaucratic reaction, with all its trials and purges, its falsifications and forgeries, its disconcerting lies.

This recurrence of Thermidor has always bolted the door of possibility whenever it has been opened just a fraction. However, its "dull peace with the world" has never quite made its way to the obstinate mole, who is forever born anew from his own failures. It took no more than thirty years for the flames of 1830 or 1848 to rekindle the embers kept glowing by various hidden groups. It took only a few years for Jacobin radicalism to resurface, laden with new concerns, with the Luddites, and then with the Chartist movement of the English working class.[6] Less than twenty years after the bloody suppression of the Commune and the exile of its survivors, the socialist movement was already being born again, as if a timeless message had spread from generation to generation down a long line of conspiratorial whispers.

Whether they be failed or betrayed, revolutions are not easily wiped from the memory of the oppressed. They are prolonged within latent forms of dissidence, spectral presences, invasive absences, in the molecular constitution of a plebeian public space, with its networks and passwords, its nocturnal assignations and its thundering explosions. "One might imagine," warned an astute observer after the collapse of Chartism, "that all is peaceful, that all is motionless; but it is when all is calm that the seed comes up, that republicans and socialists advance their ideas in people's minds."[7]

When resignation and melancholy follow the ecstasy of the event, as when love's excitement dulls under the force of habit, it becomes absolutely essential "not to adjust yourself to the moments of fatigue." We should never underestimate the power not of that daily fatigue which leads to the sleep of the just but of the great historical weariness at having spent too long "rubbing history against the grain." Such was the weariness of Moses when he stopped on the threshold of Canaan to "sleep the sleep of the earth." The weariness of Saint-Just, walled up in the silence of his last night alive. Or the weariness of Blanqui, flirting with madness in his dungeon at Taureau. Such too was the heavy fatigue which fell, in August 1917, upon the shoulders of the young Peruvian publicist José Carlos Mariategui:

> We wake up ill from monotony and ennui. And we experience the immense desolation of not hearing the echo of the least event that might liven up our minds and make our typewriters rattle. Languor slips into things and into souls. Nothing remains but yawning, despondency and weariness. We are living through a time of clandestine murmurings and furtive jokes.[8]

A few months later, this avid chronicler of resurrectional events came to find them at first hand in the old world of Europe, then in the throes of war and revolutions.

In reactionary times, obstinate progress becomes "a long, slow movement, itself patient, of impatience," a slow, intractable impatience, stubbornly at odds with the order that then reigned in Berlin, and that was soon to swoop down upon Barcelona, Djakarta or Santiago:

> Order reigns in Berlin, proclaim the triumphal bourgeois press, those officers of the victorious troops, in whose honour Berlin's petty bourgeoisie waves its handkerchiefs and shouts hurrah. Who here is not reminded of the hounds of order in Paris, and of the bourgeoisie's bacchanalian feast on the corpses of the Communards? "Order reigns in Warsaw! Order reigns in Paris! Order reigns in Berlin!" So it is that the proclamations made by the guardians of order spread from one centre to another of the global historic struggle.[9]

Then there begins the time not for a passing reduction of speed but for "inevitable revolutionary slowness," for maturation and ripening, for an urgent patience, which is the opposite of fatigue and habit: the effort to persevere and continue without growing accustomed or getting used to things, without settling into habit or routine, by continually astonishing oneself, in pursuit of "this desirable unknown"[10] which always slips away.

"At what moment in time could truth return to life? And why should it return to life?," wondered Benjamin Fondane in the very heart of darkness.[11]

When? Nobody knows. The only certainty is that truth remains "in the rift between the real and the legal."[12]

For whom? There are no designated heirs, no natural descendents, but a legacy in search of authors, waiting for those who will be able to carry it further. This legacy is promised to those who, as E.P. Thompson puts it, will manage to save the vanquished from "the enormous condescension of posterity." For "heritage is not a possession, something valuable that you receive and then put in the bank." It is "an active, selective affirmation, which can sometimes be reanimated and reaffirmed, more often by illegitimate heirs than by legitimate ones."[13]

The event is "always on the move," but "there must be some days of thunder and lightning" if the vicious circle of fetishism and domination is to be broken. The morning after a defeat can easily lead to an overwhelming feeling that things

must forever begin again from scratch, or that everything is suspended in an "eternalised present." When the universe seems to repeat itself without end, to keep on marking time, nevertheless the "chapter of changes" remains open to hope. Even when we are on the point of believing that nothing more is possible, even when we despair of escaping from the relentless order of things, we never cease to set the possibility of what might be against the poverty of what actually is. For "nobody can easily accept the shame of no longer wanting to be free."[14]

After twenty years of liberal counter-reform and restoration, the market-based order now seems inescapable. The eternal present no longer appears to have any future, and absolute capitalism no longer any outside. We are confined to the prosaic management of a fatalistic order, reduced to an infinite fragmentation of identities and communities, condemned to renounce all programmes and plans. An insidious rhetoric of resignation is used left, right and centre to justify spectacular U-turns and shameful defections, regrets and repentances.

And yet! A radical critique of the existing order braces itself against the tide, inspired by new ways of thinking resistance and events. In the vicious spiral of defeats, those engaged in defensive resistance sometimes harbour doubts about the counter-attack which is so long in coming; the hope of a liberating event then falls away from everyday acts of resistance, retreats from the profane to the sacred, and ossifies in the expectation of an improbable miracle. When the present drifts without past or future, and when "the spirit withdraws from a given era, it leaves a collective frenzy and a spiritually charged madness in the world."[15]

When it loses the thread of earthly resistance against the order of things, the desire to change the world risks turning into an act of faith and the will of the heavens. Then comes the tedious procession of smooth-talking potion sellers and charlatans, fire-eaters and tooth-pullers, pickpockets and cut-throats, relic-sellers and fortune-tellers, *New Age* visionaries and half-believers. This is what happened after 1848, when the *quarante-huitards* of *A Sentimental Education* turned to commerce or looked to their careers.

This is what happened after 1905, when disappointed militants became "seekers after God." This is what happened after May 1968, when certain faint-hearted prophets took it into their heads to play at angels, having played too much at monsters. In such situations, religious revivals and kitsch mythology are supposed to fill the gap left by the disappointment of great hopes.

Against renunciation and its endless justifications, those involved in the politics of resistance and events never give up looking for the reasons behind each loss of reason. But the disjunction of a fidelity to events with no historical determination from a resistance with no horizon of expectation is doubly burdened with impotence.

In a sense, resistance can take on an infinite variety of forms, from a concrete critique of existing reality to an abstract utopia with no historical roots, from an active messianism to a contemplative expectation of a Messiah who never comes, from an ethical politics to a depoliticised ethics, from prophecies seeking to avert danger to predictions claiming to penetrate the secrets of the future.

As for events whose political conditions seem evasive and compromised, it is all too tempting to treat them as moments of pure contingency with no relation to necessity, or as the miraculous invasion of repressed possibilities.

Thermidorian times, as everyone knows, see a hardening of hearts and a weakening of stomachs. In such circumstances, many people find nothing to oppose the assumption that everything is likely to turn out for the worst, other than their willingness to settle for the lesser of the evils on offer; when this happens, the "flabby fiends" ["les monstres mous"] congratulate each other, share a wink and pat each other on the back. Then the outgoing Tartuffe, "the old Tartuffe, the classical Tartuffe, the clerical Tartuffe," takes the "second Tartuffe, the Tartuffe of the modern world, the second-hand Tartuffe, the humanitarian Tartuffe, at any rate the other Tartuffe"[16] by the hand. This alliance of "two Tartuffe cousins" can last for a very long time, with "the one carrying the other, one fighting the other, one supporting the other, one feeding the other."

The veneration of victors and victories goes hand in hand with compassion towards the victims, so long as the latter stick to their role as suffering victims, so long as they are not seduced by the idea of becoming actors in their own version of history.

However, even in the worst droughts and most arid places there is always a stream – perhaps barely a trickle – which heralds surprising resurgences. Again, we must always distinguish between the rebellious messianism which will not give in, and the humiliated millennialism which looks instead towards the great beyond. We must always distinguish between the vanquished and the broken, between "victorious defeats" and unalleviated collapse. We must avoid confusing the consolations of utopia with forms of resistance that perpetuate an "illegal tradition" and pass on a "secret conviction."

There are always new beginnings, moments of revival or renewal. In the dark times of change and transition, worldly and spiritual ambitions, reasons and passions, combine to form an explosive mixture. Attempts to safeguard the old are mixed up with the first stammerings of the new. Even in the most sombre moments, the tradition on the rise is never far behind the tradition in decline. There is never any end to the secret composition of the uninterrupted poem of "probable impossibilities."

This obstinate hope is not to be confused with the smug confidence of the believer, or with the "sad passion" driven out by Spinoza. On the contrary, it endures as the virtue of "surmounted despair." For "to be ready to place hope in whatever does not deceive," you must first have despaired of your own illusions. Disillusioned, disabused, hope then becomes "the essential and diametrical opposite of habit and softening." Such hope is obliged constantly to "break with habit," constantly to dismantle "the mechanisms of habit," and to launch new beginnings everywhere, "just as habit everywhere introduces endings and deaths."[17]

To break with habit is to retain the ability to astonish yourself. It is to allow yourself to be surprised.

These untimely invasions, during which the contingency of events cuts a path through insuf-

222

ficient yet necessary historical conditions, make a breach in the unchanging order of structures and of things.

Crisis? What crisis is there today? There is an historical crisis, a crisis in civilisation, a stretched and prolonged crisis which drags on and on. Our ill-fitting world is bursting at the seams. As H.G. Wells predicted, the rift between our culture and our inventions has not stopped growing, opening up at the very heart of technology and knowledge a disturbing gap between fragmented rationalities and a global irrationality, between political reason and technical madness.

Does this crisis contain the seeds of a new civilisation? It is just as pregnant with unseen barbarities. Which will prevail? Barbarity has taken the lead by a good few lengths. It is becoming more difficult than ever to separate destruction and construction, the death throes of the old and the birth pangs of the new, "for barbarity has never before had such powerful means at its disposal to exploit the disappointments and hopes of a humanity which has doubts about itself and about its future."[18] We fumble our way through this unsettled twilight, somewhere between dusk and dawn.

Is it a simple crisis of development? Or, indeed, rather than a sort of discontent within civilisation, is it a sorrow that gives rise to "myths which make the earth shake with their enormous feet"? If a new civilisation is to prevail, the old one must not be entirely lost, abandoned or scorned. Not only must it be defended but it must also be ceaselessly reinvented.

The stubborn old mole will survive the dashing locomotive. His furry, round form prevails over the metallic coldness of the machine, his diligent good nature over the rhythmic clanking of the wheels, his patient smile over the sniggering steel. He comes and goes, between tunnels and craters, between burrows and breakouts, between the darkness of the underground and the light of the sun, between politics and history. He makes his hole. He erodes and he undermines. He prepares the coming crisis.

The mole is a profane Messiah.

The Messiah is a mole, short-sighted and obstinate.

The crisis is a molehill which suddenly opens out.

• • •

People turn to fortune-tellers when they no longer have prophets.
Chateaubriand

François Furet concludes *The Passing of an Illusion* with a melancholy verdict. "The democratic individual, living at the end of the twentieth century, can only watch as the divinely sanctioned order of history trembles to the core." To a vague anticipation of danger is added "the scandal of a closed future," and "we find ourselves condemned to live in the world in which we live."[19] Capital seems to have become our only horizon, fixed until the end of time.

There will be no more afterwards, no more elsewhere.
Death of the event.
End of story.
End of history.
And they all lived unhappily ever after.

But in fact there is always conflict and contradiction, there is always discontent in the midst of civilisation and crisis in the midst of culture. There are always those who refuse servitude and resist injustice.

From Seattle to Nice, from Millau to Porto Alegre, from Bangkok to Prague, from the organisation of the unemployed to the mobilisation of women, a strange geopolitics is taking shape, and we do not yet know which events will follow in its wake.

The old mole burrows on.

Hegel draws our attention to that "silent and secret" revolution which always precedes the development of a new way of thinking. Through the unreasonable detours of history, the cunning claws of the mole dig their own path of Reason. The mole is in no rush. He has "no need to hurry." He needs "long periods of time," and he has "all the time he needs." If the mole takes a backward step, it is not in order to hibernate but to bore through another opening. His twistings and turnings allow him to find the place where he can break out. The mole never disappears, he only goes underground.

mole and locomotive

Negri and Hardt say that the metaphor of the mole is a figure of modernity, they say that he has been surpassed by postmodernity. "We've come to suspect that the old mole is dead": his digging gives way to the "infinite undulations of the snake" and other reptilian struggles.[20] But such a verdict smacks of that chronological illusion whereby postmodernity is supposed to follow on after a modernity that has since been consigned to the museum of ancient history. Whereas the mole is ambivalent. He is both modern and postmodern. He bustles discreetly about in his "subterranean rhizomes," only to burst thunderously forth from the craters he makes.

On the pretext of giving up on history's meta-narratives, the philosophical discourses of post-modernity lend themselves to mystics and mystagogues: when a society runs out of prophets it turns to soothsayers instead. This is the way it goes, in periods of reaction and restoration. After the massacres of June 1848 and the 18th Brumaire of the younger Napoleon, the socialist movement was likewise seized by "Christolatry." "Look at these offspring of Voltaire," wrote one former Communard, "these former scourges of the church, now huddled together around a table, hands piously clasped in mystic union, waiting hour upon hour for it to rise up and lift one of its legs. Religion in all its forms is once again the order of the day, and has become so 'very distinguished.' France has gone mad!"[21]

Pierre Bourdieu was right to distinguish mystical affirmation or divination from the conditional, preventive and performative stance of prophecy. "Just as the priest is part and parcel of the ordinary order of things, so too is the prophet the man of crisis, of situations in which the established order crumbles and the future as a whole is thrown into question."[22]

The prophet is not a priest. Or a saint.

Still less a fortune-teller.

To ward off disaster it is not enough to resist for the sake of resistance, it is not enough to wager on the possibility of a redemptive event. We must seek both to understand the logic of history and to be ready for the surprise of the event. We must remain open to the contingency of the latter without losing the thread of the former. Such is precisely the challenge of political action. For history does not proceed in a vacuum, and when things take a turn for the better, this never happens in an empty stretch of time, but always "in time that is infinitely full, filled with struggles."[23]

And with events.

The mole prepares the way of their coming. With a measured impatience. With an urgent patience.

For the mole is a prophetic animal.

notes

1 This article is a translation of "La Taupe et la locomotive," the introduction to Bensaïd's book *Résistances: essai de taupologie générale* (2001) 9–26; the translation includes, as its concluding section, the book's short epilogue (243–48). [Translator's note.]

2 Friedrich Engels, *The Condition of the Working Class in England* (Moscow and London: Progress/Lawrence, 1973) 121 (translation modified).

3 Paul Ricoeur, *La Mémoire, l'histoire, l'oubli* (Paris: Seuil, 2000).

4 Ernst Bloch, *Thomas Münzer* (Paris: UGE, 1975).

5 Ibid.

6 See Edward P. Thompson, *The Making of the English Working Class* [1963] (London: Gollancz, 1980).

7 Henry Mayhew, *London Labour and the London Poor: A Cyclopaedia of the Condition and Earnings of Those That Will Work, Those That Cannot Work, and Those That Will Not Work*, 4 vols. [1861–62] (New York: Kelley, 1967).

8 José Carlos Mariategui in *El Tiempo* (Lima) 16 Aug. 1917.

9 Rosa Luxemburg, "Order Reigns in Berlin" (Luxemburg wrote this text on 14 January 1919, several days before her murder by the Freikorps dispatched by a social democrat Minister of the Interior).

10 Dionys Mascolo, *Le Communisme* (Paris: Gallimard, 1953).

11 Benjamin Fondane, *L'Ecrivain devant la révolution* (Paris: Paris-Méditerranée, 1997).

12 Ibid.

13 Jacques Derrida with Marc Guillaume and Jean-Pierre Vincent, *Marx en jeu* (Paris: Descartes et Cie, 1997).

14 Michel Surya, *Portrait de l'intellectuel en animal de compagnie* (Tours: Farrago, 2000) 11; see also Surya, *De l'argent* (Paris: Payot, 2000) 122.

15 Karl Mannheim, *Ideology and Utopia: An Introduction to the Sociology of Knowledge* [1936] (London: Routledge, 1960) 192–96, quoted in E.P. Thompson, *The Making of the English Working Class* 419.

16 Charles Péguy, *Clio* (Paris: Gallimard, 1931) 99.

17 Charles Péguy, *Note conjointe* (Paris: Gallimard, 1942) 123.

18 Georges Bernanos, *La Liberté pour quoi faire?* [1953] (Paris: Gallimard, 1995).

19 François Furet, *The Passing of an Illusion. The Idea of Communism in the Twentieth Century*, trans. Deborah Furet (Chicago: U of Chicago P, 1999).

20 Antonio Negri and Michael Hardt, *Empire* (Cambridge, MA: Harvard UP, 2000) 57.

21 Gustave Lefrançais, *Souvenirs d'un révolution-naire* (Paris: La Tête de Feuille, 1971) 191.

22 Pierre Bourdieu, "Genèse et structure du champ religieux," *Revue Française de Sociologie* 12 (1971): 331.

23 Hegel, *Leçons sur l'histoire de la philosophie* (Paris: Folio Essais, 1990).

works by bensaïd

With Henri Weber. *Mai 1968: une répétition générale*. Paris: Maspero, 1968.

With Camille Scalabrino. *Le Deuxième souffle: problèmes du mouvement étudiant*. Paris: Maspero, 1969.

With Charles-André Udry and Michael Löwy. *Portugal, la révolution en marche*. Paris: UGE 10/18, 1975.

La Révolution et le pouvoir. Paris: Stock, 1976.

L'Anti-Rocard: ou, les haillons de l'utopie. Paris: La Brèche, 1980.

bensaïd

Stratégies et partis. Montreuil-sous-Bois: PEC-La Brèche, 1987.

With Alain Krivine. *Mai si!: 1968–1988: rebelles et repentis*. Montreuil: PEC-La Brèche, 1988.

Moi, la Révolution: remembrances d'une bicentennaire indigne. Paris: Gallimard, 1989.

Walter Benjamin, sentinelle messianique à la gauche du possible. Paris: Plon, 1990.

Jeanne, de guerre lasse: chroniques de ce temps. Paris: Gallimard, 1991.

"L'Inglorieux vertical: Péguy critique de la Raison historique." *Amitié Charles Péguy: Bulletin d'Informations et de Recherches* 60 (Oct. 1992): 208–28.

"Charles Péguy, avant le seuil." *Amitié Charles Peguy: Bulletin d'Informations et de Recherches* 69 (Jan. 1995): 60–63.

La Discordance des temps: essais sur les crises, les classes, l'histoire. Paris: Éditions de la Passion, 1995.

Marx l'intempestif: grandeurs et misères d'une aventure critique (XIXe–XXe siècles). Paris: Fayard, 1995. *Marx for our Times: Adventures and Misadventures of a Critique*. Trans. Gregory Elliott. London: Verso, 2002.

Le Pari mélancolique: métamorphoses de la politique, politique des métamorphoses. Paris: Fayard, 1997.

With Christophe Aguiton. *Le Retour de la question sociale*. Paris: Page 2, 1997.

Lionel, qu'as-tu fait de notre victoire?: leur gauche et la nôtre. Paris: Michel, 1998.

Contes et légendes de la guerre éthique. Paris: Textuel, 1999.

With Philippe Petit. *Eloge de la résistance à l'air du temps*. Paris: Textuel, 1999.

"Leur logique et la nôtre" [on Kosovo]. *Le Monde* 7 Apr. 1999.

With Morin Edgar et al. *La Pensée-Prigogine*. Paris: Desclée de Brouwer, 1999.

Qui est le juge?: pour en finir avec le tribunal de l'histoire. Paris: Fayard, 1999.

Le Sourire du spectre: nouvel esprit du communisme. Paris: Michalon, 2000.

Les Irréductibles: théorèmes de la résistance à l'air du temps. Paris: Textuel, 2001.

mole and locomotive

Passion Karl Marx: les hiéroglyphes de la modernité. Paris: Textuel, 2001.

"Personne ne sait ce que seront les révolutions du XXIe siècle." Interview conducted by Jean-Michel Helvig. *Libération* 19 May 2001.

Résistances: essai de taupologie générale. Paris: Fayard, 2001.

"Operation 'Bullshit Unlimited.'" *International Viewpoint* 343 (Sept. 2002). Available online at <http://www.3bh.org.uk/IV/>.

"Préface." *Avril à Jenine.* By Nahla Chahal and Hala Kodhami. Paris: La Découverte, 2002.

Les Trotskismes. Paris: Presses Universitaires de France, 2002.

Un Monde à changer. Paris: Textuel, 2003.

Le Nouvel Internationalisme contre les guerres impériales et la privatisation du monde. Paris: Textuel, 2003.

Daniel Bensaïd
Département de Philosophie
Université de Paris VIII
93525 Saint-Denis
France

Peter Hallward
French Department
King's College London
The Strand
London WC2R 2LS
UK
E-mail: peter.hallward@kcl.ac.uk

Alistair Swiffen
Hertford College
Catte Street
Oxford OX1 3BW
UK
E-mail: alswiffen@hotmail.com

ANGELAKI
journal of the theoretical humanities
volume 8   number 2   august 2003

introduction

david webb

Serres' engagement with themes such as communication, science, space, time, language, singularity, multiplicity and technology places him at the heart of recent European thought. Yet his contribution is wholly distinctive, finding new and unusual paths between problems and introducing readers to unexpected perspectives. One of the reasons for this lies in Serres' own background in mathematics and science. It was once common for philosophers to begin as mathematicians and scientists. By contrast, today it is quite rare. But often this means only that philosophers, lacking experience in contemporary mathematical and scientific thought, remain beholden to an ideal that mathematics and science themselves are fast overtaking. What Serres has drawn from his experience of mathematics and science is a style of thought that departs from the familiar concerns of systematicity, proof and derivation; whereas the philosopher makes a virtue of slow analysis, the scientist searches out relations between apparently disparate phenomena and the mathematician celebrates inventiveness and elegant simplicity. For Serres, the activity of thought is not essentially explanatory, it is operational, transformative. If his work is a science of relations, these relations are themselves forms of displacement.

This concern is reflected in Serres' abiding interest in Leibniz, whose work he describes as offering "a general theory of relations," and in communication, the topic of the first in the series of five *Hermès* volumes that he published between 1969 and 1980 and a theme that lies at the heart of much of his work.[1] At stake here is

michel serres

translated by alberto toscano

THE SCIENCE OF RELATIONS
an interview

less a theory of linguistic relation than a general conception of exchange that is the condition both for existence and for the knowledge one can have of it. The body is a site of intensive communication across membranes and through and between organs and cells; the mind still more so. Society, too, exists only through such exchange. This general sense of communication was developed via information theory, which also confirmed for Serres that communication can only occur where there is a code and that codes are necessarily exclusive. Since attempts to achieve perfect transparency will inevitably fail, we live with the excluded third, noise, or, as Serres presents it in one of his most well-known books, the parasite.[2] Politically speaking, that perfect transparency is impossible means that perfect equality is also

ISSN 0969-725X print/ISSN 1469-2899 online/03/020227-12 © 2003 Taylor & Francis Ltd and the Editors of *Angelaki*
DOI: 10.1080/0969725032000162675

impossible, which underlines the seriousness of the question of *how* we communicate – this is one reason why the issue of teaching is so important for Serres.

The themes of communication, translation, distribution and disorder addressed in the *Hermès* volumes received a fresh and perhaps decisive treatment in Serres' return to Lucretius in *The Birth of Physics*, a text published in the same year as *Hermès IV, La Distribution*.[3] In his study of Lucretius, Serres brings together atomism and Archimedean mathematics to reveal a rigorous science based on differential principles and non-linearity. Atomism is shown to be a theory of flow; that is, of material communication or relation. Order emerges not by design but as the outcome of regularities formed within vortical currents and turbulent flow, which is itself the result of an uncaused deviation in the path of atoms as they fall, the clinamen. In the Lucretian universe, or multiverse, there are no universal laws governing the movement of atoms, beyond the principle that they find the path of least resistance along a descending path. All order, and therefore all the laws that describe order, are local in both space and time; though any particular configuration or world will spiral in decline towards a form of entropic death, the clinamen will always ensure fresh turbulence and the birth of new order elsewhere, at another time.

For Serres, Lucretian atomism is a materialist model whose general principles are reiterated not only in different worlds with different physical laws but across difference discourses; thus morality, history, linguistics and economics can all be interpreted according to the model of non-linear flow. Since this model is not a body of universal law, this is not reductionist. Moreover, since science does not abstract directly from nature, there is no epistemological barrier to its concepts and methods appearing elsewhere; often, they were already operative there, albeit implicitly. Abstraction, for Serres, begins not with the substantial objects of experience but with the processes by which they enter into relation with one another. Although certain forms of relation recur, the specificity of the relations themselves necessarily varies from case to case and can only

be determined locally. There is therefore no universal logic or epistemology; only relations which themselves define a shifting temporal, spatial and discursive topology. Similarly, Serres does not regard disciplines as isolated from one another, each with their own concepts and methods, but rather approaches history as a field in which to explore the complex and continually changing terrain between science, philosophy, literature and other branches of culture.[4]

If Leibniz presents the world as a continuous sea in which each point communicates with every other, Lucretius reminds us that the sea is a place of treacherous currents whose successful navigation demands local knowledge of local conditions.[5] In a rich and mobile body of work, they mark the two tendencies whose interrelation Serres elaborates with remarkable invention across and between a variety of disciplines and themes. The possibility of such inventiveness lies, he might suggest, in the very complexity of the relations explored, which may be understood as a turbulent material flow in which thinking and writing themselves participate. But to achieve it still requires a mind that is both without prejudice and attentive to the sense that things bear in themselves.

notes

1 The reference to Leibniz comes from Serres and Latour, *Conversations on Science, Culture, and Time* 108; cf. Serres, *Le Système de Leibniz et ses modèles mathématiques* (1968) and Serres, *Hermès I* (1969).

2 Serres, *Le Parasite* (1980).

3 Serres, *La Naissance de la physique dans le texte de Lucrèce* (1977); *Hermès IV, La Distribution* (1977).

4 Serres, *Hermès V, Le Passage du nord-ouest* (1980).

5 Serres, *Hermès II, L'Interférence* 10.

the science of relations: an interview[1]

michel serres

Peter Hallward: *Like many thinkers and intellectuals of your generation (I have in mind Lévi-Strauss, Foucault, Braudel, a few others) you were deeply marked by the experience of the war and by the unprecedented acts of violence that accompanied it. Was your initial orientation towards mathematics, and in particular your interest in modes of pure formalisation (the identification of structures indifferent to any interpretation or content) linked to this experience in some way?*

Michel Serres: It is difficult to make much of a connection between my personal history and my commitment to mathematics. I began with mathematics for a simple reason: one cannot be a philosopher without also possessing the most all-encompassing scientific background possible. I began my studies with mathematics and then moved on to physics; in the past ten years I have been studying biochemistry, with the aim of acquiring a fairly ample range of scientific knowledge. Almost all philosophers went through a version of such training: Aristotle, Plato, Descartes, Leibniz … It is a tradition in the history of philosophy: you cannot do philosophy without having a very solid and varied knowledge "in the horizon of the sciences." This is the case with Kant, with Bergson, with Russell, etc. In reality, mathematics is the universal language of the sciences – hence the importance of a mathematical apprenticeship.

This approach to philosophy has no relation to the war. War had the contrary effect, in fact: it forced me to abandon my mathematical apprenticeship. Hiroshima is the major event of the war because, for the first time, scientists found themselves forced to pose fundamental ethical questions. Many scientists of my generation left physics for biology, so as not to preoccupy themselves any longer with the nuclear question – this accounts for the explosive growth in biochem-

istry, both in Great Britain and France. I myself turned towards philosophy in order to get out of the sciences.

P.H.: Braudel and Lévi-Strauss adopted a "structuralist" perspective, in the broadest sense of the term, partly so as to avoid thinking the events of the war in their immediate historicity – this wasn't the case for you?

M.S.: I do not belong to the same generation as Braudel and Lévi-Strauss – when the war began I was nine and when it ended fifteen, so it was not an adult experience for me. By contrast, they had an adult reaction to the war. This is a decisive gap, which was then repeated between my own generation and the next. What it generated at the time, for example, was an overestimation of political problems, since those of the generation after mine did not see, as I had, how politics can end up in corpses and bombardments. That's why my generation was less disposed to be directly involved in politics.

P.H.: What did you first look for in contemporary mathematics, in particular with respect to the Bourbaki group and the project of thorough formalisation?

M.S.: In my time, there was an important scientific revolution, which is what confers meaning upon a changing discipline. It is when a discipline changes that its meaning becomes visible. This happened with what was called the passage from classical mathematics to formalist mathematics, in the manner of Bourbaki. It was a very important stage in the ongoing reflection upon the object and methods of mathematics. This revolution changed the vantage point, or the point of attack, of mathematics. The idea of a "logicism" that took its cue from axiomatic systems was already well known long before the war. Here we were dealing with a revolution that concerned the comprehension of the very objects of mathematics, a comprehension that was more set-based, more operational and more abstract. The margin of abstraction was indeed greater. It was possible to see sets of objects all at once, as it were, rather than needing to describe them one by one.

P.H.: Was it along these lines that you arrived at your own conception of structure?

M.S.: I was not a structuralist in the same way as Lévi-Strauss and Jakobson, since they were structuralists in the linguistic sense of the term. I, on the other hand, was a structuralist in the mathematical sense of the term. I considered it necessary to consider things as sets and to see which operations united the elements of a given set. This description could be followed by a second one, and one could then see the analogy between the two. For example, in Molière's *Don Juan* one can see how exchange functions in the opening scene in which Sganarelle praises tobacco, in the relations with women, in the scene with the beggar, etc. – the same operation is repeated on different terrains, but each time it is the same basic operation of exchange that takes place.[2]

Little by little, I abandoned this perspective, because a second mathematical revolution came to pass: this was the information revolution, i.e. algorithms (the Turing machine). I'm lucky: in my life I've been witness to two great mathematical revolutions. I am a child of Bourbaki and Turing.

At that time, I was beginning to study physics, that is, to understand the problems regarding information. I was struck by the concept of background noise: in any dialogue whatsoever, there is a convention between the counterparts, which dictates that we should struggle against the noise that would otherwise hamper our conversation. This was a relatively novel concept of communication. It was then that I parted ways, breaking with the vulgate shared by most philosophers of the time, which was broadly speaking a Marxist one (especially with Althusser at the École Normale), and which sought to foreground problems of *production*. I said no, the society of tomorrow will be a society of *communication* and not a society of production. The problems of production are virtually resolved in the West, and it is the problems of communication that will now take centre stage.

That is why I wrote the five volumes of *Hermès* (the god of communication), *The Parasite* (the obstacle to communication), as well as a book on angels (the messengers, the commu-

nicators). Hermes is a single operator of communication, contrary to the angels, who constitute a multiplicity of operators. There is thus a constant analysis of this phenomenon of communication in my books.

P.H.: Would it be correct to say that you've moved from a formalist conception, which regarded itself as indifferent to all content, to any idea of meaning or of "world," towards a conception in which, roughly speaking, form and content partake in a unique and infinitely polyvalent expression, a generalised communication of sorts?

M.S.: Just as the first mathematical revolution was a formalist one, and allowed an abstract grasp of large sets, so the second (the algorithmic revolution) allowed for a description of singularities [*singularités*] of some very singular things. These two revolutions are almost antinomies of one another. It's not by accident that I worked on Leibniz, who spent his entire life trying to unite a very abstract kind of work to a great monadic singularity, trying to grasp the latter by the former. The project of capturing both the universal and the monadic singularity has always provided the horizon for my own work – whence my current preoccupation with biochemistry, which tells us that it is from the universal structure of DNA that singular individuals derive.

P.H.: Despite the obviously contemporary character of your examples, is it the case that your conception of philosophy is classical, i.e. pre-Kantian, more or less? I mean, isn't it precisely a neo-Leibnizian conception, in which what is at stake is grasping the world in an immediate way, without passing through the categories of a more or less reasoned re-presentation of the world?

M.S.: In *Hermès IV* there is a piece on Kant and the theory of the heavens where I show that Kant was the first to think the fractal object. But we are no longer dealing with the same world. Ever since the beginning of the nineteenth century, we do not live in the same world; the human body is not the same, and neither is our understanding of the universe and its constituents (atoms, molecules, cells, stars, galaxies …).

P.H.: But what of the idea that the world is the bearer of its own intelligibility, which we can access not because we are in a privileged position to represent and classify objects, but because we partake of it, because we are part of it, because we can think it, in its very substance? That I know the world in the way that it knows itself?

M.S.: Yes, I do indeed think that many operations of knowledge are already at work within the objects of the world.

P.H.: Then in what sense can we say, for example, that we are no longer dealing with the same world as Kant?

M.S.: I don't think there is anything contradictory about the notion that the theory of knowledge I am proposing provides an account of the evolution of the object of this same knowledge.

P.H.: Does this theory still have a specific place for hermeneutics as such? If we do in fact know the world immediately, as it knows itself, then can scientific explanation account for those problems traditionally associated with the interpretation of meaning?

M.S.: That is a genuine question. More and more, the hard sciences allow singularities to appear, and they are increasingly aware of the knowledge that proliferates within each and every singularity. For example, when I was young it seemed that the San Andréas fault closely resembled another fault in Japan. Today when one studies the San Andréas fault, one discovers a tree of fault lines that is extraordinarily complicated, and which has nothing in common with the fault line that runs by Tokyo. These fault lines are really very singular, very unique. Another example: when I was young, you could find the general schema for the liver or the hip in an anatomy manual. Today, by means of magnetic-nuclear resonance, you can obtain an image of Peter's liver when he was eighteen years old, or of Michel's at seventy. A

schema that was geometric and abstract has in a sense been replaced by an extremely singular image, and all of a sudden the knowledge of the liver, for example, proliferates, along with all of its possible singularities. This is just a single instance of the profoundly algorithmic movement that today affects all the sciences; you can find it equally in mathematics, in physics, in the work of scientists concerned with the place of the singular in the physics of appearance [*la physique de l'apparence*], if you will.

Fundamentally, what is interesting in hermeneutics is finding meaning in the singularity of a given work. Today, in a certain way, there is indeed a rather interesting point of fusion between, on the one hand, an undertaking aimed at singularity within the sciences and, on the other, what is announced in the humanities through studies of *Le Père Goriot* or *King Lear*, for example. I think the effort to bring such singularities to light is basically shared by these two intellectual enterprises.

P.H.: Can the full singularity of these various elements be identified without referring it back in the end (or in the beginning) to a single absolute principle? In your writings, for example, does the singular not figure as the instance of one or another of the various principles that reappear systematically throughout your work, somewhat like a mode, to use Spinoza's vocabulary, of an effectively absolute substance that would express itself through communication, turbulence, chaos, noise, and so on?

It seems to me that there are two dominant tendencies in your philosophy, which I sometimes find difficult to reconcile. On the one hand, there is a "particularising" aspect, so to speak, which insists on the contingent complication of networks, on the fundamental opacity of every geographical or intellectual territory, on the irreducible labour of navigating a path between the various obstacles that we face in the "forest" of thought – hence all the work that distinguishes your project from anything resembling a Cartesian approach to philosophy. But, on the other hand, you often refer to holistic totalities that sometimes resemble absolute principles of sorts. Of course, we are dealing with dynamic, self-differentiating principles, but the absence of limits to their effectiveness makes these principles de facto *absolute. I have in mind those moments in your book* Genesis, *for example, where the emergence of singularities seems to issue from noise itself, where every form is nothing but an ephemeral organisation of a more fundamental chaos. Or those moments when the fundamental nudity of man, such as you conceive him, as being nothing, puts him face to face with the whole [*le tout*]. You say, for instance, that "the relation of nothing to everything offers up the secret of begetting, of becoming and of time," that "man is blank and undifferentiated" and for this very reason "capable of anything."*[3]

M.S.: I am currently preoccupied with some rather anthropological problems, if you will – since I'm now reaching the end of my life I am moving on to these sorts of questions. I quickly recognised that there is a fundamental difference between man and animals. There is a sort of specialisation in the detail of the animal organism. The ape is very specialised in order maximally to exploit a determinate niche, just like a starfish or an octopus. If you compare the hand to the claws of the crab or the tentacles of the octopus, you become aware of the extreme specialisation of the animal limb when compared to the hand. There can be no history of the crab; we are always dealing with the same operation. But we cannot say what the hand is for, and therefore it can do anything – draw a bow, play rugby, make signs, fight … The hand is de-specialised.

Basically, I believe that the fundamental concept is that of de-differentiation. Because man is de-differentiated he has no niche; his niche is the world, he has moved beyond the stage in which he exploited a specific niche. That is our singularity. The human singularity implies de-differentiation. This de-differentiation is organic, it appears long before the invention of tools, but we can only perceive its importance thanks to anthropology.

P.H.: So when you say that, on the one hand, I am anyone, no one, empty, and, on the other,

that I am extremely complicated, a very complex being, who has travelled a lot, lived a lot, whose experience it would be very time consuming to decipher or navigate – are we dealing with the same thing, the same kind of being?

M.S.: Yes, it's the same thing. It's very clear that the more specialised an organism is, the more it seeks out a stable niche, one that would be in harmony with its specialisation. The more de-differentiation functions the more you are completely lost in a world in which you can have any experience whatsoever. The hand is an extremely precise model for this situation. The work of the hand is not over, far from it; we can still find a thousand and one uses for this object which has no function. We have no niche but the world.

P.H.: I hope you'll allow me one last variant of this same question: what is the precise relation between order and disorder? Often it seems that order arises from disorder like Venus from the waters, or like messages emerging from background noise. Elsewhere, it seems that disorder itself is in some sense caught in what is, strictly speaking, a primitive conflict between order and disorder. Once again, are we dealing with an irreducible dualism or with a dynamic, self-differentiating unity?

M.S.: I can't answer this question without bearing in mind certain historical considerations, since there was a moment when, in the fields of physics and biology, there arose something akin to a school of thought (inaugurated in particular by Francisco Varela) which spoke of the generation of order through noise. Many people threw themselves into this idea, but it did not bear the fruits promised at the time. In my book *Genesis* there is something like an echo of this period, though I swiftly abandoned the idea whereby order could be born from noise once I realised that this theory is devoid of results or applications. It revealed itself to be a sterile path. It is therefore very difficult to reply to your question in general terms. We are beginning to understand certain things related to this question in biology, or, say, physics, but we don't yet have a global answer. For example, those who seek to understand how DNA emerged from the pre-biotic soup have yet, as far as I know, to find an answer.

P.H.: I suppose the solution would be to approach this question in terms of time *– the time of becoming, precisely, which would allow us to think the transformation of disorder into order?*

M.S.: Exactly. That is Darwin's response. It is also Bergson's response. But ever since Darwin and Bergson, the appreciation of time has changed. I will address this in my next book. In effect, neither Einstein nor Bergson possessed an adequate measure of time, whereas we do have one now. For example, we can now say, basing ourselves on almost certain evidence, that DNA began 3.5 billion years ago, that the earth began 4.2 billion years ago and the universe 13.6, and so on … It's extremely difficult to have any intu-itive picture of what is involved in such expanses of time; indeed, it's not something that earlier thinkers knew anything about. I believe we must begin to re-think time, taking these orders of magnitude into account. There's a great deal at stake when we say that such and such a human gesture dates from 120 or 200 thousand years ago, that the general organism emerged around six million years ago. And what does this mean? That time is constructed out of things, that it must be understood in terms of this real density or expanse.

P.H.: That is precisely Bergson's intuition – that time has nothing to do with an empty space. Time itself is not the element in which things come to pass, it's the very passage of things, their becoming. It is things themselves that "flow" from time.

M.S.: Indeed. But neither Bergson nor Deleuze truly anticipated the effects of this simple reflec-tion on quantity, which changes a lot of things. In your own body, for example, some of your neurons date from eight million years ago, but some date from the reptilian age, i.e. from hundreds of millions of years ago; your DNA is

original with respect to that of your parents, but the fact of DNA dates from four billion years ago. And the atomic constituents of your body are thirteen billion years old.

P.H.: What then is the relationship between this biochemical aspect of the cognitive operation and the act of thinking, of being conscious, of taking decisions?

M.S.: It would be something like the difference between ten to the power of six and ten to the power of minus six: it involves an incredible time-scale. Thinking, in the sense that we discuss it, as the cogito, as culturally influenced cogni-tion, etc., is relatively recent.

P.H.: To come back indirectly to my previous question: does this reflection on temporality separate you in some fundamental sense from the neo-Leibnizian thinking of substantial communication and pre-established harmony? From a Leibnizian perspective, the complexity of elements in their spatialisation – be it physical, geographical, cultural, etc. – is perfectly compatible with their essential isolation: elements relate only to God, whom they express. This is surely a decisive way of resolving the apparent tension I mentioned a moment ago, between particular complexity, on the one hand, and the "empty" or indeterminate relation of all-and-nothing, on the other. Monads, as you explained many years ago, are not distributed within an empty space but "are instead in God, conceived as a spiritual place that is neither measurable nor divisible. Behind phenomenal [i.e. merely apparent] spatiality, real opera-tions play themselves out in the zero of the place, in the absence of measure, of division, of situation and of distance [...]. The [divine] doublet omnipresence–copresence brings the rela-tional path back to zero."[4] But this obviously presumes the immediacy of divine, or creative, action. By conceiving the relation between noth-ingness and the all through time – since I am nothing, I can become everything – are you rejecting a new version of Leibniz's "substantial communication," a new version of creative unity?

I suppose that my question is always the same one: in the end, are you a thinker of the creative One, or are you instead a thinker of creative relations?

M.S.: We live in a world of networks, in which relations are active and sometimes creative, and where, if we bracket the God hypothesis, we must in effect *navigate*, as you put it. Or perhaps there could be a God-function, which would be a way for us to tell ourselves that somewhere there exists a knowledge that would resolve all these questions, but which would be like an integral of which we only possess the differentials. Perhaps some day there will be a knowledge that will permit us to grasp the complexity of these relations, but there isn't one now. In this respect, however, it is interesting to suppose that there might be such a knowledge: one calls it God, and draws the consequences. In any case, I think the seventeenth century certainly did have an idea of God of this type: the idea that there exists an integral of human thinking, an integral of clear and distinct knowledge.

Incidentally, this is why I always asked Deleuze the following question: in what space do you draw your plane of immanence? If there is a *plane* of immanence it must indeed be somewhere. I got no reply. But if he wanted to say that there's no such thing as transcendence, then he shouldn't have used the term "plane." If you think that only immanence exists then there is no plane; otherwise, if there is a plane it must indeed be placed somewhere, and we must ask ourselves in what direction and how – and so there is a transcendence. One could say that all of Deleuze's thought refuses this idea of transcendence but that its every expression presupposes it.

P.H.: I would like to move on now to questions of ethics or morality. You say that "the morality of relations is based on the science of relations."[5] What does this mean? Does relation as such lead to a morality?

M.S.: Yes, relation establishes something, and it's very simple. No one exists before someone has told them "I love you." Before that, he or she

has yet to exist, or has existed very little. It's an example of how relation creates something. Relation is creative. I believe that relation precedes being.

My great dream, my life's dream, which perhaps I will not have the chance to carry out, is to write a great book on prepositions, because prepositions describe all possible relations. It's a shame that written French has no post-positions; in spoken French one often says things like "I am for" [*je suis pour*] or "are you against?" [*est-ce que tu es contre?*], and so on.

P.H.: But can one think the "with" as such, qua pure relation, without thinking the action of relating along with the substance of what is related or brought together? Can we isolate prepositions from verbs and nouns? Must we not, by definition, think the "with" with other elements of language?

M.S.: One can do without everything but prepositions. In computational linguistics, among the ten most frequently used words in French, four are prepositions (*de*, "of," tops the list), that is, words that create relation. Now, philosophy has only ever spoken with nouns and verbs (being, having ...), but it never speaks of prepositions. The verb itself is often bare, for example in English, where the verb *to get* does not mean very much by itself, but where you can create *get off*, *get on* ... It is the preposition that plays the determining role. *To take* means nothing: *to take off* or *to take away* is a different matter. You see, philosophy rarely or never speaks real language. It's as though it always spoke in a telegraphed language – "arrive tomorrow Euston station come take my luggage."

P.H.: Heidegger's works on language, and on being-with, did they have any value for you?

M.S.: I was so busy with sciences and techniques that it was very difficult to throw myself into an author who refused them wholesale. There are two kinds of philosopher: there are philosophers who shackle you and philosophers who free you. Once you are "in" Hegel it's very difficult to speak otherwise than as a Hegelian, whilst with

Leibniz you are free. Leibniz never gave me much trouble; he is very intuitive, he throws open many doors and closes none. In a certain way, Heidegger is very confining. Once you follow Heidegger's reasoning you become a Heideggerian.

P.H.: I come back to the question of a relational morality. I'm thinking, here, instinctively, of people who developed the means to analyse or clarify relations that otherwise ("naturally") would have remained obscure, for example, relations of domination, oppression, repression – I mean thinkers in the line of Marx, Freud, Fanon, etc. Left to myself I tend to conceive of relation in light of the simple assumption that, in the midst of the systematic injustice in which we live, every future reconciliation must pass through a preliminary antagonism or accusation – in short, that a Desmond Tutu is only possible after a Nelson Mandela. But you are very distant from a conception of justice that passes through accusation and judgment; you insist that "we are all accused and accusers," indifferently.[6] Is this really true, in the world as it now stands?

M.S.: Very often, those who overthrow oppression very quickly turn to oppression themselves. I've had very regular experience of this.

P.H.: But what of Gandhi? Mandela? Martin Luther King?

M.S.: To a certain extent, King, Gandhi and Mandela never fought against oppression. They lived as if oppression were not taking place at all. They were rather on my side, they were proponents of absolute non-violence, at least King and Gandhi. They never took up arms. They never seized the weapons of the enemy in order to overthrow him. I agree, they tried to understand relation, they made accusations. But their great success lies in the fact that they tried to understand relation without being locked in the Hegelian dialectic of master and slave, in which the slave only ever dreams of becoming the master. Gandhi and King possessed a true science of relations. Take Gandhi's great speech

on salt. To have found that salt was the key to this affair was a magnificent discovery: the English are making us pay taxes for something that belongs to us.

P.H.: There is also in your work a rather classical insistence on moderation and restraint, on poverty. But you don't identify very clearly the precise mechanism of this restraint, I mean a mechanism that might have a real impact in the present circumstances, dominated as they are by corporate globalisation, by the presumption that there is no alternative to the way things are, etc.

M.S.: Most people today, faced with the power of the market, of globalisation, take refuge in cultural exception. It is they who are restricted, if you will. Now, in order to attack globalisation, it's far better to remain universal, to play the universal against globalisation. For example, the Americans impose their system of measurement, but the only universal system is the metric system, because it refers to the meridian and to astronomy: this indicates how American-led globalisation is a form of imposed particularity. The only way to attack such globalisation is the universal. The only effective thing is universal thought, it really is.

P.H.: One last question along these lines: it seems to me that sometimes you affirm a sort of ethics of genius or of heroic innovation, in which innovative and courageous invention "is the only true intellectual act, the only act of intelligence"[7] – and therefore, I suppose, the only act worthy of moral consideration. You insist on the value of rarity. Do you conceive of morality on the basis of what's exceptional?

M.S.: It's not a question of genius, but it's true that the only true intellectual act is to invent. Now, it is equally true that nothing works better than the university model: it generates honest, industrious and precise people. How old are you, Mr Hallward?

P.H.: I'm 34.

M.S.: I have just one piece of advice for you: take the university model and chuck it into the sea.

P.H.: It's a tempting thought! And how will I make a living?

M.S.: You can make a living by teaching, etc., but you need to be careful that, as far as your own thinking is concerned, you've thrown away the model. The university model is the best possible model, that's why it's dangerous; the better it is, the more we must keep our distance. Why? Because it forbids invention, it forbids it absolutely. If you invent then you will be excluded from the university, one way or another. The university is the great inhibitor of intelligence, precisely because it is its perfect model. The professors are admirable, the École Normale is magnificent – throw it all overboard. Because after you reach a certain age there is only one lesson of intellectual morality, which is to forget this entire model as quickly as possible. I am not saying that this is the sufficient condition for invention, but it certainly is a necessary condition.

P.H.: And you, an honoured member of the Académie Française, an employee of Stanford University, doesn't your own trajectory rather refute what you've just said?

M.S.: But I was excluded from the field of philosophy at your age, I was barred from teaching philosophy. I moved to history, and taught in a history department my entire life. All of my books are outside of traditional philosophy, as the university understands it.

P.H.: I move on now to my very last questions. You edit a large and growing collection of works of French philosophy. How do you understand the specificity of this tradition? What makes it "French"?

M.S.: It's difficult to say, because whatever trait I present, you'll tell me that, yes, in England we do that too, etc. Simply, there is an historical tradition, written in this language, and not only by the French, but by the Swiss, the Germans (as you know, Frederick II studied his philosophy in the French language), etc. There is certainly a constant concern with science, there's always that. There is also an enduring ideal of clarity and transparency.

What separates us from you English speakers is the status of the language. When I speak or write in English I have a great admiration for this language, for a genuine reason, which is that I'm an old sailor. When you speak English, you find yourself adrift on an immense sea of words, tossed about by waves and fluctuations: Shakespeare is the open ocean. The French language is relatively small, and when you speak it you find yourself skating on an icy lake.

P.H.: Unfortunately, as soon as you begin to speak of philosophy, the English language becomes extremely restricted!

M.S.: So why's that? Because one's ideal of rigour is always the reverse of the fundamental quality of one's language. Since the English language is extraordinarily rich, when it comes to philosophy it needs to narrow itself. It becomes very analytical. Whilst we, on the other hand, we need to free ourselves, because our language is frozen solid. The French language is already analytical.

P.H.: And to finish: your current projects?

M.S.: At present, I'm working on all of the problems of biology, of the living. I would like to end my work with these questions of life and anthropology. I read a lot in the life sciences, I spend a lot of time in biochemistry labs, it's been my passion in the last six or seven years.

notes

1 This interview was conducted in Paris on 12 September 2002.

2 Cf. Serres, "Apparition d'Hermès: Don Juan," *Hermès I* 233–45.

3 Serres, *Troubadour of Knowledge* 47; Serres, *Genesis* 47.

4 Serres, *Hermès I* 160.

5 Serres and Latour, *Conversations* 193.

6 Serres and Latour, *Conversations* 192.

7 Serres, *Troubadour of Knowledge* 92–93.

works by serres

"The Geometry of the Incommunicable: Madness." 1962. Trans. Felicia McCarren. *Foucault and His Interlocutors*. Ed. Arnold I. Davidson. Chicago: U of Chicago P, 1997. 36–56.

"Humanisme, philosophie et poésie de la Renaissance." *Études Philosophiques* 23 (1968): 185–95.

Le Système de Leibniz et ses modèles mathématiques: étoiles, schémas, points. 1968. Paris: Presses Universitaires de France, 1982.

Hermès I, La Communication. Paris: Minuit, 1969.

Hermès II, L'Interférence. Paris: Minuit, 1972.

"Géometrie/Algèbre: l'eau solide – le jeu du loup." *Barroco* 6 (1974): 21–35.

Hermès III, La Traduction. Paris: Minuit, 1974.

"India (the Black and the Archipelago) on Fire." *SubStance* 8 (1974): 49–60.

Jouvences sur Jules Verne. Paris: Minuit, 1974.

With François Dagognet and Allal Sinaceur (eds.). *Cours de philosophie positive.* 1975. 2 vols. By Auguste Comte. Paris: Hermann, 1998.

"Discours et parcours." *Critique* 31 (1975): 365–78.

Esthétiques sur Carpaccio. Paris: Hermann, 1975.

Feux et signaux de brume: Zola. Paris: Grasset, 1975.

"Jules Verne's Strange Journeys." Trans. Maria Malanchuk. *Yale French Studies* 52 (1975): 174–88.

"Laplace et le romantisme." *Le Préromantisme: hypothèque ou hypothèse?* Ed. Paul Viallaneix. Paris: Klincksieck, 1975. 319–25.

With François Dagognet and Allal Sinaceur (eds.). *Philosophie première.* By Auguste Comte. Paris: Hermann, 1975.

"Analyse spectrale." *Critique* 32 (1976): 557–99.

Hermès IV, La Distribution. Paris: Minuit, 1977.

"Michelet: The Soup." Trans. Suzanne Guerlac. *CLIO* 6 (1977): 181–91.

La Naissance de la physique dans le texte de Lucrèce: fleuves et turbulences. Paris: Minuit, 1977. *The Birth of Physics.* Ed. with an introduction and annotations by David Webb. Trans. Jack Hawkes. Manchester: Clinamen, 2000.

"Exact and Human." Trans. Winnie Woodhull and John Mowitt. *SubStance* 21 (1978): 9–19.

"The Algebra of Literature: The Wolf's Games." *Textual Strategies: Perspectives in Post-Structuralist Criticism.* Ed. Josué V. Harari. Ithaca: Cornell UP, 1979. 260–76.

Hermès V, Le Passage du nord-ouest. Paris: Minuit, 1980.

Le Parasite. Paris: Grasset, 1980. *The Parasite.* Trans. with notes by Lawrence R. Schehr. Baltimore: Johns Hopkins UP, 1982.

Genèse. Paris: Grasset, 1982. *Genesis.* Trans. Geneviève James and James Nielson. Ann Arbor: U of Michigan P, 1995.

Hermes – Literature, Science, Philosophy. Ed. by Josué V. Harari and David F. Bell. Baltimore: Johns Hopkins UP, 1982.

"The Origin of Language: Biology, Information Theory, and Thermodynamics." *Oxford Literary Review* 5.1–2 (1982): 113–24.

Détachement: apologue. Paris: Flammarion, 1983. *Detachment.* Trans. Geneviève James and Raymond Federman. Athens: Ohio UP, 1989.

Rome: le livre des fondations. Paris: Grasset, 1983. *Rome: The Book of Foundations.* Trans. Felicia McCarren. Stanford: Stanford UP, 1991.

Les Cinq sens. Paris: Grasset, 1985.

"Corruption – The Antichrist: A Chemistry of Sensations and Ideas." Trans. Chris Bongie. *Stanford Italian Review* 6.1–2 (1986): 31–52.

L'Hermaphrodite: Sarrasine sculpteur. Paris: Flammarion, 1987.

Statues: le second livre des fondations. Paris: Bourin, 1987.

"Simone Weil." *Cahiers Simone Weil* 11.4 (1988): 297–98.

(Ed.). *Eléments d'histoire des sciences.* 1989. Paris: Larousse, 1997. *A History of Scientific Thought: Elements of a History of Science.* Oxford: Blackwell, 1995.

"Literature and the Exact Sciences." Trans. Roxanne Lapidus. *SubStance* 18.2 (1989): 3–34.

"Panoptic Theory." *The Limits of Theory.* Ed. Thomas M. Kavanagh. Stanford: Stanford UP, 1989. 25–47.

science of relations

Le Contrat naturel. Paris: Bourin, 1990. *The Natural Contract.* Trans. Elizabeth MacArthur and William Paulson. Ann Arbor: U of Michigan P, 1995.

Discours de réception de Michel Serres à l'Académie française. Paris: Bourin, 1991.

Le Tiers-instruit. Paris: Bourin, 1991. *The Troubadour of Knowledge.* Trans. Sheila Faria Glaser with William Paulson. Ann Arbor: U of Michigan P, 1997.

With Bruno Latour. *Eclaircissements: cinq entretiens avec Bruno Latour.* Paris: Bourin, 1992. *Conversations on Science, Culture, and Time.* Trans. Roxanne Lapidus. Ann Arbor: U of Michigan P, 1995.

La Légende des anges. Paris: Flammarion, 1993.

Les Origines de la géometrie: tiers livre des fondations. Paris: Flammarion, 1993.

Atlas. Paris: Julliard, 1994.

Éloge de la philosophie en langue française. Paris: Fayard, 1995.

Les Messages à distance. Montréal: Fides, Musée de la civilisation, 1995.

"La Leçon de 'Clio.'" *Amitié Charles Péguy: Bulletin d'Informations et de Recherches* 75 (July 1996): 114–22.

"Nous avons perdu le monde." *Zellige* 2 (July 1996). Available online at <http://www.resus.univ-mrs.fr/;slzeus/liens/michel_serres.html>.

Nouvelles du monde. Paris: Flammarion, 1997.

"La Rédemption du savoir." Interview conducted by Luis Join-Lambert and Pierre Klein. *Quart Monde* 163 (Mar. 1997). Available online at <http://www.agora.qc.ca/textes/serres.html>.

"Science and the Humanities: The Case of Turner." Trans. Catherine Brown and William Paulson. *SubStance* 26.2 (1997): 6–21.

Et al. (eds.). *Le Trésor: dictionnaire des sciences.* Paris: Flammarion, 1997.

(Ed.). *A Visage différent: l'alliance thérapeutique autour de l'enfant meurtri.* Paris: Hermann, 1997.

"A Michel Serres Interview (parts I & II)." Interview conducted by Catherine Dale and Gregory Adamson. *The Pander* 5 (spring 1998). Available online at <http://www.thepander.co.nz/culture/mserres5.php>.

"Inauguration." Agen, 24 Sept. 1998. Available online at <http://www.resus.univmrs.fr/;slzeus/liens/inauguration.doc>.

With Nayla Farouki (eds.). *Paysages des sciences.* Paris: Pommier, 1999.

Variations sur le corps. Paris: Pommier, 1999.

Hergé mon ami. Casterman, 2000.

Retour au contrat naturel. Paris: Bibliothèque Nationale de France, 2000.

Hominescence: essais. Paris: Pommier, 2001.

"Le Virtuel est la chair même de l'homme." Interview conducted by Michel Alberganti. *Le Monde* 18 June 2001.

En amour, sommes-nous des bêtes? Paris: Pommier, 2002.

L'Incandescent. Paris: Pommier, 2003.

Michel Serres
Académie Française
23, quai de Conti
75006 Paris
France

Peter Hallward
French Department
King's College London
The Strand
London WC2R 2LS
UK
E-mail: peter.hallward@kcl.ac.uk

Alberto Toscano
Sociology Department
Goldsmiths College, University of London
New Cross
London SE14 6NW
UK
E-mail: a.toscano@blueyonder.co.uk

David Webb
Philosophy Department
Staffordshire University
College Road
Stoke on Trent
Staffordshire ST4 2DE
UK
E-mail: d.a.webb@staffs.ac.uk

notes on the contributors

sepideh anvar

is a freelance translator who works from Chinese and French into English. She lives in Paris.

andrew asibong

is based in the French Department of King's College London, where he is completing a Ph.D. thesis entitled "Metamorphosis and the Métèque," a study of the politics of fantastical transformation in contemporary French and francophone fiction, theatre and film.

alain badiou

teaches at the École Normale Supérieure in Paris; his books include *Théorie du sujet* (1982) and *Being and Event* (1988).

daniel bensaïd

teaches at the University of Paris VIII (Saint-Denis); his books include *Marx for our Times* (1995) and *Résistances* (2002).

bruno bosteels

is Assistant Professor in Romance Studies at Cornell University. His research centres on questions of literature and politics in Latin America, as well as on contemporary critical theory and philosophy. His book on Badiou and politics has been accepted for publication by Duke UP, and he is finishing another manuscript, *After Borges: Literature and Antiphilosophy.*

ray brassier

is Research Associate at the Centre for Research in Modern European Philosophy, Middlesex University, and a member of L'Organisation Non-Philosophique Internationale (www.onphi.org).

emma campbell

recently completed a Ph.D. on Old French saints' lives at King's College London. Her research interests include medieval literature, philosophy and the study of gender and sexuality. With Robert Mills she has co-edited an essay collection entitled *Troubled Vision: Gender, Sexuality and Sight in Medieval Text and Image* (forthcoming) and has published articles in *French Studies* and *Comparative Literature.*

monique david-ménard

teaches at the University of Paris VII (Denis Diderot); her books include *Hysteria from Freud to Lacan* (1983) and *La Folie dans la raison pure* (1990).

sean gaston

received his Ph.D. from the Department of English at the University of Melbourne. He is an independent scholar living in Britain and has published on Derrida and Levinas. His most recent publication is "Derrida and the Ruins of Disinterest" in *Angelaki* 7.3.

andrew goffey

is Senior Lecturer in Media, Culture and Communications at Middlesex University. He wrote his Ph.D. on Gilles Deleuze. He has published articles on recent French philosophy and on the relationship between philosophy, science and culture; he is currently writing a book on biopolitics.

peter hallward (editor)

teaches at King's College London. His publications include *Absolutely Postcolonial* (2001) and *Badiou: A Subject to Truth* (2003).

nick hanlon

is completing a Ph.D. on Baudrillard at Pembroke College, Cambridge. He has published articles on Sade and Baudrillard, as well as a study of "Death, Subjectivity, Temporality in Baudrillard and Heidegger" forthcoming in *French Studies*.

michel henry

taught at the University of Montpellier III (Paul Valéry); his books include *The Essence of Manifestation* (1963) and *I Am the Truth* (1996). He died in July 2002.

jane hiddleston

is a lecturer in French Studies at the University of Warwick, where she teaches French thought and francophone literature. Her book *Reinventing Community* (2004) analyses notions of community in the work of French philosophers such as Derrida and Nancy alongside the literary works of North African immigrant writers. She is currently working on the Algerian writer Assia Djebar.

christian jambet

teaches at the lycée Jules Ferry and the Institut d'Études Iraniennes (University of Paris III); his books include *Logique des Orientaux* (1983) and *La Grande Résurrection d'Alamût* (1990).

philippe lacoue-labarthe

teaches at the University of Strasbourg II (Marc Bloch); his books include *The Subject of Philosophy* (1979) and *Typography* (1989).

guy lardreau

teaches at the Lycée Carnot in Dijon; his books include *L'Ange* (1976, with Christian Jambet) and *La Véracité* (1993).

françois laruelle

teaches at the University of Paris X (Nanterre); his books include *Une Biographie de l'homme ordinaire* (1985) and *Principes de la non-philosophie* (1996).

diane morgan

is Senior Lecturer in Cultural Studies at University College Northampton. She is the author of *Kant Trouble: Obscurities of the Enlightened* (Routledge, 2000) and co-editor, with Keith Ansell-Pearson, of *Nihilism Now!: "Monsters of Energy"* (Macmillan, 2000).

forbes morlock

teaches in the English and Textual Studies Department at the Syracuse University London Centre. His first attempts to come to terms with Jacques Rancière's *The Ignorant Schoolmaster* appeared in the *Oxford Literary Review* (vol. 19, 1997).

jean-luc nancy

retired from teaching at the University of Strasbourg II (Marc Bloch) in 2002; his books include *The Sense of the World* (1993) and *Being Singular Universal* (1996).

jacques rancière

is Emeritus Professor of Aesthetics and Politics at the University of Paris VIII (Saint-Denis); his books include *The Nights of Labor* (1989) and *Disagreement* (1998).

clément rosset

teaches at the University of Nice; his books include *La Philosophie tragique* (1960) and *L'Objet singulier* (1979).

michel serres

is a member of the Académie Française and teaches at Stanford University; his books include *Hermès* (1982) and *Hominescence* (2001).

bernard stiegler

teaches at the Université de Compiègne and is director of the Institut de Recherche et Coordination Acoustique/Musique (IRCAM); his books include *Technics and Time* (1994) and *Passer à l'acte* (2003).

alistair swiffen

is a newly appointed tutorial fellow in Modern Languages at Hertford College, Oxford. He studied French at Downing College and Trinity Hall, Cambridge, where he completed a Ph.D. on the ethical principles developed by Gérard de Nerval, Robert Desnos and Jacques Lacan in their depictions of madness. He is currently researching the link between Lacan's theorisation of madness and the ideological theories of Slavoj Žižek, Jacques-Alain Miller and Louis Althusser.

alberto toscano

is lecturer in the Sociology Department at Goldsmiths College, University of London. He is the co-editor (with Nina Power) of Alain Badiou's *On Beckett* and the translator of Badiou's *Handbook of Inaesthetics* and *The Century*. He is the author of several articles on contemporary philosophy, political theory and aesthetics.

nicolas truong

is a journalist who works for *Le Monde de l'Éducation*, in Paris.

david webb

is Senior Lecturer in Philosophy at Staffordshire University. He edited the English translation of Michel Serres' *The Birth of Physics* and has published several papers on Heidegger and more recently on Foucault and Cavaillès. His current research is on the scientific background to Foucault's archaeology.

ANGELAKI
journal of the theoretical humanities

BEST NEW JOURNAL
Council of Editors of
Learned Journals 1996 Awards

Modern Language Association Convention,
Washington, D.C.

Transcript of the presentation

This year's Best New Journal is *Angelaki*.

One judge called *Angelaki* "A strong and surprising publication that is interested in a wide range of cultural studies issues from harder-theory perspectives," while another praised its "speaking-to-the-moment stance." *Angelaki*'s "position papers" and "substantial essays, addressing current concerns in cultural theory" zero in on "interesting and problematical topics and fields," with results that are "resourceful," "rigorous," and "lively."

Another judge remarked on *Angelaki*'s physical strengths: "The covers and small format are attractive, and the two-column layout is readable, the paper good." The following remark, however, sums things up best: "I put *Angelaki* at the top because I find it refreshingly alive, buzzing with critical energy."

Angelaki 36A Norham Rd
Oxford OX2 6SQ UK

E-mail: editorial@angelaki.demon.co.uk
http://www.tandf.co.uk/journals/
routledge/0969725x.html

vol. 6, no. 2
gift, theft, apology

Publication: August 2001. Pages: 206.
ISBN: 0415 27110 X

Editor: Constantin V. Boundas
   Trent University

Contents

vol. 6, no. 3
general issue 2001

Publication: December 2001. Pages: 238.
ISBN: 0415 27111 8

Editor: Pelagia Goulimari
   Oxford

Contents

vol. 7, no. 1
aesthetics and the ends of art

Publication: April 2002. Pages: 262.
ISBN: 1 899567 06 02

Editor: Gary Banham
                Manchester Metropolitan University
Curator: Sharon Kivland

Contents

vol. 7, no. 2
inventions of death: literature, philosophy, psychoanalysis

Publication: August 2002. Pages: 214.
ISBN: 1 899567 07 0

Editor: Roger Starling
             University of Warwick

Contents

vol. 7, no. 3
general issue 2002

Publication: December 2002. Pages: 190
ISBN: 1-899567-08-9

Editor: Pelagia Goulimari
Oxford

Contents

vol. 8, no. 1
general issue 2003 I

Publication: April 2003. Pages: 180
ISBN: 1-899567-09-7

Editor: Pelagia Goulimari
Oxford

Contents

The World of Learning ONLINE
www.worldoflearning.com
Available Now

Instant access to educational contacts around the globe

- Librarians
- Professors
- Deans
- Curators
- Chancellors
- University presidents
- Rectors

Locate academic institutions of every type, world-wide

- Universities and Colleges
- Schools of Art, Music and Architecture
- Learned Societies
- Research Institutes
- Libraries and Archives
- Museums and Art Galleries

Additional features of The World of Learning online

- Multi-user product
- Fully searchable
- Updated throughout the year

Free trials available from launch date
For further information e-mail: info.europa@tandf.co.uk